**Technology
in Education:
Looking Toward 2020**

TECHNOLOGY IN EDUCATION SERIES

Technology in Education: Looking Toward 2020

RAYMOND S. NICKERSON
BNN Laboratories, Inc.

PHILIP P. ZODHIATES
Education Development Center, Inc.

LEA LAWRENCE ERLBAUM ASSOCIATES, PUBLISHERS
1988 Hillsdale, New Jersey   Hove and London

Lawrence Erlbaum Associates, Inc., Publishers
365 Broadway
Hillsdale, New Jersey 07642

Library of Congress Cataloging-in-Publication Data

Technology in education: Looking toward 2020 / edited by Raymond S.
   Nickerson and Philip P. Zodhiates.
      p.   cm.
   Bibliography: p.
   Includes indexes.
   ISBN 0-8058-0214-2.   ISBN 0-8058-0297-5 (pbk.)
   1. Educational technology—Congresses.   2. Intelligent tutoring
systems—Congresses.   3. Computer-assisted instruction—Congresses.
I. Nickerson, Raymond S.   II. Zodhiates, Philip P.
LB1028.3.T397   1988
371.3 '07 '8—dc19   88-212126
                                                                        CIP

Printed in the United States of America
10   9   8   7   6   5   4   3   2   1

Contents

Preface

The Educational Technology Center of the Harvard Graduate School of Education convened a 13-member panel in Manchester Village, Vermont, to consider the long-term future of information technology in American education. The task before the "2020 Panel" was to envision a state of affairs in the early part of the 21st century in which technology would play a major role in elementary and secondary education nationwide and to describe what it would take to get there. Panelists were asked to consider research, development, hardware and software environments, preservice and inservice teacher education, technical assistance, organizational and cultural changes in the institution of schooling, and anything else that would be necessary to achieve the vision.

Our purpose in establishing the panel was to contribute to a long-range national agenda for research, development, and application of information technology in education. The goal was to help mobilize public and private support for such an agenda and to help establish a realistic framework for thinking and planning by legislators and policy makers at the federal and other levels of government. Above all, the aim of the panel was to deepen and enrich policy makers' and school people's understanding of technology's potential role in education—the dangers and drawbacks as well as the opportunities.

PANEL SPONSORSHIP

The primary sponsor of the panel was the Office of Educational Research and Improvement of the U.S. Department of Education. Additional support was provided by the Carnegie Corporation of New York, the Office of

Technology Assessment of the U.S. Congress, and by members of the "ETC Industry Group," six computer manufacturers who have been associated with and supported the work of the Educational Technology Center: Apple Computer, Inc., Control Data Corporation, Digital Equipment Corporation, Hewlett-Packard, International Business Machines Corporation, and Texas Instruments.

THE ORIGINS OF THE "2020 PANEL"

Neither the "2020 Panel" nor this book would have been possible without the vision of Charles Thompson, former director of the Center for Learning Technology at Education Development Center, and later Co-Director of the Educational Technology Center (ETC) at Harvard. The "2020 Panel" has its origins in a paper that Christopher Dede, Philip Zodhiates, and Charles Thompson wrote on Intelligent Computer-Assisted Instruction (ICAI).[1] The writing of the ICAI Report provided the authors with an opportunity to evaluate recent educational applications of artificial intelligence, and to think about future directions in the field and the potential of the technology to transform the traditional classroom roles of teachers and students.

Upon completion of the ICAI paper, Charles Thompson began to explore ways of following up on what the authors had learned about recent developments in the area of intelligent tutoring systems and came up with the idea of organizing a panel under ETC auspices to explore the future of AI-based applications in education. As plans for the panel matured, however, the original narrow focus on artificial intelligence quickly broadened to accommodate a wider spectrum of information technologies.

The target date of 2020 was chosen for a number of reasons. For one thing, we wanted the panel to have an impact on the design and development of information technology, and it was our belief that a shorter time frame would have less of a chance to influence future developments in educational technology. After all, we knew that the next generation of technology, which will be in widespread use within a decade or so, is already under development. There was also the danger that a shorter time frame would limit the imagination of panel members; they would be too constrained by what is already available or thought to be technically feasible. We hoped that focusing on a target date 30 years or so from now would free participants' imaginations of present-day technological constraints. Finally, "2020" seemed an especially appropriate name for a panel charged with looking into the future. In addition to suggesting

---

[1]Dede, Christopher J., Zodhiates, Philip P., and Thompson, Charles L. "Intelligent computer-assisted instruction: A review and assessment of ICAI research and its potential for education," (Topical Paper 85-25), Educational Technology Center, May 1985.

the possibility of wisdom and foresight, the name mocked our aspirations for
achieving perfect vision.

Panelists were selected to represent a cross section of disciplines and perspectives. Participants included researchers in the area of computers and education, cognitive and developmental psychologists, as well as leading figures in
the intelligent CAI or intelligent systems community; scientists, mathematicians, and computer scientists; and practicing educators and others who understood both the constraints on and opportunities for introducing new technologies
into schools.

THE "2020 PANEL" MEETING

In preparation for the conference in Vermont, Raymond S. Nickerson, the chair
of the "2020 Panel" effort, circulated a short paper that offered a starting point
for thinking about the purposes of education and of technology's role in
American schools. In the paper, which appears here as Chapter 1, Nickerson
asked the panelists to articulate a vision of a desirable end state in the year
2020, and to define the research, development, and related activities that would
be needed to make it happen.

Participants were also asked to write a paper on a topic of their choice and
to exchange drafts before the conference. Preliminary papers were circulated
in time for panel members to prepare for the meeting in Manchester Village.

The purpose of the conference was not to present papers but to use the drafts
panel members had written as points of departure for a broad exchange of
ideas. Later, participants had the opportunity to revise their papers in light
of the 2-day discussion.

The panel's deliberations in Manchester Village returned repeatedly to
the question of the proper ends of schooling, and much of the panel's discussion of technology and its potential for education took place within this
larger philosophical context. There was broad consensus with Nickerson's
assertion that "the first question we should ask is not 'What can technology do?' but rather 'What should be done.' Only after we have a reasonably clear idea of what it means (or should mean) to be educated and of
what we would like an educational system to accomplish, should we turn
to the question of what role or roles technology should play in the educational
process."

The themes that emerged from the 2-day meeting had at least as much to
do with schools and with how the vision of a technology might be put into practice, as with the vision itself. This dual focus on education and technology grew
out of two circumstances: the presence on the panel of people who were especially knowledgeable about educational institutions and the deep interest of even
the most technology-minded members of the panel in issues of curriculum,

pedagogy, and implementation. As a result, the discussion on the future role of technology in education was tempered by a note of caution, with even the most optimistic among the participants acknowledging the magnitude of the challenge facing those who hope to use technology to bring about change in schools.

A ROAD MAP TO THE BOOK

The Technology-Dependent World of 2020

Thomas Landauer predicts the development of "powerful cognitive tools" that will enable us to do such things as calculus and linear programming and to find any piece of information we want in a matter of seconds. According to Landauer, the presence of an "omnipotent and omniscient technology" able to perform many of the cognitive tasks now performed by people will have profound effects both on employment and education. For one thing, people will be replaced in many intellectual activities by machines. For another, technology will degrade the intellectual content of most jobs; problem solving will cease to be an activity in which most people engage, instead becoming the province of the few. Cognitive aids will also change the ways in which we accomplish intellectual tasks. Machines, for example, will be able to help us compose (not just type) letters and plan (not just draw) buildings; and search, recursion, and iteration will be the common ways of solving problems. In Landauer's view, by 2020 the workplace will have been radically transformed, with workers divided into three camps: a small cadre of very elite technologists, inventors, and artists; a large number of people involved in human service activities; and a third camp composed of managers of production and capital.

In a world in which most people are engaged in service-type activities rather than problem solving, education would have to be restructured, Landauer says, "to prepare people to please each other, and to solve problems about social and artistic matters." Schools would emphasize the humanities—a common core of languages, art, music, and social interaction skills—and downplay mathematics and the sciences, domains heavily oriented toward problem solving.

Technology in the Service of Individual-Centered Learning

Howard Gardner envisions using technology to individualize the education of students who come to school with a variety of skills and predispositions. Gardner presents his theory of "multiple intelligences" as an alternative to the reigning "uniformist" view of cognition, which describes the mind as a single entity and defines intelligence solely in terms of logical-mathematical thinking. In contrast to the unitary view of mind, which implies that all students should tackle subject matter "in the same way and in the same order," Gardner's pluralistic theory of intelligence would require schools to prepare students for depth rather than breadth, so that each child might possess at least one area of "deep knowledge." Schools and communities would be expected to provide learning opportunities that match the interests and abilities of students. Technology's role would be to "assess the intellectual proclivities and achievements" of students, to store and update information about educational opportunities for students in the community, and to "match students with appropriate curricula" and "optimal pedagogical approaches."

Less Is More: Using Technology to Increase Understanding

Andrea diSessa dismisses the usual implications drawn from the "information explosion," namely, that "everyone needs to learn more and more, and faster and faster." Instead, he proposes that schools reduce the scope of what they cover in the curriculum in favor of teaching fewer things in greater depth, and emphasizing competence, theory building, and the skills of synthesis and problem solving. In addition, diSessa would have schools teach "mid-level" domain-specific knowledge, which he contrasts to both knowledge of scientific facts and higher order thinking skills.

In diSessa's view, computers serve two functions. One is as intrinsically motivating educational devices; the other is as a medium of invention and construction. diSessa reminds us that a large part of students' enjoyment and sense of accomplishment, both in school and out, comes from competent performance in the building of things.

Enhancing Mathematical Thinking

Alan Schoenfeld addresses the question, "What mathematics and what thinking skills should one teach in 2020?" He points out that although the subject matter of mathematics is constantly undergoing change, the process of doing mathematics and thinking mathematically has remained invariant over the years. It is this ability to think mathematically that Schoenfeld would have schools teach. According to Schoenfeld, thinking mathematically includes mastering mathematical facts and procedures, learning problem-solving strategies, being able to assess progress towards a solution, developing appropriate beliefs about the use of mathematics, and mastering learning skills.

Schoenfeld also explores the use of computer-based tools that provide students with simultaneous multiple representations of mathematical concepts. These representations might include the on-screen simulation of a real-life event, its graph, and the equation of a function that generates the graph. He describes one such system, a tutor for "Green Globs," a computer game whose purpose is to help students improve their knowledge of algebra and their understanding of the relationship between functions and graphing.

Computer-Based Apprentice Tools

Wallace Feurzeig believes that schools have a responsibility to help children "become active practitioners in some discipline area." Although he acknowledges the importance of a common curriculum for all children, Feurzeig wants education to help young people achieve competence in a particular knowledge domain.

Computer-based tools can help schools achieve this pedagogical goal in two ways, according to Feurzeig. First, computers can introduce children to formal thinking procedures in the context of playful activities such as writing simple programs for controlling robots or writing poems. Second, computers can bring children into closer contact with the work of real practitioners. By 2020, Feurzeig envisions the availability of computer-based tools that are similar but simpler versions of those used by scholars, scientists, and artists. These "apprentice tools" will help bridge the gap between schooling and work, initiating "the student in the actual processes used by experts to perform real tasks."

The Role of Computer Science
in Precollege Education

Elliot Soloway argues that the main purpose of teaching computer programming at the precollege level is to provide students with synthesis skills, the kinds of skills one needs to build things. Programming, Soloway asserts, "is an excellent vehicle for teaching and learning these skills [because] in writing a computer program what one is actually doing is creating an artifact that will serve some end. This artifact is a mechanism, that when turned on, will do something." The experience of designing a tool that does something useful is a radical departure from the usual analysis-oriented activities that students now engage in, Soloway says.

Technology and Cognitive Research

Lauren Resnick and Ann Johnson examine current efforts to build computer-based intelligent tutors in the areas of reading, writing, and arithmetic. These software development projects are implementing and testing theories, such as "automaticity" and "scaffolding," that have emerged from cognitive science research.

Resnick and Johnson point out that efforts to develop intelligent tutoring systems, in which the machine builds a model of what the student knows and chooses instructional steps, are hampered both by our incomplete understanding of human learning processes, and more fundamentally by a machine's inability to really "know" any of its users. Nonetheless, they believe that AI systems can still be effective learning devices as long as human teachers remain a central part of the student's instructional environment. Whatever their limitations, Resnick and Johnson believe that computers are becoming "everyday partners in work and leisure, extending human intellectual power."

Technology and Knowledge Transfer

Roy Pea proposes a new approach to the problem of knowledge transfer. Unlike the dominant theory of transfer, which looks for the existence of objective "common elements" that connect what people already know with a new situation, Pea's "interpretive perspective" suggests that elements perceived by an individual to be the same between a past and present situation are not intrinsic in the nature of things, but are "read" in terms of that individual's culturally-influenced category system of problem types. Pea argues that knowledge transfer requires "situation analysis, a determination of the ways in which prior knowledge bears on the situation because the problem reminds the thinker of previous problem cases or types."

One educational implication of Pea's perspective is that schools ought to make greater use of everyday situations in constructing problems for students to solve, and to make the links between the outside world and the classroom more explicit. Another way that schools can foster knowledge transfer is to do a better job of integrating learning across the different subject areas.

Equity Concerns

Shirley Malcom warns that unless explicit efforts are made to develop educational applications of technology that benefit the least advantaged members of society—the poor, racial and linguistic minorities, the physically and learning disabled—and to provide them with equal access to technology-based resources, the gap between the "haves" and "have nots" is likely to increase. Malcom points out that lowered cost and greater physical access to computers will not by themselves be sufficient to improve the lot of disadvantaged students. Technological developments, Malcom argues, must be accompanied by a concern for equity. She states, "If we have a tool that may help [students] overcome previous disadvantage and reach their educational potential, we have a moral obligation to give priority to this purpose."

Malcom views as promising the strategy used to develop successful computer-based products for the physically disabled. The development of these products, she points out, was "driven by human need" and involved users in their "conceptualization, design, and testing." She calls for similar efforts at "leveling the playing field" on behalf of learning disabled, limited English proficient students, and other disadvantaged children. Such an effort, Malcom argues, requires several ingredients: research that is sensitive to the needs of different groups of learners, teacher training that fosters the integration of technology into the curriculum, a teacher workforce that is broadly representative of the student population, software that is appropriate for different learning styles, strategies for involving parents in their children's learning, and the ready availability of computers at little or no cost.

Educational Technology and School Organization

David Cohen's concern is with the impact—or more precisely, lack of impact—of technology on the organizational structure of schools. The computer is only the latest new technology to be introduced into schools, Cohen reminds us. He argues that the history of older new technologies, such as paperback books and educational television, suggests a general proposition about the relationship between technology and educational change, namely, that technology does not drive change but only provides opportunities for change. For opportunities to be seized, the introduction of technology must be accompanied by organizational changes. But for school organization to change, the incentive structure that determines how teachers teach and students learn must first be overhauled. The record of past educational technologies, Cohen says, shows that serious adoption of a new technology occurs only at the margin, where "there is both support for change and no powerful opposition to it."

The Technology-Rich Classroom of the Future

The charge to the panel was to envision a state of affairs in the early part of the 21st century in which technology would be playing a major role in elementary and secondary education. One participant who addressed this issue directly, William Bossert, described his vision of a classroom in which a number of informational and intellectual resources were made available to children. In Bossert's view, high-quality data and audiovisual access to libraries and museums would deepen students' intellectual engagement with the world outside the school while avoiding the usual logistical headaches associated with field trips. In the future, he says, "a field trip to anywhere can be as easy as pressing a key on a student's personal processor." The technology would make museums and libraries more accessible, particularly benefiting less advantaged students. "If major museums and libraries had digitally encoded copies of their possessions and simple means of network access, there need be no rich or poor schools,"

Bossert says. "Suppose the Museum of Comparative Zoology could be accessed remotely by network, with catalogs, high resolution graphics, and perhaps even specimen data available. The access would be selected by catalog for older children or by pictorial maps for younger students." After a class visit to the museum, a student could "return" electronically to browse through the exhibits, by looking at the catalog or moving over a map.

In addition to promoting links between the classroom and the external intellectual environment, Bossert wants to use technology to encourage intellectual exchanges among students within a classroom. Appropriately designed computer programs would make possible the solution of complex problems by a group of students, while helping "level the abilities within a group so that less able students might take on tasks that would be viewed by others as meaningfully furthering the group activity," Bossert suggests.

Bossert's vision focuses on learning tools for students. By contrast, Jim Minstrell's classroom of the future would be full of electronic aids for teachers. One machine would help the teacher perform organizational and management tasks: keep track of appointments and deadlines, and stay abreast of articles of interest to the teacher. A second machine, a teaching assistant, would help the teacher prepare the day's physics class. The machine would be adapted to reflect the teacher's particular preferences and instructional style. This device would be connected to the phone line and monitor student progress wherever students log on, at home or at work; it would also be able to describe students' thinking, diagnose their difficulties, and suggest instructional strategies.

Toward a Common Vision

Our goal has been to produce a document that is not merely a collection of individual chapters, but a statement of a shared vision about what can and should be done to advance the application of technology to education over the next few decades. Towards that end, Ray Nickerson prepared a synthesis of the 2-day Panel discussion in Vermont, which appears here as the final chapter. The purpose of the final chapter is to highlight certain themes while providing the chairman with an opportunity to articulate his own vision of technology in education in 2020.

Philip P. Zodhiates

Foreword

The Educational Technology Center at the Harvard Graduate School of Education started in October of 1983 with a mandate to explore the ways in which the new information technologies could be used to help improve the learning and teaching of mathematics, science, and computing at the primary and secondary levels. In responding to the challenge of this mandate, we decided that the best use we could make of the human resources available to us would be to focus our efforts on exploring the capabilities and the potential of the technologies that are now, or were very soon to be, available in schools.

After two years, the Center was well established, had acquired a certain degree of momentum, and had fashioned a research style of working collaboratively with practitioners. It was by then clear that our research activities would contribute in a serious way to the ongoing public discourse on computers in education. On the other hand, it was also clear that because the focus of our activities was on present-day schools with present-day teachers, we were not going to be in a position to have much to say about the likely influence of technology on the long-term direction and shape of education in this country.

Although we recognized that time and resource limitations would prohibit our giving adequate attention to this issue ourselves, we believed that we could make a contribution by convening a panel of thoughtful people from various corners of the education community to think, talk, and write about these matters.

It was clear from the beginning that the success of this effort would depend on the choice of both chair and staff for the panel. Happily, Raymond S. Nickerson of BBN Laboratories, Inc. agreed to serve as chair, and Philip P. Zodhiates of Education Development Center, Inc. as chief staff person to the panel.

With Ray Nickerson and Philip Zodhiates, we identified an initial set of people whose thinking we wished to bring to bear on the subject, and we invited them to join the panel and to nominate others who would complement the perspectives represented in the initial group. We regard ourselves as most fortunate in attracting to this enterprise the extraordinary collection of people that agreed to join the panel.

We charged the panel with the task of envisioning powerful, desirable roles for technology in the educational system of the United States in the year 2020 and reflecting on what it would take to reach that state. We invited them to address any dimensions of the problem they considered important — moral, social, and political as well as technological — and to respect the complexity of the educational system we were asking them to think about.

This book is the result of the efforts of the panel. We feel that it is a diverse collection of reflections on the future of technology in education, each of which is characterized by uncommon thoughtfulness. We found the role we played in creating the 2020 panel gratifying. We found the panel's work challenging and provocative. We trust that you will as well.

Judah L. Schwartz

Charles L. Thompson

1 Technology in Education in 2020: Thinking About the Not-Distant Future[1]

RAYMOND S. NICKERSON
BNN Laboratories Inc.

The year 2020 was picked as the focal year for the Educational Technology Center panel on the future role of technology in education not simply because of its alliterative usefulness for purposes of constructing titles or themes, but because 35 years is about as far into the future as we dare try to look. Considering how technology has moved since the arrival of the digital computer about 35 years ago, it would seem foolhardy to attempt to look in any detail at what the world will be like much beyond that date. Even on that time scale there is little reason to believe that we can predict much with very great accuracy. Perhaps we can, however, develop some plausible scenarios. And to attempt to do at least that much is imperative, if we would hope to impact intelligently the course the future takes. The purpose of this paper is to propose a perspective for thinking about the future, not so much with the intent of predicting it as with that of helping to shape it.

First some assumptions:

- There are many possible futures. If this were not true, there would be little point in this type of exercise.
- Not all possible futures are equally probable.
- Not all possible futures are equally desirable.
- What is most desirable among the possibilities is not necessarily most probable in the absence of some concerted effort to make it so.

---

[1]Background paper for Educational Technology Center (Harvard) Panel on Technology in Education in 2020, for meeting Oct. 15-17, 1986.

We need to try to understand better what the possibilities are and what the factors are that will determine which of them will be realized. We need to identify preferred futures among the possibilities, and to consider what can and should be done to increase the probability that the actual future will be among the preferred ones.

Some of the possible short-term future trends in technology are quite easy to see — at least in nonspecific ways — and seem to be probable. Among those that would appear to be highly relevant to education are the following:

- The speed of the devices used for computing and for storing information will continue to increase, while their size, power requirements and cost will continue to decrease. These trends have characterized computer technology for several decades and will probably continue to do so for the foreseeable future.

- Computer systems that realize orders of magnitude increases in computing power by exploiting parallel multi-processor architectures will become increasingly common.

- Remote wireless terminals will provide access to computer networks and thereby to central repositories of information of nearly every conceivable type.

- Microprocessor-based computing power will be everywhere — in household appliances, in hand tools, in games and toys, in clothing.

- Software will be available for an increasingly extensive array of applications and much of it will have potential for serving educational purposes.

- Software also will be developed that will permit the supplementation of conventional text with dynamic graphics, including process simulations, that should enhance the effectiveness of expository material.

- Multimedia communication facilities, allowing the mixing of text, images, and speech will become widely available.

- User-oriented languages and "front ends" to applications software will become increasingly easy for people without technical training to use. How soon truly natural-language capabilities will be available is difficult to say; however, systems with useful aspects of natural language and limited speech input and output capabilities will proliferate.

- Computer-based information services addressed to a diversity of objectives — job posting, want ads, selective news, information searches — will also proliferate.

- Increasingly powerful tools to facilitate interacting with very large data bases — both for directed searching and for browsing — will be developed.

It seems clear that such developments have great potential to influence, perhaps transform, education. It is very easy to imagine innumerable ways in which educational applications of them could be made. Consideration of those possibilities is not, however, the best way to begin thinking about the future roles of technology in education in the future. The first question we should ask is not "What can technology do?" but rather "What should be done?" Starting with the feasibility question runs the risk of selecting the problem to fit the solution in hand, which may not be the problem one should be trying to solve. The fact that technology makes a particular educational objective feasible is not, by itself, an adequate reason for establishing that objective.

What kind of educational system should we be striving for? What should the goals and objectives of education be? These are the first questions we need to ask. Then come questions of method and of the kinds of actions and resources that are needed to expedite the realization of those goals. Only after we have a reasonably clear idea of what it means—or should mean—to be educated, of what we would like an educational system to accomplish, should we turn to the question of what role or roles technology should play in the educational process.

What does it mean—or what should it mean in today's world—to be educated? Here is one answer: An educated person should be a knower, a thinker, and a learner. Becoming educated means acquiring (a) domain-specific knowledge, (b) generally useful cognitive skills, and (c) the ability and desire to learn.

The teaching of domain-specific knowledge has long been recognized to be a primary objective of education. Some people would claim that the teaching of thinking skills has also been a major objective for a very long time. There seems to be a growing consensus among many educators and researchers, however, that at least the latter objective has not been widely realized and that there is a need not only to put greater emphasis on the importance of higher-level cognitive skills (e.g., reasoning, problem-solving, decision making) that are assumed to be useful across a wide variety of content domains and in meeting the challenges of everyday life, but to find more effective ways to develop them. Much of the research supporting this view has focused on the teaching of "strategies" or "heuristics" for thinking critically and creatively. Some of it has also focused on the development and enhancement of certain "processes" (observing, comparing, classifying, forming and testing hypotheses) that are assumed to be fundamental to the development of intellectual competence. Unfortunately, some of the discussions of these needs have tended to treat the teaching of domain-specific knowledge and the teaching of general thinking skills as mutually exclusive possibilities. An alternative position, and the one taken here is that it is the proper business of education both to ensure the acquisition of domain-specific knowledge—and lots of it—and to develop students' ability to think.

The third objective mentioned above (that of enhancing students' ability to learn and their interest in doing so) is no less important than the other two; indeed the case can easily be made that it is fundamental to them. If one has effective learning skills and a deep interest in learning, one surely will acquire domain-specific knowledge and perhaps thinking skills as well. If one lacks learning skills, not only will one's educational progress be limited in school, but, more importantly, one will be poorly equipped to meet the challenge of continuing learning that today's information-rich and rapidly moving society presents. To be well prepared for the future requires not only having learned a lot but being able to learn effectively on one's own.

In addition to producing people who know a lot, who can think well, and who can learn, education should serve several purposes. It should, for example, equip one to participate meaningfully and responsibly in a democratic society. The importance of an informed intellectually capable citizenry is a very old theme and an argument that Thomas Jefferson made most eloquently in defense of the idea of universal public education. Paradoxically, while modern communication technology has made it possible for the average citizen to be far better informed, especially about newsworthy events, than his counterpart of a few centuries or even decades ago, it has also increased greatly the importance of critical judgement. Television and other mass media can be effective tools for statesmen and demagogues alike, and part of what it means to be a good citizen today is to be able to interpret and assess rationally the countless messages that vie more or less continuously for one's attention. Inasmuch as many of these messages are indirect, not necessarily verbal, and very subtle, this requires more than familiarity with the language and the rules of logic. It requires a nontrivial understanding of human thinking and especially of the various ways in which opinions and attitudes can be influenced.

Education should also provide one with the knowledge and skills that will be useful in acquiring a trade, vocation, or profession. That is not to suggest that an education should provide a person with a trade, vocation, or profession, but that it should prepare him to acquire one. And it should greatly increase the individual's options with respect to the kind of professional or vocational training that becomes possible.

Most importantly, education should affect one as a human being in substantive ways. It should greatly extend one's horizons and broaden one's perspective. It should increase one's appreciation of other cultures, other viewpoints, other life styles. It should deepen one's sensitivities to other people's rights, feelings, preferences, and hopes. It should make one more understanding and tolerant of individual differences and more capable of settling disputes in nonviolent ways. And it should heighten one's curiosity and inquisitiveness; as a consequence of one's education, the world should be a far more interesting place than it otherwise would be. Whether or not education, as we know it, does have these consequences may be questionable; whether it should, in my view, is not.

What about instructional method? Are there some general principles upon which we might expect a significant amount of consensus? Here are some possibilities:

- Instruction should be individualized. It is unreasonable to expect all students to learn at the same rate, to have the same difficulties in mastering any particular subject matter, to have identical interest patterns, and to have lock-step changes in their levels of motivation. The lecture approach to instruction, which treats a sizeable class of students as though all its members were identical with respect to learning ability, interest, existing knowledge, and other variables important to learning, is bound to be grossly inefficient from the point of view of the individual learner. That is not to argue that lectures can never serve a useful purpose. However, an educational process that relies solely, or perhaps even primarily, on lectures for instruction has very little to recommend it except possibly economics, and even then only if the value of the teacher's time is much more heavily weighted than the value of the student's time.

- Instruction should be adaptive. Again, it is not realistic to expect all members of any collection of students to master a set of materials at the same rate and by means of precisely the same sequential thought process. Different students will have difficulties with different aspects of the material and will require supplementary information and help at different times. Ideally, an educational process should be able to adapt to the moment-to-moment ability of the learner to assimilate the information, comprehend the concepts, principles, and relationships, and master the skills as required to attain the learning objectives.

- Instruction should be interactive. The student should be able to ask, as well as to attempt to answer, questions. This is not to suggest that instruction should be totally nondirective and without structure or teaching objectives. However, the implementation of a curriculum should be sufficiently flexible to permit the student frequently to pursue avenues of special interest, to engage in inquiry, exploration and discovery. There should be much opportunity for dialog and for situations in which teacher and student have the relationship of collaborators in an exploratory process. The learning environment should permit and facilitate hypothesis testing and experimentation.

In addition to such general principles about instructional method, there are several themes that have emerged or seem to be emerging from educational research that relate to specific aspects of learning and instruction. Any thinking about the role of technology in education in the future should take these themes into account.

- *Constructivism.* Learning is best described not as a process of assimilating knowledge but as one of constructing mental models. The learner's role is seen as necessarily an active one. It is questionable whether there is such a thing as passive learning. If new information is to be retained it must be related to existing knowledge actively in an integrative way.

- *The importance of conceptual understanding.* Much of the knowledge that students are expected to acquire in school, especially in mathematics and science, is procedural. One learns how to perform certain operations in an algorithmic fashion. If knowledge of how to carry out specific procedures is not accompanied by an understanding of why the procedures work, the student may fail to see the applicability of the procedures in situations other than those in which they were acquired.

- *The role of preconceptions.* Learning is incremental and transformational. We learn by building on what we know, and by modifying what we only thought we knew. Even when the topic is new (e.g., an "introductory" course) students approach it with many preconceived ideas. Some of these preconceptions are very likely to be misconceptions, which is to say, they are likely to be inconsistent with what the course is intended to teach. If substantive misconceptions are not identified and corrected, the mental edifice that the student constructs is likely to be unstable because of its shaky foundation. Individualized and adaptive instruction means, among other things, instruction that is highly sensitive to what the individual student already knows, and does not know, with respect to what is to be learned.

- *The importance of connecting in-school and out-of-school learning.* Research is showing that a major impediment to learning in school is sometimes a failure of either the teacher or the student to connect the material that is being taught in the classroom with what the student has learned or is likely to need to know in everyday life. More specifically it has been shown that students often bring to the classroom knowledge that is directly relevant to what they are expected to learn but they fail to see the connection and the learning process suffers as a consequence.

- *Emphasis on metacognition and self-management techniques.* Metacognitive skills have been receiving increasing attention by educational researchers, as has the idea that effective thinkers and learners take considerable responsibility for managing and monitoring their own thinking and learning activities. Metacognitive skills are assumed to be identifiable and learnable. They include planning, directing attention, assessing comprehension, controlling anxiety, and a variety of other aspects of managing one's intellectual resources and monitoring one's cognitive performance. Evidence is accumulating to support the notion that a significant difference between more and less effective problem-solvers and learners lies in the different degrees to which they have acquired and learned to use to advantage such metacognitive skills.

- *The need for lifelong learning.* There have always been advocates of the idea that one's formal schooling should be considered as only one phase of a lifelong process of learning. This fact notwithstanding, in the popular view education has been something one *gets* during one's youth and *uses* for the rest of one's life. The untenability of this view becomes increasingly apparent as the rate at which society changes increases. The fact that specific job skills can, and do, become obsolete over very short periods of time is one practical reason for stressing the importance of lifelong learning.

Another theme that has been prominent in the educational research literature in recent years is the potential of technology to facilitate instruction and learning. It is this theme that provides the focus for the panel.

The possibility of using computers and related technology for instructional purposes has been of interest to some researchers and educators for at least two decades. Early hopes for computer-assisted instruction have not been realized, however, and the impact of technology on instruction and learning to date has not been great. To the extent that a major impediment to the educational exploitation of computer technology has been financial, that impediment is rapidly disappearing with the development of powerful and relatively inexpensive personal computers. Application of this technology to education will be less and less limited by hardware costs. The cost of software development will continue to be a limiting factor, but that too will become increasingly important as the software base expands.

Exactly what the impact of technology on education will be in the near-to-mid-range future remains to be seen. The challenge to this panel is to develop a better understanding both of what that impact *could* be and of what it *should* be and to identify the factors that will determine what it *will* be. We want to see more clearly what the possible futures of education are and to understand better how to increase the likelihood that the future that is realized is among the more desirable of those possibilities.

Meeting this challenge will require more than simply trying to understand where computer technology is headed — although it will require that. It will be necessary also to pay close attention to what researchers have been learning about learning and instruction, and a great amount of educationally relevant research has been going on in the recent past. It will mean thinking hard about educational goals, about what it means or should mean to be an educated person, about the purposes that education should serve for the individual and for humankind in the aggregate. Only in the context of a perspective that is broad enough to encompass these types of considerations can we approach the question of the not-distant future roles of technology in education with some hope of helping to shape developments for the better.

Following are examples of the specific questions that suggest themselves as one attempts to think, with the foregoing considerations in mind, about how education could or should be influenced by technology over the next few decades.

- Should the purpose of education change in the near-term future? If so, how?

- How will the domain content of education change over the next 35 years? How should the curriculum change to accommodate the new knowledge that will be acquired over that period?

- What changes might we expect with respect to literacy demands? Will it be important for students in 2020 to become literate with respect to a much broader range of representational media, and in particular, electronic media? What will/should be the role of the traditional book? How pervasive will be the use of electronic storage and transmission of information of various sorts?

- What are computers likely to be like in 2020? What are they likely to be able to do? How much computing power might we expect it to be economically feasible for the average student to have? How much might we expect him to be able to carry easily on his person? What kinds of software are likely to be available? Will machines have extensive speech and natural language capabilities?

- How might technology be exploited to make possible the development of new and qualitatively different ways of representing information so as to make it more conducive to human assimilation?

- What are the characteristics of an environment that is highly conducive to learning? How can technology facilitate the development and maintenance of environments with these characteristics?

- How can technology be used to individualize instruction, to make it more appropriate to the capabilities, limitations, and interests of the individual learner, and more adaptive to the educationally relevant characteristics of the immediate learning situation?

- How should technology be used to develop interactive and mixed-initiative learning environments? How does one design environments that provide an effective balance between directed instruction and student-guided exploration and experimentation?

- How might technology be used to help motivate learning?

- How can technology be used to increase the probability of students understanding the basic concepts, principles, relationships, and processes that constitute the subject matter of their learning? How can it be used to help ensure that the understanding that is obtained is more than a superficial one?

- How can technology be used to facilitate the integration of knowledge across traditional disciplines and conventional subject-matter domains?

- How can it help bridge the gap between what is learned in the classroom and what is learned in everyday life? How can it increase the probability that knowledge acquired in the one context will be applied effectively in the other?

- How can technology be used to develop more effective techniques for assessing what an individual knows about a given topic and for probing the depth of understanding?

- How can technology be used to facilitate the development and enhancement of reasoning, problem-solving and decision-making skills, and intellectual competence in the most general sense? How can it be used to make people more effective learners?

- How do we make sure that the use of technology in education does not have a dehumanizing effect (cerebration at the cost of socialization)?

- What are the risks of making people smarter without making them better? If we did suddenly find ourselves with educational tools that were far more powerful than any we have known in the past, would we know how to use them to the benefit of humankind? Suppose it were possible to teach math and science, say, many times as effectively as we have been able to do heretofore. Would the use of this new found power make the world a better, safer, more pleasant place in which to live?

- Should the role of the teacher change over the next few decades? How?

Over the past century, the methods used in agriculture and manufacturing have changed dramatically in this country. Means of transportation and communication have been developed that could hardly be imagined a century ago. Medicine has been revolutionized, as have the means of waging war. Educational methods have changed very little by comparison. Although it would be rash to attribute this difference to the relative lack of application of technology to education, there can be no doubt that the degree to which technology has impacted education pales by comparison with its use in these other areas.

It seems clear that technology has the potential to affect education in significant ways in the foreseeable future. How that potential will be realized, and whether education will be better as a consequence, remain to be seen. The basic assumption underlying the establishment of this panel is that the answers to these questions are, to a large degree, within our control. The future, and in particular the future of education, will be what we make it. Technology is expanding the possibilities; human choice will determine the actualities.

2 Education in a World of Omnipotent and Omniscient Technology

THOMAS K. LANDAUER
Bellcore

In the next 35 years technology will change human life in many ways. I want to raise questions about how the role of education may be changed by the new ways in which people will interact with the world. I am particularly concerned with a new and rapidly developing kind of technology that I call *cognitive tools.* A cognitive tool is a technological device that helps people do cognitive tasks, in Ray Nickerson's words, helps them to know, think, or learn. We have grown accustomed to technology that aids physical tasks, and practiced in worrying about implications for unemployment and education. We frequently are told, for example, not to worry about automation because it will free people for the more interesting and challenging mental activities that only humans can accomplish. I believe the next 35 years will see dramatic encroachment on these "only humans can do" domains by machines. Not only will machines replace us in humdrum activities like posting ledger accounts and copying letters, but they also will interact with us intimately in all kinds of intellectual activities, from composing (not just typing) letters to planning (not just drawing) buildings.

These developments will raise three questions especially relevant to education. One is what will education be for when new tools do many of the old tasks for which the "basics," literacy and calculation, are the present tools? A second question, in some ways prior, is what kind of mental tasks should technology help us with, and how? In terms of efficiency, economics, or human gratification, what tasks or parts of tasks are really better reserved for an educated human mind, and which should be taken over by or aided by what kinds of information-processing help? A third question is how will education fit into the new ways of living that will surely evolve as more and more of our current activities are done by machines or with their help? An important special case is to wonder about the extent to which new information-processing devices will preempt some of the current roles of education as a side effect.

Most of these new tools are not yet even imagined, and in many cases my discussion merely points to a prediction that people will start to invent them. But many cognitive tools with important potential consequences will undoubtedly be in laboratory use in 10 years. An old Bellcore rule-of-thumb predicts an average of 15 years from lab to home. Count another 10 years for penetration of the market and replacement of old technology, and the year 2020 is about the right place to look for major effects.

What the actual changes and effects will be, we cannot predict with any confidence. What we can do, however, is to consider what new possibilities may face us, and what radical alterations in life and society may be inherent in them. Thus, the approach I take here is not a cautious evaluation of what is most likely but the painting of what I believe to be a realistically plausible technological future that would force major changes in education. The view of the future that I offer is predicated on an optimistic assessment of probable progress but does not depend on an uncritical acceptance of hyperbolic claims for artificial intelligence or imaginary hardware devices. With a few exceptions, the technology I project requires only improvement and extensive development and application of existing scientific and engineering knowledge and methodology.

COGNITIVE TOOLS: OLD AND NEW

Most of education can be seen as the provision of tools for doing cognitive work or play. Reading and writing are tools for communication and for learning. Mathematics is a set of tools for problem solving. For millennia such tools have been based on a crude but crucial technology consisting of conventional marks on paper, augmented by extremely difficult-to-learn mental skills. Learning to use these tools well takes tens of thousands of hours of patient instruction and practice. By current standards for new cognitive tools, such a requirement is appalling. Imagine an ad for a computerized spreadsheet whose small print advised that 100,000 hours of practice would be needed for successful operation!

The substantive contents that are taught in schools can also be seen as cognitive tools. At present, the primary technologies for information access, reading coupled with library access, are extremely slow. For most important mental tasks, acquiring the knowledge needed at time of use is not feasible. (Only professors on sabbaticals can hope to get away with it.) Moreover, the digestion of information from reading and its transformation into useful new thoughts or problem solutions depends on the possession of vast amounts of prior knowledge by which to interpret it. Thus, having lots of knowledge is an important tool for acquiring and using more knowledge, as well as for its own direct application. Choosing the body of knowledge to be implanted by schooling has been a difficult and hotly debated topic. Because school learning cannot be more than a small fraction of the knowledge used throughout life, designing it to be maximally useful as a tool is the central concern of curriculum planning. Obviously, the availability of new sources of information and much more powerful tools for its ready access is going to have dramatic influences on curriculum.

What kinds of cognitive tools are forthcoming? Consider some harbingers. A relatively new tool with rising currency among a certain class of professional thinkers is a variety of programs that helps them do symbolic mathematical manipulations. Examples are the programs MACYSMA and muMATH. Recently, hand-held calculators with similar functions have become available. Feurzeig (this volume) describes such a tool being developed for classroom use. With these programs or calculators one can state an algebraic expression and ask the machine to perform any of a large number of routine, but error prone and boring, manipulations. For example, it can find factors, roots of polynomials, or multiply out large expressions. It even helps with simple changes of variables, substitutions, and the like. All these are much more tedious and prone to human error than mathematicians sometimes pretend. Indeed, applications of such programs to check classical computations have found serious errors in formulae in use for decades (for a readable account, see Pavelle, Rothstein, & Fitch, 1981).

So far, such tools have been aimed primarily at professional users of mathematics, not at ordinary folk. Most current implementations are very far from "user friendly." But it can be only a matter of time, and probably a short time, much under 35 years, before we all have them. The symbol-manipulating skills of ordinary arithmetic and algebra that are painstakingly (painfully?) taught in the schools use technological aids now, but terribly primitive ones based on paper and pencil. These are bound to be replaced by portable devices that will do the dirty work for us. The ancient hand tools for formal thinking will give way to power tools.

(I know this suggestion is likely to lead to murmurs of moral indignation. It always seems like cheating when technological prosthetics are introduced into mental activities. I wonder what outrage greeted the earliest uses of writing as a crutch for arithmetic? Of course, whatever we are well used to and were taught in school is natural and god-given, and what is introduced this year is a form of decadence.)

This issue has already been faced to some extent (National Science Board, 1983), and it would be good to know the answers from experience and experiment. What has been the effect on the teaching of arithmetic skills of the introduction of the hand-held calculator? Is it safe to allow children to grow up without being able to do mental (or pencil and paper) addition, multiplication, division, and subtraction? (I, for one, gave up long ago doing square roots without electronic help, and larger roots have always required everybody to fall back on log tables or slide rules. Where will it all end?)

An intriguing idea is that new tools will not just help people do mathematics and other cognitive jobs more easily but in the same way they used to, but they will also lead to fundamental alterations in the way problems are solved. (See Pea, 1985, for a cogent discussion of this topic.) A particular example is simulation. For practical purposes, much of problem solving is more easily accomplished by using simulation methods, or trial and error techniques. For nontrivial problems, such methods require enormous numbers of precise calculations and cannot be done with paper, pencil, and brain. Their use is currently restricted to those with access to large computers for problems whose economics are justified by some large-scale business or scientific use. With the cheapening of computers these techniques will become available to the masses. Spreadsheet programs may well represent the first wave of a tide. Quite possibly we will want to teach people the skills and ways of thinking necessary to take advantage of such tools.

The kind of stepwise sequential iterative procedure that one uses in traditional computer programs, and in many simulation approaches, is a rather different style of thinking and problem solving from the closed-form solutions of logic and mathematics that we have customarily taught in schools. One can debate whether "procedural" or "declarative" methods of expressing and solving problems are "better," but it is certainly true that sequential iterative (and more so, recursive) approaches and search methods for complex problems were not very convenient to use in previous eras. For problems of any size, literally thousands of steps may be involved, each having to be performed correctly to achieve a useful answer. People simply cannot do that very well using paper and pencil because of their own lack of speed and accuracy. One might even hazard the conjecture that much of mathematics was invented largely to skirt this practical problem, that calculus, for example, was primarily a trick to avoid arithmetic! The need was to find a way to answer practical geometry or accounting problems that the cognitive tools of the day, paper and pencil, were not up to. From a practical perspective, most of the problems of navigation and engineering, even many fundamental principles of physics, could have been expressed naturally and calculated with sufficient precision by iterative numerical procedures if only better tools for doing the calculations had been available.

The calculus was, of course, one of the greatest intellectual accomplishments in human history. But it is at least worth asking to what extent it and other systems for arriving at closed-form symbolic problem solutions will remain as dominant in the future. Even in deep areas of basic research in science, engineering, and mathematics itself, methods of exploration, derivation, and proof that rely on the carrying out of vast numbers of conceptually simple steps with the help of computers are already commonplace. But probably more relevant to education is to consider everyday mathematical problems, ones used by ordinary citizens. Take, for example, the task of computing compound interest. A direct way that, I hazard, appeals to a fair proportion of the public would be to calculate the interest for period 1, add it to the principal, calculate the interest for period 2, and so on. It is quite an easy and direct method to understand, and each step is easy to accomplish with everyday mental skills. But to calculate the interest for 20 years compounded daily and get it right is near impossible. Thus, those who can master it—probably a disappointingly small minority—have been taught to derive or at least apply a formula that relies on the calculus. Now that we could easily supply a machine that would do the iterations accurately, might it not make sense, at least for some people and some applications, to teach people how to set up the problem as a straightforward iteration? If we found that to be true, what other kinds of mathematical tasks might also be easier for people to manage with new, artificially aided techniques?

Another such invention is a better kind of book. Putting books on-line in "hypertext," or in some other much better form that makes them vastly easier to navigate and learn from may change things dramatically. Suppose you have a book in which you can find just the information you want when you need it, that if asked leads you through questions and exercises, or to background, explanatory, or related material. Suppose you have a library composed of such wonderful books, all interconnected and jointly indexed. Then you might do much more of your learning on your own than you do now. If learning on your own were made much easier, education as we know it, which consists largely in providing guidance and discipline, might whither.

A somewhat less certain prospect that is emerging in the computer applications business is that of machinery whose use is "transparent." By this is meant something whose operation can be grasped easily without formal instruction. Methods for designing equipment are emerging that, though not solving the problem completely, are making many new products much easier to learn and operate. Engineers used to design new pieces of important equipment, such as power shovels or locomotives, with almost no attention to ease of operation. No one winced at the notion that operating the new machine would require a 7-year apprenticeship. Nowadays, the expressed attitude, at least, has come full turn. The goal is to make a new piece of equipment easy enough to learn that flipping through a few pages of instructions, or having the machine talk to you, should be enough to get you started doing useful work. Human factors psychologists have discovered that, by doing early prototyping and iterative redesign, things that start out being hard to operate can be made easier by orders of magnitude.

Some of education, if you will count such things as typing classes, has been devoted to laboriously teaching people how to use difficult-to-operate machinery. I think we can anticipate a great reduction in that need as our methods for building easier-to-use devices and systems improve. One reason for a firmer prediction in this direction is that the rapid obsolescence of new technology provides a strong economic motive to invest in the research and development needed to make machines transparent.

The typing example raises its own miniproblem. Possibly by 2020 all computer systems will accept speech input (but I disbelieve they will accept truly "natural" language as their usual mode of intercourse, given that natural language is highly ambiguous and imprecise.) Nonetheless, we can anticipate a rather interesting trajectory toward that target. It is going to be some time (estimates vary wildly; mine is at least 10 years) before widely useful speech recognition becomes available in any quantity. During that time, and probably for at least 10 years afterwards, interaction with the increasingly omnipresent computer will require operation of a keyboard. Typing is going to be one of the most important cognitive tools for the next few decades but then may disappear entirely as a useful skill. This is a rather interesting example of a phenomenon I think will become quite common and pose an enormous challenge for education. Changes in technology will themselves be much more rapid. The notion of training now for use later will be called more often into question. But more of that later.

The serious issue is: What shall we teach our children, when we know that the way we solve problems now may not be the best way to do them next year? Should we teach for whatever tool is on the market, best, or cheapest now? (e.g., teach to hand-held calculators with reverse Polish notation now?) Should we try to create national standards for such tools, guaranteeing by law that they stay constant for 10 years so that school training will be of some value? (e.g., temporarily outlaw symbolic or iterative calculators?) Or, do we simply omit teaching such skills at all and hope that sufficient instructional materials will come with future commercial devices?

The development of computer-based symbolic math tools was done by mathematicians for mathematicians. But we are already seeing much more systematic approaches to cognitive tool development, in which psychologists and educators are teaming up with computer scientists to invent new information-processing methods that serve as mental aids. For example, the Cognitive Science research group at Bellcore has the invention of such aids as an explicit goal. The belief is that current hardware and software technology is already up to the task of providing an enormous number of enormously helpful new aids, if we only knew what we wanted them to do. The strategy is to analyze what people find difficult in performing intellectual tasks and then find ways to have a computer make it easier (see Landauer, in press). Often the invention step is almost trivial once a good analysis of the human difficulties is at hand. An example of this scenario occurred with respect to the next domain of new cognitive tools that I want to mention, information retrieval.

Reading and writing are tools of information transfer. When the transfer involves keeping the information around for any length of time between production and consumption, we customarily talk of storage and retrieval. Books, libraries, and lately, magnetic tapes and discs have been the storage devices. Methods for finding the information in large collections thereof began with early books. Some early inventions in this field were the replacement of "sequential access" scrolls by "random access" pages, page numbering, the idea of separate books for separate topics, tables of contents, indexes, libraries, catalogs, and concordances. Recent additions include abstract services, permuted term indexes, and query languages. So far, electronic technology has changed the situation primarily by making much larger stores of information of certain kinds available much more quickly to expert users. Those who can afford the fees and have the expertise can, from their desks, search the abstracts and titles of literally millions of articles in their field of interest, or billions of bits of information about stocks or some commercially inventoried product in a matter of minutes. We need to consider how this growing availability of information itself will affect our lives and our educational institutions.

Techno-sages see us all, within not many years, having access over our "telephone" lines to virtually all the libraries, data bases, and newswires of the world. It is quite certain that the technology will be here. The cost of mass storage and transmission devices continues to plummet. There is reason to believe that most of America, at least, will be glass fibered with gigabit-per-second switched lines by early in the 21st century. This means that, should they so desire, people will be able to dial up their favorite movie, or the contents of the Library of Congress, at a reasonable cost.

An outstanding question, of course, is whether anyone, and if so who, will want such floods of information. Currently, the success of people in searching for information in large data bases is probably no better than it was in libraries hundreds of years ago. From what we can tell, it has always been a toss up whether people found what they were looking for in large collections, and it still is. The likelihood of finding something in the first place you look is around 10 to 20% (see Furnas, Landauer, Gomez, & Dumais, 1987). The proportion of relevant documents returned by searches using the best current indexing and retrieval methods is almost always well below 50% (Salton & McGill, 1983). And you usually get many more things to look at that you do not want than that you do. Modern electronic technology makes all this happen faster and on a larger scale, but with no greater success rate.

We looked into the matter by studying in detail how people describe information they want in a number of domains. What we observed is that failures to find are almost always caused by human use of terms that the retrieval system does not recognize. Librarians, systems analysts, and information-retrieval designers have always underestimated the seriousness of this problem. One inventive solution was straightforward; just install lots more names, i.e., index terms—we call them aliases—for each of the objects in an information retrieval system and have the system know with what likelihood what objects are intended by each name. Impractical with paper and print, this technique is easy with a computer. Trials, reported in detail elsewhere (Furnas et al., 1987), have shown that this trick can increase human success rate in information retrieval by factors of three to five. (The difficulty, of course, is in collecting all the terms, typically around 30, that people will want to use for each object. But that too can be automated; Furnas, 1985.)

The method here relies only on standard computer science technology and works well for modest-sized data bases. To make it a practical device for every person for the huge data collections of the future will require some major advances in common computing environments. In particular, these improved retrieval methods will work much better when massively parallel machines become commonplace. If we extrapolate from past developments in the computer world, we should certainly see this happen well before 2020. We can thus anticipate that much easier and more effective retrieval of much vaster quantities of knowledge will be with us by then.

The main point I want to make, however, is not to predict this or any other "gee whiz" bits of future. The moral is that information-processing technology, computers, switches, and high-capacity transmission, etc. make possible the invention of new cognitive tools that will let people perform mental tasks much better than they could before. This realization, I believe, is going to spark an explosion of attempts to help people remember and think better. Let me conclude this section by asking you to imagine that everybody has a device that makes it genuinely easy to do calculus and linear programming, and another that allows them to look up any piece of information they want in a matter of seconds. What do we teach such people in school?

WHAT SHOULD COGNITIVE TOOLS DO AND WHAT SHOULD THEY BE LIKE?

This topic is possibly only tangential to our main purpose in understanding the effect of technology on education. It does not involve so much how education will be changed by technology as how the wisdom of education ought to influence technology. A case could be made, however, that those with wisdom and responsibility for the training of mental abilities should be involved in the specification and design of the tools that those mental abilities will use. This is partly because the educational activities that educators must plan and execute depend heavily on the available tools and partly because experts in education know a lot about what is needed, desirable, and practical in cognitive tools. And, perhaps, because they will have to interact with the outcomes of inventions and development of such tools, it would be desirable for educators to be involved in their creation.

Let me try to illustrate the kind of question I have in mind. What is fundamentally better, reading or listening? Twenty years ago an anthropologist friend of mine predicted that by now students would not be taught to read, because the tape recorder would have replaced books. It hasn't happened, but maybe only because the tape recorder is such a clumsy tool. Perhaps future developments will make his prediction come true. But, do we think this is a good goal to pursue? Is there something fundamental in the act of reading, or perhaps of writing, that makes it a better medium for human information transfer than the medium of speech and hearing? What is the better way to set down thoughts and to send them to someone else (or to oneself): handwriting, typing, or talking?

Some people who have access to electronic mail think it is a better way of communicating than face-to-face or telephone conversation for many purposes. Suppose this is true. How much of the superiority involves the use of the text format, and the possibility of scanning it, and so forth, and how much is simply due to the convenience of storage for later consultation and easy transmission? If text is fundamentally important, then we will have to continue thinking about how to teach people to read.

Let us put this question in a somewhat different way. Why was text and print invented in the first place? Is it a second-rate substitute for talking and listening, invented solely to get around the technological problems of evanescence in sound waves, or does it exploit a higher capacity sensory and mental channel for input, storage, or manipulation? Is there a better way of answering such questions than the marketplace alone?

It would, of course, be sad to think that a new technically illiterate population could not avail itself of our rich cultural history: old art, old writing, and old science. But if we look at the way most people get their information about the world now—from television, movies, radio, and telephone—it may be hazardous to believe that they will always retrieve past glories by reading. We need realistic preparation for the possibility that other modes will be the dominant choice.

WHAT WILL LEARNING
AND EDUCATION BE FOR?

I believe that by 2020 a good portion of the cognitive tasks now performed by people will be capable of performance by machine. We are fond of claiming that there are things that only humans can do, or asserting that machines will free people to do ever-more "intelligent" tasks that they prefer, but a lot of this is merely whistling in the dark. For one thing, it is far from clear that most people would "prefer" to do their own deep thinking, or that they would want to be taught how to do it, if machines could relieve them of the necessity. The view that thinking will never go the way of manual farm labor is tempting and comforting for professional intellectuals, such as those who write and read books like this one, people who engage in difficult thinking not just because they have to, but because they enjoy the activity and excel at it. But it may be a seriously egocentric, elitist notion arising from a temporary phase of historical evolution in which human intellectual skills have been of paramount value. If my conjecture is right, by 2020 only a select few will have extensive need or desire to be educated for difficult mental work, whereas everyone will have greater need to learn history and "civics," morals and manners, and the leisure arts.

At this point, I must interject a small caveat about my own argument. As applied science comes more and more to run the world, everyperson's need to evaluate the claims of "experts" becomes more acute. People today seem to be having serious difficulties discriminating science from science fiction. As science grows more esoteric and specialized and is often done by anonymous computers, what means of evaluation will be available to its consumers? It seems doubtful to me that the average person could ever know enough to understand the detailed arguments of science on most important topics. Perhaps the only reliable protection and guidance will have to be provided by social institutions, e.g., Surgeons General, National Research Councils, and the like. But surely the knowledge that evaluation is necessary, the attitude of scientific scepticism, and some general knowledge of what evidence and credentials do and do not support what claims, must be a critical part of future general education. It would also seem desirable for people to have some understanding of the world they live in, to be able to see the machines and objects they use and interact with as natural phenomena rather than as manifestations of incomprehensible magic. Thus, education in Science and Technology as an enlightening subject matter, and as a type of humanity, "science appreciation" if you will, should be a continuing goal.

Nevertheless, in the main, the popular demand for technical knowledge and formal problem-solving skills will, I believe, be reduced rather than increased as the result of advancing technology. Almost all farming activity has disappeared from the daily life of most people, despite a rich tradition of love for the soil and its honest toil. So it may well be with "information work." Already a great deal of "deskilling" has occurred in formerly intellectually demanding office occupations; single activity "word processing" and "message" centers have reduced the content variety of secretarial and clerical jobs. A substantial move away from both blue-collar and traditional white-collar work toward "service" occupations is well under way. In thinking about education for the future we need to consider very seriously what people will be doing with their lives, both in work and in recreation.

The number of people who are engaged in truly intellectual activities, like computer programming—or what takes its place—will decline as machine intelligence takes over more and more. Machine intelligence is already being used to solve mathematical and physical problems that have resisted scientists for hundreds of years. Thus even in science, the touching faith that only human creativity can prevail begins to seem naive. There is a hope, to which I subscribe, that the power of technology can be used to make work more enjoyable and gratifying. But there seem to be powerful economic and social forces, and perhaps even common preferences, that favor the intellectual deskilling of employment. Work "enrichment" is often resisted not only by management but by workers as well, and as a historical/statistical fact has not been a popular movement. The Volvo experiments in craft-team manufacture, for example, like the Swedish laws prohibiting boring work, have not been widely copied.

By the target date of our title, I think the working population will have divided itself essentially into three camps. Camp one will be a very small cadre of elite technologists, inventors, scientists, and artists. As always, the front lines of these occupations can be occupied only by a very small percentage of the population. Because the bits left for human mentation will be harder than now, the remaining human practitioners will be even more strongly selected high-end outliers. The problems they work on will be much more esoteric, because all but an occasional novel problem will be soluble by anyone with the help of machinery. Traditional problem solving, for the few who continue to do it, will be harder and perhaps more important, but it will no longer constitute a paying job for large numbers of people.

The second camp will be people in occupations involving human-to-human interaction where motivational concerns are critical. Human motives have much to do with instinctive, biological values, with the sight, sound, smell, and actions of other humans. I predict that the very involvement of difficult, individual human effort in the production of a goods or service will become its main determinant of value, because it will be the only thing that is truly scarce. This has already begun to happen. Witness the great growth of fancy restaurant cooking and eating, where the criterion of quality escalates constantly to require that the product involve a great deal of human skill and attention. Witness the skyrocketing earnings of star athletes and entertainers; that is, occupations that fulfill emotional and pleasure-giving functions, and that are defined as valuable by the provider being a human, will become a much larger part of the scene.

The third camp will be the managers of production capital and activity. How the ownership and management functions will be assigned is an area in which it is less safe (if possible) to hazard guesses. Nonetheless, it seems likely that the traditional role of schools in forming values and in teaching methods of interpersonal relations will not only remain pertinent but perhaps will take on a much more central role.

If this scenario is even partly true, it will raise some troubling social and educational issues. For one thing, there is a question of the elite versus the rest of us when technology has become more difficult and fallen into the hands of fewer people. Will those who are capable of understanding and pushing the rarified technology be the masters or the servants? Even in the short run, how will the possession of technology and technical know-how be distributed in the population? Already we see access to computers very skewed, the affluent parts of society offering them to their children and the poor being left behind. How will this distort our society, our values, and our lives? Already we see an alarming trend for interest and talent in computer technology to be the near exclusive province of males. What are the implications and the remedies for this? This is a pressing current problem for education that probably will get worse.

A danger exists, I believe, in viewing computer skills as an issue of vocational training. Acquiring a taste for computer methods and competence should be viewed as a basic intellectual tool. Intellectuals of the future, be they musicians, artists, or scientists, will want new skills to use the computer methods that will surely come to augment human intellect in these pursuits. We must be sure these skills are distributed in an effective and fair manner.

Ray Nickerson at the outset described education as the provision of knowledge and the ability to think and to learn. It is worth considering the extent to which future citizens are going to need or want these offerings. How much and in what ways will most people really need to think, how much and how will they really need or want to learn? If most people are primarily engaged in interpersonal activities and entertainment rather than in the work and living problem-solving activities of the past, the things they will need and want to know may be very different. At risk of heresy, I hazard a guess that the intellectually rigorous activities of schooling are almost always aversive to the majority of students, and the social activities appealing. How should education respond if economic and personal needs for mental skills wane and those for social skills wax? What kind of restructuring of education would it take to prepare people to please each other, and themselves, to solve problems about social and artistic matters, and to be ready to easily acquire that kind of knowledge? Will reading, writing, and calculation still be the basic skills we don't know how to teach? Or will we be more concerned with ethics, esthetics, games and athletics, learning for the pleasure of it, group dynamic and conversational skills, and purely expressive art?

Let me raise just one more relatively short-term issue. The rapidity with which, even now, work and recreational activities are changing is staggering (think just of calculators, electronic cash registers, word processors and spreadsheets, skateboards, sailboards, mountain bikes, and VCRs). It used to be that a few people in each generation were laid off jobs because of technological change. Soon almost everybody can expect to change the way they earn their living or enjoy themselves every 10 years or so. This can only accelerate. It is getting harder to think of technical things to teach in school for 12 years that will still be useful when the time comes to apply them. It is even hard to choose continuing education topics. For example, courses on the operation of local telephone companies are not easy to plan, because the technology changes so rapidly that an instructor can hardly say anything that will be true in a few years. The alternatives often being adopted are either to make new methods much more self-evident than in the past, so less training is needed, or to provide very "local" ways of teaching, including computer-based "embedded" training, so that learning becomes an integral part of the job. Thus technical education loses its separation from work (and play).

Some Concluding Speculations.

On the one hand, all the issues raised previously should make us wonder whether much of the technical and intellectual content of education as we now know it has long to last, or whether it was developed for a different world. I have suggested the possibility that the acquisition of high-powered mental skills may become appropriate for only a small fraction of students. On the other hand, I have speculated that a complementary effect of the same factors may be to make the social and "self-fulfillment" functions of mass education much more important. Education always and everywhere has served the politically and economically dominant needs of society, be they the perpetuation of religion, oral history, craft, art, or military skills, or relatively lately, the imparting of "basic" knowledge. Social skills have always been an important component. The development of universal education was probably driven at least as much by the need of industrialized societies for well-behaved workers as by any real requirements for technical training or the desire of the populace to be informed. Thank goodness, the purely disciplinary role of schools seems to be in decline, but the need for inculcation of prosocial attitudes and behaviors is at least as great in our fluid mass culture as it was when social control was lodged more securely in small communities and families.

As the industrial and office life of recent centuries is transmuted into the service and recreational life of the next, the demand for personal adjustment skills, interpersonal relations skills, group and societal process knowledge, shared cultural knowledge and experience (replacing the socializing influence of clan and family) will probably become much stronger. Individuals will need and want to learn such things in pursuit of their own happiness, and societies will need citizens so educated to preserve domestic and international tranquility. These needs will grow as people spend fewer hours in relatively lonely and closely supervised activities on assembly lines and in front of terminals (this is predicated on the assumption that the current growth of individual terminal work will be transitory). Nor should we underestimate or denigrate the likely increase in the future role of schools, or what replaces them, as recreational or "cultural" institutions, in which children spend time safely and happily under adult supervision, places where the individual "life of the mind" can be nurtured, but also places where social contacts are made and the social "business" of life is carried out.

Thus, oddly enough, at least one view of the probable effect of increasing technological power, and an increasingly technological society, is that daily living, and education as its reflection, will eventually become less technical and more social in its goals and content. This suggests that an exclusive or dominant concern in educational research and development on intellectual problem-solving skills or on scientific and technical knowledge might be a mistake. Although these will probably be in great demand over the next few decades, by 2020 the "humane," "social," and "cultural" aspects of education may be in greater need of cultivation.

REFERENCES

Furnas, G.W. (1985, April 15–18). Experience with an adaptive indexing scheme. *Human Factors in Computer Systems, CHI'85 Proceedings*, 131–135.

Furnas, G.W., Landauer, T.K., Gomez, L.M., & Dumais, S.T. (1987). The vocabulary problem in human-system communication. *Communications of the Association for Computing Machinery, 30,* 11, 964–971.

Landauer, T.K. (in press) Research methods to support creation of computer systems for effective human use. In M. Helander (Ed.), *Handbook of human–computer interaction.* Amsterdam: North Holland.

National Science Board Commission on Precollege Education in Mathematics, Science, and Technology. (1983). *Educating Americans for the 21st century.* Washington, DC: National Science Foundation.

Pavelle, R., Rothstein, M., & Fitch, J. (1981, December) Computer algebra. *Scientific American,* 136–152.

Pea, R.D. (1985) Beyond amplification: Using the computer to reorganize mental functioning. *Educational Psychologist, 20,* 167–182.

Salton, G., & McGill, M. (1983). *Introduction to modern information retrieval.* New York: McGraw-Hill.

3 Mobilizing Resources for Individual-Centered Education

HOWARD GARDNER
Harvard Graduate School of Education
Boston Veterans Administration Medical Center

INTRODUCTION:
A CRITICAL MOMENT IN AMERICAN EDUCATION

The period of the middle 1980s marks a special moment in American educational circles. For the first time in a generation, the quality of public education in America is undergoing considerable scrutiny. There is little question that, as a consequence of these discussions, education will change—indeed, it has already begun to change. Even as the pressures mount for educational reform, insights about the nature of the teaching and learning processes are issuing forth at an accelerating rate from the research community—not only from researchers in education but also from workers in cognitive science and neuroscience. A major question for our time is whether the findings from educational research will address, and satisfy, the needs of educational reformers; and, if so, what form the end result may take.

In light of the record of previous reforms, and of plausible theories of human nature, ample grounds for pessimism exist. It is possible that the call for reform will peak, if it has not already done so, and that the changes made will turn out to be chiefly cosmetic. Despite the good intentions of planners, reform may fall victim to facts of economics (e.g., a depression) or of demographics (e.g., an influx of poorly prepared students whom the schools are unwilling or unable to serve; or a cohort of poorly trained teachers) or of cultural trends (e.g., the effects of drugs or of the mass media will overpower the effects of schools). In such cases, of course, prognostic exercises like this one, however stimulating for the participants, will prove to be exercises in futility.

Even if the pressures for reform succeed in bringing about significant change, it is possible that the changes will not be to our liking. Indeed, my own belief is that the most likely changes are ones that, while relatively easy to implement, will be of educationally dubious quality. In this chapter I first sketch the results of a less palatable (but more likely) reform, which I term *uniform*; in my view this type of reform reflects a certain set of assumptions about cognition and education, assumptions that are shortsighted and dubious. I contrast this "uniform approach" with one I find far more congenial — and "individual-centered" reform. On my reading, the facts about human development and learning support an "individual-centered approach"; the advent of new technologies and resources, human as well as mechanical, enhance the likelihood that such an individual-centered approach could in fact be implemented. In the latter part of this chapter I put forth some proposals about how to conceptualize and implement such a form (and reform) of education.

A "UNIFORMIST" VIEW OF COGNITION

Deeply entrenched in Western thought is the view that the mind is best conceived of as a single comprehensive and coherent entity. There are of course countless variations of this theme and many proposals of different human faculties as well. Yet a line of thought that originates with Plato and runs directly through Descartes to Kant argues powerfully that human mental activity is best conceived of as unitary: whatever variations may occur ought to be conceived as wrinkles on a single mental theme. And central to this view of the mind is a belief that logical-mathematical thinking underlies all respectable forms of thought.

As philosophical traditions were converted into empirical research programs about a century ago, these habits of thought recurred in the incipient field of psychology. The most dramatic and pervasive example occurred in the attempt to measure, and to model, human intelligence. If mind is unitary, then intelligence (or, at any rate, high intelligence) is the property of the excellent, or expert mind. And if psychology purports to measure mental processes, it ought to concern itself with the measurement of intelligence. In effect, this is how the reasoning proceeded in Alfred Binet's laboratory in Paris, and, shortly thereafter, in the schools and military ranks of America as well.

Lest I be accused of putting forth a caricature of views, I must stress that there have always been those who have questioned the unitary view of intelligence, and those who have called for a broadening of what should be tested, if not how it should be tested. However, this plea for pluralism has always been a minority position within the psychology, education, and measurement communities. Somehow, the reservations about intelligence and intelligence testing were swallowed whenever it came to any kind of mass undertaking. It is simply easier to have a single intelligence test, to add up the scores of subtests, and to come up with a single score that serves as an index of intellect. And although such successor measures like the SAT also recognize in principle a variety of cognitive capacities, there has been an analogous tendency to sum the scores and to regard the total as a measurement of intellect. Such are the ways of what David Riesman (1986, personal communication) has termed *low meritocracy.*

EDUCATION FROM A
UNIFORMIST PERSPECTIVE

Nowhere have the implications of the Uniformist view been more clearly evident than in the schools and universities of our country. Though lip service is routinely paid to plurality and diversity, in fact the one-dimensional view of mind and intelligence has dominated over the decades. Indeed, this conventional wisdom was stated quite emphatically in the original national curriculum study, the report of the 1893 Committee of Ten.

According to this group, headed by President Eliot of Harvard, every subject taught at all in a secondary school ought to be taught in the same way and to the same extent to every pupil so long as he pursues it, no matter what the probable destination of the pupil may be, or at what point his education is to cease (Ravitch, 1985). Interestingly, this remark is quoted favorably in a report submitted recently in one of the United States (Indiana, 1986, p. 48).

In putting forth such positions, educators are not calling for a single academic course: Even in the most uniformist of settings, a variety of course offerings and a smattering of electives will always be available. Rather, it is commonly believed that there is a hierarchy of material within each subject matter as well as a hierarchy across subject matters (with math and science occupying the top). All students should tackle this hierarchy in the same way and in the same order for as long as they are in school, and their position along the hierarchy should be regularly charted. Correlatively, students' intelligence and academic merit can be assessed by their performances on this commonly shared curriculum.

Indeed, a not-too-farfetched scenario of the schools can be put forth. At first youngsters should master the basic skills — acquire literacy and a few other cognate competencies. Those who succeed here can advance to critical thinking. The ones with a successful academic record will be encouraged to take college entrance examinations, to attend college, and to seek professional training as well. Others who fall short will occupy vocational roles in less prestigious pockets of the society. Rewards fall to those who are "the best and the brightest," and these traits tend to be assessed by the standardized tests that punctuate the academic calendar.

Now it must be remarked, once again, that few people express total satisfaction with such a state of affairs. There is a recognition, particularly among parents and teachers, that "school smarts" do not necessarily translate into "street smarts," and that some talents and abilities are not adequately gleaned from a glance at the school record. But these are seen as regrettable wrinkles in a generally serviceable system, rather than as fundamental or fatal flaws.

There is one overwhelming advantage to such a uniformist vision of education. If in fact the mind is relatively uniform and subject matters can be taught in the same way to the mass of students, then the task of educators becomes radically simplified. Rather than developing many courses and then crafting and recrafting them in light of the abilities of specified students, or groups of students, it becomes possible to fashion a common "core curriculum" and to assess students' success with it using the same yardstick. With the advent of increasingly sophisticated equipment, it also becomes possible to deliver this educational material through computer technologies, and to employ these same technologies for the purposes of assessment and placement. This mentality also gives rise to the practice of ranking students, teachers, schools, and even communities in terms of their performance on common (if "low meritocractic") measures, such as scholastic aptitude or achievement tests. In this particular instance there is an unusually cozy fit between the American obsession with ranking and quantification, and the kinds of statistical manipulations that can be readily performed on the results of standardized testing.

A PLURALISTIC VIEW OF THE MIND

Whatever the venerability and "commonsense attractiveness" of unitary views of the mind, they have received little convincing support in recent years from studies in the neurosciences and the cognitive sciences. On the basis of a review of sizeable literatures in these fields, I have concluded that a unitary view of mind represents a severe distortion of what has been established through scientific studies in psychology, education, brain science, and computer science (Gardner 1983, 1985).

Without reviewing these reviews here, let me simply mention the impressive confluence of views. In artificial intelligence the search for a general problem-solving algorithm has given way to the devising of expert systems, which have built into them intensive and detailed knowledge of specific domains. In educational psychology, the difficulty of obtaining transfer has once again pointed up the importance of subject-matter knowledge and the need specifically to train aspects of critical thinking, rather than expecting that it will simply emerge from casual modeling or from disparate problem solving.

The results are especially striking in the areas of science most familiar to me. In developmental psychology, the belief in broad stages and structures that cut across disparate domains of knowledge has been shaken, stimulating a renewed respect for the need to acquire specific skills in particular domains. Studies of special populations, such as autistic children, learning-disabled children, and gifted children have shown that, as often as not, talents or deficits are restricted to a specific area, like mathematics, music, or language. Finally, and perhaps most persuasively, mounting evidence from neuroscience points to the amazing specificity of particular neural structures and neural systems, which, either at birth or over the course of development, become "dedicated" to highly specific forms of information processing.

Once again, in the interest of fairness a contrasting point of view should be noted. Not a few scientists continue to cling to the hope that, even if a unitary form of intellect is a receding dream, some more general mental operations or capacities may exist (Anderson, 1983; Newell & Simon, 1972). Indeed, convincing evidence for such capacities would be extremely desirable from every point of view, and particularly to those charged with the education of the mind. Yet even those nostalgic for a uniformist perspective recognize that much of the knowledge must be domain specific; that critical thinking and metacognitive skills ought to be applied to specific forms of information; and that these general skills are difficult to train, often resist transfer, and require constant use if they are not to atrophy.

Despite an emerging consensus that intellect is best viewed as pluralistic, there is anything but agreement about the optimal nature and number of divisions. Schemes range from the divisions of the brain into two faculties (corresponding to the two cerebral hemispheres); to the positing of 150 different vectors of the mind (Guilford, 1967); to the identification of thousands of cortical modules that subserve minute skills such as line or phoneme detection (Mountcastle, 1978).

THE "MULTIPLE INTELLIGENCES" PERSPECTIVE

My own view is that there can never be a definitive list of mental faculties. Lists will (and must) differ depending on the uses to which they are to be put. In my own case, proceeding from an educational perspective, I have identified seven sets of capacities, which I term *intelligences*. These capacities, viewed as relatively autonomous information-processing devices activated by specific environmental contents, include linguistic, logical-mathematical, musical, spatial, bodily-kinesthetic, interpersonal, and intrapersonal intelligences. As a general argument for plurality, this list suffices; but in my own applied educational work I have found it advisable to deal with much finer grained capacities, at least two dozen subskills or "subintelligences" (Malkus, Feldman, & Gardner, 1987). Were I to work particularly within one intellectual domain, I might well want to identify an even larger number of component capacities.

Each intelligence is based initially on a biological potential, latent in every normal member of the species but differing in its degree of expression as a joint consequence of genetic and environmental factors. In exceptional individuals it may be possible to view intelligences in isolation, but in all normal individuals (and in all normal activities), blends and combinations of intelligences are featured. Moreover, following the years of early childhood, intelligences are never encountered or cultivated in pure form. Rather, they come to be involved with a range of symbol systems (like spoken language and picturing systems), notational systems (like maps, musical or mathematical notation), and fields of knowledge (ranging from physics to abstract painting). It is scarcely a misrepresentation to assert that education involves the cultivation of intelligences as they have come to be embodied over the millenia in various culturally contrived systems.

To the psychologist and the biologist, it would be optimal if educational studies could focus simply on the individual mind. Our task would then reduce to a fostering of each of the intelligences in whatever way seemed most appropriate. However, as a result of collaborative work with David Feldman of Tufts University (Feldman, 1980, 1986) and Mihaly Csikszentmihalyi of the University of Chicago (Csikszentmihalyi, in press; Csikszentmihalyi & Robinson, 1986), I have become convinced that it is necessary to take into account at least two additional perspectives: the perspective of the *domain*—an epistemological view—and the perspective of the *field*—a sociological view.

Let me illustrate these novel terms with two brief examples. In any educational regime one must ultimately deal with at least three separate constituents: the mind of the learner, the organization of an area of knowledge, and the particular social roles and institutions that permit, and ultimately determine, involvement and success within a particular culture. Thus in the case of an individual training to be a mathematician, one must take into account his or her own logical-mathematical skills (an "intelligence" analysis); the current organization of mathematical knowledge (a "domain" analysis); and the particular roles (mathematician, scientist) and institutions (universities, private industry, publications, prizes, recreational activities) wherein mathematical behaviors might be performed (a "field" analysis). Similarly in the case of music, education involves the interplay among an individual with a certain degree of musical *intelligence*, the organization of particular *domains* of music (jazz, classical, etc.), and the delineation of particular roles (performer, composer, listener) and institutions (orchestras, academies, composing guilds, and the like) within the musical *field*.

Evidence has mounted, then, from numerous disciplines in support of a pluralistic conception of the mind. However, claims as to the nature and delineation of the actual mental faculties are numerous and often inconsistent with one another. In my own case, as noted, I began with an identification of seven primary mental faculties or *intelligences*. Educationally oriented projects have convinced me, however, that at least for certain purposes it is necessary to break the intelligences down into much finer fragments. Similarly, collaborative work has convinced me that it is insufficient simply to take into account the level of intelligences: Equally crucial to the educational equation are the structure of the domain of knowledge and the constitution of the surrounding social fields in which all learning and performance must ultimately be expressed.

EDUCATION FROM A PLURALISTIC PERSPECTIVE

The notion of a genuinely pluralistic education is at once exciting and yet potentially so overwhelming as to be disheartening. If there are really as many human faculties as I have suggested, it would certainly be desirable to develop them all to the fullest possible extent. Yet, given the finitude of time and resources, such a panoramic education is simply not feasible — or perhaps one should say, *no longer* feasible. One could randomly select a few of the fields to foster, but such a procedure would be extremely difficult to justify. One could provide a panoramic education to a privileged few, but that would be suspect on grounds of equity and quite possibly unsuccessful even under the ripest of circumstances. Defying the evident constraints, one could attempt to provide a panoramic education for all; yet, unless new ways are discovered to condense educational experiences radically, this attempt to provide all things for all people would risk providing only a superficial veneer of knowledge. Finally, one could attempt some form of match between individuals and particular subject matters and social roles, thereby gaining the most mileage for the individual and for the educational system as well.

In confronting these educational options, one inevitably encounters issues of educational values. Although the latter "matching" alternative seems the least objectionable one, and — at any rate — the one for which I will ultimately argue, it is necessary to confront a reasonable objection. Our ideal of education remains (for many) the Renaissance individual who was prized for his versatility. Perhaps it is wrong to withhold from any individual the opportunity to follow as many directions as possible. And certainly a premature streaming would seem to forego rather than to maintain options.

It is difficult for anyone reared in our cultural tradition to dismiss entirely this line of argument. We would all like to develop as many of our faculties as possible, and certainly we want the same for our children. Yet in the current context I think it is necessary for us to acknowledge a cruel truth: It is simply impossible for anyone, no matter how gifted, to gain competence across the range of domains of knowledge. Perhaps 500 years ago, or even 100 years ago, such synoptic knowledge was possible. But knowledge has accrued at such a rate that even within specific fields, like physics or mathematics, it is futile for the most gifted individual to encompass all that is known.

As already noted, we must therefore face a difficult set of choices. We can elect to offer an entire diet of options to individuals, knowing secretly that this smorgasbord approach is destined to fail. Or (except in the rare case of the omnibus prodigy), we can begin at a relatively early age to make suggestions about which course of study and learning makes sense and suggest options that seem most positive (and most possible) to all concerned.

At issue here is another set of contrasting values — the relative advantages of knowledge-in-breadth, as opposed to knowledge-in-depth. Certainly, it is important to rear individuals who possess at least some knowledge about a variety of topics (and I indicate next some possible steps toward that end). Yet it seems to me that, at present, the more compelling need in our society is for each individual to possess at least one area of "deep knowledge."

I have reached this controversial conclusion for the following reasons. First, the prospects of deep knowledge across the board is, for the most part, no longer feasible. Second, the advent of mass media has made it relatively easy to pick up a smattering of knowledge about many topics, while paradoxically making it less palatable to probe deeply into any single one. Third, the most important milestone in education involves the location of some area, some topic, some discipline, with which one feels an affinity and into which one can probe deeply (Walters & Gardner, 1986). Once such a connection has been forged, the opportunity arises for other kinds of comparable links to be forged subsequently with other kinds of topics. In contrast, without such an integral connection to at least one area, the chances that an individual will ever become involved in the pursuit of knowledge are slim indeed.

In the light of these admittedly vexed considerations, I have reached the following conclusions. During the preschool years and in kindergarten, youngsters ought to be exposed to the widest possible set of materials and encouraged to play (if not to work!) with all of them. This exposure will not only ensure that children have at least the opportunity to interact with all manner of materials but will increase the likelihood that they will forge some kind of meaningful connection to at least one body of knowledge or competence (see Malkus et al., 1987).

There is a core set of skills — principally the basic literacies of reading, writing, and calculating — that should constitute a primary agenda of the elementary grades. These activities should be introduced in as naturalistic a setting as possible and all children should master these basics in as comfortable and individualized a manner as possible. Allowances should be made for students who have difficulties in one or more of these areas and alternative routes to mastery should be explored whenever possible.

Beyond this core, on which later learning will depend, much of education should be elective — elective in terms not only of *which* activities are pursued but also of the *ways* in which those activities are presented. Some of this training can occur in schools as we have traditionally known them, but much of it can (and should) take place in the homes, outside school, and in the wider community. Identification of this course of study will be a joint mission of a number of specialists, the parents, and before long the student himself or herself.

With age and experience, curricula should take on an increasingly individual flavor; by the high school years, well over half the students' time ought to be spent in those areas they choose to pursue. (I should not have to stress that these areas ought to be pursued in as rigorous a fashion as possible, and that electives should in no wise be equated with permissiveness). But what, then, of common experiences for students, and of the development of breadth and synthesizing powers as well as expertise in specific domains and fields?

As a democrat, I am fully committed to the provision of common experiences and common knowledge for all students. My chosen vehicles are classes in civics, current events, and ethics, in which all students—whatever their areas of strength—will participate on a regular (perhaps daily) basis. It is here where students should come to realize that, whatever their differences in backgrounds, aptitudes, or cognitive profiles, they must know about certain common themes and engage in discussions of social and political matters with all their peers.

As for the development of broader powers of mind, such as the capacity to synthesize, it is my own view that the potential for such integration probably exists, in at least certain youngsters, from early in life. Yet, the ultimate development of these capacities probably presupposes a relatively full exploration of one or two areas, which can then be extended outward, rather than an explicit training of synthesizing modes of thought. These are pure speculations, however; we desperately need work on the nature and cultivation of synthesizing powers.

In opting for considerable depth learning as a principal feature of the individual-centered school, I do not mean to minimize the importance of breadth. Students ought to have some sense of the range of human knowledge and the wide gamut of ways of knowing.

One promising way to achieve breadth as well as depth is to conceive of the learning cycle as a set of alternating emphases. Following the aforementioned period of wide-ranging exploration in early childhood, middle childhood should become a time of increasingly deep penetrations into areas of interest and inclination. Early adolescence, in turn, is a time when student attention turns once again to the broadest kinds of issues and to the widest set of possibilities—a period tailor-made for breadth. Further oscillations, within college and professional studies, should yield students who are comfortable with the span of knowledge—though they will not know many areas in detail—and who have also explored at least one area with depth and penetration.

Clearly, taking a pluralistic view of intellect as a point of departure, I have proposed a set of values, a course of study, and a range of options that differ widely from those currently available in the schools. It will be necessary to create a new set of roles to carry out these procedures and also to use existing (and still-to-be-devised) technologies in novel ways. There will be need for considerable "stretch" on the part of all concerned, but the result should be an educational system that is richer and more powerful than any we have known so far.

ROLES IN THE PLURALISTIC SCHOOL
OF THE FUTURE

The school of the future must be so organized that it can regularly and accurately assess the intellectual proclivities and achievements of its students. In
addition, the school must devise curricular and vocational options that are
matched to the maximum extent possible with the interests and abilities of the
students. The school should make as many of these options available as possible within its own walls, while assisting the students in effecting relevant connections outside of the school. Finally, teaching and supervising in school should
be so organized to ensure that the various connections are being forged successfully and that the joint goals of students, parents, teachers, and the community are being met.

From one perspective, the preceding missions have been implicitly undertaken by many of our best schools. Nothing that I have mentioned falls completely outside the realm of what has already been achieved in one or another
educational setting. On the other hand, viewed in the context of current
American society, with an impending teacher shortage, declining enrollments,
mounting problems in the motivation and management of students, and
decidedly limited financial resources, the same picture can be viewed as utopian. It may be possible, however, to so mobilize human and technological
resources that at least part of the aforementioned vision can be realized.

I propose the development of the following roles in the school of the future
(see also Gardner, 1987):

The Assessment Specialist. Although considerable expertise has been developed
within our society for the administration and evaluation of standardized examinations, a pluralistic view of intellect calls for a much more flexible approach to assessment. Most of our current instruments focus heavily on linguistic
and logical capacities: These tests are so designed that they can be readily
handled by individuals with strengths in these two intelligences, but they may
routinely miss students whose intellectual talents lie in other areas.

I have called elsewhere for instruments of assessment that are "intelligent-
fair." It should be possible to assess spatial or musical or personal skills (or their
component "subskills") in ways that *directly* tap these abilities, without the
need to approach them through the "lenses" of logical-mathematical and
linguistic intelligences. Considerable use of observational instruments, checklists,
videotapes, and the like should have the effect of highlighting, or at least giving some weight to, such nontraditional, less academic intelligences.

Assessment has generally been considered an activity that occurs outside
of regular schooling and carries the implication of a more objective, less "interested" form of evaluation. From my vantage point there is no need to so
isolate assessment. I would prefer to see a range of assessment instruments, from
daily or weekly spot-checks, to longer term projects, to portfolios that encom-

pass materials assembled over months or even years; ultimate evaluation ought to be based on a congeries of such instruments, some of which would be so unobtrusive that they would remain invisible to students and to casual visitors in the classroom.

Let me describe one such assessment effort, currently being undertaken with my colleague, David Feldman, and others at the Eliot–Pearson School at Tufts University (see Malkus et al., 1987, for further details). In Project Spectrum, a research effort at the preschool level, we are attempting to document the range of intelligences (and "subintelligences") exhibited by a classroom of 3- and 4-year-olds. The classroom has been equipped with a wide range of toys, puzzles, games, special "nooks," and other inviting paraphernalia, all so designed to attract the interest and exploratory appetites of young children. The youngsters have the opportunity to interact with these materials throughout the school year. In addition, we have devised more "targeted tasks" that allow trained researchers to look in finer detail at specific forms of intellectual competence.

At the conclusion of a full year in the classroom, parents receive a Spectrum Report, a succinct essay that describes the child's current intellectual profile and working styles and provides as well some suggestions about which educational opportunities might be followed up at home, in school, or throughout the wider community. It is hoped that parents (as well as subsequent teachers) will use their information to plan educational options and activities for the child in future years.

Project Spectrum is founded on the assumption that, as early as the preschool years, children differ from one another in their configuration of intellectual strengths, and that knowledge of these differences can prove instructive to those charged with the education of the child. It is possible, of course, that such information could be misused in various ways—for example, to "stream" a child prematurely, to assume that a child lacks a talent in an area where he or she simply has no interest at this age, or to discern a link between a child's trait and an adult role where in fact none has been demonstrated. Such, alas, are the risks of any fine-grained assessment; the best response to them may simply be "eternal vigilance" as to their possible occurrence. To my mind, however, the benefits of more complete knowledge of a child's capacities, and the greater likelihood that children will "connect" to meaningful contents at an early age, outweigh the risks entailed in an early assessment.

In addition to ours, a number of research laboratories have been experimenting with new ways of assessing potential and achievement across the entire age range of school. Some of these means of assessment are relatively straightforward and require little in the way of additional training or expense. Yet it is clear that supervision of an assessment program, decisions about how to assess particular children, and what sense to make of the resulting profiles are tasks that require specialized training. Stephen Kaagan, Commissioner of Education in Vermont, has estimated that up to 25% of the student's time in the school-of-the-future will be spent in assessment activities (Kaagan & Wolkomir, 1986). Even if this estimate proves on the high side, there is still little question that assessments will be an important component of any future schooling. It is therefore essential to develop a cadre of assessment specialists and, if it is not feasible to assign one to each school, to have such a specialist available at least on a rotating basis.

The Student–Curriculum Broker. Assessing the student's potential and achievement is of course only a part of the school's responsibility—a function that brackets the central teaching mission of the school. Important decisions must be made regularly about *which* courses of study to pursue, as core curricula and as electives, about which activities ought to be engaged in after class, and about which vocational lines ought ultimately to be explored by the student.

The matching of student to curricular options is the particular obligation of the student–curriculum broker. This individual must be knowledgeable about the various domains of knowledge appropriate to students of a particular age. Thus the elementary school broker should be acquainted with curricula objectives for the basic skills and the elective areas. At secondary and tertiary levels, separate specialists might be needed for natural science, social science, and artistic and humanistic pursuits.

On the basis of findings from the assessment specialist, as well as other lines of information about the student's abilities, interests, and aspirations, the student–curriculum broker offers suggestions about which course of study should be pursued. Drawing on the same sources of information, the broker also attempts to select that approach—be it teacher centered, self-administered, gleaned from a book, or obtained through interactive technology—which seems most appropriate for each student at his or her current stage of development. Should this role be properly filled, we would have a happy situation where students would pursue courses for which they have aptitude and interest, doing so in ways congenial to their cognitive styles.

As described, a large part of the curriculum broker's role consists in the recommendations of courses. Note, however, that the broker can be of value even in a school that pursues a uniform curriculum. For even in this instance, it is still possible to present "core curricula" to students in ways that conform most closely to their particular intellectual strengths and working styles. To be sure, evidence in favor of "aptitude-treatment" interactions is still on the modest side (see Cronbach & Snow, 1977). Yet, it is my firm expectation that, as we learn more about the processes involved in different intelligences and about the fine structure of different domains of knowledge, we will be in a favorable position to recommend appropriate learning techniques, whether in a "uniform" or an "individual-centered" school.

The School–Community Broker. Traditionally it has been the schools' responsibility to devise (or select) curricula and to make them available to students.

Ideally, there ought to be in every community an additional agency that serves as a repository for information about the full range of learning options available to a resident throughout the life cycle: apprenticeships, mentorships, software and hardware for purchase, journals, self-administered courses, clubs, friendship networks, computer networks, and the like. My own view is that such an agency is unlikely to arise spontaneously and that schools are the logical (if not the only plausible) candidates to occupy such a niche.

Such an agency is crucial for a reason to which I have already alluded. Just as the range of materials to be learned extends well beyond what is humanly possible to encompass, so, too, the number of educational options available to individuals today is staggering. Some of us are so overwhelmed by the innumerable options that, like the proverbial centipede, we are at least temporarily immobilized. The granting to the school of the "brokerage" responsibility would be an appropriate move, making available to students early in their lives some initial entrées to the educational opportunities featured in their wider community.

Although much of this information can be made directly available to students, it is clear that some form of guidance is needed, particularly early in the school years. The burden of the school–community broker is to gather the widest set of options for students and to aid in the process of matching students with these opportunities. In a sense the school–community broker carries out on a wider scale the responsibilities that are ceded to the student–curriculum broker within the walls of the school. The sphere of the school–community broker is the "field" in Csikszentmihalyi's sense, whereas the sphere of the student–curriculum broker is more properly the "domain" in Feldman's sense.

The school–community broker assumes an additional responsibility, however. It does not suffice simply to make the initial connections for the student, say, to a local dance company or insurance agency. It is crucial to follow up on this connection, to make sure that it is operating properly for all parties concerned, and to confirm that some educational benefits are in fact accruing to the student. Such a follow-up activity is of the essence. In fact, it becomes the chief determinant of whether a particular communal option should be maintained, strengthened, or eliminated from consideration.

As I have described them, the trio of assessment specialists, student–curriculum broker, and school–community broker, appear to be three separate vocational roles. I should indicate, therefore, that these roles have been conceptualized quite apart from their particular instantiations. The roles might be occupied by traditional workers, such as school psychologists, or by one or more newly trained kind of specialists, such as an all-purpose "educational broker." The roles might also be conceived of simply as functions of an institution — e.g., assessment, curriculum guidance — without any reference to the means whereby these functions are realized. Or they might be assumed, wholly or in part, by classroom teachers or subject-matter specialists.

Subject Teachers and Master Teachers

In my version of events, far from undercutting the teacher, implementation of the preceding roles should free teachers to do what they are most skilled at doing—teaching various subject matters to students and serving as role models of scholarly and personal qualities. Teachers would be expected to be experts in their particular subject domain. In addition, they would either specialize in a pedagogical approach that would be particularly suited to one kind of student, or they would develop a repertoire of teaching approaches that could be matched to the varying needs of a diverse student body.

A select group of teachers would be designated as master teachers. Some would model teaching for new subject-matter teachers and would monitor their progress during their early years of teaching. Other master teachers would have a wider and hitherto unprecedented responsibility. It would be their function to oversee the entire educational process, to make sure that the efforts of the assessment, curricular, and community specialists are being properly orchestrated to provide the maximally beneficial experiences for students. In the event that a serious disservice was being done, these master teachers would have the power to order revisions in assessment, curriculum, or community matching, as well as in style and content of teaching. Obviously, it would be important for master teachers to use this "reassignment" option sparingly and to attempt to achieve desired reforms through evolutionary rather than revolutionary means.

DEPLOYMENT OF RESOURCES: HUMAN AND TECHNOLOGICAL

The attentive reader of this chapter will have noticed that, until this point, very little has been said about the role of technology in the school of the future. This choice has been deliberate, and it is not merely dictated by my limited knowledge of all but the simplest technologies. I wish rather to make the point that, at least until now, technologies are best seen as tools of the school's purpose rather than as independent actors in the educational process. Even the most elaborate and sophisticated technology is unlikely to be of use in the school unless it serves a well-motivated need. (And perhaps not even then, if one is to believe David Cohen's pessimistic analysis elsewhere in this volume.) Thus, it is against a background of the kind of school that we want, mind that we are trying to cultivate, and roles that belong in a prospective school, that the niche of technologies is most properly addressed.

These warnings having been registered, it is apposite to say a few words in conclusion about the role of technologies in the "individual-centered" school of the future. When it comes to the assessment of students, certain uses of technology come readily to mind. It is quite likely that many aspects of assess ment can take place directly with computers. For example, in the case of "adaptive testing," a student's response to a set of items at a given level of difficulty triggers "on-line" a decision about which family of items ought to be presented next. At a more macroscopic level, a classroom could be so designed that information about student's choices of materials and behaviors with those materials could be automatically recorded electronically and fed into a central computing facility. All information relevant to assessment—from responses on objective tests to "free play" with blocks, bells, or books—would then be drawn on in the fashioning of an assessment profile. Comparisons of profiles across years, or classrooms, could be readily made. Of course, the quality of the profile would be no better than the quality of the materials provided to students and the quality of the computers that yield the ultimate profile.

The use of technology for school–community brokerage is as readily envisioned. Information about the full range of educational opportunities within the community, and about the record of successes and failures with prior uses of these opportunities, could be readily kept (and updated) in a central data base. This data base could then be drawn on in recommending options for particular students. Once again, the entire process of linking assessment and brokerage could be automated; and once again, the only limitations inhere in the quality of thought that went into the linkage of cognitive and stylistic profiles with recommended activities.

To my mind, the greatest challenge and the greatest technological opportunity lies in the area of curriculum. Perhaps it was once a virtual necessity that all students study history or physics or music in the same way, but this rigidity need no longer obtain. It should now be possible to match students with appropriate curricula and, ultimately, to optimal pedagogical approaches within those selected curricula. I see the new technologies playing an indispensable role in this area. The technologies can provide the kinds of information that are most congenial to a particular student's cognitive strengths, offer the kinds of supplements needed in areas of special difficulty, and ultimately assist in the assessment of learning by means appropriate to the student's cognitive profile. Meanwhile, as an interim method, it should be possible to generate "templates"—rich sets of problems designed for exploration by students who display certain cognitive profiles.

Because every subject domain differs from every other, it may not be possible to offer general pedagogical prescriptions in this area. In my view, it will be necessary for "domain specialists" to work in consort with psychologists, educators, and technologists in the preparation of materials that are at once educationally sound and suited to different learning strengths and styles. We should be under no illusion that this process will be easy to carry out. In all likelihood it will be expensive and time consuming. But the possibilities of enhancing learning for many students who might otherwise be deprived of knowledge makes this effort worthwhile and, in fact, essential. Perhaps, armed with the proper use of the powerful new technologies, we may succeed in making learning more efficient and thereby open up the possibility that individual students may master several domains of knowledge, after all.

It may seem that these descriptions border on the utopian. Indeed, in a time of unprecedented demands on finite financial resources, they may not be readily implemented. Yet to my mind, the chief obstacles are not ones of resources, but rather ones of will.

It should be possible today to make significant strides toward an individual-centered school. We already know a good deal about the range of human intelligences. Unobtrusive methods, such as the use of checklists, can provide at least a rough-and-ready assessment of individual cognitive profiles. Good teachers — and, in particular, teachers of special education — have already developed ways of teaching that are targeted to different kinds of student learners; it should be possible to assemble this information and make it far more widely available. Booklets of community resources already exist in many places and their preparation (and conversion into data bases) would be worthwhile summer projects for students in those communities where they do not exist. Finally, the concepts involved in this way of thinking are already intuitively familiar (and congenial) to many teachers and should not arouse undue opposition.

Rather, to my mind, the chief obstacles to the adoption of this approach come from prevalent attitudes within certain powerful pockets of contemporary American education. Ignoring the many lines of evidence reviewed in this chapter, most educational decision makers have committed themselves to an evaluation of education, and of educational progress, in terms of the most simplistic unidimensional metrics. This mentality leads to the publication of scores — scholastic aptitude tests, standardized achievement tests, etc. — in the newspapers, and the concomitant evaluation of students, teachers, principals, superintendents, districts, and entire states and nations in terms of their distance from the mean. Of course, as has often been pointed out, it is possible for everyone to come out ahead at this game — simply by appropriate statistical manipulations — and, in the meantime, the issues of what education is, and what it can be, are ignored.

No single educational approach can provide all the answers, and an individual-centered approach, even if fully adopted, would doubtless have its weaknesses as well. At least, however, this tack grows out of a view that recognizes diverse forms of intelligence, diverse types of knowledge, and diverse styles of learning. It is pluralistic, in the best sense of that term. How welcome it would be if technology — which is so often condemned for it inhumanity — could be mobilized to help insure that each individual achieves his or her full intellectual potential.

ACKNOWLEDGMENTS

For their helpful comments I wish to thank Joseph Walters and the members of the 2020 Panel. The research described herein was supported in part by the Markle Foundation, the Rockefeller Foundation, and the Spencer Foundation.

REFERENCES

Anderson, J. (1983). *The architecture of cognition.* Cambridge, MA: Harvard University Press.

Cronbach, L., & Snow, R.E. (1977). *Aptitudes and instructional methods.* New York: Irvington.

Csikszentmihalyi, M. (in press). Society, culture and person: A systems view of creativity. In R. Sternberg (Ed.), *The nature of creativity.* New York: Cambridge University Press.

Csikszentmihalyi, M., & Robinson, R. (1986). Culture, time, and the development of talent. In R. Sternberg & J. Davidson (Eds.), *Conceptions of giftedness.* New York: Cambridge University Press.

Feldman, D.H. (1980). Beyond universals in cognitive development. Norwood, NJ: Ablex.

Feldman, D.H., & Goldsmith, L. (1986). *Nature's gambit.* New York: Basic Books.

Gardner, H. (1983). *Frames of mind: The theory of multiple intelligences.* New York: Basic Books.

Gardner, H. (1985). *The mind's new science: A history of the cognitive revolution.* New York: Basic Books.

Gardner, H. (1987). An individual-centered curriculum. In *The schools we've got and the schools we need.* A publication of the Council of Chief State School Officers and the American Association of Colleges for Teacher Education.

Guilford, J.P. (1967). *The nature of human intelligence.* New York: McGraw-Hill.

(State of) Indiana. (1986, March). *Schooling for the twenty-first century.* Unpublished report.

Kaagan, S., & Wolkomir, J.R. (1986, March). *Three forces of today shaping the schools of tomorrow.* Paper presented at a Colloquium at the Harvard Graduate School of Education.

Malkus, U., Feldman, D.H., & Gardner, H. (1987). Dimensions of mind in early childhood. In A.D. Pellegrini (Ed.), *The psychological bases of early education.* Chichester, UK: Wiley.

Mountcastle, V.B. (1978). An organizing principle for cerebral function: The unit module and the distributed system. In G.M. Edelman & V.B. Mountcastle (Eds.), *The mindful brain.* Cambridge, MA: MIT Press.

Newell, A., & Simon, H. (1972). *Human problem solving.* Englewood-Cliffs, NJ: Prentice-Hall.

Ravitch, D. (1985). *The schools we deserve.* New York: Basic Books.

Walters, J., & Gardner, H. (1986). The crystallizing experience: Discovery of an intellectual gift. In R. Sternberg & J. Davidson (Eds.), *Conceptions of giftedness.* New York: Cambridge University Press.

4 What Will It Mean To Be "Educated" in 2020?

ANDREA A. DISESSA
University of California, Berkeley

The line of argumentation in this chapter is straightforward. First, I argue that what it will mean to be educated in 2020 is much more under our control than might be expected. Second, I discuss some of the directions we might profitably pursue given the degrees of freedom suggested in the first argument. Many of these involve computers in significant measure, but many come just as much from a progressing sense of what a good education should be, independent of the means used to achieve it; a change in goals is as important as a change in means. Finally, I look at some roadblocks and some more practical matters concerning who really has the power to bring about educational change. My concern is mostly with science and mathematics education at the precollege level, but my remarks are not intended to be exclusively aimed in that direction.

SETTING GOALS

It is fashionable to argue that the needs of our technological and information-intensive society are creating demands, indeed, perhaps fomenting a crisis in our educational system. The "information explosion" means that we need faster and better thinkers, able to scan, digest, assess, and act on a bewildering bombardment of facts. If I looked, I am sure I could find a statistic that says something like "the amount of information that will be discovered in the next 20 years will surpass the total in all our previous history!" The implication seems obvious: Everyone needs to learn more and more, and faster and faster.

There is a degree of truth in these statements. Certainly in engineering, for example, information has a very fast turnover, and being an engineer means constantly learning more. Still, taking these arguments at face value is misleading. Take a case in point. I do not recall being particularly lazy in my university and postgraduate career.[1] If "time on task" is the dominant variable, my cohort and I were near ceiling. I was also lucky enough to have access to some of the finest teachers and learning resources. But, suppose through technology, better cognitive science, and so on I could have learned another 30%. I have no doubt that such an accomplishment would make headlines in the evaluation of an educational experiment. Yet, would that make a dent in keeping up with the information explosion? Not unless it were a 30%-per-year increase in productivity, compounded! If the accomplishments of our culture and the educational challenges of the future are viewed only as the accumulation and management of information, I am quite sure we are lost.

The problem is that the "information explosion" as a concept is indifferent to the quality of the information. But, as T.S. Eliot reminded us, knowledge can get lost in information, and wisdom can get lost in knowledge. I argue strongly that what we need is a little bit more wisdom, not a dramatically increased ability to keep up with an ever-escalating pile of pure information.

There are less poetic ways of thinking about this. Science has always made progress by, occasionally in a profound insight, unifying scores and scores of individual "facts" into a parsimonious theory. Given our genuinely limited cognitive abilities, the way to keep up with a pile of facts is to build a few theories of the right kind, not simply to manage in a less insightful way the grand pile of facts. So I come to a major desideratum for an educated citizen in 2020, which I discuss further in the next section—we want to produce more theory builders, more synthesizers, more strategy inventors than fact managers.

There is another, deeper fallacy in conventional uses of the concept of the information explosion. The presumption is that our needs for education drive the educational establishment. Indeed, the extreme version is that our inability to keep up with needs will precipitate an educational crisis. I believe the fact is that we will muddle through more or less well according to how well we educate our youngsters. To be sure, there may be a cataclysm precipitated by our inability to manage our increasing power over the environment earth, but the problem is that such threats feed back into what we do only minimally. To take a prominent example, the threat of nuclear war barely suffices, and only from time to time, to get the leaders of the world together to talk about the issue. The idea that a better educated populace would produce statistically more competent and wiser leaders, or at least a more rational selection of them, does not have much force in getting down to brass tacks in improving education. We may have lots of crises, but they are very unlikely to be inter-

---

[1]It may seem irrelevant and self-indulgent for an academic to consider how he might have been better edcuated. But, we often learn best from what we know best. And I insist that it is not irrelevant if those who succeed in learning can succeed better.

preted as crises of the educational system as long as there is any more proximal cause — some particular person made the wrong decision, some safety device was designed improperly. Proximal causes will be perceived as just plain causes every time. Big, diffuse but underlying causes hardly ever get the blame.

(It could be argued that if compelling demonstration could be made for some particular, cost-effective route to improving education, in contrast to the plethora of competing options, the political establishment would follow along. This is a possible but difficult road to follow. One of the main reasons is testing. This follows the same pattern as the information explosion in that facts are easy to see and measure. Things get pretty blurry when one moves into knowledge and understanding. Wisdom or the ability to learn, of course, are essentially beyond measurement at present. Serving on a panel for the National Academy of Sciences, I had a chance to look in some detail at the science tests that are ostensibly measuring the achievement of our educational system. The really discouraging thing is not so much that the tests are all, give or take a little, the same in the kinds of things tested for and the way in which they test for them, but that the testing establishment is deeply and seriously invested only in better statistical techniques, better "validation," etc., with hardly a word about testing for different things or about significantly more legitimate ways to examine than the multiple choice tests.)

Consider business and industry. The typical response to problems — even if, as is unlikely, those problems are seen as stemming from inadequate education — is to manipulate the variables at hand. Move the business, automate, diversify, or consider the failing line of business a loser and get into a more profitable line. If the educational need is obvious, critical, and above all well defined, one might consider in-house training. But training is as far as it goes — education is just one of those things one has to compensate for, not deal with.

This is not to fault industry. Their concern is the short, or possibly, medium term. They haven't the resources nor the means at hand to make a serious stab at big, underlying causes. So, at best, one gets little programs here and there based on one or another bright idea.

Our look to the future should not obscure the fact that we have for a long time, if not always, suffered from the constraints of limited education. The future will be more of the same, not some sudden realization that we are suffering from limited skills and limited intellectual accomplishments. There is always room for more and better at the top; nobody questions how much our country benefits from truly exceptional individuals. But it is not just at the top. There is every reason to believe our productivity and quality of life would be enhanced by improved education at all levels. To take a trivial example, I have personally never seen a case where the superior skills of a secretary, up to Ph.D. credentials, were not appreciated and productively utilized.[2] Even

---

[2]"Overeducation" is a problem of expectations and desires, and of arranging reasonable compensation. It is not a problem of waste except in the case of unutilized learning produced by overly specialized education.

people of "menial" status would contribute more efficiently to our civilization with better intellectual skills. Anyone who has the least faith in our political system must admit it depends in a weak but not trivial way on the decision-making abilities of every voter. Our society could benefit now and could just as much have done so in the past, from a better educational system. This is not something new or something about to strike us with great force.

The problem, to summarize, is that the deficits of education are, have been, and will continue to be uncoupled from the problems they cause. The lack of coupling is informational—education as a distant, diffuse target is almost the last thing blamed in looking for causes[3]—and the lack of coupling is instrumental—big, diffuse targets are very hard to muster an attack on from any individual point where the difficulty is manifested.

Thomas Landauer (this volume) advances another version of this notion that education is uncoupled from social productivity. However, there is a central difference in our views. He presumes that education for the most part simply will not matter in purely instrumental terms. In contrast, I presume it really does and will continue to do so in government, decision making more generally, social fabric, continued scientific and engineering innovation, etc. The decoupling I see is in public inappreciation of the real coupling. Landauer's future visions are an extreme example of the case. And the other decoupling is real and instrumental, but directed inversely: Knowing our society's challenges does not, I claim, tell us anything very specific that must be done educationally.

I have come to a major point of articulation in my argument. Educational change will not be driven in any direct way by needs or specific problems. Therefore, we can, and we must, shape goals and images for education in large measure out of our own initiative, out of the best ideas and means that we have for improving education. No scanning of future job needs, no scenarios of manpower deployment, no present or near-future goal setting in terms of standardized tests can suffice to define for us the job at hand. We have the opportunity and the obligation to consolidate the best thinking on learning and education into images and workable programs, and to engage in the best spirit of social dialog to convince and find ways of enacting our proposed reforms. It is not, nor will it become, obvious what should be done. It is as much up to our imaginations and our will in fashioning productive new goals as it is a matter of improving our means.

Before pursuing my list of candidates for top (new) goals, I should add a caveat or two to the perhaps unbounded sense of freedom I have engendered. First, there is no doubt that there must be some sense of continuity in our fashioning new goals. An obvious concern for continuity is that we must maintain a curricular line for the specialists and professionals who need to progress

---

[3]This is not to say schools are not criticized. But it is only a vague sense that they just ought to be better behind such criticism. Only educators argue that lack of industrial productivity means we simply must spend more Federal money on schools.

to the top levels of our educational system. I assume a rough invariance in the higher levels. Graduate education, for example, is likely to remain the discretionary province of the professors that teach at that level, and that fact provides some constraints on what is done at lower levels. These constraints percolate down into undergraduate school, and even, a bit, into high school. Similarly, education at the undergraduate level for those who are expected to begin work immediately in fairly narrow, technical positions is to some extent constrained. Yet, I think the vast majority of schooling, particularly below college years, should have as a goal producing the best possible general education, preparing students to learn specialties, without teaching them only specialties. And more specialized needs can also be achieved in ways that better pursue the goals listed in the next section.

More subtly, public values in education constrain the goals we might propose. If accountability in education comes down to arithmetic achievement test scores, I project nothing much will have come of our effort to change education. More positively put, changing the public's image of good education is part of the agenda for change I am proposing.

With these caveats in mind, then, I reassert my claim that what in particular we teach is dramatically less important than the general intellectual development education engenders. Of course, saying this also brings the obligation to say a bit about what one looks for in terms of general intellectual development. I have already brushed past this in referring to skills of theory building, synthesizing, making judgments about state of knowledge, etc., but I make my primary run at these issues next.

GOALS FOR 2020

Less is More

Let me begin proposing goals to pursue by continuing to counter misleading aspects of the notion of an "information explosion." Namely, it seems we should aim at teaching more and more, more and more quickly. Efficiency, thus, is a byword and that, in turn, can set our goals for the use of computers. On the contrary, I feel strongly that a high priority is to reduce the scope of education, at least as measured by standard curricular measures. The central proposition is that developing knowledge and understanding is an incredibly complex and delicate matter. More specifically, public education as a projection of the popular image of what it takes to master any particular subject matter has vastly underestimated the complexity of the task. The mistaken attitude is that all it takes is a mastery of a properly organized collection of facts. Instead, learning is better viewed as conceptual change.

Contemporary research is beginning to be quite specific about past underestimates of the difficulty of the task of learning. One particular manifestation of this work has shown that the development of knowledge in science involves what is an almost entirely ignored "complication." Students come to courses with very well-developed prior conceptions that can interfere with learning (Clement, 1982; McCloskey, 1983; McDermott, 1984). More insidious, these prior conceptions may be almost entirely invisible to standard practices of measuring achievement. So, for example, the best students may apparently competently master a domain by the "objective" standards of current exams but may entirely fail to change their fundamental beliefs about the subject matter when we bother to ask questions framed in terms of the basic mechanisms, rather than in terms of more superficial numerical results or algorithmic performance. My own work has shown that even the students themselves may be quite aware of these problems at some level. They tell me they did fine in high school physics, they got A's, "but really didn't understand the stuff at all" (diSessa, 1985).

The details of this story are interesting and important to the state of contemporary research. But for the purposes here, I assert that it is evident already and will only become more so that deep changes in conceptualization are difficult to bring about and need a good deal of time. If, as I have already claimed, the particular things studied are less relevant than we once thought, then this assertion about conceptual change brings some direction in this new freedom. The short message is, depth rather than breadth. If we need not teach everything, at least we should teach something well.

There are side effects of underestimating the difficulty in bringing about conceptual change. Exceptional physics students that I have interviewed at least knew they did not understand the physics taught in high school. The less gifted are in serious danger of thinking they do understand! Wisdom and judgment can hardly be cultivated on the basis of disastrously misguided senses of what understanding feels like, senses developed from overoptimistic coverage in the curricula, and on the basis of pats on the back for reasonable achievement on "objective" criteria that have little correlation with deep conceptual change. The weakest students, not having the time to achieve even multiple-choice-test-sanctioned understanding, are entirely out of the arena of competent intellectual functioning. When will they ever develop skills of judging what is and what is not known and understood? Curricula designed without the deepest concern to bring students to levels of understanding that they (and we) can really appreciate can at best produce intellectual dilettantes and at worse foster legitimate feelings of alienation from an artificial task.

Slogans are two edged. Whereas they provide an easy handle on an argument, they also hide any subtlety that may be involved. Let me counter a few misgivings of "less is more" in this context that stem from too simple a reading.

If we are to teach less, one may ask which subjects should be left out. Yet, at that scale, one need not reduce "coverage" at all. Certainly I believe most if not all the standard subjects should be included in a good education, especially in view of the broad goal of increasing students' synthetic and adaptational skills. Elementary schoolchildren should learn mathematics, science, language, history, and so on. Yet within each of these, there is plenty of opportunity to dig in somewhere, while leaving out some of the currently exorbitant pile of "facts." It may well be, and, indeed, I expect that more depth in learning may end up increasing coverage. This may happen in three ways. Motivationally, students who have achieved some true competence in an area may find a thirst to acquire more. Secondly, teachers may find that learning even one topic deeply in each subject may catalyze an understanding of what the subject is about that will facilitate learning more in the area. (More on this in the section on Learning at All Levels.) Thirdly, the preceding two mechanisms may mean children are much more attentive and competent to learn outside of standard "forced-learning" situations like school. In the light of these considerations, a refined slogan might be "breadth will follow from depth."

Is "less is more" applicable to all subjects? One may argue that some literary and cultural pursuits are by definition exercises in breadth. Certainly it makes no sense to learn about literary style by spending all of one's time learning a particular one. I am also on less secure scientific ground in asserting that depth is centrally important in some of these areas compared to science and mathematics. Yet, I believe similar considerations will be found to apply to all subjects, but in varying degrees and in varying ways. I expect that learning about literary style will benefit from learning what constitutes the coherence of what we call style rather than only from getting a feeling for an endless stream of styles. Learning about the world's cultures similarly should benefit from abstracting and synthesizing cultural dynamics, to the extent we can do that.

Perhaps the underlying issue here is to get a better understanding of what one should mean by depth. Certainly I do not mean learning all the technical little details, say in a mathematical exposition, or learning exactly how many men Napoleon lost on his trek into Russia. The notion of depth that is relevant has more to do with getting a grasp of the central ideas in an area that organize and give access to other aspects of it. It has more to do with the central conceptual changes that need to occur before students can "live" comfortably in a new world view. If these intuitions of depth turn out to be valid, but turn out looking more like a particular kind of breadth in some areas, I will still feel happily vindicated. If, on the other hand, there exists no such notion of depth at all, if there is no point of intellectual leverage except in masses of information, then "less is more" will simply have been proven wrong.

Like most of the goals I list, technology does not define the direction here. In fact, the "obvious" first hopes for new technology are almost always for efficiency. But in crafting models for the use of computers, we should insist that depth of understanding be a central lesson. I and others have taken on this task, and I think it proper to elevate its importance more widely. One of the most attractive options is that technology itself will open up more subjects that are roughly along the current curricular trajectories, but that are more learnable and provide students and teachers with easier routes to assessing the *quality* of understanding acquired. One of the general trends that I hope will develop is that there will be a moving away from subject matter, facts, etc. toward more active, intellectual skills. Perhaps the most important property of these new skills in the light of the present goal is that students be able to see and appreciate the powers of the skills they acquire.

Colleagues and I have explored computational geometry as such an area (Abelson & diSessa, 1981). I can give two examples where depth is easiest to see in our goals. First, we expect students to be able to synthesize geometry — not only understand how it works from a distance; they must be able to implement it, make a working model on a computer. Second, we expect students to discover and come to understand *new* geometries. We expect them to have learned enough of the "geometry game" that mathematicians play that they can do more than play by the rules: they can make up their own rules in a meaningful way. The state of the art in my experience is that we can currently get bright high school students this far into mathematics, activities one reserved for advanced undergraduates and beyond. By 2020 I would like to see average elementary schoolchildren doing the same kind of thing.

Programming itself may be another example of an area where depth of understanding and competence can dominate breadth and coverage. It is already true that some children know much more about programming than their teachers, something that almost never happens in, say, mathematics.[4] This undoubtedly happens for a number of reasons, but among them is that some children, after reaching some degree of competence, find a particular area for programming that draws them in and becomes a place in which they can really specialize. The properties of programming that are important for this to happen are: (1) There is a core of not very difficult knowledge to master — understanding part of the programming language per se; (2) then there is a very great deal to be learned in a very great many contexts for programming in which the student may already be a specialist, at least with respect to interest; (3) and finally, learning in the particular contexts must be relatively easy to acquire without a lot of instruction. So a child can learn a little about procedures and variables, become passionate about a certain kind of interactive game, and then learn on his own the many "tricks" and pitfalls in programming such games. Standard school subjects are often quite deficient with respect to (1) and (2), so (3) almost never happens.

There is a great deal to say about each of the three stages listed previously. With respect to (1), current languages still are in a rather primitive state, and frustratingly few students get over the initial competence barrier. But if we work on it, there are prospects for substantial improvement in the next decades. With respect to this and with respect to (2), especially the role of interest patterns,

---

[4]In the worst cases, this may be true trivially in that teachers know little about programming. But I am not talking about such cases.

I have more to say shortly. Regarding (3), evidently becoming an expert in something does not guarantee depth in a practical sense. Becoming expert in a trivial enterprise is not obviously laudable. Yet, with some guidance, finding a substantial domain in which to program and learn seems a surmountable problem.

One as yet essentially unexplored area that offers intriguing possibilities in the development of student expertise in programming is "expert systems." Very generically, I am talking about the embedding of expertise about something in a "computational object" ("program" is too restrictive a word) that may even dynamically exhibit some of that expertise. A handful of companies are already making money and solving problems by applying artificial intelligence techniques in this way. Such an externalization of knowledge about almost anything may have profound effects on the attitudes of its "programmers" toward learning and on their understanding of knowledge. A childhood passion for dinosaurs may turn into a wonderful exploration of biological classification and archeological puzzle solving if turned into the attempt to automate the classification process.

Although it may seem implausible for children to do this, note that to be useful as a learning device, the expert systems do not need to be practical — they need not really "work" without the student's careful handholding of the system. Moreover, as technology and the understanding of the principles behind such systems advance, they get much easier to build. We have already had high school students duplicate some of the earliest projects in artificial intelligence. I describe very briefly such a program in the section on Computational Media. I do not think it at all beyond hope that by 2020 young students will be able to regularly externalize expertise on a computer and thereby develop both their own particular expertise and also their sophistication about knowledge and learning.

Aesthetics

Curriculum is usually argued for on the basis of its general importance or on the basis of some "logical" trajectory toward well-defined goals at an advanced level. Much of the mathematics curriculum is defined on the basis of its relevance to a rational approach to calculus, seen as the pinnacle of public school math, reached just at the end of high school or the first year of college. I have tried to undermine the presumption that any necessary pinnacles of that kind exist. And, even granted a goal such as learning calculus, vast amounts of freedom still exist. How much trigonometry, a subject studied just before calculus, is really necessary to begin calculus? How much algebra is really needed, and, going farther back, is the extensive and proof-oriented approach to plane geometry really cost effective? A more realistic guess about the origin of these prerequisites is that some of each of these may be necessary, but that the dynamic of curriculum development is that once a subject is named the slot gets filled, if not bloated, by someone's estimate of a "complete" treatment, independent of its original motivation.

Instead of intrinsic curricular justifications of this kind, I propose as a second new goal that subject matter be chosen on the basis of aesthetic criteria — the perceived beauty and enjoyment that students will feel having learned the subject. This may sound highly controversial, yet I think it a better criterion than imagined prerequisites to prerequisites to competent professional work, work (like professional mathematics) that the vast majority of students never approach, and work that especially the talented ones who will become professionals could approach just as effectively in radically different ways.

Motivation is the obvious justification for trying to develop subjects whose raison d'etre (aside from a weaker demand of legitimacy as a mathematical or scientific subject) is student aesthetic approval. It is a powerful justification; gaining access to things that engage and please us keeps many a child struggling to master his two-wheeled bicycle, and school could well learn this important lesson. Einstein said, "Love is a better teacher than duty." But a subtler reason than motivation to pursue aesthetics may be more profound: Learning any system in the context of tasks that we understand enough to be motivated strongly to wish to master means that we get important feedback from our successes and failures. If you understand at least the results of your attempts, if not precisely the mechanism that accomplishes those results, you are in a position to debug, to gradually improve, your mastery of the system.

I can illustrate. Arguably the best idea in the development of Logo (Papert, 1980) is that children perceive it to be about pictures. Children know a great deal about drawing and assessing good and bad approximations to their intentions. In using a computer language to make that happen, then can observe the pictorial effects and get essential feedback on the sequence of commands or program that they thought would engender a desired effect. I do not believe anyone has proposed, let alone carried out, a study of how much programming children learn in Logo with turtle graphics, compared to how much they would learn without it. The experiment may not even be doable, but, I would say, that is no shame. The only result that I would believe is that the more pleasing and accessible the domain (be it drawing with turtle graphics or some new more motivating and understandable domain in which to program), the more effective the instruction in programming.

It is worth pointing out that competent performance is the goal that almost always draws people into learning a skill. This means that if we deprive students of the opportunity to engage in competent performance of the skills we teach them, even if those skills are attractive enough to get them engaged in the learning task itself, then we will have cheated them and will likely pay the price. Schools need to become places where children feel they are competent and get to enjoy their competence, even if it means repetition, apparent inefficiency, and so on. The alternative is the present situation, where students are kept off balance, where the least sign that competence is developing means it is time to move on to the next topic. We need exercises after "mastery," in addition to exercises toward mastery.

Following student aesthetics and competence will inevitably lead to a kind of individualization far preferable to more standard approaches to "personalized instruction." Manipulating the presentation of subject matter for personal preferences, but choosing it for intrinsic reasons that we can hardly explain to children, let alone convince them to embrace—that is like putting a little sugar in the Cod liver oil. Not only should we start closer to their own desires, but in the exercise of competence beyond mastery, children will inevitably show far more of their own personality and style than is possible in the best of circumstances when all the learning is going on in the darkness of incompetence. Howard Gardner, elsewhere in this volume, also speaks of the need and advantages of deep personalization, and of more possibilities, technological or not, in this regard.

Computers have two very special roles here. First, there are the most intrinsically engaging of all educational (for my purposes, mathematical and scientific) materials. This is, of course, provided children are given control of the machines rather than vice versa. To cite a single but telling example, computers in the schools are probably the only educational innovation that has ever had schoolchildren picketing the school board and instigating their own fund-raising activities (as happened in my previous home town in Massachusetts)! The second role is, for me, equally obvious. Besides skill for pure aesthetic pleasure or competition, making things is the ultimate expression of competent performance. And computers are a strong candidate for the most flexible, universally manipulable medium of invention that is available to humans. I give a single example to illustrate the general point of this section, and this particular point about computers.

One of the most successful units that we developed for a high school summer program was about vector geometry. Probably the essential reason for the success was that we taught the subject in the context of getting a computer to draw three-dimensional images. No sooner did students get a minimal competence than remarkable creations began to spring up, creations like games and animations: 3-D space war, geometric ray wars,[5] where paths of light rays were bent and reflected by optical objects (implemented, of course, with vector operations), and even animation of choreographed three-dimensional dances of geometric shapes like cubes, tetrahedrons, etc.

Present-day computer technology makes these attempts sometimes less than mind boggling in execution. Inexpensive machines are still much too slow to allow complex, smooth, real-time dynamics to be programmed simply in high-level languages. And the resolution and color characteristics of displays are

---

[5]War is not a theme we encouraged, but students don't wait for our sanction on things they like and feel competent to engage in.

limited. But by 2020, cheap supercomputers ("super" by today's standards) and the likelihood of very high resolution, limitless colors and textures, and even genuine three-dimensional images will provide orders of magnitude more attractiveness in the final product than was necessary to spur our high school students on. I imagine students programming for fun simulations of the quality of the J.P.L. simulations of the Voyager flybys of Jupiter and Saturn.

More generally, if we wish students to engage in creative activities like scientists, artists, engineers, and designers, we must expect to provide tools to help them at a level they can control. Computers are craftable into such tools, which can take drudgery out of these intrinsically attractive activities.

If we can manage the trick of not turning computers and programming into a dull, devitalized activity to conform to norms, and to provide for easy testing, they can be one of our best aids in bringing students' aesthetics seriously into play.

Learning at All Levels

I have already mentioned that my initial desideratum, "less is more," is not intended to be taken literally. Like everyone else, I would like my students to learn more. "Less is more" really means learning more in ways that are much more difficult to describe than subject-matter topics of the usual type in curriculum. This section is about a particular slice of "deeper understanding" that goes roughly under the rubric of "higher order" knowledge.

There is probably a reasonable consensus in the educational research community, if not in practice, that a shifting emphasis toward higher knowledge is a high priority for education in 2020 — problem solving, learning to learn, and so on. What I want to do here is make some slight refinement on that background, give my own version of "higher order knowledge." The point is that not everything that anyone can make up in this category actually makes sense, is teachable, and will genuinely give students leverage in being the flexible, resourceful, reflective, quick learners that we would like them to become.

One of the generic problems of higher order knowledge is that, the higher the order, the weaker the knowledge. Thus, if you know lots of specific things about physics, you are much better off with those "strong" (particular) methods than using more general heuristics. $F = ma$ is usually a good deal more powerful in a mechanics problem than "think of a similar problem you've solved." Now, we all find ourselves in situations where our knowledge is limited, and we need to use weak, general methods, especially weak general methods for learning. But, on the other hand, we should never put ourselves permanently in situations in which we are restricted to weak general methods, not if we can help it. In coming to areas we know little about, we should want to be people who can build competence rather than people who are merely better than most in the first stages of the encounter.

Thus, we want students to acquire competence at all levels of knowledge; and through reflecting on the nature of that knowledge that makes it powerful, and the paths taken to acquire it, they should get better at acquiring competence at all levels. Another way of saying this is that we all should have skills at higher levels, but that we should not have the preference for using the highest level possible. Instead, we should use the highest level necessary but push to find out what really makes the field tick; we should not be dilettantes satisfied with the first easy conquerings in a new field that we can make by effectively using what we already know.

Following this general line, most have come to the conclusion that we should set the goal that our students, as Nickerson puts it in his introduction to this volume, be knowers as well as learners. The cast I give here follows on the claim that knowing any particular thing is not the point. Instead, the point is "learning by doing at the metalevel:" The best way to learn about learning is to do it seriously, i.e., learn something in particular and be reflective about it.

One advantage of the slogan "learning at all levels" is that we are less in danger of squeezing out the middle in the obvious squabble over how much emphasis to put on "high level," how much on "low level." If I were in an argumentative mood, I might propose that middle-level knowledge is more important than higher level knowledge because it provides flexibility (a degree of transferability) without falling back on the weakest principles. I might propose that many previous attempts at teaching higher order skills aimed in the right direction but overshot the mark. But, because one does not hear talk about the virtues of midlevel knowledge at all, as opposed to both "higher order thinking skills" and "really knowing the (low level) stuff," I content myself with giving a sketch of what the idea is intended to mean, and with giving some examples of midlevels. I characterize first and exemplify afterward.

Midlevel knowledge is domain specific, much more specific than "general learning skills," problem-solving heuristics like "divide the problem into subproblems," or, more technically, ideas like "means/ends analysis." But it is at the same time less particular than facts or theories or conventional curriculum topics. Midlevel knowledge will use a language of description that easily crosses these lower level boundaries, and it will typically deal with a domain at a relatively high level of abstraction. Although I do not take the following characteristics to be defining, I believe they are properties that midlevel knowledge can have for a learner:

- It will be orienting, giving a student a broad view of what is going on in a field and providing a framework into which more specific ideas can fit.
- It will be strategic in the sense that it will say more about what can and should be done with particular knowledge than is inherent in a presentation of the knowledge per se.
- It will be synthetic, joining multiple views, providing ways of seeing them as the same.

- It will be generative, not closed and limited to the particular ideas it describes, but relatively easily extendable to other ideas and to genuinely new ideas the student might invent.

- It will provide a sense of relative importance, not just assert truth or prescribe specific action.

I like to think that much of the educational task can be viewed as finding the things that students already know that can be of value in teaching a new thing. In this model, midlevel knowledge might or might not exist; it is difficult to say in advance what people know that might be relevant to an area. Midlevel knowledge may be very different from field to field, and in locating it, a sophisticated taste will be required to identify things like "importance," and to judge whether a common abstraction will really turn out to be insightful and generative, or trivial. On the other hand, I believe there is a lot of midlevel knowledge waiting for us to uncover, and although it is not presently the case, I believe there are scientific principles for assessing the efficacy of knowledge of this kind. I believe it also possible to give students an effective sense for the character and power of this kind of understanding, and the ability to invent their own.

Midlevels #1. One of my favorite examples involves a personal experience that occurred when I was learning algebra. I was slogging through all the details of an exposition of "the quadratic equation." It occurred to me that what was going on was a hairy complicated derivation whose precise point was that, once it was done, I'd never have to do it again. The notion of solving a whole class of problems at once, a class defined by the form of the equation, had never occurred to me.[6] In fact, I believe this to be one of the epistemologically novel aspects of algebra compared to mathematics taught earlier. The experience was synthetic in preparing for me a common approach to many new things to come. Once I saw the lesson of the quadratic equation in that light, I had a powerful insight into some of the magic of mathematics. More specifically, I knew that the details of the derivation were probably a lot less important than I had thought—it was orienting and provided a gradient of importance. Though the derivation technique "completing the square" is a generalizable and useful technique, I do not believe the textbook was really trying to nor should it have tried to teach that as the main point of the quadratic equation. That the writer of my textbook had not thought it might be important to tell me that I was seeing a different class of problem being solved is symptomatic of the neglect of the middle levels of understanding.

---

[6]I actually got quite excited by this insight and spent a lot of time explaining it to my peers. Perhaps the reason was that I could see it was at a different level, not just another insight, but a different kind of insight.

One should give as much care to, and even choose, subject matter for its middle-level points at least as much as for its low-level points.

Midlevels #2. My second example is a bad choice for a middle level, bad at least if one wants to teach calculus so that it extends naturally to ideas important in physics. When the concepts of integral and derivative are introduced, one is always given the interpretation of an integral as "the area under the curve." But, this fails miserably to generalize to the set of ideas necessary to understand the concept of integral in physics. There, one sees many new things, line integrals, Gauss's theorem, Stokes theorem, etc., which, given a better middle-level view than "the area under a curve," are all examples of the same basic strategy.

Consider the following view of derivatives and integrals: If you have some locally computable quantity {e.g., the difference of a function's value from the beginning to the end of a small interval, $f(a) - f(b)$}, and you can arrange it so that in adding up a bunch of these guys, all the intermediate values cancel {adding a change in value over two successive intervals, $[f(a) - f(b)] + [f(b) - f(c)] = f(a) - f(c)$}, then you have a wonderful theorem of the form, "adding up locally computable things {derivatives} gives you a global quantity of the same form {change in value of a function—the integral}." This idea is not quite as intuitively accessible as "area under the curve." But it is dramatically more extendable. It avoids unnecessary relearning, which often needs to take place on the walk from calculus to physics class. It is strategic and generative in the sense that it supplies the key idea in proving the fundamental theorem of calculus and also all those other theorems at the same time. Even new and nonstandard operations are comprehensible in this frame. It is also more representative of the kind of thinking mathematicians do. After all is said and done, the central gist of a topic, the key ideas and a sense for the kinds of problems that can be solved in that way and those that cannot be are vastly more important to flexible learners than the low-level details—except on current final exams![7] Table 4.1 gives an idea of the breadth of this intuitive conceptualization. We have managed to teach bright high school students and first-year undergraduates the last two topics, with applications in mathematics and physics; the former group had not yet learned calculus. It's not magic; it's picking the right conceptual frame.

Midlevels #3. I had a short argument with a colleague about the importance of simply having a lot of facts in one's head. He argued that if one had not

---

[7]Having the right midlevel conception should remind the reader of Wertheimer's insightful solutions to problems, as compared to sufficient solutions. Insightful solutions are ones that illustrate cleanly the general reasons for things turning out the way they do, thus providing understanding that transcends the particular problem.

Table 4.1   Mathematics within the Scope of "Cancelling at Boundaries"

The Fundamental Theorem of Calculus (late high school/early undergrad. mathematics):

Quantity: The difference in values of a function at endpoints of an interval.

Local Version: $[f(x + \Delta x) - f(x)]/\Delta x = f'(x)$

Global Version $f(b) - f(a)$

Cancellation at boundary in adding up local quantities:
(by arithmetic)
$f'(x) + f'(f + \Delta x) = [f(x + \Delta x) - f(x)]/\Delta x + [f(x + 2\Delta x) - f(x + \Delta x)]/\Delta x$
$= [f(x + 2\Delta x) - f(x)]/\Delta x$

Generalization: The "sum" of the local differences (derivatives = f') times Δx is the global difference.

Notation: $\int_a^b f' \, dx = f(b) - f(a)$.

Gauss's Theorem (freshman physics):

Quantity: The flow of fluid out from a volume.

Local Version: The flow of fluid out from a small region.

Global Version: The flow of fluid out from a large region.

Principle of Cancellation at boundary of small regions:
The flow out from one small region into a neighboring one is the flow into the neighboring one (across the common boundary), which is the *negative* of the flow *out* from that region (across the common boundary).

Generalization: The sum of local sources of fluid equals the net flow out from a region.

Notation: $\int_{Volume} \vec{\nabla} \cdot \vec{f} \, dv = \int_{Surface} \vec{f} \cdot d\vec{S}$

Stokes Theorem (freshman physics):

Quantity: "Rotation" around a loop.

Green's Theorem (advanced calculus, advanced undergraduate physics):

Path Integrals in Complex Analysis (second year college mathematics):

Vector Singularities and "Index" Theorems (advanced undergraduate or graduate mathematics):

The Gauss-Bonnet Theorem in Differential Geometry (advanced undergraduate or graduate mathematics):

had a lot of experience with trigonometry, one would never recognize that an expression like $\sin(\Theta)\cos(\phi) + \cos(\Theta)\sin(\phi)$ might be insightfully simplified to $\sin(\Theta + \phi)$. One traditionally learns and proves a slew of similar formulae in high school trigonometry. Having an important part of my doctoral thesis in physics depend on similar (though rather more complex) simplifications, I was sympathetic to the argument. However, in this case my colleague demurred when I remarked that there is a simple, general way to learn and remember the whole class of such formulae at once. Euler's formula, $e^{i\Theta} = \cos(\Theta) + i\sin(\Theta)$, plus a bit of strategic insight—namely, all those trigonometric formulae can be simply derived from the formula—does the trick. Certainly, there is great economy in this unified approach. And one is unlikely to be able to remember all the implied "angle addition formulae" in any case. We proceeded to derive the specific formula at issue, which, in fact, neither of us could remember precisely. One can appreciate why Euler had this little emblem engraved on his tombstone.[8]

There are certainly fine points. How much sophistication does it take to understand Euler's formula? The rebuttal may be that it does take sophistication, but who of those that need trigonometric identities will not have that sophistication when she needed them? Certainly, in my case, by the time I needed trigonometric identities of this kind in physics, I also knew complex numbers. There might be other reasons to prove a plethora of trigonometric identities one at a time, though I cannot think of any. In general, one should demand strong justification before pursuing an eclectic approach over a unified one.

I do not say that judgments about when a unified approach is possible or profitable are easy. And I am sure one will not always draw the same conclusion, favoring an expert's parsimonious solution. Yet, I think so little consideration is given to these issues, practically and in terms of cognitive research, that more consideration could not hurt.

I could continue with instances. For example, Piaget showed that children spontaneously develop a strong sense of proportionality by adolescence. Yet, the general and powerful mathematical theme that follows from that sense, linearity and linear approximations, is hardly visible in any beginning or intermediate texts of physics or mathematics. Similarly, ideas of local as opposed to global views of a situation find root in a child's sense of his bodily or social neighborhood. I believe these could give reason to fundamental differences in physics between conservation laws (global laws) and laws of motion (local and differential laws). These all deserve elaboration, but instead, I close this section with a technology- and future-oriented example.

I find it intriguing that one of the few domains in which there appears to be a spontaneously growing research base on midlevel knowledge is computer programming (Owen, 1986; Soloway, this volume). Researchers are uncover-

---

[8]He actually used a more specific form for his epitaph, $e^{i\pi} + 1 = 0$. This contains all the most important quantities of the real and complex number system, 0, 1, π, e, and i, and nothing but them, in the same expression.

ing and documenting many kinds of midlevel knowledge such as plans, plan fragments, strategic but programming-specific knowledge, orienting knowledge toward programming environments, etc. I would like to think this is because of some special relation between programming and midlevel knowledge that we can take advantage of pedagogically. Perhaps programming just happens to be particularly rich at middle levels, and we can use it to exercise students' general acquaintance with them. Elliot Soloway develops this line elsewhere in this volume. Perhaps programming involves an explicit representational system that is simply more adapted than, say, text and pictures, to represent midlevel knowledge. We should know if this is true by 2020.

None of the preceding is what people usually refer to as "higher level knowledge." Instead, understanding anything well at these middle levels is often identified with "maturity" in a field and is assumed to come magically. I am proposing that we seek to understand this "maturity" and set the goal of having students who are more mature in this way. 2020 is not too soon to expect to see substantial changes in the intellectual confidence and in the flexibility of learning and knowing that students should exhibit from being more knowledgeable at all levels.

Computational Media

My final proposed goal for near-future education is the only one that is driven directly by technology. It is a goal that is subordinate in some ways to both the aforementioned — it will help provide domains (indeed, it may be one!) to exercise deep understanding, and it will go a long way toward engaging students and teachers in personally valued intellectual pursuits. But this particular goal involves changing the fundamental infrastructure of knowledge in our society and, in particular, in education. As such, it may have deep effects on the realizability of a much broader set of goals and subgoals than can be listed here; for example, who produces educational materials and what are our popular images of an educated person.

For centuries, the dominant mode of representing knowledge has been text. This is not because text is, in principle, the best way to represent knowledge, but because there simply have been no economic competitors to spreading knowledge through the printed word. It is not just a matter of spreading knowledge either. Text is a personal tool that liberates in its production as well as in its dissemination. Thinking is augmented by having writing as an intellectual prosthetic.

What I propose is that computation can become a new medium, a new mode of self-expression and dissemination of knowledge. Beginning with text processing, itself a nontrivial advance, computers can add, for example, seriously useful nonlinear presentation methods. One imagines hypertext worlds in which documents connect easily to other documents or to themselves in multiple ways, in which one can choose the perspective one wishes to take on a document, and the document appears different accordingly. Computers can add general methods of presenting dynamic information, like simulations, and they can provide significant possibilities of interactivity for the first time. Television and films provide dynamic but not substantial interactive capabilities.

Computers are not now such a medium. "Computer literacy" is a bad joke without a good body of "literature," without the sense that it is essential to be able to express one's self in the medium. For computers to become a medium, we must undertake a number of serious and difficult developments.

Standardization. A popular medium must provide a backbone of commonality that can be easily adapted to specialized needs. Thus, most in the United States speak English, and it would be much less valuable as a medium of common exchange if there were dozens of competing languages. More specifically, any would-be medium must serve the needs of common folk for common tasks, as well as the needs of specialists and experts. English does this simply by adding specialized vocabulary, but preserving grammar and syntax. In comparison, although Visicalc is great for business, it is not a big deal for kids or for family life.

Integration. The medium must accomplish a maximal range of tasks easily. Thus, with text, you can write a book, jot notes, make an outline, etc., without needing a different "language" for each task. On the other hand, with contemporary computer systems, you do have separate languages for tasks like programming (a programming language), data bases (data base languages), drawing, dynamic graphics (animation systems), text processing, outlining, etc.

Simple Utility. Everyone should be able to make some positive use of the medium. Even if children cannot write books, they can sometimes use written language profitably, and they can use spoken language profitably from the earliest stages. Arguably, written language is as difficult as it is to learn precisely because it is less useful than spoken language for beginners.

Reconstructibility. Though I mentioned it already, it is important to underline the characteristic that each individual can use the medium for his own purposes and rebuild it. Motion pictures are unlikely to be a popular intellectual medium in this sense, because it is too difficult and expensive for individuals to make things for themselves. Compare, again, jotting notes, writing letters, etc.

Programming is central to the task. If we cannot make programming easy and accessible, computers will not have reconstructibility or generality and thus fail as an intellectual medium. If we cannot change programming from something that is quite general, but so far from many useful activities (text editing, data bases, etc.) that individual and special-purpose tools must be built for all of these, then it will never be a true medium in this spirit, but only a metamedium, reserved for experts.

Let me concretize these considerations with a fantasy. Imagine a biology class in 2020 starts a unit on leaves. The "textbook" they are using comes on a plastic disk that fits into the small, portable, personal computers the students use as a substitute for paper and pencil. The book has several presentations on leaves that the class can choose from, depending on their interest level in the particular topic and the amount of background the students have in biology and in other areas like mathematics, artificial intelligence, etc. Actually, the different presentations are not stored, but they are computed on the basis of selected parameters. The chapter includes a fairly standard exposition on leaf morphology and metabolism, though it has dynamic and interactive pictures that allow selective explanation and zooming in on various substructures of the leaf. The book also contains a rather large data base of pictures of leaves suitable for student exploratory analysis. All the leaves in the data base are classified by date and geographical location, and many are already classified by species. The students and teacher happen to be particularly interested in leaves for some reason and decide to spend a substantial amount of time working on a research project.

The selected project is to study the effect of rainfall and acid rain on leaf size. First, the students collect other data bases containing rainfall and acidity data from geography and current events books. (Note how important it will be to have a common format for the data, or at least to have a uniform medium and programming available to convert if necessary.) They decide on a geographical region and range of species that represents a good overlap of the available data, and a few students set to work writing a program to sort through each data base, selecting the data that is relevant and organizing it in a form that is most convenient to their current pursuits.

After taking a graphing utility from their mathematics text and writing a few simple programs to translate the data from the form produced by their data bases to the form needed for the graphing tool, results begin to emerge. Some species are affected by both amount of rainfall and acidity dramatically more than others. Someone gets the bright idea that this may be related to genus and begins sorting data to check that hypothesis. Others notice they have only a few leaves of certain species and wonder if the conclusions they are drawing are valid. The teacher decides to pursue this point with the class and brings out some statistical tools that, in the end, tell the class there really is a sampling problem for some species.

Noting that there are additional unclassified leaves in the original data base, some students want to proceed classifying them to help resolve small sample problems. A group of hackers decides to automate the classification process, not so much because it would save time over manual classification, but because they simply like making relatively fancy programs. The superhacker in the bunch is assigned the task of writing a program to translate the pictorial encoding of the leaves into a computationally tractable format, say a turtle program to draw the leaf. Other students write little analysis programs to compute things like number of lobes and some general size and shape parameters of the leaf. They all store the computed information in the original data base entries so everyone can make use of their newly generated data. Finally, as a group, they try a number of heuristic techniques of taking the parameter sets and turning them into classifications, playing around until the program agrees for the most part with what they can do by manually inspecting the leaves. In the course of improving the program, quite an interesting debate arises about how closely what the program is doing resembles what they as humans do to classify.

Time is running out in the term, so the teacher assigns each student to write a report on the project. They do this quite easily by taking snatches of data, graphs, leaf pictures, and textual analysis from the class project book that contains all the experiments the class did. Then they paste those snatches together with interspersed explanation rationale and conclusions.

What are the most fantastic aspects of this fantasy? We (the M.I.T. Logo Project) have already taught high school students enough pattern-recognition A.I. to engage in tasks similar to classifying leaves, namely, recognizing written letters. I have had conversations comparing machine and human strategies with these students. If good high-level languages and substantial computational power become generally available in schools, I believe many if not most students could engage in such activities. There are no insurmountable barriers, economic or technical, to the availability of such systems. Indeed, we have a prototype computational system in operation in which one could write textbooks that include all the capabilities just implied: full programming capabilities entirely compatible with personal work environments, moving and interactive illustrations, tools that may be "clipped" out of the book for use elsewhere, and extendable data bases including numerical, textual, and pictorial information (diSessa & Abelson, 1986). Even computer-based, pictorial leaf data bases exist. Oddly, I think the most implausible aspects of this story are that schools will accept activities like the aforementioned as central to their mission, that teachers can be trained and will accept the challenging new roles of guide and co-investigator, and that we will find ways to standardize and provide economic incentives to producers and distributors of materials with such open properties.

I do not underestimate the difficulties in turning computers into a general intellectual medium and building the right economic and social niche for it. This is not something that will happen automatically or be forced on us by circumstances in the future. Like the other goals we should set for 2020, it will not happen unless we think about it, decide that it is worth doing and that we are capable of doing it, and then set our minds to doing it.

SOME WORRIES

In closing, I discuss briefly a set of worries about the practicability of realizing any of the aforementioned goals. These all center on who is the "we" that will set and pursue these goals. In fact, the wisdom, power, and will to decide to pursue any such goals is widely distributed, and it is not at all obvious that "we" can really think about them, decide to act, and then act effectively to realize them. David Cohen (this volume) has given an extensive treatment of some of the obstacles to change. Following are some constituencies and commentary on their special roles with respect to other coalitions of "us."

Politicians. Much of what I have proposed to think about will take significant research and development. Will politicians gracefully accept "our" consensus that great gains can be made and are worth the monetary and political price?

Textbook Manufacturers, and Curriculum Legislators. Between the research and the development that needs to be done and the practical implementation at the local level is a power block that defines and often profits from the particular choice of curriculum. Whereas this is to some degree a public affair, if "we" wish to teach different things, the public must understand and support the initiative. Still, there are so many details and practicalities that it will be a very severe mistake not to realize that a special group holds a lot of the chips.

Domain Specialists. Mathematicians have always had a special role in defining the mathematics curriculum, scientists in science, etc. I have argued that this is appropriate, but only in the proper degree. Domain experts will have to give up some of their power and prestige in defining curriculum, particularly elementary curriculum (far from their vested interest in preparing professional mathematicians and scientists). They will have to do this in deference to the understanding that there are specifically educational issues, particularly the importance of not relying on contemporary images of professional practice or even competence in a particular subject area as the final measure of educational value. My perhaps optimistic hope here is that a new professional class of educators will develop, a new class that can, in part, be trusted to uphold the integrity of domain instruction, that can be trusted to listen to and understand domain experts, but who can speak authoritatively on the needs and possibilities of teaching things that are not the first instincts of domain specialists as they see it from their valuable but somewhat arcane perspective.

Cognitive Researchers. Science does not know much yet about aesthetics, or about knowledge at the scale that can prescribe effective midlevel conceptualizations. But these are things that may be handleable by researchers as a group. In a broader social context, it is all too easy for scientists to stop short of practical realization of their ideas, and to think scientific evidence and results are interesting and compelling to nonscientists. To declare goals and constraints without arguing for those goals in terms that are generally understandable, and without showing how those constraints can be negotiated, will ensure a divided "we" and goals that end as exhortations to others. If physicists have an obligation to worry about the social consequences of their work, how much greater is the obligation of cognitive scientists?

Teachers. As Carl Berger says, teachers are where the rubber hits the road. Even the most technophilic educator needs teachers at least to stand out of the way. Those of us who see essential roles for teachers, perhaps even more demanding than in the nontechnologically intensive past, need ways of understanding and engaging teachers as part of the "we" whose goals I have been proposing, and as part of the team that realizes them.

SUMMARY

I have argued that in looking toward 2020, we have the possibility and even the obligation to decide what being educated should mean. We may agree at the start that we would like to help nurture knowledgeable, thoughtful, versatile, creative, responsible, and even wise individuals. But, it is less easy to say exactly what those qualities entail, how we should go about instilling them or balance conflicting goals, like depth and breadth. To help in this task, I have proposed a short list of subgoals that are more instrumental, without losing the important quality of raising our sights beyond our current means. I have argued we want and need to consider teaching less, to teach more deeply what it means to know. I have argued that, more than at any time in history, we have the possibility to engage students' own goals and aesthetic senses in what is taught. I have argued that we have a better sense for the range of knowledge, from detailed, subject specific, to intermediate levels that broaden and generalize understanding within a discipline, to high levels that allow us to enter new areas without fear and allow us to get the last ounce of efficiency from what we already know. Finally, I have argued that it is profitable to consider extending text with computation to a new, general medium of knowledge expression that will, in a highly nontrivial way, affect even what we call literacy. Changing the currency of representing knowledge will have profound effects on the scale of decades, at least.

These goals are properly timeless and timely. Educational goals should not be at the mercy of the latest technological whimsey. But on the other hand, new capabilities should reorder our priorities in that although we might desire many things, the efforts we exert should have the serious possibility of paying off in ways that were, until now, out of our grasp.

Finally, setting goals is not only an intellectual task but a highly social one that will involve many constituencies. Deciding on and willing the pursuit of our future selves, as I have sketched in my images here, will take serious discussion among politicians, curriculum power brokers, domain specialists, cognitive scientists and technologists, teachers, and the public.

REFERENCES

Abelson, H., & diSessa, A. (1981). *Turtle geometry: The computer as a medium for exploring mathematics.* Cambridge, MA: MIT Press.

Clement, J. (1982). Students' preconceptions in introductory mechanics. *American Journal of Physics, 50,* 66–71.

diSessa, A. (1985). Learning about knowing. In E. Klein (Ed.) *Children and computers, New directions for child development (No. 28).* San Francisco: Jossey–Bass.

diSessa, A.A., & Abelson, H. (1986). Boxer: A reconstructible computational medium. *Communications of the ACM, 29,* (No. 9), 859–868.

McCloskey, M. (1983, July). Intuitive physics. *Scientific American,* 122–130.

McDermott, L.C. (1984, July). Research on conceptual understanding in mechanics. *Physics Today,* 24–32.

Owen, D. (1986). The naive physics of computation. In D.A. Norman & S.W. Draper (Eds.), *User centered system design: New perspectives on human-computer interaction.* Hillsdale, NJ: Lawrence Erlbaum Associates.

Papert, S. (1980). *Mindstorms: Children, computers, and powerful ideas.* New York: Basic Books.

5 Mathematics, Technology, and Higher Order Thinking

ALAN H. SCHOENFELD
The University of California, Berkeley

OVERVIEW

In broad terms, this chapter deals with the following question: How might technology be harnessed (or directed) over the next few decades to improve the teaching of mathematics in particular, and higher order thinking skills in general?

The first section begins with an exploration of which aspects in mathematics (and to some degree other fields) may be important to teach over the next few decades, and an explanation of the reasons for focusing on higher order thinking skills. The second section deals with the general potential of technology and some of the ways that technology can be used to support and enhance human cognition. In the third section I discuss the current plans of the Berkeley Functions Group (see acknowledgments), which is in the process of developing a computer-based tutor for the discipline-specific and metacognitive aspects of cognition in relation to functions and graphing.

WHAT MATHEMATICS (OR PHYSICS, OR BIOLOGY, OR WRITING SKILLS) AND WHAT THINKING SKILLS SHOULD ONE TEACH IN 2020?

Readers who are comfortable with the "process rather than product" perspective and believe in the importance of such things as heuristics, metacognition,

67

and belief systems may consider this explanatory preface to be an unnecessary detour. In my experience, however, many talented professionals conceive of their responsibilities as teachers of subject matter in very constrained terms. Their idea is that if you teach subject X, your job is to lay out the details of subject X—period; that is, they see a teacher's obligation as presenting the facts and procedures that comprise knowledge of the domain as coherently as possible, making sure the students master those facts and procedures. I argue here that laying out the subject matter, although an essential part of the endeavor, is only one facet of it. These opening paragraphs are intended to make that point.

To begin, I would like to stretch our allotted 30-plus years (to the year 2020) by a factor of 3—if you will, exchanging the clearsightedness of a 2020 vision for the farsightedness of a vision of 100 years hence. Can we predict what mathematics would be important to teach a century from now?

If you take the point of view that what counts is the subject matter, the task is hopeless. At the college and certainly at the professional level, today's mathematics is almost completely different from the mathematics of a century ago. Moreover, the pace of change is increasing dramatically. A century ago, mathematicians could not have predicted today's mathematics. In turn, we have no way of knowing what mathematics will be important at the tail end of the 21st century. Does that mean that the task of deciding what to teach is impossible?

I think not. Rather, the dilemma indicates that a focus on subject matter misses something critical. There is an invariant, but it is not the product of mathematics; it is the process of doing the mathematics. There are constants across the centuries that bind together the mathematics of 1887 with that of 1987 and will undoubtedly be central to doing mathematics in 2087. If you don't believe this, I propose the following thought experiment. Take any of the greats in mathematics from the past and imagine them alive today. Mathematics has changed drastically since their time. Would these people be completely at sea in modern mathematics, totally lost because the subject has changed so much?

It's not likely. One has the sense that, despite the differences between contemporary mathematics and the mathematics of their times, Descartes, or Gauss, or Euler would—after a brief adjustment period, of course—be perfectly at home and productive in today's mathematics. This would also be true a century from now. That being the case, we see that understanding the subject matter qua subject matter is only a part of what comprises understanding mathematics or thinking mathematically. The consistencies across centuries lie in what it is to *do* mathematics. I argue that the great mathematicians of the past can be characterized as possessing the following predilections:

1. to receive structure, to see what makes things tick, and how they are internally and externally connected;

2. to abstract and perceive uniformities in objects and systems that are super-ficially different; and

3. to use abstraction, formal systems, and other mathematical methods of inquiry as fundamental means of investigating these structures and relationships.

These predilections, one may be confident, will be the bedrocks of mathematics in 2087.

Taking this view of mathematics — that mathematics is a verb (something you *do*) as opposed to a noun (something you *master*) — causes a radical reconceptualization of the goals of mathematics instruction. If you hold the "mastery" point of view, your goal as a mathematics instructor is to have your students learn and be able to employ the techniques determined by the curriculum. Depending on grade level, those techniques may be factoring polynomials and solving mixture problems, or solving differential equations and related rates problems. But either way, the instructional approach is the same; the teacher demonstrates the technique, trains students to use it, and tests them on closely related problems. In this case, the instruction is considered successful when students can perform the requisite operations, and perhaps only those operations.

From my point of view, the facts and procedures typically mastered in mathematics curricula are the "vocabulary" of mathematics, the tools of the trade, which, like all tools, are only meaningful when they are used. Consider this analogy to understanding language. Anyone who understands English possesses a core vocabulary and has mastered certain rudiments of grammar. Yet, understanding extends far beyond vocabulary and grammar; a meaningful measure of a person's linguistic competency is his or her ability to communicate via spoken and written language. Can that person get the gist of a well-presented (written or oral) argument and in turn express what he or she wishes to express in a straightforward and coherent way? Similarly in mathematics, the meaningful measure of mathematical understanding is the individual's ability to correctly apply mathematical thinking in the appropriate situations.

I can hardly claim that this perspective is new; the seeds of it are in Descartes' (1625–1628) *Rules for the direction of the mind,* and they take root in Pólya's (1945, 1954, 1980) writings on problem solving. Because we are looking ahead to the future, let me again cast back into the past for a sterling and timeless example: Harold Fawcett's (1938) explorations of *The nature of proof.* For most students, a course in plane geometry consists of an exercise in memorizing definitions and proofs that were discovered a thousand years ago. The material has not changed, is memorized and forgotten, and bears no relation to the students' thinking outside the geometry classroom. However, Fawcett saw geometric reasoning as a process in which making definitions promotes clarity and provides a solid foundation from which to draw accurate and unambiguous conclusions. These skills are useful in real life, such as disentangling the nonsense of a political campaign, or trying to decide (as judges and jurors do all the time) whether a particular action is legal or illegal, or determining whether certain actions (e.g., building a "star wars" system) are within the bounds of a treaty your country has promised to respect. Fawcett's (1938) statement is lucid and to the point:

> The real value of this sort of training to any pupil is determined by its effect on his behavior. . . . [W]e shall assume that if he clearly understands these aspects of the nature of [deductive geometric] proof his behavior will be marked by the following characteristics:
>
> 1. He will select the significant words and phrases in any statement that is important to him and ask that they be carefully defined.
> 2. He will require evidence in support of any conclusion that he is pressed to accept.
> 3. He will analyze that evidence and distinguish fact from assumption.
> 4. He will recognize stated and unstated assumptions essential to the conclusion.
> 5. He will evaluate these assumptions, accepting some and rejecting others.
> 6. He will evaluate the argument, accepting or rejecting the conclusion.
> 7. He will constantly re-examine his assumptions which are behind his beliefs and which guide his actions. (pp. 11–12)

My perspective is that learning mathematics—that is, learning to think mathematically—involves developing a certain analytical predilection, a mathematical *weltanschauung*. It means mastering the tools of contemporary mathematics in service of that "urge to mathematize and analyze." It also involves having strategies for mastering the domain, making progress on difficult problems within the domain, and becoming an efficient, resourceful problem solver. My goal for mathematics instruction is that students gain such skills. The spectrum of skills suggested previously are now more systematically elaborated.

My studies of mathematical competence (see my 1985 *Mathematical Problem Solving* for details) have resulted in a framework for the analysis of mathematical performance that includes four qualitatively different aspects of mathematical behavior. These categories are hardly unique to mathematics. Indeed, I argue here that they are germane to competent performance in any problem-solving domain, and that instruction in all problem-solving domains should take them into account. A parallel argument has been made by Collins, Brown, and Newman (in press). In a review of programs in reading, writing, and mathematics, Collins et al. abstracted "four kinds of content we think it critical to teach students about any subject area." Three of their categories coincide with mine, and we each endorse the other's fourth. The union of the two frameworks follows. I now give a telegraphic version of the five kinds of content that should be in any curriculum. To emphasize the generality of the framework, I then give examples from mathematics and writing to illustrate each category.

Category 1: Domain Knowledge. It goes without saying that mastery of basic facts and procedures lies at the heart of expertise in any discipline. In mathematics for example, one finds definitions and facts ("a polynomial is . . ."; "the sum of polynomials is the same, independent of the order in which they are added") and procedures ("you multiply two polynomials as follows . . ."). In writing, there are also rules of grammar and procedures for creating simple declarative and compound sentences. Little more needs to be said about domain knowledge, save that in most curricula, this kind of knowledge is the primary if not the sole focus of instruction. The rest is largely ignored.

Category 2: Heuristic Strategies. These are nonalgorithmic procedures, "rules of thumb" or "tricks of the trade" for making one's way through complex tasks. Such procedures are not guaranteed to work or even be relevant to the task at hand; but if they do work, they often help one to make significant progress. In mathematics the foundational work for our understanding of heuristic strategies is due to Pólya (1945, 1954, 1980), whose descriptions of these domain-specific techniques has kept armies of mathematics education researchers busy for decades. Typical heuristics include: procedures for making sure you understand a problem before jumping into its solution, trying to exploit the solutions of easier but still related or analogous problems, trying to decompose the given problem into a collection of simpler problems, establishing subgoals, etc. Note that at this level of description the techniques appear to be domain independent. Research indicates, however, that the means of implementation are very much domain specific. For example, one instantiation of the "making sure you understand" heuristic is a problem-solving strategy all in itself; you make sense of a problem with an integer parameter n by plugging in different values of n and seeing the behavior that results. There are a dozen other understanding strategies, each as complex as this; at best, they bear a surface similarity to each other. Hence, delineating and teaching strategies are not easy tasks, but they pay large dividends when properly done.

The writing literature is chock full of heuristic strategies that are directly analogous to those in mathematics. There are general homilies, such as "make sure you have something to say, that you know what it is, and that the paper says it." At the same general level, there are suggestions such as those for writing military instruction manuals: "Tell them what you're going to tell them. Then tell them. Then tell them what you told them." There are general procedures, for example, drafting a detailed outline for helping to make sure that a paper is well structured. There are methods for getting out of writer's block, such as "free writing." At the more detailed level of paragraph construction, there are suggestions regarding the nature of topic sentences, elaborations on them, summaries of paragraph content, and transitions to the next paragraph or idea.

Each of these is a nonalgorithmic suggestion that may or may not work for a particular individual in a particular situation. If it does, however, it can lead to significant progress.

Category 3: Executive Control. The argument here is that what counts is not just what you know; what counts is how you use, or fail to use, what you know. A common failing of novice problem solvers is that they go off on wild goose chases while working on a problem. Often, they pick one approach and persevere with it, despite clear signs that the effort is not yielding progress. Such perseverance may keep them from using other methods they know and have successfully used in other circumstances, causing them to fail. Students may simply wander all over the map. For example, one student's attempt to solve a complex algebraic equation meandered in interesting ways. Each step was logically correct in that it was a legitimate transformation of the equation that came before. But a close look revealed that the equation the student was working on after seven transformations was more complicated than the equation he set out to solve. The student, lost in step-by-step operations, had lost track of where things were going.

In contrast, competent problem solvers may try a wide range of potentially fruitless approaches when working difficult problems. But by vigilant attention to what helps and what does not — in essence, by good resource management on line — they can make progress where others would not. Research indicates, for example, that college mathematics faculty take three or four times as long to read a calculus problem before beginning to work on it than their students. This is not because they read more slowly, but because they postpone jumping into working on the solution until they know what they are doing. (See Chapters 4 and 9 of Schoenfeld, 1985, for details.)

The general idea of executive control is that there is a feedback loop that consists of monitoring one's actions on line, assessing progress, deciding whether change needs to be made, and taking action if the situation is deemed problematic. The mathematics examples indicate that competent performance is closely linked to good executive behavior, and that failure is often linked to an absence of it. Again, there are clear analogues in the writing process. Novice students will begin writing an essay before they have thought out the main ideas they wish to express. Or they may get carried away by the flow of their writing, only to notice after much time and many paragraphs that they have lost their original theme and thus must discard all they have written. They can also be insensitive to contradictions in what they have written, or to the completeness and coherence of their arguments. Of course, when experts write, the process is hardly error free. But experts exhibit a much greater sensitivity to how things are going along the way. There may be wrong turns, but they are caught more rapidly (or the paper is altered accordingly); and although contradictions or incomplete arguments may occur, the writer is on guard for them.

Category 4: Beliefs. In the introductory discussion, I characterized part of thinking mathematically as having certain predilections: to perceive structure, to see "what makes things tick" and how they are internally and externally connected; to abstract and perceive uniformities in objects and systems that may appear on the surface to be different; and to use abstraction, formal systems, and other mathematical methods of inquiry as fundamental means of investigating such structures and relationships. If you view mathematics this way, you may engage in "mathematical behavior" in circumstances where such behavior is appropriate, for example, along the lines previously quoted in the selection from Fawcett. But if you think of mathematics solely as a discipline that provides prepackaged solutions for prepackaged and formally stated problems, you may not use it when it is appropriate, even when you are perfectly capable of doing so.

One's notion of mathematics determines whether, and if so, how one uses mathematics in situations for which it is appropriate. For example, in my research (see, e.g., Schoenfeld, 1985, Chapter 5), there is clear evidence that students who do not place much faith in the results of mathematical proofs will make conjectures that flatly violate results they, themselves, have just proved. Another example about the predilection to analyze and justify mathematically comes from Ed Williams (personal communication, June 1986). Williams was one of the organizers of a mathematics contest for talented high school students. One of the problems on the examination was the following: "Which fits better, a square peg in a round hole or a round peg in a square hole?"

Like Williams, I took the question to mean "In which case does the plug cover a larger proportion of the hole?" A brief calculation showed that the peg-to-hole ratio is $2/\pi$ (which is less than $\frac{2}{3}$ or about .66) for the square peg in a round hole, whereas the peg-to-hole ratio is $\pi/4$ (which is greater than $\frac{3}{4}$, or .75) for the round peg in a square hole. For that reason, I said, "it's the round peg." Judah Schwartz interpreted the question differently. He took the word "fit" in the problem to mean "fit tightly" and looked at the points where the plug is tangent to the hole. The tangent line for the round peg coincides with the side of the square, whereas the tangent line for the square peg is not defined, so Schwartz's answer is also "the round peg."

More than 300 students took the test, and most drew sketches comparing the two situations. Almost all chose the round peg as the answer. However, of those 300-plus students—the best of the province, taking a formal mathematics test—only 4 provided any justification for their answers. (The sketches drawn by the others were rough and did not contain the seeds of mathematical arguments.) Apparently, most students felt there was no need to explain their answer. For the mathematician, it is inconceivable to answer the question without a computation. Every question contains an implied "why?" and is not answered until the implicit request for justification has been explained, preferably with irrefutable arguments such as the computational ones aforementioned. In contrast, many students believe that answering a mathematical question means giving an answer, because that is what the question specifically requires. The research indicates that students pick up their beliefs about mathematics from their classroom experiences with mathematics. It follows that instructors and instructional designers (including designers of technology-based systems) should pay attention to the beliefs that students develop.

Once again, there are clear parallels to beliefs about writing. As in mathematics, people have beliefs about the writing process, and those beliefs have strong effects on those individuals' writing. For example, what kind of work is required to produce a paper once you have outlined the main ideas in it? It depends. I am all too aware of my personal answer to that question, working on the final draft of this chapter. One version of this first section was thrown out completely, because the rhetorical device that opened it got me into trouble. Another version landed me in the right ballpark, but it was in serious need of revisions. The third version was in close to final form, but needing work. You are reading the fourth, modulo changes by editors. Each of the four versions, thanks to the fact that I work on a text processor, contained myriad minor revisions on line—various adjustments in sense, grammar, tone, and conveyed meaning. Now my view of the writing process is that revisions are an essential component of writing, and I allow time for them. In fact, I keep the five draft versions of *Mathematical Problem Solving* on my bookshelves at home as a tangible reminder of the evolutionary and dialectic nature of the writing process. (Some day, if time permits, I would like to do an exegesis of that process.) Yet mine is just one model, and there are very different models of the writing process. Another model holds that once you have the ideas worked out, you should be able to write a paper more or less linearly from start to finish, translating the ideas into prose. When you have reached the end, you are done. This model, or some version of it, is held by a large number of students. Possessing such beliefs about the nature of the writing process determines the amount of time they allocate to writing tasks—and ultimately, the quality of the papers they produce.

Category 5: Learning Strategies. One assumes that a major purpose of instruction is to help students develop into autonomous learners, so they will be better able to learn about new domains or acquire new skills. In mathematics, there are strategies for learning to read, conceptualize, and write mathematical arguments. One must learn that each statement in a mathematical argument is an answer to an often tacit question. The author is trying to go some place; it is your job to figure out where. The result is that it takes a long time to read a mathematical argument. An hour or two per page in a journal is not atypical, and it may take quite a while to read a page in a textbook. The means of mathematical reading is quite different from reading, say, a newspaper article. After each major assertion, one stops to ask why that assertion was made, instead of a weaker or a stronger one, and where the argument is going. This kind of approach to reading mathematics is clearly learned behavior. There are similar ways to conceive of and write mathematical arguments. Mason, Burton, and Stacey (1982) suggest a three-phase sequence: Convince yourself, convince a friend, then convince an enemy. Again, the parallels to writing are clear. Mason et al.'s suggestion points to a comparable learning strategy for writing in any domain: If you put the pen (or keyboard) down for a moment and approach your own words as a naive but critical reader, you will get useful feedback on your own writing processes.

My sense of "domain competency" is that it is essential to address the five aspects of content described previously. As noted before, this view is quite similar to the views expressed in Collins, Brown, and Newman (in press). Subject matter is one of four categories they discuss in their presentation of a general framework for evaluating learning environments. That framework, which also includes discussions of teaching methods, lesson sequencing, and the sociology of the learning environment, merits careful consideration.

For the purpose of this chapter, a very sketchy discussion of these last three categories is given and serves as a backdrop for the discussions in the sequel. Collins, Brown, and Newman (pages 11–13) suggest there are six teaching methods that "are critical to expert teaching and that become interwoven in good teaching."

- Modeling, showing how and why an expert does a task.
- Coaching, observing students as they work and correcting their performance on line.
- Inquiry, a strategy of questioning.
- Articulation, getting students to articulate their own knowledge and reasoning.
- Reflection, replaying and abstracting students' work, and contrasting that with expert performance.
- Exploration, pushing students into a mode of trying to do the activity better on their own.

They point to three aspects of lesson sequence that may be useful:

- Scaffolding and fading, to allow students to develop greater autonomy as they master subsets of the required skills.
- Increasing complexity, as the student becomes more competent.
- Increasing diversity, so that the student learns when and where the skills he or she has learned are relevant and useful.

Finally, they address the sociology of the learning environment and factors that may affect the way instruction is received and/or perceived as being relevant to the world outside of school. In this category, they stress the importance of:

- situated learning,
- intrinsic motivation, and
- sociological (and cognitive) effects of cooperative and competitive learning.

This latter topic, specifically the role of small-group learning both for sociological and cognitive reasons, is also addressed in Schoenfeld (in press). There, I advance the idea that, in addition to being more culturally "real" and reflecting mathematical work in the real world, small group work has the advantage of having students operating precisely in their "zone of proximal development" (see Vygotsy, 1978).

TECHNOLOGY AND ITS POTENTIAL:
WHAT ROLES MIGHT TECHNOLOGY PLAY
IN 2020?

In the previous section I focused on aspects of performance and learning in mathematics and other disciplines, and a brief review of a framework for evaluating instructional environments. In this section, I focus on interesting things one might do with technology. The connections bewteen the two sections are not drawn explicitly, but they should be apparent.

Some caveats are always in order when one tries to play futurist. An amusing and somewhat chastening book is Cerf and Navasky's (1984) *The Experts Speak,* which offers a compendium of amazingly wrong predictions about the future. In particular, three of the quotes in the book regarding the future of computers are well worth repeating. The first is a one-word comment from Sir George Bidell Airy (Astronomer Royal of Great Britain; holder of the K.C.B., M.A., LL.D., D.C.L., F.R.S., and F.R.A.S.), estimating for the Chancellor of the Exchequer the potential value of the "analytical engine" invented by Charles Babbage: "Worthless." The second is a remark attributed to Thomas J. Watson, IBM board chairman in 1943: "I think there is a world market for about five computers." The third comes from Ken Olson, president of Digital Equipment Corporation, in a 1977 presentation to a convention of the World Future Society: "There is no reason for any individual to have a computer in their home." Of course, one can balance these pessimistic predictions with equally wild predictions from equally respected experts about the effects of computers. Some of these optimistic statements claimed that robot slaves would replace humans in doing all the drudgework in American homes and factories by the mid 1960s, and that artificially intelligent programs far surpassing human intelligence would be commonplace by about the same time.

When playing futurist one should be mindful of prior claims about technological revolutions in the schools. For example, we were told in no uncertain terms that educational TV would completely change the face of American education, and its influence has been minimal. Even so, there is reason to believe that in the case of computers significant changes are in the offing. As Andy diSessa has pointed out, we should not predict the future of computers in schools by linear extrapolation from the present. Consider the impact of an earlier technology—pen and paper—on schooling. Could we have predicted the effects of mass literacy by extrapolating from what happened in classrooms where students were allowed to read and write for a total of 15 minutes a week?

The main issue, then, is to see in what ways computer-based technology can or might effect fundamental changes. Borrowing an argument from Roy Pea (1985, 1987), we explore the notion of computers as transformers of cognitive functioning rather than as amplifiers of it. The pen-and-paper analogy mentioned in the previous paragraph provides an appropriate place to begin.

Transcendent technologies do more than simply amplify your potential, allowing you to do things more efficiently than you could without them. In addition, they enable you to do some things differently and other things you simply could not do before. Consider for a moment the contrast between a literate and preliterate society. Given the physiological limitations on individual cognition (short-term memories [STM] of 7 ± 2 chunks, the amount of time required to enter a piece of information in long-term memory [LTM], the volatility of memory, etc.) and on communication (no permanent records, and personal contact required for information to be passed from one person to another), the potential achievements of individuals in a preliterate culture, and of the culture itself, are necessarily severely constrained. Access to written records of cognition does more than expand the degree to which tasks can be carried out; it enables individuals and their society to do things hitherto impossible. For example, I can use paper and pencil to do computations that I cannot do mentally. In that way, paper and pencil technology serves as an amplifier of my capacity. But I can also put down dozens of items on paper and scan all of them for connections. In doing so, I overcome the limitations of short-term memory and perform acts I simply would not be capable of performing otherwise. I can write something and return to it a week (or a month, or a year) later and, after a quick brush-up, pick up where I took off—thus defeating not only STM limitations and the need for rehearsal, but the fallibility of LTM. Most important, I no longer need rely either on my own limited capacities or the capacities of those who can help me in person. By virtue of the written word, Gauss and Descartes are my personal tutors; and knowledge is cumulative, in a way that far exceeds the memory capacity of any human or society of humans relying on memory alone.

Technology is obviously going to make it easier to do things in the future (calculators a decade ago, spreadsheets today; dynamic economic models and who knows what else tomorrow?); its amplifier potential is clear. However, it is also important to think in terms of its transformational potential, to think about ways in which technology will enable us, either as individuals or as a society, to do things differently or do new things altogether. Whether based on graphite and paper or on silicon chips, cognitive technologies, "extracortical organizers of thought" à la Vygotsky (1978), allow us to be more than we are without them.

At present, one can point to few examples of computer technology that have had demonstrable impact on large numbers of people. Perhaps the best example of a potentially universal tool is the text processor. Text processors fulfill a need and, in their amplifier role, make it easier to do things that one could have done before. (I am a poor typist, for example. The ease of error correction combined with the accessibility of an automated spell-checker makes writing much more pleasant.) But writing with word processors is not just easier, it is different. For some writers, the ease with which they can edit sentences, shift paragraphs, and reorganize whole sections of a document produces different writing patterns. For others, the medium offers new potential. For instance, free writing, dumping in text without worrying about editing it, is easy to do on computers with little or no "overhead." If you don't like what you've written, you can get rid of it. If you like it, you can exploit it. Some writers use text processors in this way to overcome a writer's block. A second exemplar is the computer language Logo. In the best of circumstances, Logo (Papert, 1980) offers a mathematically rich microworld. It is a universe in which certain conceptual ideas (e.g., procedures, variables, mathematical structure, debugging) are salient and learning about them is more "natural" than in the real world. Similar claims have been made about programming in general; by being forced to think logically, students pick up new and valuable modes of thought. I am chary of such claims (studying geometry was supposed to do the same) when they are thrown about casually. But I believe that with some thought one might discover a nugget of truth to them, and that with some care, as in Fawcett's explorations of geometry, one might find ways of making the right connections.

To return to the main question in this section, what might technology do for us in 2020? Despite the cautions in my opening paragraphs, I suspect that one should try to be visionary (or at least listen to those who are) because we are just getting started in this game. To some degree, both languages like Logo and tools like text processors are vehicles of empowerment. The individuals who take to them gain mastery of the tool, of the environment (to some degree), and develop a sense of themselves as being more powerful because of what they can do with the tool. People like Alan Kay take this notion one step farther. Rather than giving people tools, he argues, one should give them media that contain the ingredients out of which they can create their own tools. From such media will emerge both ownership and power. Whether in the form of a Dynabook (Kay's vision of a briefcase-sized computer with everything you could ever imagine in it) or an easily usable language like diSessa's Boxer (designed to be flexible enough so that people can make their own tools with it; see diSessa & Abelson, 1986), such means of empowerment should be developed and explored.

Ownership and power, what one might more generally call the engagement aspects of computational media, are important things to look for in what technology can offer. These correspond to what Pea (1987) has called the purpose functions of technology, the aspects of technology that involve people in its use. By virtue of getting people involved, these purpose functions provide other things as well. A third exemplary program to which we return in the next section of this chapter is Sharon Dugdale's "Green Globs" (see Dugdale, 1982, 1984). Green Globs is a game in which students shoot at targets ("globs" or other objects on a coordinate grid) with algebraic equations. After the students define a curve algebraically, the curve is drawn, and each glob explodes when a curve passes through it. Students become skilled at the game by developing an understanding of how to make a curve do what they want, that is, by learning how to pick the coefficients that will produce a curve shaped in a particular way. The game is interesting and attractive. Students get hooked, and in playing the game, they learn important mathematical lessons. In sum, purpose functions are vitally important. The benefits they confer are not only individual as in the preceding examples, but social as well. Students develop communication networks in which they revise each others' work, share the best examples, improve on them, compete via electronic mail, etc. These kinds of group communications provide the hook that gets students involved in activities that become increasingly important to them.

We now turn to the issue of subject matter. Here, the framework outlined in part one of this chapter takes a central role. If one looks for the appropriate uses of technology for educating, whether in mathematics or other disciplines, one expects the technology to be harnessed in ways that promote (a) mastery of facts and procedures of the discipline, (b) problem-solving strategies relevant to the domain, (c) good executive behavior, (d) appropriate belief structures about the domain, and (e) the development of useful learning strategies. The key question is: what can we do, in any of these categories, that is extremely difficult or just too expensive to do without the help of technology? A few quick illustrations are given here. More follow in the second part of this section and in the discussion of our software under development.

Mastery of the Subject Domain

Technology has much to offer students in helping them master basic subject matter, both in routine facts and procedures. Indeed, good old drill-and-practice CAI has a useful role to play in providing low-cost training or refresher work in basic skills. More interesting, however, is what aid technology can offer students in developing the cognitive support structures that underlie the substantive understanding of mathematical notions. In particular, much of mathematics is concerned with the analysis of dynamic situations and the use of multiple representations. Computer-based media are ideally suited for both types of situations. For example, one difficulty with graphing is that students tend to think of graphs as static, gestalt entities—the curves that result when you join the dots after plotting enough points of $y = f(x)$. This perspective, a natural consequence of students' pencil-and-paper experience with graphing functions, leads to difficulties. For instance, students have trouble interpreting the behavior of constant functions. With the help of computer-based technologies,, real-time graphing is easy. The Eureka software developed by the ITMA project in Great Britain (1984) runs a simulation of a man taking a bath. Students can turn a tap on or off, turn the drain on or off, and have a man get in or out of the tub. As they do, the water level in the tub changes dynamically in real time. Next to the simulated bathtub is a coordinate graph in which, again in real time, the water level of the tub is plotted as a function of time. Discussions are structured so that students are led to explore the relationships between the properties of the graphs and their corresponding simulations. As the students converse, some things that are normally very hard to grasp without the dynamic simulations become absolutely clear. For instance, when nothing at all is happening in the bathtub (i.e., the water level is constant), the graph keeps moving and produces a constant function. A once-difficult concept is now easier to understand. Similarly, Bob Tinker's (1981) software does comparable things for real-time, real-live actions. A sensor measures a student's distance from a microcomputer. On demand, the computer produces real-time graphs of distance, velocity, and acceleration versus time. Students can try to match each other's distance, velocity, or acceleration graphs. In doing so, they get a bodily, kinetic sense of what otherwise may seem purely abstract concepts. These are promising directions for technology that should be explored.

The programs just described simultaneously demonstrate two representations of the same phenomenon, allowing students to make connections between those representations. Extending this idea, we can present as many as four or five simultaneous representations of the same phenomenon: a real-live event, its on-screen simulation (perhaps showing only salient variables), a verbal description of the event, its graph, and the equation of a function that generates the graph. With simultaneous representations, students can learn to interpret events demonstrated in one representation and explore those same events in other representations. Thus, students might come to see (a) how all the representations are linked, and (b) that different representations might be useful in answering particular questions about such events. At a more straightforward, practical level, software under development at the Educational Technology Center (Kaput, 1985) shows three representations of proportionality relationships: sets of icons representing the relationship (say "three people for each house"), a table of values showing number of people opposite that of houses, and graph of the pairs (houses, people) in a Cartesian coordinate system. Seeing all these demonstrated simultaneously and working through a curriculum that helps them focus on relationships may well make it easier for students to see things that are otherwise quite difficult to see.

Problem-Solving Processes and Strategies

There are few examples in this category, and a great deal of room for progress. A small number of computer-based tutors focus on thinking efficiently in a domain, for example, the geometry and LISP tutors developed by John Anderson and colleagues (Anderson, Boyle, & Reiser, 1985) at Carnegie–Mellon University. In standard geometry instruction, the rigid two-column print format for geometry proofs gives students the impression that deduction is a linear process. In contrast, the geometry tutor provides an explicit representation of the search space for proof problems and thus gives students a much better sense of the nature of mathematical deduction. The LISP tutor has similar properties regarding programming processes. However, both tutors constrain students to solve programming problems in "ideal ways," imposing their own problem-solving style on the students.

In this author's view, that rigidity is problematic. A far less rigid approach to tutoring at the level of strategy was taken by Burton and Brown (1982) in their development of a computer-based coach for the game, "How the west was won." The coach identified students' procedural difficulties, such as their difficulties in using the distributive law for multiplying across parentheses. In addition, it identified the strategies the students were using to play the game and offered better options when it had them. Such prototyping of strategic tutoring needs to be extended substantially. (I should also note that I have kept my examples to mathematically related topics. If one goes outside of mathematics, there are curricula focusing on writing skills that use computers as vehicles, major tutorial programs in medical diagnosis, etc.)

The examples in the preceding paragraph place the burden of teaching or enhancing strategic behavior squarely on the shoulders of the technology itself. That is quite a substantial burden. A different use of technology is as follows. One can exploit technological tools to carry out difficult and time-consuming tasks. This frees up cognitive resources so that students (perhaps with the help of teachers or others) can focus on problem-solving processes. One software tool developed along these lines is the "Geometric Supposer" (Yerushalmy & Houde, 1986). The Supposer allows students to define geometric constructions on given objects (e.g., a procedure designed to trisect an angle) and then to reproduce those constructions on new objects. If a student has defined a procedure for trisecting an angle, the Supposer will repeat the student's construction on new angles, allowing the student to see if the construction works in those cases. This kind of tool makes a once-costly operation, performing the construction, relatively trivial. The result is that the student no longer worries about the overhead of performing the construction, which is done by the machine. The student can focus on whether it works and why. Properly exploited, this tool allows for an interesting dialectic between deduction and empirical experimentation. It allows students to test hypotheses empirically, discover which ones might work, and then think about how they might be proved. In that way, the technology can be used as part of a strategy-oriented environment.

Another example of a technology-assisted focus on strategy involves the use of computer-based symbolic manipulation packages. Tools such as muMath or MACSYMA will perform quite complex calculations. With these tools, finding the roots of a 23rd degree polynomial, inverting a 16 by 16 matrix, or finding the indefinite integral of a complicated function are relatively trivial matters. The machines can be used to perform drudgework computations, freeing students to focus on conceptual issues. Don Small has described one clever use of such technologies. In a calculus class, he had worked some standard graphing problems, where students studied horizontal and vertical asymptotes of functions, critical values, and so on. In this course, the most complicated rational function one is likely to graph is of the form $P(x)/Q(x)$, where P and Q are factorable polynomials of degree 3. Having worked a few such graphs, Small marched his class into a room with a terminal. He wrote the equation of a rational function $P(x)/Q(x)$ on the board—but where P and Q were of degree 16 and 17, respectively, and not neatly factorable. The task for his students was to graph the function. They could ask any computational question they cared to and he would obtain the answer with the help of the symbolic manipulation package. The students could have asked numerical questions forever: Give me $f(0)$, $f(0.01)$, $f(0.02)$, etc. But this is inefficient and uninformative. With the tool to do the drudgework, the students were able to focus on learning which questions to ask—and thus learn about effective strategies. Small reports that the students began inefficiently, plotting lots of points between the first two vertical asymptotes of the function. As they moved from left to right, they got better and better at choosing points, observing which choices provided vital information and which were probably unnecessary. In doing so, they learned a lot more about graphing than they had the old-fashioned way, plotting by hand. (note that this kind of activity could be entirely computer based, with a coach similar to the coach in "How the west was won.")

Metacognition and Executive Control

A search for environments that focus directly on developing metacognitive skills yields almost nothing. I can point to one notable attempt along these lines, a piece of software called Algebraland (Brown, 1984) developed at Xerox Palo Alto Research Center. The task for students is to solve algebraic equations, which appear in a "problem window" on the screen. Confronted with an equation to solve, students choose the operation they wish to perform (combining terms, distributing, or expanding one side of the equation; adding, subtracting, dividing, or multiplying both sides of the equation by the same term), and the machines does the work. This makes them "managers" rather than "doers," allowing them to focus on their choice of operations. In addition, the machine also keeps a record of the students' steps so the students can review their work. Finally, it provides a graphical representation of the students' search for a solution. Examining the graphical representation of their solutions allows students to see whether their approach has been efficient, been circular, had unnecessary detours, etc. By making the students' path to a solution a tangible and visible object, Algebraland provides the students with a means for reflecting on their work, and perhaps improving it. (That, at least, is the theory. Whether the environment is sufficiently motivational to induce people to engage in such reflection, and whether the representations are actually useful, are empirical questions.)

There is little else in technology I can think of that deals directly with issues of metacognition. Our plans for one such environment are discussed in the next section.

Beliefs

Mathematics is dull and boring, and school mathematics has nothing to do with the real world. Everybody knows that.

Most people hold this belief. Part of the reason is their experience with school mathematics, which is often dull and dry and not connected to the real world or to one's personal life. Hence, one important aspect of belief directly addressable by technology is the notion of engagement (related to ownership, power, social use, and motivation) discussed earlier. Any piece of technology that gives people a better sense of what mathematics is about, makes it more enjoyable, or manages to integrate mathematical thinking into the real world in a nontrivial, profitable way is a big win. Independent of their other virtues, programs like Green Globs or Logo help with regard to belief.

The case for Logo has been made well and at length by Papert (1980). Here is one example. Among the pernicious and nonmathematical beliefs that students pick up in ordinary instruction is the idea that "in mathematics it's right or it's wrong"—and that if it's not right, it's worthless. However, in Logo students write programs that are near misses. They are not always right, and they can be fixed. As the result of such experiences, students come to understand that doing mathematics is a dialectic process, one in which you can make progress, refine your understandings, and ultimately come up with the right ideas. In addition, both Logo and Green Globs have a role in social environments. Green Globs, for example, has an explicit provision for saving students' "best shots." Students see one another's attempts, learn from them, and try to improve on them. (Sharon Dugdale has shown us shots taken by high school seniors that were far more interesting and imaginative than ours.) And in both Logo and Green Globs, students who continue to refine their skills can become more proficient than their teachers. That is quite different from the traditional classroom where the authority lies in the hands of the teacher, and students' habitual deference to experts' authority can result in their becoming passive memorizers of others' mathematics.

Three other ways in which technology may be exploited to help modify beliefs are as follows. First, my work on students' understandings of geometry indicates that in typical instruction there is the potential for students to develop an inappropriate separation between the worlds of deductive and empirical geometry. In the formal realm, students learn to write proofs to confirm relationships that are either intuitively obvious or that have clearly been known for centuries ("prove that base angles of an isosceles triangle are equal."). However, they will engage in guess-and-test empiricism when working new construction problems. The two worlds remain separated: Students will even ignore the results they have just deductively proved and will make conjectures that contradict their own assertions when working constructions. In my own problem-solving courses, I try to combat this unfortunate separation by having students work problems where their intuitions come up short, and where deduction helps them arrive at the right answers. But a broader approach, with more potential for real discovery, is possible with the help of technology. For example, the Geometric Supposers offer a world in which constructions are cheap, and empirical evidence is seen to be quite useful but not definitive. Properly exploited, they can be used to help students develop a sense of balance regarding the roles of empiricism and deduction. Students can test many conjectures and learn that not all constructions that look good actually work. Because it takes little effort to try out their constructions, they can also do a lot more guessing and will (again, in the best of circumstances) generate conjectures that are new, outside the scope of standard text materials. Such excursions take an ordinary mathematics classroom into the realm of discovery, and into an environment where the students are doing their own mathematics — not memorizing someone else's. (See Schoenfeld, 1987, for a more extensive discussion of this idea.)

Second, mathematical tools enable people to make sense of the real world. Over the past few decades, there have been revolutions in statistical analysis techniques and models of real-world phenomena. Statistical analysis kits are now accessible on microcomputers. Projects that have students gather information about objects important to them and analyze the data in interesting ways may induce students to see connections between the formal mathematics they study and the real world (Swift, 1984). Similarly, calculators, other like tools, and in the not-too-distant future symbol manipulation packages can free students from the need to work problems that only have integer coefficients and integer answers. The potential for mathematical modeling — taking real situations, abstracting them, analyzing the abstractions, and then interpreting the results in the real world — is much greater than ever before. If we exploit that potential by designing interesting curricula that take advantage of accessible technology, we may be able to break down some of the barriers between school mathematics and the real world.

Third, simulations offer the opportunity to deal with manageable versions of reality, or with abstractions of reality in which particular ideas can become more salient or easier to understand. When people playing games with the "Dynaturtle" (diSessa, 1984) make predictions based on their misconceptions about particle motion, they get to see the results of those predictions immediately. Consequently, they may begin to notice where their misconceptions differ from what actually takes place. Pilots use flight simulators before flying certain airplanes. People who are learning how a steam generation plant works can see the results of their actions (closing a valve sends a backup flow of water into another pipe, etc.) in a plant simulation called STEAMER (Hollan, Hutchins, & Weitzman, 1984). Though it is mostly conjecture at this point, one can imagine simulations of chemical bonding, of various physical worlds, of economic exchanges, etc.; these may give people manageable subworlds in which they can develop their intuitions about complex objects.

Learning Strategies

I wish there were more to say about this. To some degree this category overlaps with those of metacognition and executive control. Some of the attempts using learning strategies (e.g., the work on Algebraland) point in the right directions. The Berkeley functions group's development work (described next) may, if we are on the right track, do likewise. Collins, Brown, and Newman (in press) observe that this is a very much underdeveloped area. As they note, good teaching practice often implicitly models good learning strategies. For example, inquiry teaching poses the kinds of questions students should learn to pose for themselves. And the "convince yourself, convince a friend, convince an enemy" sequence discussed by Mason, Burton and Stacey (1982) applies as much to learning about a domain as it does to constructing a convincing mathematical argument. But much more needs to be done in this area. We know precious little about good tutorial strategies, and even less about good strategies for learning.

MORE ON GLOBS:
NOTES ON REPRESENTATIONS, A TUTOR,
AND A METATUTOR

In this section I discuss our work on a computer-based tutor for graphing algebraic functions. It is our stab at a limited part of the technological future. Our work was motivated by Sharon Dugdale's Green Globs programs, which were mentioned earlier in our discussion of exemplary software.

Green Globs consists of a number of different games sharing a common format. For the sake of simplicity, we consider only the simple game that has the student shooting at target globs on a coordinate grid. (These comments apply to the other games as well.) The goal of the game is to generate a graph that passes through as many of the globs as possible. Students type in the equation of a function, which is then graphed. The globs intersected by the curve explode, and the student receives a score that increases exponentially with the number of globs hit. Hence, there are rewards for hitting as many globs as possible with one shot. If the student is successful with a shot, he or she can move on to try to hit different globs. If the student is unsuccessful, the globs that were missed remain unexploded; the curve remains on the screen or the student can choose to erase it. Thus, the game offers students an opportunity to modify previous attempts (e.g., by systematically varying the coefficients) and try again. Figure 5.1 (from Dugdale, 1984, p. 83) shows some sequential displays from a game of Green Globs. We note that the person whose shots are recorded here is highly skilled.

Green Globs is interesting and motivational. Students win by developing a good sense of how to generate curves with particular properties, which are displayed on the grid. The students who become skilled at the game learn the relationship between the algebraic and graphical representations of a function. Moreover, they may well learn to "push graphs around." It is certainly useful, for example, to know that you can translate a graph upward by adding 1 to its equation, move it one unit to the left by replacing (x) by $(x + 1)$, and so on. In the best of all possible worlds, the students learn a great deal about the relationships between algebraic functions and their graphs. (Because this is a gaming environment, there is no explicit control in the environment of what students do or don't learn. If the game is used in an instructional setting, the teacher might have goals or a curriculum with specific intentions.)

With expanded computational power at our disposal (we are using Xerox workstations, quantum jumps more powerful than the micros on which Green Globs runs), we are embedding a game similar to Green Globs in a computer-based tutorial and exploration environment. Our intention has been to capitalize on the solid intuitions that led to the development of the original game. We hope to develop a rich computational environment that, while preserving the motivational aspects of the game, will provide the cognitive and metacognitive support structure to help students develop solid understandings about equations and graphs. We expect as well that the environment will serve as an experimental medium, allowing us to test ideas about computer-based tutors and environments. In the sequel, we discuss three aspects of our environment that are in various stages of prototyping.

Providing Support Structure for Underlying Cognitive Skills.

A major goal of Green Globs is to have students recognize the relationships between the forms of equations and the shapes of their graphs. Similarly, one hopes to have students become adept at pushing the equations around, to pro-

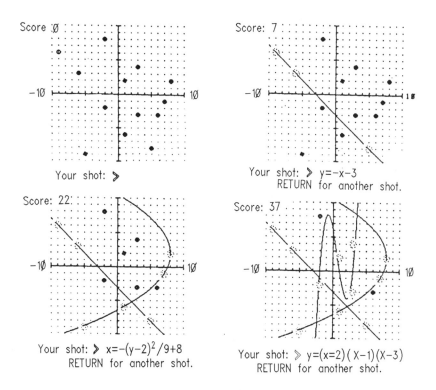

FIG. 5.1 *Note.* From "Computers: Applications Unlimited," by Sharon Dugdale, p. 83, *Computers in Mathematics Education,* 1984 NCTM Yearbook.

duce specific changes in the shapes and positions of their graphs. An additional goal is to have students know more than one algebraic form corresponding to a given type of curve, for various forms may be differentially useful. In one form it may be easy to read the properties of the graph from its equation, for example, whereas another may be more amenable to symbolic manipulations. One hopes that as they become familiar with the domain students will become proficient both at working with different forms and at recognizing which forms are useful to what ends.

We illustrate these comments with a brief discussion of parabolas. Consider first parabolas whose equations are written in the form

$$\text{Form 1:} \quad y = ax^2 + bx + c.$$

People familiar with the properties of this general form know that the coefficient a determines the width and direction of the parabola, and that changes in c result in vertical translations of the parabola. Other properties of this form are less transparent. Changes in b have a somewhat mysterious effect, leaving the width unchanged but moving the vertex, whereas variations in a change the width and possibly the direction of the parabola and move the vertex. To determine either the roots or the vertex of the parabola, you have to do some algebra. In contrast, the form

$$\text{Form 2:} \quad y = a(x\text{-}b)^2 + c$$

allows one to read off the vertex immediately; moreover, changes in a, b, and c now produce clear shifts (in width and direction of the parabola, movement along a horizontal axis, and movement along a vertical axis, respectively) in the graph. The roots are still mysterious, and the form may not be terribly convenient for algebraic manipulations. The form

$$\text{Form 3:} \quad y = a(x\text{-}b)(x\text{-}c)$$

(when the parabola is factorable) is, again, useful for some things and not others. You can read the roots off the equation directly, but it takes some practice to envision the graph as a function of **a, b,** and **c.**

The screens of our prototype machines are large enough to simultaneously display a number of windows for student work. In particular, the screen will easily accommodate a game board (with something like an enhanced version of the original Green Globs game), a "playing field" (a coordinate grid in which the student is free to play with a variety of functions and graphs), and space for tutorial dialogues. Students play for keeps on the game board. They can, however, move to the playing field if they want to try out some ideas or explore the behavior of particular functions. The playing field comes with a graphing tool kit, in which there are simultaneous displays of the graph of a function and the standard forms that represent it algebraically. If they wish, students can call up template forms for basic functions such as the parabola. All three of the forms just given appear on the screen, with the default function $y = x^2$, and the graph of $y = x^2$ appearing on the coordinate axes. The coefficients in any of the forms can be varied easily, using a mouse on a sliding scale. As the coefficients are changed, the graph changes in real time. Our expectation is that students will then be able to trace the effects of varying the coefficients on the shape of a curve (e.g., changing c in Forms 1 and 2 produces clear effects, whereas changing a or b in Form 1 does not.). In addition to linking each algebraic form to the graphical form, we have also linked the algebraic forms to each other. Thus, the student can see how the factored and expanded algebraic forms that correspond to the same graph compare to each other — and can also see, for example, that the factored form cannot be used when the parabola moves above the x-axis and its roots become imaginary. In this way, we hope to make tangible some of the relationships that, under ordinary circumstances, take a long time for students to perceive.

In a similar vein, we would like for students to develop a sense of what one can and can't do with geometric objects, such as the standard quadratics. Can you make a parabola pass through five randomly chosen points in the plane? On the playing field, students can call up standard objects ("give me a parabola") and then do things to them — pick them up and move them, make them narrower or wider, etc. As the graphs are modified, the linked algebraic forms change automatically, so that the students see (a) what one can and cannot do with the objects themselves, and (b) how the physical transformations result in alterations of the corresponding algebraic forms.

A Graphing Tutor

A major goal of Green Globs is to have students develop an understanding of the relationship between the algebraic and geometric representations of functions. The game is fun, but that's not enough. In a pure gaming environment, there are no guarantees: The right information may be present in the environment, but students might miss it or might fail to make the connections one hopes they would make. On the other hand, a purely didactic environment ("here's how to play the game") can sour a good game with the result that nobody likes it anymore, and nobody gets anything out of it. Dugdale's work with Green Globs includes a serious concern about the classroom environments in which the game is played. We have similar concerns about the technological environment in which our version of the game is embedded. We seek a good middle ground, where the game remains motivational but where the students get the right kind of help when necessary or appropriate.

Putting technology aside for the moment, we can imagine a best case scenario in which a talented human tutor is available to work with a student as the student plays Green Globs. For the reasons already mentioned, the tutor would not try to cram information down the student's throat. Rather, the tutor would serve as a resource when students wanted help and would occasionally go beyond the students' request to make suggestions that would improve their game. In general, tutorial interventions would be kept to a minimum so that the student continued to enjoy playing the game. However, particular kinds of situations would trigger a tutorial intervention, or better, an inquiry as to whether the student would like help. One such situation can occur when something unexpected happens—for example, when the student tries to shoot a straight line in a particular direction and it goes someplace else. In our best case scenario, the tutor, serving as consultant to the student, might hear an exclamation of dismay when the shot went awry. She might respond with "Something wrong?," offering help if the student wanted. (For example, the student might have forgotten that lines that move "down" have negative slopes.) Another type of situation that calls for intervention occurs when students stabilize on a suboptimal strategy and do not appear to be making progress. For example, we observed one pair of students who played game after game picking off points two at a time with straight lines. That is good practice for a while, but there is something wrong if the students, who have studied far more complex curves, are using the same method a month later. In the social environment that surrounds the game in classrooms, these students would see others scoring better with more complex curves; they would also see wonderfully complex shots in the "hall of fame." This would provide motivation for moving on to more complex techniques. A talented tutor might bring such things to students' attention—not pushing, but letting the students know that there were other things for them to try when they were ready. When the students were ready, the tutor would be available to lend a hand. The tutor would be available for brush-up sessions as well.

We are working on the design of a computer-based tutor for the Globs game. Our intention is to endow it with the attributes described in the previous paragraph. The tricky part is balancing among multiple constraints. The tutor needs to be:

- knowledgeable—able to provide the right information about graphs and equations;
- responsive—able to sense when the student is having difficulty with a particular idea and offer help; and
- unobtrusive—so that its help is appreciated when offered and the motivational aspects of the game are not lost because of too much meddling.

As Sleeman and Brown (1982) emphasize, diagnosing students' difficulties on complex intellectual tasks is an extraordinarily difficult enterprise. What you see as a (machine) tutor are the student's actions, what the student tried. What you need to figure out is the student's *intention*, for you can only do troubleshooting if you know what the student was trying to do. (If you try to remediate a problem the student doesn't have, all hell breaks loose.) Once you know the student's intention, there is still the question of whether the student's failure to take a particular approach was caused by an absence of relevant knowledge and skills, or by the failure to invoke them. And, of course, diagnosis is only the first part of the story; selecting appropriate teaching strategies for instruction or remediation is hardly a trivial matter. Fortunately, we have a leg up on the first problem, that of determining the student's intentions. One of the components of our system is a "playing field" where students can explore the properties of various functions before returning to the game board to play for keeps. One option on the playing field will be to identify the points one wants to hit (say by clicking on them with a mouse) and then take a practice shot. (This is like calling your shots in billiards. We might include a scoring bonus for making the shots you call.) In this perfectly natural way, students will state their intentions, and a major diagnostic problem is solved. If this approach works, constructing the first part of a fairly sophisticated tutor may be within reach. The second part, providing the tutor with good pedagogical skills, is also a matter of concern. We are working on "remote systems" that allow human tutors to interact with students on the machine so that we can explore the pedagogical strategies used by those teachers.

A Metacognitive Tutor

Figures 5.2 and 5.3 show the record of a student's work in one game of Green Globs. The student's first nine shots, labeled in sequence from (a) through (i), are shown in Fig. 5.2. After shot (i), she cleared the screen. Her next 14 shots, labeled in alphabetical order starting with (j), are shown in Fig. 5.3. Note that soon after starting the game the student abandoned the goal of playing for the highest possible score. In Fig. 5.2, she tried to hit the three points nearest parabola (g) with one curve, and on shots (q) through (w) in Fig. 5.3, she focused on hitting the three points in the lower right-hand corner of the coordinate grid.[1] In both Fig. 5.2 and 5.3, we see the student working hard to generate a parabola of a particular shape and position.

What I find interesting is the way she went about the task. Figures 5.2 and 5.3 offer a wealth of information. The shooting task is iterative, and the traces of prior attempts remain on the screen. Hence, after a few shots there is more than enough evidence on the screen to indicate the results of varying a single parameter. Reflecting on Fig. 5.2 and 5.3 as they stand, you can discover a great deal. And if you set about doing things systematically, varying just one parameter at a time, you can figure out how the parabolas behave.

There were no signs of such behavior on the student's part. Just the opposite, she was rather impulsive, rushing to try a new shot ("What if I try . . .") as soon as the evidence from a previous shot was displayed. She clearly had some goals in mind: hitting a particular triad of points with a parabola. What is not clear, however, is how she used the feedback from prior shots to shape her next attempts. At times she varied one parameter in the parabola, at times two. For example, in shots (d) and (e), she seemed to be exploring one parameter systematically, but then in (f), she shifted gears and then in (g) did something radically different. One is reminded of the algebra student whose work was mentioned in the section on executive control; in both cases the student's work seems to make sense locally, but it is hard to gain a sense of global progress.

In this section, I focus the discussion at the metacognitive level and away from the level of subject matter. I am *not* concerned with the question of whether the student could have been taught a foolproof procedure for getting a parabola to pass through three designated points; I am sure she could have been taught such a procedure in less total time than she spent playing the game. What I am concerned with is a metacognitive issue. How did the student use the knowledge she did have? In particular, how effective was she at taking advantage of the information available to her on the screen?

As noted before, the student did not seem to capitalize on the information

---

[1]This shift in the student's goal structure is important. It indicates that Green Globs offers significant intrinsic as well as extrinsic motivation. Although the initial goal is to get a high point score, students will often put that goal aside temporarily in the service of another goal—to learn how to manipulate a particular curve.

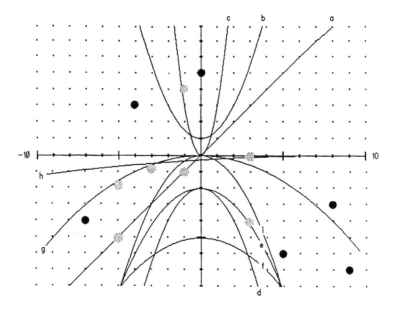

Label	Equation	Number of Globs Hit	Comments
a	Y = X	2	Type in quickly, without consulting screen.
b	Y = 1/2X² + 1	0	Also type in quickly.
c	Y = 3X²	1	
d	Y = − (1/2X²) − 2	0	Said "Maybe I should make it bigger, one fourth."
e	Y = − (1/4X²) − 2	1	
f	Y = − (1/8X²) − 5	0	Changed two parameters at once.
g	Y = − (1/16X²)	2	Interviewer prompts to "move graph over."
h	Y = − (1/16X − 1/2)²	1	Interviewer says that "1/16 squared" made flat graph.
i	Y = − 1/3X²	0	Reviews sequence of parabolas before choosing 1/3. [Chooses to clear screen of current graphs, leaving only the globs which have not been hit yet.]

FIG. 5.2

available to her; nor did she seem to be organized or systematic. Of course, human behavior should not be organized, systematic, and reflective all the time (how boring it would be!). But there are often times when a small dose of any of the three would pay tremendous dividends. As in the previous section of this chapter, we can imagine the best case scenario in which a talented human tutor was available to work with this student as she played the game. This tutor, rather than focusing on subject matter (e.g., "I'll show you how to hit any 3 globs with a parabola"), would focus on metacognitive issues. If the student had ignored some valuable information or failed to capitalize on it, the tutor might bring it to the student's attention. She might point out how the student

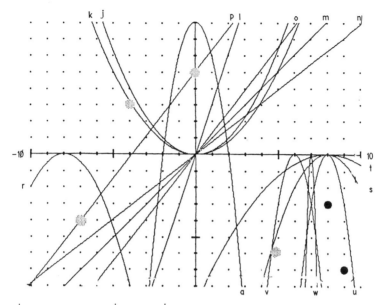

Label	Equation	Number of Globs Hit	Comments
j	$Y = 1/4X^2$	0	Interviewer asks "What is a slightly smaller number
k	$Y = 1/5X^2$	1	than 1/4?" Student chooses 1/5.
l	$Y = 3X$	0	Trying to hit (0,5). Interviewer says "You can use
m	$Y = X$	0	straight lines." Student quickly tries 2 lines.
n	$Y = 7/9X$	0	Tries to determine particular points and slope.
o	$Y = 9/7X$	0	Interviewer says "We want rise over run, y-intercept."
p	$Y = 9/7X + 5$	2	Interviewer says "Move it up by adding."
q	$Y = -(2X^2) + 8$	0	Student changes back to parabola, shifts along y-axis.
r	$Y = -1/2(X + 8)^2$	0	Interviewer notes that student first adds 8; student
s	$Y = -1/2(X - 8)^2$	1	backspaces and changes to " - 8."
t	$Y = -1/7(X - 8)^2$	0	
u	$Y = -3(X - 8)^2$	0	Interviewer suggests using 6 or 7.
v	$Y = -3(X - 6)^2$	0	
w	$Y = -3(X - 7)^2 22$	0	MIstyped equation crashes program.

FIG. 5.3

was getting close to a discovery and then lost it. She might replay aspects of the student's work and show where it might have led, had the student followed up on it. Or if she saw the student being impulsive or unsystematic, the tutor might gently bring this to the student's attention.

Such work would not be easy for a human tutor, and to develop a computer-based tutor with similar skills is a decidedly nontrivial challenge. We think that developing such a tutor is an interesting and possibly achievable goal, and we are exploring ways of making progress towards it. One vehicle for such explorations will be our remote tutoring system. We will use it to explore human metacognitive tutoring at a distance and see if we can replicate some of the aspects of the human tutoring in our computational environment. Whether or not we succeed, we expect to learn a fair amount about good human teaching in the process.

Brief Summary and Discussion

Making no reference to technology, the first part of this chapter offered a broad characterization of what it means to think mathematically—and by extension, a broad characterization of five important aspects of thinking in any problem-solving domain. Those five aspects of the framework are: (1) mastering the facts and procedures of the domain; (2) learning problem-solving strategies; (3) developing executive or metacognitive skills; (4) developing a set of perspectives consistent with using the tools of the trade; (5) having some good learning strategies. Illustrations of each category were given in both mathematics and writing, to indicate the general applicability of the framework.

The second part of the chapter focused on technology, somewhat independent of subject matter. It discussed the role of technological tools as empowering devices, and the power of cognitive technologies to enable people to do things differently, not just better. It then pointed to a few ways in which technology, either standing alone or in the context of a larger environment, might be used to foster some of the aims outlined in the first section. In the third part, we outlined some of our development and plans for a tutorial environment (with tool kit, subject-matter tutor, and metacognitive tutor) around the game of Green Globs.

Some concluding comments and caveats are appropriate at this point. It should be noted that our discussion is quite speculative, the details are sketchy, and a tremendous amount needs to be done before the ideas discussed in the third section can be translated into reality. Though I am confident of the solidity of the framework presented in the first section, its validity is anything but firmly established. Its present status is that a number of independent researchers in several fields have converged on similar perspectives, and there is good reason to suspect that something important lies behind that convergence. More to the point, it should be stressed that the framework is a beginning and not an end. Even presuming that it is more or less right, an enormous amount of work will be required to flesh out the details. (More than a decade of my work in mathematical problem solving has barely scratched the surface.)

Difficult as that endeavor may be, it will be easy in comparison to the work required to build the kinds of computational environments described here. The obstacles will not be technological: By the time we really know what we are doing, the computational power to achieve our aims will be accessible. Rather, the obstacles will be psychological. The best contemporary models of cognition in complex domains are still quite rudimentary, and the best models of human interactions (with other humans or with machines) much more so. This chapter contains many assertions about our intentions, our wish to understand the ways that talented and sensitive human tutors work, and how to capture some of that behavior in a computational environment. Those assertions are, in fact, a statement of purpose. It goes without saying that fleshing out our intentions will be a major research endeavor.

Finally, this perspective represents just one part of one vision of 2020, and a narrowly focused one at that. I have not dealt with the issues of creativity, equity, or the integration of technology into people's lives or into the schools, just to name a few. As the other chapters in this volume make all too clear, those are significant and difficult problems. Intentionally, this chapter does not stand alone; it stands in the context established by the others. We can only profit from the interplay of the sometimes complementary and sometimes contradictory perspectives expressed in them. One thing about the future is certain: It will have plenty of room for accommodating the pluralistic views in this volume, and many more.

ACKNOWLEDGMENTS

The computer-based environment described in this chapter is the product of the Berkeley Functions Group. Members of the group, in alphabetical order, are: Abraham Arcavi, Laurie Edwards, Marty Kent, Bill Marsh, Mark Nakamura, Al Schoenfeld, and Jack Smith. Special acknowledgments go to Marty Kent for his work as programmer and idea generator for the computational environment, and to Laurie Edwards for performing the student interviews and generating Fig. 5.2 and 5.3. The work described in this chapter was supported by the National Science Foundation through NSF Grant MDR-8550332. NSF grant support does not necessarily imply NSF endorsement of the ideas expressed in this chapter.

REFERENCES

Anderson, J.R., Boyle, C.F., & Reiser, B.J. (1985 April). Intelligent tutoring systems. *Science, 228,* (26) 456–462.

Brown, J.S. (1984). Process versus product: A perspective on tools for informal and communal electronic learning. In S. Newman & E. Poor (Eds.), *Report from the learning lab: Education in the electronic age.* New York: Educational Broadcasting Corporation, WNET.

Burton, R.R., & Brown, J.S. (1982). An investigation of computer coaching for informal learning activities. In D. Sleeman & J.S. Brown (Eds.), *Intelligent tutoring systems* (pp. 79–98). London: Academic Press.

Cerf, C., & Navasky, V. (1984). *The experts speak.* New York: Pantheon.

Collins, A., Brown, J.S., & Newman, S. (in press). The new apprenticeship: Teaching students the craft of reading, writing, and mathematics. In L.B. Resnick (Ed.), *Cognition and instruction: Issues and agendas.* Hillsdale, NJ: Lawrence Erlbaum Associates.

Descartes, R. (1625-1628/1964). *Discourse on method and rules for the direction of the mind.* In R. Descartes, *Philosophical essays* (L.J. Lafleur, Trans.). Indianapolis: Bobbs–Merrill.

di Sessa, A. (1984). *The third revolution in computers and education.* A report for the Committee on Mathematics, Science, and Technology Education, Commission on Behavioral Sciences and Education, National Academy of Sciences. Manuscript available from author, School of Education, University of California, Berkeley.

diSessa, A.A., & Abelson, H. (1986). BOXER: A reconstructible computational medium. *Communications of the ACM, 29*(9), 859–868.

Dugdale, S. (1982, March). Green Globs: A microcomputer application for graphing of equations. *Mathematics Teachers, 75,* 208–214.

Dugdale, S. (1984). Computers: Applications unlimited. In V.P. Hansen (Ed.), *Computers in mathematics education (1984 Yearbook of the National Council of Teachers of Mathematics)* (pp. 82–88). Reston, VA: National Council of Teachers of Mathematics.

Fawcett, H.P. (1938). *The nature of proof (1938 Yearbook of the National Council of Teachers of Mathematics).* New York: Columbia University Teachers College Bureau of Publications.

Hollan, J., Hutchins, E., & Weizman, L. (1984, Summer). STEAMER: An interactive, inspectable simulation-based training system. *The AI Magazine,* 15–27.

ITMA Collaboration. (1984). *The Micro as a teaching assistant.* Essex, UK: Longman House.

Kaput, J. (1985, August 30). *Multiplicative word problems and intensive quantities: An integrated software response* (Tech. rep.) Cambridge, MA: Educational Technology Center, Harvard University.

Mason, J., Burton, L., & Stacey, K. (1982). *Thinking mathematically.* London: Addison–Wesley.

Papert, S. (1980). *Mindstorms.* New York: Basic Books.

Pea, R. (1985). Beyond amplification: Using the computer to reorganize mental functioning. *Educational Psychologist, 20,* 167–182.

Pea, R. (1987). Cognitive technologies for mathematics education. In A. Schoenfeld (Ed.), *Cognitive science and mathematics education.* Hillsdale, NJ: Lawrence Erlbaum Associates.

Pólya, G. (1945). *How to solve it.* Princeton: Princeton University Press.

Pólya, G. (1954). *Mathematics and plausible reasoning* (2 Vols.). Princeton, NJ: Princeton University Press.

Pólya, G. (1980). *Mathematical discovery* (2 Vols.). New York: Wiley.

Schoenfeld, A. (1985). *Mathematical problem solving.* New York: Academic Press.

Schoenfeld, A. (1987). What's all the fuss about metacognition? In A. Schoenfeld (Ed.), *Cognitive science and mathematics education.* Hillsdale, NJ: Lawrence Erlbaum Associates.

Sleeman, D., & Brown, J.S. (1982). Introduction: Intelligent tutoring systems. In D. Sleeman & J.S. Brown (Eds.), *Intelligent tutoring systems* (pp. 1–11). London: Academic Press.

Swift, J. (1984). Exploring data with a microcomputer. In V.P. Hansen (Ed.), *Computers in mathematics education (1984 Yearbook of the National Council of Teachers of Mathematics)* (pp. 82–88). Reston, VA: National Council of Teachers of Mathematics.

Tinker, R.F. (Ed.) (1981). *Hans on: A forum for science and technology educators.* Cambridge, MA: Technical Education Research Centers.

Vygotsky, L.S. (1978). *Mind in society.* Cambridge, MA: Harvard University Press.

Yerushalmy, M., & Houde, R. (1986). The geometric supposer: Promoting thinking and learning. *Mathematics Teacher, 79*(6), 418–422.

6 Apprentice Tools: Students as Practitioners

WALLACE FEURZEIG
BBN Laboratories, Inc.

INTRODUCTION: EDUCATIONAL GOALS

Education ought to be directed to helping young people make an informed commitment to life and work by helping them learn who they are and what they might become. As well as imparting a base of fundamental knowledge and building a foundation for learning in the major subjects—the arts, sciences, history, language, and mathematics—education ought to have another goal, one that is orthogonal to this, and of comparable importance. We should help children make a serious commitment to becoming good at something they have to work at, that takes time, and that requires a significant investment of thinking. We ought to help students *acquire a practice*. We would like them to become active practitioners in some discipline area, however narrow, and we would like them to share their development with others. We'd like to bring the culture of practitioners into the classroom. The burden of this chapter is to suggest how information technology might contribute to this purpose.

Technological Contributions

Our thesis is that computers can make real contributions to education in at least two ways. The first is propaedeutic. Computers can be used to create highly motivating learning environments that help students acquire early the habits of serious thought and work so necessary for intellectual development. This can be accomplished in part through playful activities. The work of children is play. Sophisticated play is also an important element of adult learning and creativity at the highest levels.

The other contribution is designed to help bridge the gulf between school and real intellectual work. School curricula often present the standard subjects in an intellectually impoverished and uncompelling way, teaching ways of thinking and doing that are distinctly different from those used by practitioners. School math is not a model of real mathematics and school science is not genuine science. Education should be directed to grounding knowledge in experience and in contexts of use, and computers can be used to create and support the knowledge sources, learning environments, and instructional tools necessary to foster this kind of cognitive development.

Computers are the most general-purpose machines invented by man. They are our first knowledge machines. Their capabilities for knowledge representation, dynamic simulation, graphic presentation, and interactive communication provide enormous potential for modeling systems of all kinds. We are beginning to realize and demonstrate some of the rich cognitive and educational benefits made possible by exploiting the technological capabilities of computers more fully and thoughtfully. Computers can model systems with complex structures and behaviors in varied ways and at all levels of detail. Models can incorporate facilities for explaining their own operation as well as facilities that enable users to modify the operation of the models. Tools and models of this kind can be made transparent and accessible to students for exploration, study, and analysis. Design tools can give students capabilities for building their own models. Instructional tasks and projects designed around the use of these tools can contribute greatly to motivating an understanding of the issues at the heart of learning and thinking within all the disciplines.

By 2020, information technology will have become so integral to everyday life and work, and will have so transformed how we do what we do, that it will inevitably affect both what is taught and how. Computer-based tools will have become central and essential for work in all the disciplines. Because of the continued advances in technology, relatively inexpensive computers will have the performance power, devices, communications, and software tools required to support applications employing extensive computation, real-time simulation and control, interactive displays, and artificial intelligence. Thus, many computer-based tools used by scholars, scientists, and artists will be accessible to schools and homes, at least in simpler counterparts and low-cost versions. This means it will be possible to bring students, during their formative years, into closer contact with the work of real practitioners.

The prospects for advancing education through information technology require, for their success, a great deal in the way of nontechnological developments. These include such things as creating the necessary human resources, primarily skilled teachers who like to teach and who are knowledgable in the subjects they teach and in the use of the computer tools they teach with. This chapter focuses entirely on technological aspects and does not address the other essential constituents of educational change. Making allowances for these, our assertion is that the achievement of order-of-magnitude improvements in the quality and productivity of education will be greatly facilitated by, and in some areas will actually require, the intelligent use of technology. Furthermore, dramatic improvement in education is not merely a luxury greatly to be desired — rather, it is fast becoming a necessity.

Current Educational Problems

The United States has very serious mathematics and science education problems. School math drags on for years and gets nowhere. The curriculum content is mathematically impoverished. The unnaturalness and lack of commonsense characterizing current mathematics teaching have been well described (Davis, 1984; Whitney, 1985). Children should be experiencing genuine mathematics and science during their formative years. Instead, despite some pretentions to teaching "problem solving," the math class remains dedicated to the acquisition of computational skills like those exhibited by current hand calculators. It even fails here. A long-term longitudinal study of elementary mathematics students in representative schools in the United States, China, and Japan found that Japanese first graders already show the same level of competence as U.S. sixth graders (Stevenson, Lee, & Stigler, 1986). The study also found that parents of the American students appeared complacent and unconcerned about their children's level of mathematical knowledge and skills.

Elementary science education is even more disastrous. The science specialist, a scarce resource in the schools of 20 years ago, has practically vanished. More than half the teachers of precollege science and mathematics are not certified in the subjects they teach. More than 7,000 of the 14,000–15,000 high schools in the United States have no physics course (Melmed, 1986). Children learn very little physical and biological science, even surface-level factual knowledge. Few have the opportunity to engage in genuine exploration, investigation, and experimentation during their school years. Despite our continued excellence in science research, we are becoming a nation of scientific illiterates.

We are losing out in higher education as well. The current level of output of mathematics PhDs is not sufficient to replace college faculties. Over half the science and mathematics graduate students in United States universities are non-U.S. citizens. Some foreign students stay in America, but even with the brain drain the U.S. numbers are decreasing. Contributing to increased international participation in science research is a good thing, but the declining numbers of American mathematicians and scientists should be a matter of national concern, if only for the reason that a loss of scientific preeminence could have long-term material implications that affect our national quality of life. If these educational losses continue to erode our science and technology base, we could descend to the status of a major second-rate power.

Let us hope that we will recognize the criticality of our educational problems and make a serious and intelligent response. The current widespread complacency concerning these problems could very suddenly be replaced by a sense of their urgency and priority. This might happen as a consequence of the substantial demands created by new information technology for workers with scientific, mathematical, and linguistic competence. Or perhaps a new Sputnik threat will direct dramatic education and training imperatives. . . .

The technology of computers will be central to the success of these efforts. This chapter describes two distinctly different computer-centered approaches with uniquely powerful educational benefits. The first one introduces children to formal thinking procedures in the context of playful activities, such as writing simple programs for controlling robot turtles or generating poetic grammars. It is designed to provide a conceptual foundation for teaching mathematical and logical ways of thinking in terms of programming ideas and activities. Students work with an extraordinary instrument, a powerful programming language, which effectively provides a facility for actively constructing their own knowledge. Virtually all mathematics and major parts of the content of the elementary science and language courses can be effectively developed under this approach. The other approach is designed to support the venerable paradigm of apprentice training using new methods and tools made possible by computers.

PROGRAMMING AS A CONCEPTUAL
FOUNDATION FOR TEACHING THINKING

The experience of school math has given generations of students the view that, as well as being both formidable and dull, mathematics is far removed from anything genuinely real or interesting in the world. The appropriate use of computers can profoundly change that experience and perception. The computer can serve as a mathematics laboratory to foster an experimental approach toward solving problems. Programming ideas and experiences can be structured to provide a natural foundation for teaching the notions and art of logical thinking. The entire content of elementary mathematics can be developed in terms of programming in a new kind of presentation that asserts a central role for technology in supporting serious mathematical, cognitive, and educational purposes.

Many tasks in this presentation may not seem to be part of the subject of mathematics because their content is so very different from the school math children are familiar with. A rich variety of tasks that are interesting to children readily lend themselves to programming. These may be drawn from language, art, music, and other domains and topics in areas of personal interest to students, often of their own choosing. They include such things as building semantic grammars for generating and producing gossip, poetry, jokes, or songs;

making and breaking "secret codes" defined by functional composition; designing and drawing tiling patterns with a program-controlled robot turtle; developing strategies for a turtle with sensors to circumnavigate objects on an obstacle course; and many other constructive projects. Children can even construct their own robots—the Logo programming language has recently been integrated with the Lego electronic construction kit to enable children to develop computer-controlled dynamic models of many kinds of devices (Ocko & Reznick, 1986).

Aside from art and shop work, school activities are seldom directed to producing things that have interest outside of school, that students feel is really theirs, that they designed and made. Programming activities like the ones just described are an exception. At the same time, these activities are natural sources for rich learning experiences. They engage students in reflective problem-solving work involving strategic planning, precise formal thinking, and constructive design. Students do not feel burdened by the need to acquire mathematical knowledge in contexts such as these because it is important for accomplishing their purpose.

Many students find work with computer-controlled robots, display devices, and animated sprites especially compelling. For example, students learn to use the Logo programming language to control a robot device, the Logo turtle. They learn a repertory of Logo commands for directing the turtle—for example, to move forward or back, turn to the right or left, position a pen to start or stop drawing its path as it moves, turn its lamp on or off, sound its horn, and test whether or not its touch sensors are in contact with an external object. The Logo turtle is most often used as a drawing device for children. However, its use is not limited to the development of pictures and patterns. Programming projects based on the use of these wonderful toys can introduce, in a concrete and comprehensible way, beautiful, and, at times deep, mathematics.

An Example of Logo Mathematics

As an example, consider the turtle path reversal problem (Feurzeig & Lukas, 1972). This problem introduces elementary students in an engaging way, to the algorithm for inverting a functional chain. This is a powerful algorithm—it is the basis for matrix inversion and the solution of linear systems. It has important applications in thermodynamics and system design. It ought to be given a memorable name, such as "the theorem of return." The task is easily stated and grasped. The student is first asked to direct the Logo turtle out of the room and around the corner where it is no longer visible. He is then asked to bring the turtle back, i.e., to issue the Logo commands that will return it home.

Students are typically taken aback by this because they can no longer see the turtle. How can one control what one cannot see? (The task thus provides a concrete metaphor for scientific inference, by introducing the idea that the mind's eye can transcend the limitations of the senses.) The students have the complete list of the Logo commands that took the turtle from home to its current invisible resting place. But even a bright student often lacks the initial insight of how to use this information. However, once students are asked how they might bring the turtle back to where it was "the time before last," they often get a flash of understanding. If the last command was to move the turtle forward some number of units, they can undo that by moving it backwards the same amount; if it was to turn right some number of degrees, they can undo this by turning the turtle left that same amount. They see that the complete plan for returning the turtle home is to undo the sequence of actions that the turtle took in proceeding to its final location, and that this is accomplished by performing the *opposite* actions in the reverse order.

After they implement the sequence of commands that return the turtle home, students are given the task of generalizing their solution. They are asked to write a Logo program to reverse *any* path defined by a sequence of turtle commands. Then, generalizing this, they are asked to describe a plan for a program that reverses turtle paths generated by *arbitrary* Logo programs, comprised not only of turtle commands but also of Logo *programs* that may themselves contain turtle commands. Recursive generalization tasks like this occur naturally in Logo programming work of all kinds and at all levels. Powerful mathematical skills are fostered in the course of developing rich mathematical content.

Rationale

The epistemological basis for this kind of presentation, mathematics in the context of programming, lies in the fundamental correspondence between the concepts underlying mathematics and the concepts underlying computation and programming. Programming languages can be designed to serve students as natural instruments for mathematical expression and communication. Logo is an example of such a language. Its syntax is built on the powerful foundational base of recursive functions. The simplicity and transparency of its form reflect its inherent mathematical structure. Its constructive power mirrors the creative power of mathematics: Logo functions are used as building blocks to construct more complex functions that become, in turn, elements of larger and more powerful constructs—very much in the way mathematicians build powerful theorems out of simpler ones, often only a few steps removed from the primitives.

The heuristic aspects of programming activity, which arise from the nature of machine interaction, are equally important. Students find the activity of building their own programs compelling. Programming provides highly motivated models for fostering the development of the principal heuristic and metacognitive skills. For example, it lends itself naturally to discussing the relation of formal procedures to intuitive understanding of problems. It provides a wealth of examples for implementing heuristic precepts such as formulate a plan, find a similar but simpler problem, and divide a problem into tractable parts (Polya, 1962). It provides models for the contrast between the global planning of an attack on a problem and the formal detail of an elaborated solution (Schoenfeld, 1985). In programming work, students directly confront the disparities between their intentions and their actions. The concrete form of the program and the interactive character of Logo programming allow the debugging of errors in one's own thinking to be identified as a definite, constructive, and plannable activity. This is a highly motivating and uniquely valuable learning experience.

The use of Logo is also relevant to what is perhaps the most difficult aspect of mathematics for a teacher: helping the student strive for self-consciousness and articulateness about the process of solving problems. Math students can seldom say anything about how they work towards the solution of a problem. They lack the habit of discussing such things and they lack the language necessary to do so. A semantically rich well-structured programming language provides a vocabulary and a set of experiences for discussing mathematical concepts, problems, and experiences. Programs are more discussable than traditional mathematical materials: One can talk about their development; one can talk about their relationship to one another and to the original problem.

Applications and Extensions

The intent of this approach is to exploit programming to teach mathematical thinking, not to teach programming as a subject in its own right. A stronger claim would be to teach *thinking* rather than mathematical thinking. But thinking has to be about *something*, it does not exist in vacuuo. There were attempts in the 1960s to develop artificial intelligence programs with *general* problem-solving capabilities. This quest proved to be a modern-day philosopher's stone. To be effective, AI applications require domain-specific knowledge as well as powerful inferencing methods. The same holds for the approach described here. One might seek to exploit programming to teach thinking in the context of some specific discipline area other than mathematics, but one cannot teach thinking by itself, abstracted from content.

Because of the fundamental connections between the foundations of mathematics and the concepts underlying computation and programming, mathematics is a natural context for Logo presentations. Logo-based teaching sequences for primary and secondary mathematical topics including number systems, functions, algebra, logic, and problem-solving strategy have been under development since 1966 (Feurzeig, Lukas, Grant, & Faflick, 1971; Papert, 1972). Elementary-level Logo mathematics courses in introductory geometry and algebra are being developed currently (Clements & Battista, 1987; Feurzeig, 1986). A substantial and beautiful treatment of Logo-based mathematics has been developed for undergraduate-level curricula. The topics covered include random motion, branching processes, space-filling designs, vector operations, topology of curves, spherical geometry, and general relativity (Abelson & diSessa, 1981). Computers and programming ought to be established as integral to the presentation of the entire mathematics curriculum well before 2020.

The richness of non-numerical topics open to programming can be exploited to develop curriculum sequences in the arts and sciences, language study, and other subjects, not only in mathematics. Extensive Logo-based materials have been developed for the visual arts curriculum (Reggini, 1985). Another highly developed curriculum, a foundational course in language and linguistics centered on Logo programming ideas and activities, has recently been described (Goldenberg & Feurzeig, 1987).

Because cognitive skills are domain dependent, one should not expect that the problem-solving competence acquired in one domain will transfer to others. Thus, it is not surprising that Logo programming skills do not directly transfer to problem solving in other domains (Pea & Kurland, 1984). In this regard, however, note that elementary Logo courses often teach little more than the syntax of Logo commands. This enables students to write simple turtle-drawing procedures, but it does not develop programming skills at a level required for writing nonsuperficial programs. Thus, though there is little reason to look for transfer of cognitive skills from Logo to other domains, a decisive experiment has yet to be done.

Logo programming can be expected to have stronger effects on the development of transferrable *metacognitive* skills. These are components of learning that may be domain independent, and that function as executive processes to monitor the progress and products of cognition. They include skills such as comprehension self-monitoring, time management, and reflectivity. There is evidence that the use of Logo to teach programming facilitates the transfer of reflectivity and self-monitoring in children (Clements & Gullo, 1984; Miller & Emihovich, 1985).

STARTING YOUNG

Computers will have a profound impact on education. They will become a strong force for educational change by providing a source of new ways of doing things, of new things to each and new ways to learn. Our argument is as follows. Computers are destined to become the universal intellectual worktool. By 2020, computers and information technology will have become central to the practice of all the disciplines — in the sciences, arts, professions, and trades, everywhere in the workplace. It is not that the old ways of doing things will have completely vanished so much as that the powerful new tools and methods made possible by computers will have become deeply established in all facets of work. The new technology will provide scientists, engineers, physicians, mathematicians, musicians, economists, historians, linguists, architects, and writers with power tools so useful and valuable that important parts of their work will become unthinkable without their use.

These tools will be designed principally for professionals and expert practitioners. However, young students who have acquired a foundation of knowledge and skills in inquiry and problem solving—the objective of the comprehensive Logo curriculum projected before—could learn the use of novice versions of these tools, designed for simple tasks. Activities centered on the use of these tools can be made compelling to students because the tools are authentic (they enable one to do something real), engaging because they are interactive, and productive because they invite the user to make something. The creation of simpler versions of these tools, designed for use by students and supported by such activities, could, in principle, enable them to gain early experience with the real practice of real practitioners. This development, by helping to bridge the gap between schooling and work, would motivate and give credibility to school programs. Thus it is plausible that it would enhance students' learning benefits during their formative years when habits of thought and work are established and key intellectual commitments made.

It may seem strange to propose to restructure education in the image of technology, but this would not be the first time this has happened. Two earlier technologies, writing and books, have become so fundamental and integral to intellectual activity and to education that their technological origins have been forgotten. Information technology has the prospect of affecting learning with comparable impact.

The Impact of Technology on the Disciplines

The program depends fundamentally on two projected developments: the emergence of computers and information technology as the crux and center of future intellectual and everyday life activities, and the accessibility of this technology to beginning students. Computers have only begun to make their most important contributions to the disciplines, within the sciences, arts, trades, and professions. Their impact on applications has been apparent for some time. Their real potential, on the creative and productive aspects of scientific, artistic, and scholarly thought and work, is only beginning to be apparent. Technology will catalyze intellectual change; it will profoundly transform thinking and practice in many fields. The continued development and integration of supercomputers, parallel computers, and computer networks will accelerate these developments.

Technology is beginning to provide instruments and environments that impact very directly and centrally on creative intellectual work in science and engineering. New computer facilities support the development of powerful methods for designing engineered systems that are too complex to be developed by conventional methods, e.g., the use of digitally simulated wind tunnels for advanced aerodynamic systems design, in place of real wind tunnel simulation of physical airplane models.

Computers are already transforming the way science is done in America. Computer modeling is becoming a standard tool for experiment and theory. It is being used to model extremely complex processes, ranging in scale from the inner structure of the proton to star cluster formation and decay. It can be an illuminating source of creative insights about the structure and behavior of complex phenomena, such as those shown in nonlinear dynamic processes, that were previously inaccessible, and it has made possible the solution of problems previously thought unsolvable. It can be expected to provide dramatic breakthroughs in physics, chemistry, genetics, economics, meteorology, pharmacology, demography, and other fields.

Computers will become increasingly important to mathematicians and physicists as basic research tools. This is already beginning to happen in areas such as mathematical chaos, nonlinear dynamics, fractals, and cellular automata. Some of this work has great theoretical importance as well as rich applications. For example, it was learned only recently that the basic elementary functions—sine, cosine, exponential, quadratic—exhibit chaotic behavior in the complex plane and thus that chaos, far from being an isolated phenomenon, is extensive and fundamental throughout mathematics. This was a surprising result whose implications have yet to be fully investigated and understood. The graphic outputs produced by the computer in studies of chaos, fractals, and automata are typically very beautiful. Progress in these areas would not have been possible without the use of powerful computational and graphic display facilities as essential investigative tools. Yet, the computational methods required to show these behaviors are now accessible to high school students, and these areas are open to genuine research investigations at high school level. In the context of dynamic computer modeling and animated graphics, many topics in physics and biology also lend themselves to study at this level.

Powerful computer environments and tools were first developed in the service of mathematics and science. Computers have recently begun to impact scholarly work in other disciplines. New systems for associative storage and retrieval enable interactive access to vast knowledge sources (connections are triggered by following semantic linkages), facilitate browsing, guide research probes along associative paths chosen from displayed alternatives, and assist in indexing, abstracting, and report generation. These capabilities have given rise to the first developments of a species of tool known as scholars' workstations (Yankelovich, Haan, & Drucker, 1986). These tools will evolve into the libraries of the future for scholars and students. They will be readily accessible by students for research projects of all kinds. Commercial prototypes for use on personal computer systems already exist (Apple Computer, Inc., 1987).

Computers are beginning to establish a strong place in the music world through the development of professional tools for performers and composers. The best state-of-the-art digital synthesizers are capable of producing a rich variety of musical sounds including high-fidelity acoustic simulations of conventional instruments and vocal choirs (not only new sounds of obvious electronic origin). Their versatile facilities for creating, varying, and recording musical sequences, and for playing live sequences with recorded accompaniments, have made these tools highly valuable to players in the concert hall and recording studio. The same machines, used with sophisticated programs for musical composition, enable automatic translation of synthesized sounds into notated music. The composer can play either the synthesizer keyboard or the symbolic representation on the machine, revise the score with an interactive music editor, and print the manuscript. These facilities are very attractive to musically disadvantaged students as well as aspiring young musicians.

Similar kinds of design and production tools in the visual arts arena will enhance the work of architects, sculptors, animators, and graphic artists. Hardware developments such as true three-dimensional displays, light wands, and pressure-sensitive drawing devices will further augment their capabilities. But their real power will come from an enormous range of visual effects made possible by dynamic computer graphics programs coupled with photographic sequences from video, compact disk, and other image sources. These tools will give rise to new visual art forms, some of which will prove valuable for their aesthetic quality, not their novelty. The technology will also enable high-fidelity reproduction of artwork on computers to facilitate study and dissemination.

Tools based directly on the ones described, the working tools of real mathematicians, scientists, scholars, musicians, and artists, can be implemented in inexpensive versions designed for use by beginning students. These tools can be introduced into education with the sure knowledge that they are the authentic instruments used by those who personify the best goals of education, the serious knowledge users and creators. They also have the rare prospect of being genuinely interesting to students. But there is a condition: Students have to learn how to use these computer-centered tools to do the things they were designed to do. Digital synthesizers cannot be used to make interesting music by someone who has no knowledge of how to use them or what to do with them. Students have to be primed in the disciplines to enable them to use the tools of the disciplines.

The other dimension to this proposal is to create learning activities centered on the use of the tools and designed to develop organically the knowledge needed to use them more and more powerfully. We propose an old way to do this. We envisage these learning activities as present-day incarnations of apprentice-like training experiences. The role of the teacher serving this goal will be like that of the master overseer of young apprentices. The classroom will become more a laboratory, shop, or studio than a lecture room. The training can be aided, at least in part, through the use of appropriate computational environments and learning technology. The domain tools that are the principal instruments in this practicum can be augmented by learning tools and laboratory work expressly designed to support their use.

A key point about the introduction and early use of the tools is that domain knowledge is developed as necessary to serve the effective use of the tools, not the other way around. The content of the discipline is not to be taught for its own sake but to enable the student to advance the needs of a current project to be carried out with the tools. The knowledge is to give the student power to achieve a goal, it is not promoted as being inherently valuable. This is contrary to the usual school tradition, where knowledge is rarely developed to enable students to do something they are interested in. Along the way, the value of learning domain knowledge in a global and general sense, apart from its immediate instrumental value, gradually becomes apparent. Students learn that the tools are truly empowering when their use is informed and guided.

Apprentice-Learning Models

In past times people became skilled craftsmen and artisans by being apprenticed to a master and learning under his tutelage, often over a period of many years. The tasks given to the apprentice gradually increased in complexity as his skills were developed, consolidated, and integrated with previously acquired skills. At each stage, new and more difficult tasks were demonstrated to the apprentice by the master or by one of his skilled assistants. The demonstrations included detailed descriptions of the actions taken supported by explanations rationalizing the choice of actions and the response to problems encountered along the way.

The apprentice then tried to emulate the work of the expert, taking it as an exemplary model. From time to time he would experiment with the materials and procedures, and explore new options, to extend his knowledge and experience. Skills were assimilated through extensive practice, guided at times by the master or his agents. The processes of demonstration and practice were often repeated and alternated many times during each new task stage. At critical phases of their training students might be assigned projects to be carried out with little or no guidance. Their work and its products were reviewed and critiqued. As the apprentice gained proficiency, he was given increased responsibilities in making the objects produced by the shop. In the course of time he made the transition from novice to journeyman, and perhaps eventually achieved master status.

Apprentice modes of training are in use today in some artistic, athletic, skilled trade and professional settings such as the music master class, the tennis court, the machine shop, the teaching hospital, and also in some graduate schools. But initial training in most task domains is largely done in school settings far removed from the real workplace. What is valuable about apprentice training is not that it is carried out in the workplace, but that it actively initiates the student in the actual processes used by experts to perform real tasks. These experiences can be realized in the schools by exploiting computer technology to develop apprentice-training tools and activities designed to motivate and prepare students for doing intellectual work within the disciplines.

We suggest that the apprentice model can be valuable for training in complex cognitive domains such as physics, mathematics, and linguistics, and not only in the practical arts, professions, and trades. Apprentice shops for early (prehigh school) training of mathematicians, scientists, engineers, and anthropologists do not exist. But they ought to, especially now that computers are becoming the working tools for the intellectual disciplines. Computers can host the teaching and learning tools to complement the apprentice-training activities of the classroom teacher. The next sections describe some kinds of instructional tools and the very preliminary work being done to develop and apply them.

Tools to Aid Knowledge Acquisition and Assimilation

A key facility for aiding students in acquiring the knowledge and skills required for solving a complex problem or performing a nonsuperficial task is an articulate expert program, a program capable of performing the same kinds of tasks that it trains and explaining its actions as it performs them. The object is to provide students with concrete models that prepare them for their own attempt to solve similar problems in the reasoned and articulate way exemplified by the expert. The domain knowledge embedded in the expert is typically in the form of rules possibly coupled with a runnable simulation model. The expert program mirrors the prescriptive role of the master in the apprentice training situation. It performs the task in the way it expects the student to emulate. As the student's capabilities grow, the expert demonstrates more difficult tasks that model the enhanced level of performance expected from the student.

The expert is articulate — as it performs a task it explains its mode of performance along the way. Each time it takes an action it can state the reason for the action, not only what the action is intended to accomplish but also why this is desirable in terms of its current goal. The goal structures employed in performing the task are explicitly represented in the rules that drive the expert. This enables rapid evaluation and execution of the rules and facilitates the generation and presentation of strategically based explanations for the expert's actions. These are couched in terms of its current subgoal structure, to better motivate the sense and purpose of the reasoning employed in performing the task.

One might expect little benefit from the effort of patterning one's own performance on that of an expert, essentially an imitative task. Why should one try to copy an expert? Won't that hamper individual creativity and inventiveness? Also, expertise is not unique — there may be different ways of performing the same task, all demonstrating expertise, but some better suited than others to the thinking and learning style of a particular student.

One part of the answer is that even the masters model the masters. For example, Einstein modeled special relativity on Maxwell's equations. Perhaps that is not surprising in physics. The physicist builds on past work, extending and integrating partial models in the search for a comprehensive theory. However, the modeling process occurs throughout the arts as well, in advanced work as well as beginning levels. Beethoven modeled his fugues on Bach's, and Michelangelo copied his first sculptures from those of his master Vasari. Even Picasso, the personification of originality and invention in art, trained himself by copying old masters at the Louvre, like generations of painters before and since. One learns to become oneself by the discipline of following paths set by others. Once a student has learned well to replicate the performance of the expert, he is on the way to finding his own way.

After the articulate expert demonstrates a task, students may try to do it on their own, working within the same computer-task environment. Guided practice facilities can support and aid the students' thinking in a variety of ways as they work on the problem. For example, expert systems can be used to serve as the students' agents in carrying out the details of task execution so that they can focus on the strategic aspects of problem solving. Expert tutors can advise students along the way by suggesting subgoals. Task-performance monitors and probes can be developed to help students become more explicit about their intentions, expectations, and inferences in the course of solving problems. Computer microworlds can be designed to foster the development of the skills of exploration, hypothesis formation and testing, and generalization. Representative instructional tools of these kinds, recently implemented for use in various elementary mathematics and science domains, are briefly described next.

The Algebra Workbench is an instructional tool designed to aid students acquire skill in solving algebra problems (Feurzeig, 1986). Its kernel is a mathematical symbol manipulation system called the algebra calculator. A student uses the algebra calculator to perform the algebraic operations he specifies (e.g., expand an expression, remove parentheses, divide both sides of an equation by a specified expression, evaluate an expression). When he works on an algebra problem (solving an equation, simplifying an expression, testing two expressions for equivalence), he need only be concerned about what operations to perform, not how to perform them — the calculator will carry out the designated operations for him. Thus, the system effectively separates the strategic and heuristic components of problem solving from the manipulative aspects and enables the student to work on tasks dedicated totally to the acquisition of these more complex strategic skills.

The system also incorporates algebra problem-solving experts with capabilities for demonstrating and explaining their performance and for critiquing the student's problem-solving work. An expert can be called by the student to perform a problem or a single step of a problem, to advise the student on how to proceed toward a solution, or to check and critique the student's work. The experts are articulate. The procedures that they employ are designed to be effective, transparent, and uniform across all problems, thus easy for students to understand and model.

QUEST (Qualitative Understanding of Electrical System Troubleshooting) is an instructional system for teaching electric circuit operation and troubleshooting (White & Frederiksen, 1985). It is built on a qualitative causal simulation of circuit behavior using device models to compute the operation of standard circuit components (battery, resistor, capacitor, switch, bulb, wire). QUEST has a facility for eliciting information from the student about his thought processes as he works on a troubleshooting task. Each time the student calls for a test or action, the system asks him to indicate what he seeks to learn from it. After the simulation is run and the test performed, the student is asked for his conclusions (e.g., about possible device or subcircuit faults) from observing the effect of the action on circuit behavior (Feurzeig & Ritter, 1987).

This probing is carried out by the system during the entire problem-solving interaction to develop detailed information about the student's intentions, expectations, and conclusions. These data can greatly extend our understanding of the student's misconceptions and difficulties over that based solely on his troubleshooting actions. The elicitation procedure is designed to be unforced and unintrusive. Responses are made easily and rapidly, by pointing at window items. The student is not expected to be deliberative about each action he takes. He can bypass the procedure at any point. This approach substantially extends the power of pure AI inferencing methods by making the student an active advisor to the instructional monitor designed to aid him. It gives the tutor very specific information about the student's misconceptions and conceptual gaps. It helps model the student's problem-solving behavior toward the pursuit of thoughtful planning and reflective analysis. This approach has a wide scope of application to complex task domains.

Tools to Aid Exploration and Inquiry

Computer microworlds are environments for aiding exploration and fostering the development of inquiry skills (Groen, 1985; Lawler, 1984). They are different from the instructional systems just described in that they do not incorporate expository or didactic facilities. Like real-world phenomena, they do not give away their secrets or explain themselves — they simply exist and behave. They can be probed, their behavior can be explored, their structure understood, their underlying operation discovered. But, unlike CAI systems, "intelligent" or otherwise, they do not teach or even advise. Microworlds, together with activities formulated for use within them, are designed as learning environments. Interactions with a microworld are designed to aid students construct knowledge through active exploration and experiment. There are no programmed scenarios or built-in agendas. Concepts like lesson and instructional sequence are not integral to this experience; they are outside and separate.

An excellent example of a highly developed microcomputer environment is the Thinkertools microworld, developed for teaching basic concepts of Newtonian physics to students at the sixth-grade level. Its other goals are to teach "the fundamentals of scientific reasoning such as the concept of a scientific law, the possibility of generalizing such laws, and the utility of alternative representations for thinking about physical systems, and to get students interested in science and build confidence in their ability to do science" (Horwitz & White, 1986).

The graphics animation and simulation packages in Thinkertools allow the user to create representations of physical objects and systems of objects on the screen and cause them to interact with each other in accordance with physical laws. It also supports computed objects such as centers of mass and measured objects, such as dials, counters, and thermometers. The laws that govern the behavior of objects on the screen are also under the control of the user. "Thus, for example, we may turn off the force of gravity—or double it; friction may or may not be present; spring constants and other parameters are variable at will. In addition, the evolution of a system may be controlled at all times by slowing down, stopping, or even reversing the flow of time. Motion may be highlighted by having selected objects leave a wake which delineates their previous positions over some period of time. Forces may be explicitly displayed as arrows drawn on the screen" (Horwitz, 1985).

Using joysticks and color monitors, Thinkertools enables students "to pilot rocket ships in space, investigate the effects of unseen forces, predict the outcome of experiments, and acquire in the process a qualitative and intuitive understanding of such basic concepts as mass, velocity, and energy." A Thinkertools curriculum in sixth-grade science has recently been developed and piloted. Initial classroom trials have shown it to be highly effective in teaching Newtonian mechanics (White & Horwitz, 1987).

Microworlds are designed to complement teaching and training by giving students an environment that allows them to assimilate, integrate, and extend their knowledge through their own explorations. This does not mean they will be able to do so. The view that exposing students to a semantically rich microworld will spontaneously generate discovery and invention is a romantic fantasy, not characteristic of responsible learning constructivists. Without the aid of appropriate activities and guidance, most students do not benefit from working in a microworld environment. They are not able to set their own goals, work through or around their own difficulties, or escalate the level of their strategic thinking. Left to themselves, they flounder. They have not learned how to function in an open nonprescriptive environment—"that takes a little longer." Skilled teachers try to overcome these deficits by providing students with the guidance and support that can make microworld experiences extraordinarily productive.

It is reasonable to ask whether such guidance and support can be made an integral part of a microworld, and whether this can be done in a way that does not do violence to its fundamental character by turning it into a prescriptive system. This idea is beginning to be explored. It has given rise to the notion of "intelligent" microworld (Thompson, 1985). This kind of system differs fundamentally from an intelligent tutoring system in that its goals and operation are based on a learning, rather than a teaching, paradigm. Its primary goals are to aid informed exploration and reflective inquiry rather than content acquisition, and its methods are nondirective. In an intelligent microworld the tutor is invoked by the student, and it must respond to the student's program, not the other way around. This requires intelligence. It requires not only that the system have a great deal of knowledge but also that it is capable of learning. The problems associated with the development of systems that learn from their students are deep and difficult, but systems with some capabilities of this kind may be extant by 2020.

ISSUES RAISED BY THE INTRODUCTION OF TECHNOLOGY INTO EDUCATION

Our proposal is to reorient education to teach the disciplines through teaching the use of the rapidly emerging new tools of the disciplines. The curriculum will be centered on computers, in the many forms they present as powerful and empowering tools for learning and doing science, music, mathematics, writing, language study, and social studies. Computers are machines for the mind. They can be used to advance learning with uniquely valuable effect. Technology will come to have a deep synergetic relationship with education — and with work and life. That is its destiny, and ours.

The details of how this will evolve are not clear. The task of designing and developing the vital source materials for this program, school-level tools modeled on those used in the practice of real practitioners, is not addressed. The idea of bringing the apprentice-training model, augmented by new learning technology, into the schools as the framework for teaching the disciplines is hardly a well-developed and worked-out plan. Some of the issues surrounding the development of this kind of educational program are very clear, however, because they are the issues that have always been central to education.

Changes in the Purposes of Education

The fundamental purposes of education are to help young people find a vocation, take responsibility for their own intellectual development, and make a commitment to themselves and to society. These purposes do not need to be redirected in the near future as a result of the new technology. Rather, technology can greatly serve to further their realization. The problem has not been so much with educational purpose as with practice. Educational activities need to be redirected to give students classroom experiences that have a credible purpose in the world outside the school.

Engagement and Commitment

The experience of computer interaction can have an extraordinary power of engagement for young people, particularly when they are working on their own projects. This process of engagement can be enormously motivating and intellectually productive. A young person sometimes acquires enormous knowledge about his chosen area across a remarkably short time. He becomes an expert. He may surprise adults, perhaps even professionals in the area, with his impressive knowledge. For some time it may seem that nothing else is important to him. And then, perhaps as suddenly as the interest developed, it may wane and die—that is not an uncommon pattern. But, even then, something extraordinary has been gained.

The awakening of a passionate intellectual interest that compels a personal commitment is an invaluable experience. The knowledge that one can learn on one's own, that one can be committed to learning everything one needs to about something one cares about, is empowering. Commitments may change but the capacity for commitment will have been established, and *that* is what transfers. The experience of taking responsibility for one's own intellectual development is the sine qua non for further learning.

Training for a Vocation
Versus Vocational Training

During their early and middle school years, students will become familiar with the use of the computer tools modeled on those of the disciplines and, through that, get a real feeling for the content, methods, and character of many different discipline areas. The primary purpose of teaching the disciplines is to help students learn what they need to do to become what they learn they want to become. It is not to train everyone to become a biologist, psychologist, artist, linguist, sociologist, or any other kind of ist. It is not vocational training. It is training for a vocation, one that may be outside the discipline subjects introduced in the schools.

High schools might be organized to reflect different interests in broad areas of concentration like science or art or social studies or engineering. The existence of powerful computers and discipline-oriented tools will create heightened levels of intellectual activity in the schools and serve as a force for attracting teachers with strong discipline knowledge and skills.

Integration of Knowledge Across
Traditional Boundaries

We ought to let the educational agenda be influenced by the things students are interested in, not only by what we think they need to learn. In the context of appropriate computer activities, these two apparently disparate goals can converge and reinforce each other. The scope of topics accessible to programming is enormous. Projects dealing with subjects such as food, music, sports, movies, jokes, and "managanese and whatever you please" (Poe, 1835) can readily be integrated into courses of study in the discipline areas. Interdisciplinary issues arise very naturally and serve to emphasize the unitary nature of knowledge and the relatedness of things.

For example, in the introductory course on the structure and use of language, students are assigned projects such as generating their own gossip, quiz programs, love letters, and poetry. Generative grammars are modeled as Logo programs. This transforms linguistic analysis into a constructive activity and reveals the close and deep connections between mathematical and linguistic structures (Goldenberg & Fuerzeig, 1987). Logo courses relating music, visual art, and mathematics can be developed along similar lines. Courses integrating the presentation of science and mathematics can be further unified and greatly enhanced in a development centered on computer tools and projects.

Cyclotrons for Children?

We are not proposing to introduce networks of parallel supercomputers into the elementary classroom nor to turn prepubescent children into research astrophysicists. Rather, we are suggesting that computers powerful enough to do virtually anything that enterprising educators will want to do will be standard school equipment in 2020, together with appropriately designed software tools accessible to schoolchildren.

Students will be using computers that enable qualitative changes in the capabilities and kinds of educational applications possible relative to those feasible with current-generation personal computers. These machines will have the level of capability found in today's personal Lisp machines used for artificial intelligence research and applications. This could happen a lot sooner than 2020. Powerful processor chips with speed and memory capacity capable of supporting large and complex programs are already commercially available in systems costing only a few thousand dollars.

High bandwidth computer communications networks will become well established, not only throughout the workplace, but in libraries and schools. Electronic communication will support the creation and transmission of multimedia information—text, pictures, speech, music, animated displays, and computer programs. The use of such technology will be economically feasible for schools. High-fidelity speech synthesis and recognition devices operating in real time, and high-resolution computer graphics displays will enable clear communication. Instructional designers will employ a variety of representations using object-oriented graphics, sprites, spread sheets, and animated three-dimensional displays. This will enable conceptually complex material to be modeled in semantically transparent presentations that are inspectable, manipulable, and modifiable by users.

Visual Programming Environments

Acquiring a level of fluency in the use of a programming language sufficient to empower students to work on the development of interesting, cognitively rich programs is a nontrivial task. Even Logo, the most accessible language, poses some difficulties to beginning students, mainly because its program structures cannot be displayed and run graphically. Visual programming environments will be developed for Logo, and for other powerful languages of the future, to make their most difficult objects and processes more readily comprehensible by teachers and students (Goldenberg, 1986). Visual metaphors and iconic constructs designed to show the structure of complex programs more transparently than is possible with equivalent symbolic representations will help students see what parts are necessary to complete a structure and how the parts must communicate. This is fundamental to the development of the skills of cognitive design and constructive approaches to inquiry and problem solving.

Structure Versus Freedom

Achieving an appropriate balance between giving students the direction they need and permitting them the freedom to explore and to make their own instructional decisions is the fundamental problem of the teaching art; it must be confronted by designers and users of learning tools as it is by human teachers. Teaching should allow for and accommodate to individual differences among students and to the changing needs of any individual student during different phases of his or her own development.

This strongly suggests two requirements for the development of learning technology: flexible locus of control distributed among student, teacher, and computer, and instructional interactions that support directed, nondirective, and mixed-initiative modes of instruction with a variety of selection and sequencing options. Traditionally, instructional technologists have favored the development of systems supporting directed instruction under computer control. There is strong persistence of that emphasis in current, and often technically sophisticated, "intelligent tutoring systems." Early use of a programming language provides an environment that supports nondirective student-controlled experiences as well as all the other mode/locus combinations. This makes it possible to introduce the issues of thinking and learning through projects that enable students to actively construct their own knowledge, allowing us to build an early cognitive foundation for later training in the disciplines.

Individualization and Socialization

Computer capabilities for individualization of instruction will always be limited by the fundamental difficulty of understanding the student's state of knowledge, misconceptions, conceptual gaps, learning difficulties, and procedural bugs (Sleeman & Brown, 1982). Even if a program were capable of building a complete student model (the central problem of intelligent tutoring systems development), the very specific use of such knowledge to aid the student's learning is a hard educational problem in principle. Certainly, this problem does not have unique solutions across students or even for the same student at different times.

As instructional programs gain greater competence, they will be able to better diagnose student difficulties and instructional needs, and to adapt responsively in accordance with such diagnoses, at least (and perhaps, at most) in well-structured instructional situations with precisely delimited goals. It should be recognized, however, that instructional activities that give students facilities for constructing tasks and solutions to problems on their own (such as through the use of high-level programming facilities and special purpose domain-specific languages) are the only ones that are truly individual (sometimes called "individualized"). Their use will become more prevalent as the limitations of purely prescriptive systems become evident.

Traditionally, instructional technologists have focused on the use of computers to foster individualization of instruction. But that is only one dimension of the complex processes involved in learning. The possibility of exploiting technology to create environments that foster a high level of social interactions that enhance learning, though seldom discussed, is at least equal in importance to facilitating effective individualization, particularly within the classroom milieu. We have seen elementary mathematics courses involving student programming projects where there is an incredibly high level of interaction among the students. They discuss and compare their programs, for mathematics procedures and projects, in a way never seen in traditional mathematics classrooms. The atmosphere is more like a beehive than a math class. Technology for turning kids into active learners and collaborators — that is the kind of educational impact we are looking for.

Dehumanization

The view that the extensive use of technology in schools will have a dehumanizing effect by turning students into narrowly cerebral unsocial beings reflects a lack of understanding of technology, and probably of children as well. This view was recently voiced by a school principal to J.C.R. Licklider, who responded: "Then, sir, I suppose that you are opposed to books." More than 25 years earlier Licklider had expressed a prophetic vision of the powerful intellectual synergy possible through the interaction between people and computers that would one day prove to be a boon for learning (Licklider, 1960). Licklider's vision is coming closer to fruition.

INTO THE NOT-DISTANT FUTURE

As Arthur Clarke observed in "Profiles of the Future," scientists are not very good at predicting the technological future. Their projections as to what will happen, and when, tend to be conservative because they are too concerned about the problems that have to be solved to get from here to there, and the actual paths often turn out very differently because of the profound accelerating effects of new discoveries and inventions. In the case of computer technology things seem to be different. Because of the dramatic rate of development and application of computers, scientists might predict that the new learning technologies made possible by computers will be well established throughout education long before 2020.

I envisage, instead, a process of change that will require a time span of generations from the time of the creation of the first technology-based educational programs to the production of a critical mass of young people who are comfortable and competent with computers and with the richness and variety of learning experiences they make possible. These men and women will become, in turn, the creators and teachers of the next wave. This is not a short-term development but it should be underway by 2020.

On the other hand, many things could go wrong. Educational systems have an enormous resistance to change. Schools might absorb our most wonderful learning tools and continue on their seemingly preordained courses without any lasting effect. It would be wonderful if one could look into the future and find that something very different will happen this time.

AN HISTORIAN LOOKS BACKWARDS FROM 2020

First, some considerations about the last half of the 20th century, the early computer era, a period we now regard as the first primitive awakenings of the *intellectual* portents of technology. Until then, computers had been thought of as an evolutionary extension of earlier technologies—calculating engines were like steam engines for doing large calculations rapidly. The notion that these new machines were not merely powerful abacuses but a qualitatively different thing, *idea machines, machines for the mind,* was slow in coming. It took many years for the enormous implications of that realization to take root. The period from the 1940s to the 1990s was a lull before the technology storm that accelerated the profound transformations in learning, thinking, and working that has led to a third-millenium man. Strangely enough (until one thinks about it and realizes that this was always the case, from the invention of the printing press leading to the book and the intellectual revolution of universal reading and writing), it is technology that has driven these new intellectual developments and not the other way round.

By the year 2055 we will not have been released from the ancient Chinese curse "May you live in interesting times." The interesting times ahead will continue to confront people with grave problems. The challenge of educating an intelligent, informed, and responsible citizenry will be with us as always. We will have to train even greater numbers of intellectual workers.

REFERENCES

Abelson, H., & diSessa, A. (1981). *Turtle geometry*. Cambridge, MA: MIT Press.

Apple Computer, Inc. (1987). *Introducing HyperCard*. Descriptive brochure. Cupertino, CA.

Clements, D., & Battista, M.T. (1987). *A Logo-based elementary school geometry curriculum*. Unpublished draft, Kent State University, Kent, OH.

Clements, D., & Gullo, D.F. (1984). Effects of computer programming on young children's cognition. *Journal of Educational Psychology, 76,* 1051–1057.

Davis, R.B. (1984). *Learning mathematics: The cognitive science approach to mathematics education*. London, England: Croon-Helm.

Feurzeig, W. (1986). Algebra slaves and agents in a Logo-based mathematics curriculum. *Instructional Science, 14,* 229–254.

Feurzeig, W., & Lukas, G. (1972). A programmable robot for teaching. *Proceedings, International Congress of Cybernetics and Systems,* Oxford, England.

Feurzeig, W., Lukas, G., Grant, R., & Faflick, P. (1971). *Programming languages as a conceptual framework for teaching mathematics*. Bolt Beranek & Newman Report No. 2165, Cambridge, MA.

Feurzeig, W., & Ritter, F. (1987). Understanding reflective problem solving. In J. Psotka, L.D. Massey, & S.A. Mutter (Ed.), *Intelligent tutoring systems: Lessons learned*. Lawrence Erlbaum Associates.

Goldenberg, E.P. (1986). Iconic programming. In *Proceedings of the Logo 86 Conference*. Cambridge, MA.

Goldenberg, E.P., & Feurzeig, W. (1987). *Exploring language with Logo*. Cambridge, MA, MIT Press.

Groen, G.J. (1985). The epistemics of computer-based microworlds. *Proceedings of 2nd International Conference on Artificial Intelligence and Education,* University of Exeter, UK.

Horwitz, P. (1985). *Description of Thinkertools*. (Tech. Note). BBN Laboratories, Cambridge, MA.

Horwitz, P., & White, B.Y. (1986, April). *Thinkertools annual progress report*. BBN Laboratories, Cambridge, MA.

Lawler, B. (1984). Designing computer-based microworlds. In M. Yazdani (Ed.), *New horizons in educational computing,* Ellis Horwood Limited.

Licklider, J.C.R.L. (1960, March). Man–computer symbiosis. *IRE transactions on human factors in electronics.*

Melmed, A. (1986, September). The technology of American education: Problems and opportunity. *T.H.E. Journal.*

Miller, G.E., & Emihovich, C. (1985). *The effects of mediated program instruction on preschool children's self-monitoring.* Paper presented at the annual meeting of the American Educational Research Association, Chicago.

Ocko, S., & Reznick, M. (1986). Lego/Logo. In *Proceedings of the Logo 86 Conference.* Cambridge, MA.

Papert, S. (1972, June). A computer laboratory for elementary schools. *Computers and Automation, 21 (6).*

Pea, R.D., & Kurland, D.M. (1984). On the cognitive effects of learning computer programming. *New Ideas In Psychology, 2,* 137–168.

Poe, Edgar Allen. (1835, April). *Some passages in the life of a lion: Lionizing.*

Polya, G. (1962). *Mathematical discovery.* New York: Wiley.

Reggini, H. (1985). *Ideas y formas: Explorando el espacio tridimensional con Logo.* Ed. Galapago, Dist. EMECE.

Schoenfeld, A.H. (1985). *Mathematical problem solving.* Orlando, FL: Academic Press.

Sleeman, D.H., & Brown, J.S. (1982). *Intelligent tutoring systems.* New York: Academic Press.

Stevenson, H.J., Lee, S., & Stigler, J.W. (1986, February). Mathematical achievement of Chinese, Japanese, and American children. *Science.*

Thompson, P.W. (1985). Mathematical microworlds and ICAI. In *Proceedings, Conference on Moving Intelligent CAI Into the Real World.* Burroughs Canada Tech. Rep. PPD Mtl-85-3.

White, B.Y., & Frederiksen, J. (1985, September). A system for teaching qualitative understanding of electrical circuit behavior and troubleshooting. In *Proceedings of the Second International Conference on Artificial Intelligence and Education.* University of Exeter, UK.

White, B.Y., & Horwitz, P. (1982). Thinkertools: Enabling children to understand physical laws. BBN Laboratories Report 6470, to appear in *Cognition and Instruction.*

Whitney, H. (1985, December). Taking responsibility in school mathematics education. *Journal of Mathematical Behavior.*

Yankelovich, N., Haan, B.J., & Drucker, S.M. (1986). *Connections in context: The intermedia system.* Technical paper, Institute for Research in Information and Scholarship, Brown University, Providence, RI.

7 It's 2020: Do You Know What Your Children Are Learning In Programming Class?

ELLIOT SOLOWAY
Yale University

In this chapter, I argue that students need to learn how to build things, and thus they need to be explicitly taught synthesis skills. Programming, as I have redefined it, is an excellent vehicle for teaching and learning these skills. Moreover, these skills will be ever more important when the computer becomes all pervasive in our society; soon, we will be acting on the world through the computer. People will need to know how to take advantage of the unique aspects of software technology: the almost limitless ability to develop new functionality, to mold the software to the specific needs and wants of the individual. The ability to use synthesis skills will be the Rosetta Stone for this access.

INTRODUCTION: MOTIVATION AND GOALS

The excitement and interest in computer education waxes and wanes. A few years ago, the computer literacy movement was a major force in schools. Children were taught BASIC programming, about disk drives, and about the binary numbers inside the computer. Today, there appears to be less urgency in having children know about computers per se; the emphasis seems to be on teaching students to use a computer as just another tool. However, we also need to prepare students to deal with the world of tomorrow. In doing so, we need to ask the following questions: (1) What roles will computers play tomorrow—say, in 2020? (2) What will the style of interacting be with those computers? (3) How much will people need to know about computers to use them effectively? (4) What will we teach students about computers in 2020?

The goal of this chapter is to present my position on these four questions.

I put forward the following two-step argument. First, I suggest that students need to learn synthesis skills—doing skills, building skills—*today*. In so doing, I redefine the concept of "computer programming" to better reflect what actually goes on during programming—the learning and using of synthesis skills. Next, I look a bit into the future and identify the all-permeating role computers will surely play in both our everyday lives and in the workplace. To effectively make use of computers, I argue, it will be even more imperative that we can readily use synthesis skills; we will be constantly creating software agents that will be sent out to do our bidding. In the last section of the chapter, I speculate on how the teaching of synthesis skills via programming should be integrated into the curriculum, and I speculate on the design desiderata for computing environments that would support people in developing software agents. I close with a few comments about the political and social implications of the arguments put forward here.

PROGRAMMING INSTRUCTION IN TODAY'S CLASSROOM

Teaching Synthesis Skills via Programming

In my considered opinion, schools today by and large focus instruction on "analysis skills": how to read and comprehend some topic, how to critique an essay, etc. However, there are other skills that are needed to be an effective problem solver, namely, "synthesis skills." We need to be able to build things. One often hears "oh, that student seems to have all the pieces right but can't seem to put them together." My interpretation of this common observation is that, although students can analyze a situation into some collection of components, they nonetheless have significant difficulty in constructing solutions. This is not surprising, because schools place little emphasis on synthesis skills, and because synthesis is a difficult activity to carry out. What programming is really about—or at least, should be about—is teaching students synthesis skills. These skills enable them to craft artifacts that meet needs—needs that are tailored to what each individual might want.

Current instruction in programming by and large misses this key point. If one looks at textbooks that teach introductory programming, one immediately sees that (1) the chapters in the textbooks are organized around the constructs in the particular language being taught (e.g., first one learns about the assignment statement, then about conditionals, and then about looping—or some perturbation of this order), and (2) what is taught is the syntax and semantics of the language constructs: how to form grammatically correct statements in the language, and what each of the statements does. Although textbooks often try to teach problem solving, they do so in a very simplistic—and to all appearances—ineffective manner. For example, "stepwise refinement" is a so-called problem-solving method in which one takes a problem statement and successively refines it into a solution. Textbooks often give examples of this being done; students are given beautifully drawn tree diagrams that illustrate stepwise refinement. However, what the textbooks fail to discuss is how that stepwise refinement was developed—what are the underlying strategies for developing this wonderfully clean-looking diagram (see Anderson, Boyle, Farrell, & Reiser, 1984).

Why are the current textbooks on introductory programming so weak on teaching problem solving and synthesis? The reason does not lie in the maliciousness of authors nor in their desire to keep the skills they have apparently mastered secret. Rather, there is precious little known about synthesis skills, and less about teaching them. In the last few years, however, researchers in the cognitive sciences have been studying problem solving in general, and synthesis in particular, and there is a growing literature on which to draw. In the next section I highlight the content of a "programming as teaching synthesis skills" course.

Synthesis Skills: Some Examples

In my categorization scheme, there are three classes of skills that facilitate effective artifact synthesis: (1) design skills, (2) alternative generation and evaluation skills, and (3) debugging skills (Soloway, Spohrer, & Littman, 1987). In what follows, I highlight each class in turn.

Design Skills

The process of developing a program—a software artifact—can be broken down into the following five phases.

Phase 1: Understand the Problem. During this first phase the objective is to develop an intuitive sense of what the goals of the situation are. Two key heuristics useful in this regard are: play with the problem, and simplify the problem. Play is a good thing; it enables someone to explore the space in which the problem is being framed. For example, one needs to try out concrete scenarios; if the problem calls for generating schedules, then generate a few example schedules. I explicitly remember being told in seventh-grade algebra class, "Oh, just set up the equations, that's all that's really important." On the contrary; what is important is first developing an understanding of the problem—and one very effective strategy is to play with lots of specific cases. The key here is to pick "representative" cases, e.g., the nominal case and some extreme, boundary cases. People have a tendency to forget boundary cases—the result often being that the whole design is wrong. It is usually straightforward to generate a solution when everything is fine, e.g., when the input data are correct, or when the number of alternatives is small. However, we must always be aware that nothing works as planned. We must take into consideration atypical cases.

Real problems tend to be too complicated to be solved as they are stated. There are usually lots of constraints that, though important, are secondary. For example, in building a sandbox, the color of the wood, though important, is a secondary issue. We can safely defer the issue of paint color for a bit. In general, good problem solvers try to simplify a problem before jumping into it, to solve the simplified version and then add the complications. Of course, the key is to realize which are secondary, and hence deferable constraints, and which are primary. The general principle for simplification is one of "making sure that interactions are kept to a minimum." For example, in building a sandbox, we cannot defer the constraint that it be square, but we can defer the paint color constraint. Why? The size of the sandbox is independent of the color constraint, whereas the size of the sandbox is very much dependent on the shape constraint. How did I know that? Without some experience in building wooden structures, it might be hard to know a priori what the interactions/ independencies are. However, what is important is that students learn to think about these concepts and simplify complex problems to where they are manageable.

Phase 2: Decompose a Problem into Goals, Plans, and Objects. The classic prescription for problem solving is to "break a problem down into subproblems." This admonition does not go far enough: It does not tell one how to go about the breaking-down process. I add the following suggestion: "Break a problem down into subproblems based on problems that you have already solved." We need to view a new problem as having some relationship to problems that we have already solved. Thus old, solved problems serve as partial solutions, as partial frameworks, for thinking about the new problem. We all know how difficult it is to solve a problem for which we have no or little relevant experience. Without appropriate old cases to draw on, we must resort to first principles, at best a long and tortuous route.

Analogy is paramount here: We need to search our experience for "related" problems. We have no robust theories for how humans carry out this process. Good problem solvers, e.g., good medical diagnosticians, seem to be able to search their mental data bases that often contain hundreds of thousands of cases incredibly fast, sometimes in milliseconds. Again, whereas the heuristics I can provide to help students in this process are at a rudimentary level (e.g., look for problems that have similar "surface features," look for problems that have similar "deep structure features"), the key point is that they should be doing this search process—and developing their own, special-purpose search strategies.

To lend concreteness to this phase, three entities are identified that should be focused on: goals, plans, and objects (Soloway, 1986). *Goals* are the objectives that need to be satisfied in the problem: Output the average of some numbers, find the minimal route from x to y, diagnose the fault in the car, etc. Moreover, often there are goals that need to be achieved not mentioned in the problem. To develop an effective design, however, the problem solver must make those implicit goals explicit. For example, in computing the average of a set of numbers, one must remember to sum the numbers and keep track of the number of numbers—two implicit goals.

Software artifacts are made up of actions taken on objects, which in turn generate the desired object (or state). *Plans* are canned action sequences— procedures—for achieving goals. For example, taxi drivers develop all kinds of strategies for driving in busy, complex cities such as Boston and New York. They know specific routes to take to avoid certain problem areas, or to minimize travel time. Thus, the solution to a new problem can be viewed as some composition of these special-purpose routines.

Objects are the "data structures" that are used by the plans. In the taxi example, the data are the streets and buildings through which the driver must maneuver. In architecture, the objects are the various materials used in the construction of buildings. Sometimes objects are "simple," e.g., a street or a brick. Sometimes objects are "complex," e.g., an area or a facade. Key in the problem-solving process is the choice of an appropriate set of simple/complex objects. Lego blocks would be a poor choice of objects for building a high-rise.

During this aspect of the design process, the goal is merely to lay out the space of alternatives—see what is important and what is not. Of course, one is always looking ahead and thinking about how the pieces—the plans and the objects—will fit together. The "formal" composition phase comes next. Here the goal is simply to see who the "players" are—what the relevant goals, plans, objects and alternatives are. (I explicitly deal with alternative generation and evaluation in the next section.)

Phase 3: Compose the Plans to Satisfy the Goals. Once the goals, plans, and objects have been identified, the process of putting the pieces together can begin. There are four ways that plans can be linked together: (1) Abutted: two plans are simply joined together, one next to each other; (2) nested: one plan is placed inside another; (3) merged: two plans are interwoven; (4) tailored: a plan may need some customizing for the particular application. Heuristics have been identified for knowing when to use which composition method, e.g., avoid merging because the causal interactions are very hard to get correct.

Phase 4: Implement the Plans in the Particular Programming Language at Hand. Goals, plans, and objects, and the composition methods just identified are independent of a particular programming language. Thus, during this phase, the software artifact builder must instantiate the plans and objects in some language, e.g., Pascal, BASIC, or Logo.

Phase 5: Reflect on What Just Happened. In developing a program, many events take place. The key to developing expertise is the skill of stepping back and summarizing one's experiences. Of course, so much may have happened that it is hard to sort the wheat from the chaff. Here again are important heuristics that can serve as concrete guidelines. For example, "remember the bugs you made, and remember how you fixed them." Good students of programming do this naturally; it enables them to catch themselves when they are about to make a similar mistake.

The preceding five phases do not necessarily happen in sequential order: For example, reflection can take place at any time, or informal decomposition may occur during problem understanding. There is no rigid ordering to these five activities.

These five activities are repeated in a cycle until a solution is developed. Not all the activities may be executed on each pass through the cycle, e.g., one may not carry out the implementation activity until much later in the design. Conversely, we all have had the experience that only after some work on a problem do we really understand it. In my terminology, the understanding activity is constantly being attempted.

The design process is not the clean, straightforward one portrayed in introductory textbooks. The orderly progression from problem to solution is largely a fiction, seen only when someone has solved the same problem many times. The design process, as I have portrayed it, is characterized more by exploration than by systematic progression. Thus, it does not follow that the design process is too mysterious, too dependent on "art" and intuition to teach. We simply need to appreciate the range of skills that need to be employed in the design process—and patiently unpack and identify them, and then develop methods for teaching them.

Alternative Generation and Evaluation Skills

What textbook solves the same problem multiple ways and then provides arguments for which methods would be better under which conditions? This lack in textbooks—and often in teaching—is most unfortunate: In any realistic situation, designers and engineers will always generate alternative designs and then provide the pros and cons for each design. Why should the first answer that one develops be the best one? Thus, I advocate explicitly teaching students to generate and evaluate alternatives and providing them with heuristics that can facilitate these processes. For example, one basic heuristic for generating alternatives in programming is to find a different representation (and hence data structure) for the objects in the problem. One can represent a solid diamond by either drawing the outline first and then shading it in, or by drawing successive lines at an angle. Each representation may then need different actions, different plans. Similarly, in evaluating alternative designs, one must know whether the resultant program will be substantially changed over time. If so, then one might want to avoid using the merging composition method, because it is very hard to unpack—and hence to modify. In sum, key in the process of synthesizing artifacts is the recognition that one must seek out and assess alternative solutions: Stopping at the first one is not necessarily a good design strategy.

Debugging Skills

People make mistakes. People iterate until they develop a complete solution. These basic facts of life must be faced squarely in synthesizing programs. Very few programmers can get a large program "right the first time." Thus, we need to explicitly teach students debugging skills—skills that will enable them to identify and fix bugs in their designs. For example, earlier I mentioned boundary cases as being particularly troublesome. In my classes, students are encouraged to develop test cases for their design that explore the boundary conditions. I also mentioned that merging composition is troublesome (Spohrer & Soloway, 1986). I encourage students to watch for specific types of bugs ("subgoal dropout") when they are doing a merging composition. Complex problems are seldom solved all in one go: It is as important to learn how to repair an artifact as it is to build it.

The Importance of Learning Synthesis Skills—Today

The term *programming* is neither accurate nor illuminating: "programming" comes from "program," which is the final product of the synthesis process. Programming does not convey the type of knowledge and skills that need to go into the process of developing that product, that artifact. To correct this situation one might coin another term, e.g., *synthesizing*, but that may just add to the confusion. For the rest of this chapter I stay with the term *programming*, by which I do not mean "teach kids BASIC," but rather the process of synthesizing software artifacts.

Programming a computer provides an excellent vehicle for teaching synthesis skills—but certainly this is not the only vehicle. By definition, in programming one must construct a software artifact that, when executed, will exhibit some behavior. The target language (e.g., BASIC, Logo) is well defined, i.e., it contains a small number of legal operators or vocabulary items. In addition, the notion of execution is well defined, i.e., the semantic interpretation for the operators/vocabulary items is unambiguous and specifiable. My work is directed at making the notions of goals, plans, and objects similarly well defined. I conjecture that it would be more difficult to teach synthesis skills in an English composition course. Although students must develop an essay on some topic, the target language for that expression—English—differs substantially from artificial languages such as BASIC and Logo. English has an almost infinite vocabulary from which to draw, and moreover, the semantics of those items does not directly lead to the semantics of their composition. In addition, the notions of goal and plan are potentially more diffuse in an English composition environment. In programming, there is usually some concrete goal that needs to be achieved. By contrast, the goals that need to be achieved in writing an English theme are typically more diffuse, more nebulous. Nonetheless, it would be intriguing to see what improvements might arise if synthesis skills were to be taught explicitly in an English composition class.

A more natural place to provide instruction in synthesis skills would be in math class, where students need to construct proofs and equations to satisfy specific goals. Alas, there is typically little explicit instruction in how to generate, say, geometric proofs; instead, students are shown numerous examples of proofs being generated, with the hope that they will learn the underlying implicit strategies by induction. As is well known, this strategy has been a failure.

People need to build things all the time: from financial plans, to luncheon plans, to actual hard artifacts such as sandboxes and casseroles. Currently, schools do not teach these skills explicitly. I suggest that programming, as it has been defined here, would be an excellent vehicle for teaching these important skills. Moreover, we need not—nay, we better not—wait until 2020 to teach synthesis skills. Recent research has given us enough from which a sound curriculum can be developed, now.

COMPUTERS WILL BE THE MEDIUM

Currently, people by and large interact directly with the world around them. For example, if one wants to cash a check, one goes to a bank; if one wants to buy groceries, one goes to a grocery store. However, in the near term—and most assuredly by 2020—people will be interacting with the world *through* computers. Indeed, my bank example is already almost incorrect: A person can even now sit at home and transfer funds via a computer. Grocery ordering, travel scheduling, and financial planning will all be "computer-mediated" activities. In effect, people will create software agents that will act on their behalf. For example, suppose a person is looking for a particular piece of furniture. That person will create a "software scout" that will query various data bases in search of that piece of furniture; that scout will most likely interact with other software agents—"software sellers" who have the desired object.

If this "computer-mediated action" future is an accurate portrayal of the future role of computers, then the following question must be faced squarely: How much about computers will people need to know to use them productively? Let me first advance the argument that suggests we need to know little about computers to use them effectively. Then, I present a critique of that position.

The Negative Position

The argument against needing to know much about computers goes something like this:

- Computers are things that can be useful, in the same way that cars and airplanes and microwave ovens are useful things.
- We certainly do not have to know how a car works to drive it; why should we have to know "how a computer works" to use it?
- Moreover, plenty of software packages are available that give the functionality that is needed. Thus, one surely will not need to know how to program.

Clear educational consequencies follow from this argument: There is little reason to teach children much about computers, and less reason to teach them how to program.

The Positive Position

The counter argument is that the Negative Position is too simplistic. It does not appreciate how special computer technology is, nor the style of interaction that is necessary to take full advantage of the possibilities of computer-mediated actions. Each of these points is addressed in turn.

The Uniqueness of Computer-Based Technological Artifacts

There are several properties that artifacts resulting from standard technologies (things made from wood, metal, and plastic) possess: they are usually built to carry out one function (or a very limited range of functions), and they are not very customizable by a particular user. For example, a car is used to transport, a phone to communicate. Customizing a car is not a job for just any individual: It is a labor-intensive activity that requires considerable skill. Moreover, these technologies are distinct and not integrated: One can make a call from a car, but one uses two distinct artifacts (the phone and the car) that happen to be attached.

In contrast, computer technology permits the production of software artifacts with the following properties:

1. Software artifacts are inherently multipurpose. For example, spreadsheets were developed with accounting-type applications in mind. However, the same spreadsheet system can be used for data analysis or for ecological simulations! The number of uses of a good piece of software are almost limitless;

2. software artifacts are inherently malleable. For example, frequent users of word processors, operating systems, and programming environments are quite fond of tailoring a system to their particular tastes and needs. Good software has "natural" defaults that facilitate straightforward use, but such software also provides almost limitless possibilities for customization;

3. software artifacts cry out to be integrated. Even a quick glance through the software advertisements these days shows the growing trend towards integration of software functionality. A data-base package is integrated conveniently with a spreadsheet system, which in turn is smoothly integrated with a word processor—and all that allows the creation and use of graphic materials as well. And using all this functionality is simpler than programming most VCRs. For home use, currently there is a program that does check balancing, and another that does investment planning. However, in the not-too-distant future, all of one's finances will be mediated by the computer: paying bills, making investments, and preparing tax reports. Moreover, from the very same "computer" one will be able to make airline reservations and funeral arrangements (and debit the appropriate bank accounts), and order a picnic tray or an automobile.

The Positive Position argues that the model of technology employed in the Negative Position does not recognize the uniqueness of computer technology; that is, we should not think that software is of the same "kind" as noncomputer-based products. The models we have of the latter kinds of entities do not neatly transfer over to software. Moreover, as I argue next, this new kind of artifact facilitates a new level of usefulness. Put another way, the aphorism "the past is a good predictor of the future" is neither appropriate nor useful for thinking about software: Our models of current technology do not give us good insight into this new class of artifacts.

The New Utility of Software Artifacts

The reason we do not have to know much about how cars, phones, or planes function is because we cannot do much with them: We do with them what the original designer intended. With multifunction, malleable, integratable software, however, we are no longer limited by the designer's preconceived notions of how something should be used. What the computer technology makes possible are artifacts over which an individual has much greater control. Put yet another way, computer technology provides almost limitless functionality to an individual.

How then does one use the available functionality? The simple answer would be: the designers of the software package will provide all the "commands" that a user will need. All the user need do is master the given instruction set. However, this misses the whole point. Such an answer would imply that software artifacts are just like other technological artifacts. But, how can a software designer today identify how people will use that software tomorrow? How can we expect a designer to know all the commands that a diverse group of users will want? Can a company guess today how its computer-based product will interact with other computer-based products and be used by potentially millions of people tomorrow? Clearly they can't: Software designers and companies are not so prescient that they will be able to perceive the range of uses for a good piece of software.

Thus, the increase in control/functionality is gained at a cost—perhaps too high a cost. We need to understand "computers" to a much greater degree than we do cars, to use them most effectively. Does one have to understand how the bits and bytes work inside a computer? Surely not: This kind of understanding is far removed from what the user typically wants to do. On the other hand, does one have to know how to program in BASIC or LOGO? Again, surely not: That would make the functionality unavailable!

To tap into the rich functionality that is becoming available via software technology, people will need to know how to synthesize software agents that will go ahead and help them realize their needs and intentions. Yes, people often will be able to get away with simply using the built-in functionality when they do routine, common activities. However, when people want something different, when they want to explore a new area, they will need to know how to compose and sequence the basic "commands" (spoken instructions, foot taps, iconic images, etc.) given by the software designer. In effect, the user will create new functionality "on the fly." Although most users will not create a 10,000 command sequence program, they will need to possess the types of skills identified earlier in the chapter.

Synthesizing software artifacts, albeit on a limited basis, will not just be the province of the white-collar professional. Recall my argument that we will soon be acting on the world through computers. Also recall my earlier example of creating a software buying agent that would go out scouting for a particular piece of furniture. Given the diversity of people's needs and interests, it seems implausible that one could create a prespecified set of commands that would satisfy everyone. Give someone 10 commands in a text editor, and they immediately want an 11th, or a different set of 10. People will need to be able to create for themselves "custom-tailored agents."

Software designers will create "application-specific, programming languages," programming languages with commands designed expressly for the task at hand. For example, there will be programming languages that enable a person to explore financial investment strategies and access on-line data bases of stock information. There will be programming languages designed expressly for finding, haggling for, and eventually buying various types of goods. In the technical jargon, these will be "very high-level programming languages." They will be closer to the language in which someone wants to solve a problem than to the language that instructs the computer to actually carry out the computation.

The notion of a "general-purpose programming language" will be, for everyday users, a thing of the past. There is, however, a price to pay for this specialization: A person will need to switch between languages to do different functions. It is thus imperative that we teach and learn synthesis skills that are independent of a particular programming language. We cannot be in the position of a car mechanic, say, who can only fix Pontiac engines built before the introduction of pollution control. We need to understand the generalities underlying synthesis skills, much as a good mechanic who understands the general principles underlying engines can work on almost any car engine.

There is still another cost to a user who wants to take advantage of the unprecedented functionality inherent in software: to cope with the inevitable "side effects/interactions"—both desirable and undesirable—that will occur in complex systems, a user will need to understand, at least at a general level, how a complex system works. For example, in the home of the near future where all the electrical appliances are controlled via the computer, one should be able to set the alarm on one's bedroom clock simply. However, one might also want to turn off the phone-answering machine 15 minutes after the alarm rings, unless one is in the bathroom taking a shower, and then the house should sense the shower being on and keep the answering machine on for a little longer. However, if it is an emergency phone call, the bathroom lights should flicker to alert you. Although these kinds of scenarios can get a bit silly, the point is that making use of the available functionality requires that the user not blindly fill in some parameter settings. One must appreciate the implications of choosing some set of options.

Using synthesis skills in concert with applications-oriented, programming languages will not be limited to everyday activities. The computer will increasingly come to mediate the workplace and lives of professionals in all disciplines. Whereas accountants may be pleased today with spreadsheet languages and assorted accounting systems, physicians, pharmacists, plumbers, and carpenters will soon be doing "programming" (in the sense of synthesizing software agents, creating new functionality on the fly with a particular software system). Computer-aided design, important as it is now though limited to expressly "design disciplines" such as circuit design and building design, will be an integral part of the professionals' tool kit. In fact, the "tool" metaphor may be too weak: Computer-based software systems will be prostheses, necessary components for a well-functioning system.

We cannot use our traditional model for interacting with technology and apply it to computer technology. If we do, we stand to lose that which makes computer technology so unique and powerful: the ability to be molded to the needs of the individual by the individual, and the ability to communicate and interact with a myriad of other products.

SUPPORTING THE LEARNING
AND USE OF SYNTHESIS SKILLS

I have argued that synthesis skills will be needed to make effective use of the functionality available via computer technology. In this section, I discuss two important aspects for facilitating people's use of that functionality: how they should be taught synthesis skills, and what software environments are needed to support people's development of software artifacts.

Should There Be A "Synthesis Skills 101"?

Earlier I said that programming was an especially effective medium in which to teach synthesis skills. However, it does not follow that we need to have a special, designated programming course in which students are taught synthesis skills. In fact, I suggest that programming be taught in the context of particular subject matter. For example, in a social studies course, students will use the computer to create simulations of different societies and access enormous data bases to follow research projects. There will be special purpose programming languages—"applications-oriented, domain-specific programming languages"—that are expressly designed for these tasks. Several units on programming using those languages and explicitly teaching synthesis skills would be appropriate here. Students are motivated to learn the material, because they need to use it in class. Moreover, the examples in the programming section would be relevant to the topics at hand—again, an intrinsically motivating factor.

Currently, programming is taught as a separate course at the secondary and postsecondary levels and is not integrated in any substantive way into the rest of the curriculum. Examples used in programming class are by and large unmotivating, uninteresting, and often downright silly. Calculating the average of a set of numbers is not a particularly interesting problem; students feel they can do this calculation by hand (rightfully so) and do not see any special advantage to learning to program and use the computer. Similarly, writing a program to output the Fibonacci numbers, teaches several important programming concepts, but the point of the activity is lost on the students because they do not know what the Fibonacci series is meant to represent.

The suggestion that programming and synthesis skills be taught in context might seem to contradict the earlier argument that there are domain-independent synthesis skills; after all, shouldn't there be a course that focuses on these application-independent skills? Not really. Experience precedes essence. Students first need to gain experience with the concrete situations in which they learn programming and synthesis skills; generalizations are developed on the basis of concrete experiences. Students who learn programming in the context of a subject matter *will* run across the same concepts repeatedly. Far from being a disadvantage, such reinforcement and systematic extension help facilitate transfer.

Another important reason for teaching programming in context is that students see concretely the diversity of applications for which programming can be useful. So long as programming is relegated to a specific course in a specific room at a specific time of day, students will not see the power of computing. We need to help light the fire of their imaginations by demonstrating the utility of computing across all disciplines.

Facilitating the Development of Software Artifacts

Given that people will need to create software artifacts, how can we support them? What tools will people need? Our strategy for dealing with this problem is to look first at how people solve problems. On the basis of an analysis of their strategies, needs, and wants, we will be in a better position to design a software artifact development facility.

We need to be careful here: It may well be that people's current problem-solving strategies have been constrained by "pencil-and-paper" technology; that is, what we may be observing is not some intrinsic problem-solving process, but rather one that has evolved to cope with the limitations of the current crop of problem-solving tools. The new computing technology may in fact result in changes in problem-solving strategy. For example, up to now it may have been important to know a fact (or a set of facts), because the cost of finding something out by traditional means—e.g., going to the library, finding the right reference manual, searching through the reference manual—was very high. In contrast, technology now is permitting the storage of enormous amounts of information, *on line*. Thus, access to information costs next to nothing. To take advantage of this technological development, however, we may want to teach students strategies for finding facts—and not the facts themselves.

Much can be said of people's problem-solving strategies (keeping in mind the previous caveat), but two major strategies that people employ need to be taken into account:

1. *Iterative solution development:* People usually solve a problem by successive approximation. They "plan-a-little, do-a-little," and on the basis of output/feedback from the do-a-little phase, repeat the entire cycle. If one is an expert in a field, and one has solved the same (or very similar) problem before, this plan-a-little, do-a-little process may be substantially short circuited, and the solution found "in one go." The plan-a-little, do-a-little, repeat strategy is consistent with our five-activity model of software development described earlier. In effect, each of the five ac-

tivities is carried out during each iteration; the next iteration in the design process takes into account the results of the current iteration.

2. *Reuse of previous solutions:* Expertise is built out of experience. Experts in an area can routinely call forth examples and cases of problems and solutions. Naturally, experts make use of such a "data base" in solving new problems. They retrieve relevant cases, pick pieces, and weave together a solution tailored to the unique features of the current problem. (This weaving and crafting employs the plan-a-little, do-a-little strategy.)

In contrast to the two preceding strategies, an important problem-solving strategy exists that is not employed all that often. Namely, people typically do not generate alternatives and evaluate alternative solutions but take the first solution that comes to mind. In effect, we tacitly trade off cost of execution with cost of development. So what that the first solution we develop takes a long time to work; we came to it quickly. However, as the complexity of the tasks increases, we need to take more care in developing solutions; some answers are better than others. Even now we run in a time-crunched society. There is never enough time to do everything we want. A little more planning up front might result in an *overall* more effective and satisfying solution.

The programming environment that I envision, then, must support the three problem-solving strategies aforementioned. It must facilitate: (1) the "plan-a-little, do-a-little, repeat" strategy; (2) the retrieval and reuse of relevant examples and cases; (3) the generation and evaluation of alternative solutions. Add to this list of desiderata a critically important constraint: that the system be usable! Although we cannot expect to learn to use a tool effectively without some investment of effort, the effort must be proportional to the gain. Programming the alarm clock in our "electronic house" had better be really simple to do, and easy to remember how to do.

Are there current programming environments that can achieve the preceding desiderata? No. Current programming environments by and large come with a text editor, an interpreter (or, more often a compiler), and some kind of debugging tool. This type of environment may well be suited to the hacker, but it is woefully inadequate for just about anyone else. One must remember that a program that is run for its effects as a final solution is very far down the road in "problem-solving time"; that is, the majority of activity involved in developing a software artifact precedes the encoding of the plan into the final program. Current programming environments, by and large, support this last stage of the problem-solving process.

What would a programming environment need to do to support the desiderata identified earlier?

1. *Support plan-a-little, do-a-little, repeat:* The key to facilitating this strategy would be the development of explicit "intermediate-level pro-

gramming languages" and their explicit computational support. Now problems are usually expressed in English, whereas the solution is couched in some formal programming language. But, we need to develop languages for all the levels in the plan-a-little, do-a-little cycle. There is nothing mysterious about these intermediate-level languages. They are just the standard operations in the domain of application; they are simply the representations that experts have developed for describing their experiences. Support for these languages means that people will be able to run their designs-in-progress; they will be able to execute partial designs, often partially incorrect designs. Feedback from these simulations is what, in large measure, helps to guide the design process. Experts do such simulations now, in their heads. Technology may well help nonexperts to perform at a near-expert level.

2. *Support reuse:* Experts have built up a repertoire of examples and cases; they have developed encoding schemes for those examples and cases, and they have developed strategies for indexing into and retrieving relevant ones. We need to be explicit about providing such support in the programming environment. There must be a library of cases, multiply indexed, which can be called on. We must be able to compose cases together to give a hybrid, new case. Again, technology may provide nonexperts with the tools to perform at near-expert levels.

3. *Support alternative generation and evaluation:* Substitution of one representation for another plays a key role in the generation of alternatives. For example, rather than using a set of individual rules to describe a decision situation, an integrated table of conditions and outcomes may well provide a better solution. We need to develop computer support for the identification of alternative representations and their substitution into the current design-in-progress. Similarly, simulation plays a key role in the evaluation of alternatives. Here I mean simulation in a very broad sense: Simulation can mean running the current alternatives and seeing which one is faster. However, I also mean simulating changes to the system over time, and seeing which system accommodates change easier.

4. *Support usability:* The usual engineering rule suggests that 80% of the system will be used for 20% of the tasks. In doing simple tasks, the system had better not get in the way of the user. The system needs to be learnable and memorable: When we want to do the hard task, we had better be able to relearn how to carry it out easily.

To realize the preceding mechanisms and objectives will require considerable research. We have precious few guidelines for creating systems with the capabilities just described (diSessa 1985; diSessa & Abelson, 1986). Note that the research needed to bring about these systems will not require some new research effort. Work on relevant topics is going on now. What I have attempted to do is provide a vision of how the pieces will need to fit together.

CONCLUDING REMARKS

The heart of the argument in this chapter is that students need to learn how to build things, and that they need to be explicitly taught synthesis skills. Programming, as I have redefined it, is an excellent vehicle for teaching and learning these skills. Moreover, these skills will be ever more important when the computer becomes all pervasive in our society: Soon, we will be acting on the world through the computer. People will need to know how to take advantage of the unique aspects of software technology: the almost limitless ability to develop new functionality and to mold the software to the specific needs and wants of the individual. Synthesis skills will be the Rosetta Stone that provides access to computer technology.

A serious political and social issue underlies the argument made in this chapter. The question is what is basic to human nature? Do people want others tell them what they can do? Or, do they want to create for themselves? When a company provides a software package with all the functionality circumscribed, then this subtlety supports the former view. Our argument clearly supports the view that people want to have control in their own hands and make of the software what they will. Moreover, we need only to look back at the computer industry itself for support of people's desire to constantly develop new functionality. About 10 years ago, the computer industry was selling "word processors" and "business computers" as two separate entities—never mind that the word processor was a full-blown, general-purpose computer. However, once people got their hands on word processors, they wanted more functionality; they asked if their word processors could run that accounting software. The computer industry dropped the artificial separation of the two functions and now advertises a computer that "can do it all." We need to be careful lest we even inadvertently build software that does not give human nature its due.

What I have proposed here is a far cry from what is now going on in the schools, though it is *not* a far cry from what is going on in the home and in the marketplace. There is an ever-widening gap between what is being taught in schools and what people do in real life (Pea & Soloway, 1987). The minimal role played by computers in schools today is one symptom of this gap. We need a major rethinking of what should go on in school today and in 2020. Although there are many problems with the arguments put forward in this chapter, my intent was mainly to rekindle our imaginations for what is possible. For too long we have had blinders on in education and have not set our expectations high enough. Computer technology can serve as an example of the limitless possibilities that are out there—if only we had the skills to join in.

ACKNOWLEDGMENTS

I would like to thank Ray Nickerson, and his Jobesque patience, for giving me the opportunity to air what I hope are intriguing speculations. I would also like to thank members of my research group for their comments and conversations: David Littman, Jeannine Pinto, Jim Spohrer, Lucian Hughes, and Robin Lampert.

REFERENCES

Anderson, J., Boyle, C., Farrell, R., & Reiser, B. (1984). Cognitive principles in the design of computer tutors. *Proceedings of the Sixth Annual Conference of the Cognitive Science Society*, Boulder, CO.

diSessa, A., & Abelson, H. (1986, September). Boxer: A reconstructible computational medium. *Communications of the CACM, 29*, (9), 859–869.

diSessa, A. (1985). A principled design for an integrated computational environment. *Human-Computer Interaction, 1*, (1), 1–47.

Pea, R., & Soloway, E. (1987). *Education science and information processing technology*, in preparation.

Soloway, E. (1986, September). Learning to program = Learning to construct mechanisms and explanations. *Communications of the CACM, 29*, (9), 850–858.

Soloway, E., Spohrer, J., & Littman, D. (1987). E unum pluribus: Generating and evaluating design alternatives (Tech. Rep.). Department of Computer Science, Yale University, CT.

Spohrer, J., & Soloway, E. (1986, July). Novice mistakes: Are the folk wisdoms correct? *Communications of the CACM, 29*, (7), 624–632.

8 Intelligent Machines for Intelligent People: Cognitive Theory and the Future of Computer-Assisted Learning

LAUREN B. RESNICK
ANN JOHNSON
University of Pittsburgh

In this chapter we consider some current and potential efforts in computer-assisted learning in light of major themes from cognitive learning theory. Some of the themes reflect established principles of human cognition and learning: others are currently active domains of questioning and theoretical development. In each case we consider the implications of cognitive principles for the development of computer-based instruction, as well as the consequences of these developments for theories of learning. The review and evaluation of programs offered here reflect an admittedly optimistic perspective on the technological advances made in recent years. Computers are altering the landscape of our social and intellectual environment, and they are undoubtedly here to stay. The promise for new approaches to human learning that capitalize on the capacities of "intelligent machines" seems great. Nevertheless, we conclude by raising questions about the current dominant view of the role of computers in education and suggesting that a broader conception of the ways in which machines might enhance human intelligence is needed.

The chapter can best be characterized as a smorgasbord reflecting the state of the field, organized around themes that are shared by and central to all branches of cognitive science. Our instructional examples are drawn quite opportunistically. Some derive explicitly from cognitive theory; others are built on the intuitions of artful instructors in various teaching disciplines. In many cases the design and building of computer-based instructional systems provide the occasion for fundamental theoretical examination. Most of the programs discussed here are as much laboratories for research on learning and instruction as they are programs for immediate instructional use. Continued collaboration among cognitive science researchers and instruction developers is critical to ensure the future of computer-assisted learning.

DEVELOPING AUTOMATICITY

Humans are limited-capacity learners. Although we appear to have an infinite capacity to acquire and store information, only a very limited amount of that stored information can be activated at one time. The limits on active memory place severe constraints on learning that must be taken into account in instruction. Such memory limitations should make it impossible to do complicated tasks that require the integration of many pieces of knowledge. But such performances are not impossible. One important reason is that large parts of mental activity are automatic. Automatic processes make very few demands on conscious attention, leaving resources free to focus on other task components. The burden of limited working memory capacity is particularly great when a new skill is being learned. This is because very little has yet become automated. For this reason, especially great attentional resources are needed during learning—resources that will not be needed to perform once learning is complete. An important task for instruction is providing ways to remove some of the capacity demands of complex tasks during learning. One way to do this is to separate and work on automating individual components of a complex skill before incorporating them into the more complex performance.

The best developed examples of automaticity training relevant to education[1] are in the domain of reading. For strong readers word recognition is an automatic process that allows comprehension to proceed smoothly. It is a well-established empirical fact that weaker readers are slower at word recognition and must attend very closely to "decoding" words, thus sacrificing attention that should be used for comprehension purposes (Perfetti & Lesgold, 1979). This repeated finding led to the idea that promoting automaticity and speed of word recognition would ensure positive development of reading ability, and some investigators attempted to test this hypothesis by using various speeded word-recognition drills. Unfortunately, the data from early experiments (e.g., Fleisher & Jenkins, 1978) along these lines suggested that drilling words individually could increase the speed of word recognition but not improve general reading skill.

The work might have stopped there, but several converging lines of research made it seem promising to pursue the automaticity training idea in a different form. First, a longitudinal study (Lesgold, Resnick, & Hammond, 1985) found that children in the first grade with severe automaticity problems are very likely to have difficulties in comprehension 2 or 3 years later. Early comprehension difficulty, on the other hand, did not predict later automaticity difficulties.

---

[1]There are many examples of automaticity building in technical skills training.

This suggests that automaticity difficulties may cause difficulties in *learning* to comprehend written texts; that is, comprehension skill is not fully formed and waiting to be "released" by improved word-recognition automaticity; but improved word automaticity may allow attentional resources to be directed to learning to comprehend. If that is the case, the effects on comprehension performance would be visible only after some delay, during which time reading comprehension was practiced.

Second, recent linguistic and psychological analyses suggest that focusing on words as the key units of reading comprehension — and targets of automaticity training — may be inappropriate. This research proposes that the important units in automated word recognition are not words themselves but regularly occurring spelling patterns that are smaller than words and larger than individual letters. According to this view, practice to automate recognition of recurring multiletter units *within* words should make reading more efficient by reducing the number of units needed (multiletter units instead of single letters) to recognize an unfamiliar word. These units provide direct access — without composition into whole words — to at least some aspects of meaning. Thus, it is unnecessary and inefficient to revert to the letter level or to fully encode an entire word to grasp its meaning. This seems to mean that automaticity training should focus not necessarily on word recognition but on fast and unconscious access to key orthographic patterns of the language.

Two computer-based instructional systems explore the possibilities of an approach to automaticity training that takes into account this new view of the nature of key recognition units in reading. Both of these projects treat the development of computer instruction as an opportunity for research on learning and investigate the transfer of automated low-level recognition to higher levels of reading skill. The two target different populations, but both exploit the unique environment computers provide to make practice fun and gamelike, with time constraints that encourage fast, automatic responses.

Automaticity Training for Adult Disabled Readers

The first project considered here is a set of programs developed by John Frederiksen, Beth Warren, and Ann Rosebery (1985a,b) for extremely weak young adult readers. Three systems provide practice and training in three different components of reading skill.

The first training system, called SPEED, was designed to promote automatic recognition of key multiletter units in words, using a game that simulates a car race. Figure 8.1 shows an example of the screen displays for SPEED. The program sets up the game before it begins by specifying the unit to be identified (in this case, GEN), an initial "speed" at which target words will be presented, and a goal speed, as shown in the first panel. As the game begins, the computer screen resembles Panel 2. Soon a series of words flash on the screen, with some containing the target unit, GEN. At first, the presentation speed is slow (in this case, 60 words per minute). The player must indicate if the key unit is embedded in the word by pushing a "yes" or "no" button immediately after the word is presented. The speed of presentation gradually increases with each accurate response; speed is recorded and displayed by the arrow at the bottom of the screen. Errors, signaled by an error light (Panel 3), result in a reduction of speed. Whereas a correct response cancels an error (causing an error light to go out), just alternating right and wrong responses keeps the speed constant and disallows progress toward the goal speed; this forces the player to resist sacrificing accuracy for speed. If all five error lights are on and the player makes another mistake, the car "crashes" (Panel 5), and the game ends. After a crash, the player can start over, with time constraints reset to a level that makes winning more likely. The goal is to increase speed while avoiding errors so that the car never crashes. When the goal speed is met, the player wins (Panel 4).

Other games in the series work on larger "chunks" of the reading process, always requiring judgment against an increasing speed criterion. The RACER system is designed to develop automatic decoding of entire words, and SKI-JUMP aims toward automatizing higher level comprehension processes by requiring sentence-level judgments. All the games are designed to establish and maintain accuracy while strengthening automaticity. These games exploit the gamelike potential of computer-based lessons and successfully produce increases in automaticity.

Frederiksen and his colleagues have conducted a series of careful studies—although on very small samples of students—that examine the extent to which automaticity at one level of the reading process produces advantages at higher levels. Their studies show clear transfer from automaticity in recognizing orthographic patterns to speed in word recognition. Thus, these training studies offer some confirmation of the theory that recurrent patterns rather than individual letters are key components of word-recognition skill. In addition, the extent to which training in component skills leads to improvement in more general reading abilities was tested using an inference task; learners were tested on their ability to infer the appropriate conjunction to complete the concluding sentence in a three-sentence paragraph. Subjects who were trained only on SKI-JUMP showed improvements in accuracy on the paragraph task, but only those subjects who received training in all three skills showed improvement in efficiency. Apparently, efforts to improve efficiency must include sequential training in the three-component decoding tasks.

Automaticity Training for Young Readers

The second set of programs described here is similar in concept to the Frederiksen et al. programs, but it is designed for younger readers. It also

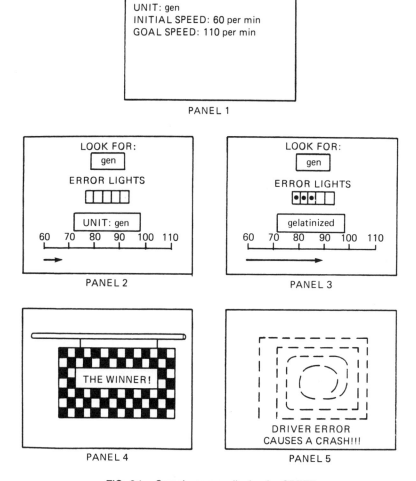

FIG. 8.1.   Sample screen display for SPEED.

operates on less sophisticated equipment and is already in commercial production and school use. Isabel Beck, Steven Roth, and Margaret McKeown have
built a series of microcomputer games in which children must engage in timed
and speeded play with single and multiletter elements of words (Beck, Roth,
& McKeown, 1985; Roth & Beck, 1984, 1985).

Figure 8.2 illustrates what a child might see in the game called CONSTRUCT
A WORD. In the left column are three word beginnings, and the other three
columns contain possible word endings. The child chooses an initial consonant or consonant group by moving a mouse around on the screen or using
a light pen. He then chooses all word endings that, combined with the chosen
word beginning, will make real words. When the child successfully constructs
a real word, it appears in the word box at the right of the screen. The challenge

is to fill the box before a timer counts down to zero. When the child beats the clock, the game ends, and the score (amount of time used and number of real words created) appears. The score serves as a baseline for the next game; that is, with each new game, the child must construct one additional word with only 10 seconds added to the clock. The goal is to construct words quickly, but the child must attend to meaning as well as to spelling patterns; not just any combination of initial consonant and ending will do. When a selection does not spell a real word, a digitalized voice box pronounces the nonword and informs the player that the word is not correct; an error message appears on the screen at the same time, providing both written and auditory feedback. During an error message (lasting 4 seconds), the clock continues to run; errors thus cause the child to lose time.

The goal of the next game, HINT AND HUNT, is to increase accuracy and efficiency in using vowels and vowel combinations to recognize words. The third game, SYLLASEARCH, introduces multisyllable words; it requires the child to identify meaningful syllable units and their boundaries, break down unfamiliar words, and synthesize syllables into potentially pronounceable words.

These carefully constructed games, useable in school settings, grow out of a body of research on automation of word recognition. But they also serve as laboratories for continuing research. They allow investigators to test theories of the development of word recognition and how it functions during comprehension. Roth and Beck (1985) have conducted transfer studies that demonstrate significant improvements in both speed and accuracy of word recognition for low-performing students. An even more positive finding indicates advances for all students in sentence-level comprehension, as measured on standardized reading tests. However, no improvements were found at the passage or paragraph level. This makes intuitive sense, because understanding whole paragraphs requires considerable mental work, and focusing on automating word recognition is probably not sufficient in itself to enable comprehension of entire passages. Still, finding transfer up to the level of sentence understanding must be considered a breakthrough. Compared with the earlier findings in which speeded practice on whole word recognition produced little transfer to comprehension, this is a very promising result.

Why should the Beck and Frederiksen programs look so promising when previous efforts to train automaticity have been unsuccessful? Part of the answer must lie in their game-like nature; they use computers in ways that capture attention through play. This probably draws on the learner's motivational resources in a way that older drill techniques could not. Furthermore, both sets of programs provide on-line adaptation—sensitivity and responsiveness to the child's competence level and reaction time. The pace of each game is monitored and modified in response to the child's performance; particular word lists can be changed; and speed of problem exposure is adapted to the child. None of this could be done without the computer; these programs represent use of the machine in a fundamental way. Although a teacher can approximate fast pac-

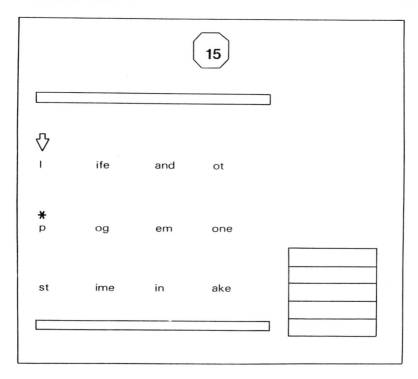

FIG. 8.2. Sample screen display for CONSTRUCT A WORD.

ing with flash cards and competitions, such activities lack the computer's moment-to-moment adaptation to learners' responses that keeps them in the zone of competence but challenges them to go further.

PRACTICE IN CONTEXT

A major difficulty with teaching focused on automating the components of a task—no matter how adaptive and gamelike the instruction—is that the components must eventually be combined into one complex task. Experience shows that this is often difficult. Components learned in isolation often prove brittle in the context of a full performance. In addition, it can be difficult to maintain motivation for practicing components. Games help but cannot totally overcome the failure of separate component practice to provide the learner with a sense of the utility and meaning of the components. An alternative way of adapting to learners' limited capacities is to provide practice in context through special forms of task sharing. In such shared practice the whole skill is performed jointly by two or more learners, or by the learner and a more expert performer. This joint performance ensures that the learner is only responsible for small pieces of the performance, those pieces that he or she is ready to do at a given moment. But these are practiced in the context of the entire performance. Practice on components is thus embedded in a more nearly natural context than in the separate components drill approach.

The idea of providing practice in context has been around intuitively for a long time. It can be seen, for instance, in the notion of on-the-job apprenticeship (cf. Greenfield, 1984; Lave, 1977; Rogoff & Gardner, 1984). The theory of "scaffolded learning" (Brown & Reeve, 1987; Wood, Bruner, & Ross, 1976) elaborates this idea from a psychological point of view. This theory, drawing heavily on aspects of Vygotsky's (1962, 1978) theory of learning, describes learning as a situation in which a skillful individual, usually an adult, provides the framework (scaffolding) within which the less skillful person, usually a child, can perform parts of a total task. In practice the task is accomplished partly by the adult, partly by the child. Together they complete the whole task, which means that whatever small bits the child is able to perform are accomplished in the context of getting the whole task done. The bits, then, come to make sense to the child through their embeddedness in a larger context; they contribute to a whole, even though the child cannot yet perform the whole. As more skill is acquired, the child assumes increasing amounts of the task until eventually able to perform alone.

Some examples from noncomputerized instructional situations convey the flavor of the scaffolding approach. First consider the process of a parent reading a book with a child who is on the borderline between being a nonreader and knowing how to read. Although the parent does a lot of the task, the child does some of it. A parent reading a picture book with a very young child usually points to pictures corresponding to words being read. Very soon, the child takes over this pointing function, as the parent continues the oral reading. Next the child may take over turning the page. Still later, when the child is on the verge of becoming a real reader, he or she may "read" (perhaps actually only respond from memory but, nevertheless, do so in appropriate context) certain familiar words or even sentences. An adept and well-attuned parent knows how much of the task to give up to the child and how much to keep. This permits the child to participate in reading a book (something quite different from simply listening to the story being read) many months and sometimes years before independent reading is possible.

A second example of scaffolding comes from school arithmetic teaching. Andrea Petitto (1985) reports a study that illustrates how the scaffolding approach can work in the classroom and how difficult it can be to adapt adequately to individuals in classroom settings. Petitto studied small group instruction on division. The teacher followed a scaffolding approach in which she provided the "commands" that identified which arithmetic steps to perform, while the children actually carried out the individual steps. Petitto provides examples of this kind of interaction, such as the following (p. 251):

Teacher: (writes 6 $\overline{)44}$ on the board) 44 divided by 6. What number times 6 is close to 44? Child: *6.* T: (writes 6) What's 6 times 6? C: *36.* T: (erasing the 6)

36. Can you get one that's any closer? C: *8.* T: What's 6 times 8? C: *64. . .48.* T: 48. Too big. Can you think of something. . . ? C: *6 times 7 is 42.*

The teacher's strategy here is to take the children through problems, giving prompts and corrections at each step of the procedure, and only gradually turning over the prompting to the children themselves. With children who had the requisite skills to perform component tasks successfully, the scaffolding approach worked smoothly and effectively. When all went well, the children carried out the individual steps without difficulty and, in the process, began to see the meaning for those steps in context. As a result they gradually took over the task of giving the sequence of "commands" themselves. They successfully learned the division algorithm and even modified it to make it more efficient. This process only worked, however, if the children could successfully perform the procedure's "pieces." With some of the weakest students, the scaffolding process broke down because the children were not able to perform the component steps reliably. The teacher then shifted attention to drilling individual components; the thread of the whole procedure was lost. Instruction that should have focused on the structure of the procedure turned instead into review of basic arithmetic facts. The context for making those facts meaningful was lost, and students were not able to learn the algorithm during the period studied.

Computer-Aided Reading

The shared-task approach to skill building is particularly adaptable to CAI. An example is the work of McConkie and Zola and their colleagues on computer-aided reading (Chrosniak and McConkie, 1985; McConkie & Zola, 1985; McConkie, Zola, & Winograd, in press). In their programs a passage drawn from children's stories, folk tales, expository writing about nature, and other relevant sources is presented on the screen. Children are invited to read the passage by themselves. If they encounter an unfamiliar word, they can touch it on the screen with a light pen. This makes the word appear more bold and visible, and the machine simultaneously reads the word aloud. What the student hears is human speech; McConkie and Zola have implemented a system that uses recorded voices to speak the desired word. A similar program developed by Warren and Rosebery (personal communication, August 1986) uses synthesized speech to pronounce needed words and phrases for weak or beginning readers.

These programs set up a situation similar to parent–child shared reading. The goal is to allow the child to focus primarily on understanding the story. Skipping over words interferes with the process of understanding, but so does taking the time to sound out words—which makes reading laborious and painful and unlikely to attract the child to reading for pleasure. The computer enables the child to ask for words with minimal interruptions to the flow of reading.

Attention can be shifted from word identification to comprehension. Children who might avoid reading because of frustration should feel more comfortable reading with this program; increased enjoyment is likely to result in longer periods of time spent reading.

Such systems raise questions involving the interaction of the technical capacity of computers with the nature of the relevant cognitive processes. For example, even though the McConkie program uses real human voices, normal intonation patterns at the sentence level cannot be duplicated. In the Warren and Rosebery program, individual words are pronounced in an odd, synthesized way. If we envision more such supportive systems that "speak" phrases or sentences for the beginning reader, the lack of intonational authenticity becomes increasingly problematic. At the sentence level, sacrifices in naturalness may interfere with comprehension—especially for immature or weak readers.

We do not know yet the limits of utility of systems such as McConkie and Zola's or Warren and Rosebery's. In these systems, it seems to be expected that the child will be able to do most of the reading but will get some help from the machine. If the situation were reversed—if the child could do very little and the machine did most of the reading—a very different system might be required, one in which (given today's technology) prerecorded speech was used with natural intonation. This would solve the naturalness problem but sharply limit the extent to which the child controlled the process. Tradeoffs of learner-control for naturalness will be the rule for some time in any computer-based instruction using oral speech. Considerable experimentation will be required to find the right combinations and compromises.

Task Sharing in Mathematics

Other variants of the shared-task idea can be proposed. In arithmetic, for example, the machine and the child might share a computational task, just as the children and the teacher did in Petitto's classroom. The machine could prompt execution of steps in a procedure and gradually delay these prompts, allowing children to select their own next computational steps and, thus, take more and more control over the full performance. Sharing could also run in the other direction, i.e., letting the child direct the machine from a menu of commands. The child could specify each step while the machine performed the computation. Thus enabled to focus on the *structure* of the procedure, the child would not be encumbered by not yet having memorized all the multiplication facts.

Another example of task sharing with a computer, Schwartz's (1983) "semantic calculator," is concerned not so much with teaching procedures as with teaching the meaning of some basic measurement concepts. In *SemCalc*, the machine performs requested calculations only when the kinds of quantities being calculated are specified. For example, it will not multiply 100 by 75 but will require a specification of 75 *miles per hour* and 100 *hours.* Furthermore, before returning a calculation result, the machine asks the user to verify that the answer will make sense as the user intended. For example, it will say, "The units of the answer are miles," and then offer either to restart the calculation or proceed. The important feature of the semantic calculator, in the current context of discussion, is that it shares the total task with the user. The machine not only takes over the calculation but also shares the comprehension monitoring task (more on this later) with the user by repeatedly asking the user to verify that the calculation to be performed will be sensible.

LEARNING AS RULE INDUCTION

There is substantial evidence that people continually induce rules that serve to make their environments predictable and explainable (Resnick, 1987; Siegler, 1978). Because of this tendency, many rules that people construct are errorful — because people engage in induction even in the absence of complete information. Instruction needs to take into account and build on this pervasive tendency to induce rules. It can do so in two ways: by diagnosing errorful rules and helping students correct them and by providing information and perhaps coaching to support correct rule induction.

Error Detection and Diagnosis

Rules that are systematic and sensible, but nevertheless inaccurate, have come to be known as *buggy algorithms* (Brown & Burton, 1978). This term results from analogy with computer routines that have "bugs" in them — small perturbations that produce consistently incorrect results. The tendency to create buggy algorithms is clearly demonstrated in arithmetic learning. Figure 8.3 shows some standard buggy subtraction algorithms. These are all very common errors made by children around 8 years of age who are learning to do subtraction. Children invent the buggy rules themselves; no one teaches them these errors. Buggy algorithms are clear evidence that people actively try to make sense of the world. But they are troublesome from an educational viewpoint because, of course, we want children to learn the right rules. A useful approach to this problem is to give learners tools for "debugging" themselves by monitoring their own performances and trying to correct them. This provides valuable learning-from-mistakes experience that both challenges and respects the child's capacity for sense making. We consider here some examples of how bug-detection programs might function in writing and arithmetic instruction.

Computer-aided Writing. One example of how the computer can support prompted and guided repairing of incorrect rules is a program developed by

1. **Smaller-From-Larger.** The student subtracts the smaller digit in a column from the larger digit regardless of which one is on top.

$$
\begin{array}{r} 3\,2\,6 \\ -\,1\,1\,7 \\ \hline 2\,1\,1 \end{array}
\qquad
\begin{array}{r} 5\,4\,2 \\ -\,3\,8\,9 \\ \hline 2\,4\,7 \end{array}
$$

2. **Borrow-From-Zero.** When borrowing from a column whose top digit is 0, the student writes 9 but does not continue borrowing from the column to the left of the 0.

$$
\begin{array}{r} 6\,\overset{9}{\cancel{0}},2 \\ -\,4\,3\,7 \\ \hline 2\,6\,5 \end{array}
\qquad
\begin{array}{r} 8\,\overset{9}{\cancel{0}},2 \\ -\,3\,9\,6 \\ \hline 5\,0\,6 \end{array}
$$

3. **Borrow-Across-Zero.** When the student needs to borrow from a column whose top digit is 0, he skips that column and borrows from the next one. (Note: This bug must be combined with either bug 5 or bug 6.)

$$
\begin{array}{r} \overset{7}{\cancel{8}}\,0,2 \\ -\,3\,2\,7 \\ \hline 2\,2\,5 \end{array}
\qquad
\begin{array}{r} \overset{7}{\cancel{8}}\,0,4 \\ -\,4\,5\,6 \\ \hline 3\,0\,8 \end{array}
$$

4. **Stops-Borrow-At-Zero.** The student fails to decrement 0, although he adds 10 correctly to the top digit of the active column. (Note: This bug must be combined with either bug 5 or bug 6.)

$$
\begin{array}{r} 7\,0,3 \\ -\,6\,7\,8 \\ \hline 1\,7\,5 \end{array}
\qquad
\begin{array}{r} 6\,0,4 \\ -\,3\,8\,7 \\ \hline 3\,0\,7 \end{array}
$$

5. **0 − N = N.** Whenever there is 0 on top, the digit on the bottom is written as the answer.

$$
\begin{array}{r} 7\,0\,9 \\ -\,3\,5\,2 \\ \hline 4\,5\,7 \end{array}
\qquad
\begin{array}{r} 6\,0\,0\,8 \\ -\,\;\;3\,2\,7 \\ \hline 6\,3\,2\,1 \end{array}
$$

6. **0 − N = 0.** Whenever there is 0 on top, 0 is written as the answer.

$$
\begin{array}{r} 8\,0\,4 \\ -\,4\,6\,2 \\ \hline 4\,0\,2 \end{array}
\qquad
\begin{array}{r} 3\,0\,5\,0 \\ -\,\;\;6\,2\,1 \\ \hline 3\,0\,3\,0 \end{array}
$$

7. **N − 0 = 0.** Whenever there is 0 on the bottom, 0 is written as the answer.

$$
\begin{array}{r} 9\,7\,6 \\ -\,3\,0\,2 \\ \hline 6\,0\,4 \end{array}
\qquad
\begin{array}{r} 8\,\overset{7}{\cancel{8}}\,6 \\ -\,4\,0\,9 \\ \hline 4\,0\,7 \end{array}
$$

8. **Don't-Decrement-Zero.** When borrowing from a column in which the top digit is 0, the student rewrites the 0 as 10, but does not change the 10 to 9 when incrementing the active column.

$$
\begin{array}{r} \overset{6}{\cancel{7}}\,0,2 \\ -\,3\,6\,8 \\ \hline 3\,4\,4 \end{array}
\qquad
\begin{array}{r} \overset{1}{\cancel{2}},0,5 \\ -\,\;\;\;\;9 \\ \hline 1\,1\,0\,6 \end{array}
$$

9. **Zero-Instead-Of-Borrow.** The student writes 0 as the answer in any column in which the bottom digit is larger than the top.

$$
\begin{array}{r} 3\,2\,6 \\ -\,1\,1\,7 \\ \hline 2\,1\,0 \end{array}
\qquad
\begin{array}{r} 5\,4\,2 \\ -\,3\,8\,9 \\ \hline 2\,0\,0 \end{array}
$$

10. **Borrow-From-Bottom-Instead-Of-Zero.** If the top digit in the column being borrowed from is 0, the student borrows from the bottom digit instead. (Note: This bug must be combined with either bug 5 or bug 6.)

$$
\begin{array}{r} 7\,0,2 \\ -\,3\,\overset{6}{\cancel{8}}\,8 \\ \hline 4\,5\,4 \end{array}
\qquad
\begin{array}{r} 5\,0,8 \\ -\,4\,\overset{7}{\cancel{8}}\,9 \\ \hline 1\,0\,9 \end{array}
$$

FIG. 8.3. Descriptions and examples of Brown and Burton's (1978) common subtraction bugs. (Adapted from Resnick, 1982. Copyright 1982 by Lawrence Erlbaum Associates. Reprinted by permission.)

Glynda Hull and her colleagues. They are specialists in English and linguistics working on the problem of teaching "basic writing" to students who enter a public university needing a remedial writing course (Hull, 1985, 1986; Hull, Ball, Fox, Levin, & McCutchen, 1985). These students write very badly indeed. The extent to which their sentences are ungrammatical, in fact, poses special problems and challenges for computer-based instruction, as we shortly see.

To say that these basic writers have trouble with standard English grammar is not to say that what they write has no regularity and pattern. Researchers have analyzed the writing of some very poor writers and discovered very systematic, regularly occurring types of errors (cf. Shaughnessy, 1977). This work has made possible the construction of a taxonomy of writing errors that could be called a *bug library*. By inserting the bug library into the memory of a computer— the same computer that serves as a word processor—writing errors can be detected through a process of pattern matching.

With this "intelligent word processor," a student composes a text and then asks the machine to scan it to pick out standard bugs. A common error in these students' writing is the addition of *ed* to an infinitive form of a verb: "I wanted to learn*ed* to write," or "I was just going to hand*ed* it to the person." Another frequent mistake is overuse of commas. Students use them to mark pauses in thinking, to add emphasis, or to divide what they believe to be separate clauses in a sentence. When the computer detects one of these errors, it calls up the passage with the error in it and displays it on the screen with the erroneous sentence highlighted in boldface type. A message appears at the bottom of the screen, as in Fig. 8.4, signaling the type of error and instructing the student to find and fix instances of the error. Note that instead of explicitly saying that the comma after "me" should be removed, the computer prompts the student to search for and solve the problem independently. The machine thus requires such active engagement that the author starts to recognize typical errors and, by repeatedly correcting them, learns to avoid *making* them. Small studies carried out in both laboratory and instructional settings confirm that novice writers do improve in this manner and that they enjoy working on these machines (Hull, 1986).

For the types of errors discussed so far, we do not need very fancy computing equipment or programming. All that is needed is a pattern matcher, which can run on relatively small machines. However, a pattern matcher sometimes cites as errors constructions that are actually appropriate grammatical constructions. For instance, the pattern matcher would flag the sentence, "The person I talked to learned a lot," for containing what resembles the past tense infinitive verb problem noted earlier, i.e., "I wanted *to learned* to write." In "The person I talked to learned a lot," *to learned* is correct. But for the computer to know that, it would have to assess the grammaticality of *to learned* as it is embedded within a larger context. A simple pattern matcher cannot make such sophisticated evaluations. And so Hull and her colleagues are adapting parsing techniques from computational linguistics to supply their already-intelligent machines with knowledge about grammar. It is reasonable to think of this as a restricted artificial intelligence system—one explicitly aimed at parsing typical *ill-formed* sentences. In large part this project can be undertaken because so much is already known about the typical kinds of errors that students make.

Error-detection in Arithmetic. It is easy to envision analogous types of error detection devices for mathematics. The first proposal for use of a computer

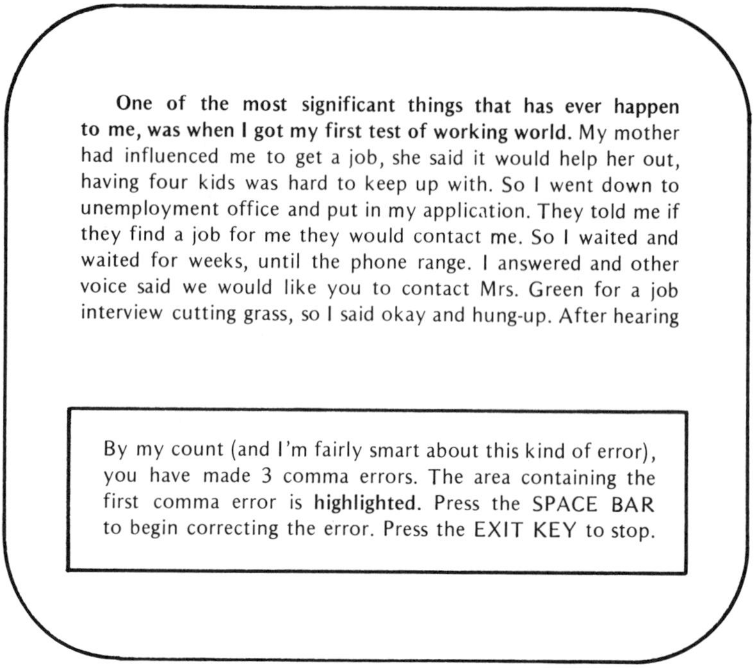

One of the most significant things that has ever happen to me, was when I got my first test of working world. My mother had influenced me to get a job, she said it would help her out, having four kids was hard to keep up with. So I went down to unemployment office and put in my application. They told me if they find a job for me they would contact me. So I waited and waited for weeks, until the phone range. I answered and other voice said we would like you to contact Mrs. Green for a job interview cutting grass, so I said okay and hung-up. After hearing

By my count (and I'm fairly smart about this kind of error), you have made 3 comma errors. The area containing the first comma error is highlighted. Press the SPACE BAR to begin correcting the error. Press the EXIT KEY to stop.

FIG. 8.4. Sample screen display from an intelligent word processor that has detected student writing errors.

in this way was made by Brown and his colleagues for subtraction bugs. There is some question, however, about whether practice on arithmetic in an environment explicitly devoted to bug detection succeeds in eliminating buggy rules during normal performances. In an instructional experiment we have run (Resnick & Omanson, 1987), an experimenter simulated a "subtraction robot," performing the actions asked for by a child but refusing to perform incorrect actions (saying "I am not programmed to do that; try something else"). Seven of the nine children selected for the experiment because they displayed systematic errors in arithmetic used the correct algorithm reliably after no more than a single refusal by the robot to act. Simply telling the children—albeit implicitly—to be careful seemed to be all that was needed to remind them of past encounters with the correct algorithm and to produce correct performance. On the other hand, most of these children reverted to their buggy algorithms a week or so later when doing pencil and paper arithmetic in the usual way, with no robot at hand to prompt them to attend more carefully. Thus, it appears that it is easy to suppress bugs temporarily by asking children to be careful, but this does not necessarily transfer to normal performance. Instead children must be taught to *routinely* monitor themselves for bugs.

An approach more likely to yield long-term effects is one in which the computer becomes a routine tool for doing arithmetic. When a child asks for an incorrect action, thereby revealing a bug in his algorithm, the computer could refuse to act, as our "subtraction robot" did. A responsive machine could also use this as an opportunity to explain *why* the buggy move does not work. Such explanations are rarely given in standard teaching practice, partly because of a continuing reluctance to show or talk about errorful performances. Their absence from textbooks is probably an inheritance from Skinnerian instructional theory, which tried to avoid all exposure to errors. In addition, teachers often are reluctant to discuss publicly a child's error, thinking it might cause the child embarrassment and discouragement. The net effect is that, although good explanations of correct algorithms are offered to children, the explanations are not tied to occasions when children are most likely to make errors. This means that the children will be unlikely to access those explanations when they are in the midst of an errorful procedure. The explanations may have been heard and even learned at some level, but they are not attached to performances; thus a child cannot draw on them in a way that might block or inhibit the buggy action and perhaps suggest a correct alternative. An interactive computer that provides explanations along with error indicators offers the opportunity to provide an explanation at the precise moment in a child's procedural behavior when it can do the most good.

Supporting Correct Rule Induction

We need not always wait for bugs to arise. It is also possible to use the computer to support proper rule induction early in the learning process. Two examples of this kind of program follow, the first from early reading instruction, the second from physics instruction.

Early Reading. The *Apprentissage* group at the Centre Mondial Informatique et Ressource Humaine in Paris (Cohen et al., 1987) has begun building a computer system that will read children's own written work back to them. Imagine a prereading child, perhaps a 4-year-old, who composes words on the screen and immediately hears those words read back to her. Preliminary observations of children using such a system show that, after an initial period of familiarization with the system, many children begin to vary spelling elements systematically. For example (translated into English), they start with *then,* change it to *ten,* and change that to *tan.* At each step the machine reads back the newly composed word, thus allowing the child to induce the role of particular letters in particular word positions. A key aspect of this system is its playful quality. By engaging in combinatorial play, the child can independently discover the principled regularity that governs alphabetic writing systems.

Rule Induction in Physics. One might consider the reading program just described as a system for helping children induce the "syntax" of spelling. In supporting rule induction it is also possible to focus on the "semantics" of a domain, i.e., its basic concepts. An example of a semantic rule induction support system is the Dynaturtle system developed by diSessa (1982). This system uses the LOGO "turtle" to create an artificial world that will behave according to the laws of Newtonian physics. In the Dynaturtle world, objects move around without friction and respond to forces placed on them in accordance with Newtonian principles. An example is shown in Fig. 8.5. The learner starts the turtle moving, and the goal is to make it arrive at a specified target on the screen. This must be done by applying forces at particular points in the turtle's trajectory. Students' initial conceptions of how different types of forces will affect the turtle's movement are not in agreement with what would happen in a Newtonian idealized world. For example, if the turtle is traveling vertically (as in the first panel of Fig. 8.5) and the student wants it to intercept a target off to the right (the circle), he or she is likely to wait until it is directly across from the target and give it a sideways "kick," expecting the turtle to make an immediate 45-degree turn toward the target, as shown in the second panel of the figure. What happens when he or she makes the hit, however, is that the turtle—in accordance with Newtonian theory—combines the new right-angle force with the continuing forward motion and goes in the direction shown in the third panel.

Through extensive exploration in this environment, fostered by problems such as requiring the learner to maneuver the turtle around a corner, people will start to learn how forces have to be applied in this Newtonian microworld. For example, they learn they can make a 45-degree turn by using two kicks — one (at 180 degrees to the turtle's motion) to stop the turtle and one (perpendicular to the turtle's motion) to make it travel horizontally. Another solution is to apply the perpendicular kick earlier so that the object moves off at an angle and hits the target (as in the fourth panel of Fig. 8.5).

This system has been only partially successful as a teaching device, however. Studies by White (1984) show that behaving in accordance with Newton's laws does not necessarily produce an understanding of Newtonian theory. This finding shows that misconceptions in physics are not simply a result of the fact that we live in a nonidealized, frictionful world—a view that many students of physics cognition once held. White shows that people can operate in an ideally Newtonian, nonfrictional world for a short time, adapt their behavior successfully, and still be unable to explain what is going on. They do not develop Newtonian *theories* just by "living in" a world where objects behave exactly as the theories say they would. This suggests that laboratories alone may not be enough for good scientific thinking to develop. Something that directs students' attention to questions of theory and interpretation will also be needed. White and Horwitz (in press) have pursued this possibility by designing a set of computer microworlds, called *ThinkerTools*, in which visual objects represent key elements of Newtonian theory, and the movement of these "theoretical objects" coordinates with the movement of physical objects.

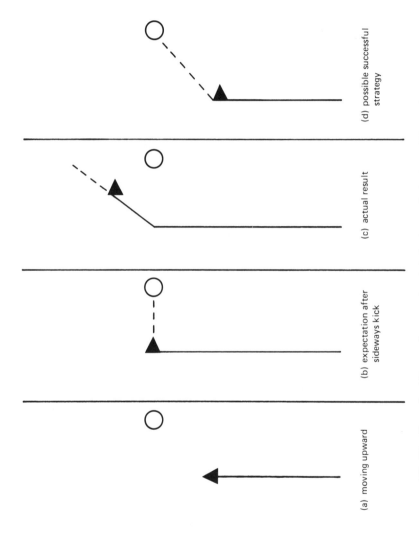

FIG. 8.5. Example of Dynaturtle semantic rule induction applied to laws of Newtonian physics (from diSessa, 1982).

(a) moving upward

(b) expectation after sideways kick

(c) actual result

(d) possible successful strategy

155

LEARNING AS THE DEVELOPMENT
OF MENTAL MODELS

ThinkerTools exemplifies a type of computer use that is becoming more widespread as computer graphics improve and as our understanding of the nature of reasoning about complex systems develops. In learning a new body of knowledge, a major task is to build "mental models" (cf. Gentner & Stevens, 1983) of complex systems and phenomena. If the mental model corresponds sufficiently well to the system itself, the learner can use the model to reason about the real world. A powerful use of computers in this process is to provide bootstrapping representations, i.e., representations that learners can manipulate and observe in ways likely to support development of their own mental models. In some cases these representations help students correct misconceptions about complex systems; in other cases they support the construction of purely abstract concepts.

Much learning requires the construction of abstractions — purely mental concepts that do not directly mirror physical or social reality. Most scientific and many social concepts are abstractions of this kind; they refer to systems of relationships, rather than to concrete features of the world, and the relationships often hold among concepts that themselves cannot be defined through ostension, i.e., by pointing out examples. Formalisms (whether expressed in mathematical notations or in systematized natural language) usually refer to abstractions rather than to ostensible reality. This complexity of reference may be what makes mathematics, physics, and similar fields so difficult for many students (cf. Resnick, Cauzinille-Marmeche, & Mathieu, 1987).

Special kinds of representational systems are required to help students construct abstract cognitive entities. These systems use at least two representations of a concept that are superficially dissimilar but possess important functional analogies. They are designed to direct learners' attention to the features that make the two representations analogies for one another even though their physical characteristics are different. By attending to these analogous features, learners can come to construct new abstract concepts that encompass — but are not fully defined by — the representations; that is, once the abstract concept is formed, the representations can be seen as nonexhaustive examples or embodiments of the concept. But first the representations must be mapped to each other to provide opportunities for the recognition of analogous features.

This notion of mapped, analogous representations as a way of supporting conceptual abstraction is demonstrated in a series of experiments using Dienes blocks as analogies to written base system arithmetic (Resnick & Omanson, 1987). These teaching experiments were done one-on-one, live, with every word of both instructor and child recorded, resulting in unusually detailed protocols of the learning processes involved for 8- to 9-year-old children. Children who possessed specific bugs were given a subtraction problem orally; they were asked to represent the top number in blocks and to make a written version of the

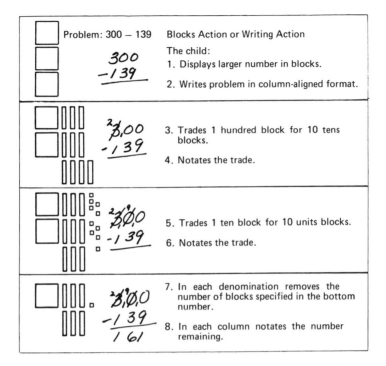

FIG. 8.6. Outline of mapping instruction for borrowing in subtraction. (From Resnick, 1982. Copyright 1982 by Lawrence Erlbaum Associates. Reprinted by permission.)

problem in column-aligned format (see Figure 8.6). This done, each child solved several subtraction problems using the blocks while making the analogous notations in writing.

The problems increased gradually in difficulty; children worked through them at varying rates, and prompts were provided until each child solved the most difficult type of problem—requiring a double trade from hundreds to tens and then from tens to units (as in Fig. 8.6)—without prompts. In the second part of the instruction, the blocks were faded out, and the children were asked to imagine the block movements and record their imagined exchanges in writing.

Through this process about one-third of the children learned the basic principles the instruction was intended to teach. This partial success of a carefully documented instructional interaction provided the opportunity to examine several hypotheses about why some children learned and others did not. The investigators carefully studied the protocols of the children. After eliminating a number of possibilities, they discovered that a particular kind of talk by the child was the only reliable predictor of learning. Specifically, it was the number of times that *quantities* were named for the tens and hundreds columns (where, unlike the units column, names of the digits do not match the value of the quantity) that predicted learning of the principles. The more children *talked* about those quantities, the more likely they were to have learned. An interpretation of this finding is that the children who talked about quantity were forced to name and attend to the very attributes that make the blocks and the writing analogous. The quantity talk in the experiment forced the construction of a higher level entity, an abstraction that makes the written and block arithmetic isomorphic.

Yoked Microworlds

The findings of the subtraction study point to a general approach to mathematics instruction that focuses on prompting children to explore analogies between written numbers and their concrete referents, thus priming the correct formation of higher level abstractions. My colleagues and I are developing a series of computer microworlds that use this approach to teach various arithmetic concepts. The core idea of these microworlds is to provide an environment in which children can explore graphic, pictorial representations of number that are carefully linked to numerical representations in a yoked fashion—so that each time the child manipulates the graphics, the computer supplies a corresponding change in the number, and vice versa.

Figure 8.7 shows an example from our STRIPS-AND-TILES program for teaching fractional parts. The notebook window" (in the lower left-hand corner) is where the child can generate numerical expressions by typing numerals on the keyboard and placing them with a mouse. In the Strips and Tiles World window, the child can generate pictorial displays of fractions. Here a unit strip is divided into a number of tiles, and that number corresponds to the denominator (in this case, 10). Any number of these tiles can be colored in; the number of colored tiles corresponds to the numerator of a written fraction. This type of fraction representation is common in regular arithmetic instruction. What the computer adds is a yoking facility in which the machine interprets the child's construction in one of the representations and automatically creates the corresponding representation in the other. Thus, in the case of Fig. 8.7, the child had constructed the fraction $\frac{1}{10}$ in the notebook window, and the machine produced its yoked counterpart in the microworld window: a strip divided into 10 tiles with 1 tile colored in. For the child's $\frac{5}{10}$, a second strip appeared, this time having 5 of 10 tiles colored in. The child might now solve the addition problem posed in the Direction window graphically by switching to the microworld window and using a mouse to move tiles around on the screen. The best solution for the problem in Fig. 8.7 would be to "lift" the darkened tile from the left-hand strip and deposit it into one of the blank sections of the right-hand strip. The computer can continue to yoke the child's graphic manipulations to her numerical ones by producing corresponding changes in the written fraction in the notebook window: changing $\frac{1}{10}$ to $\frac{0}{10}$ and

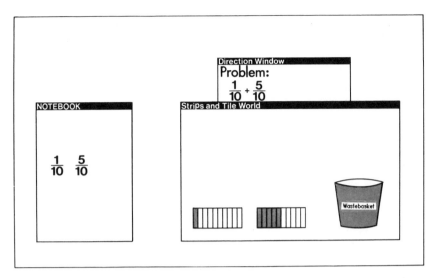

FIG. 8.7. Window image for rational number tutor.

$\frac{5}{10}$ to $\frac{6}{10}$. An empty strip can be moused away into the "wastebasket," at which time the computer will delete the $\frac{6}{10}$ notation in the notebook.

The preceding is a very general introduction to the possibilities of yoked representation. A key to developing such representations is to remind oneself continually that it is not the representations on the screen that matter in the end, but the representations built up in the students' heads — their mental models. We think that by showing at least two screen representations and forcing students (via yoking) to think about why the two go together, we can "force" the constructing of abstract representations. Recent papers by Nesher (in press) and Ohlsson (1987) develop criteria for yoked representations in the domain of arithmetic based on explicit assumptions about mathematical epistemology. Similar analyses are required to guide development of yoked representations in other areas.

Simulation Laboratories

In addition to yoked representations, valuable types of bootstrapping representations are those that use computer graphic and animation capacities to allow students to "see how things work." Such representations simulate complex or opaque systems. The simulations highlight significant features and functional relationships of the system. The models displayed need not — in fact, probably should not — be exact matches to physical reality or to experts' mental models. Rather, they are pedagogical constructions designed to provide material for the learner's cognitive construction. When students can manipulate certain elements and observe effects elsewhere in the system, the representations function as computerized laboratories.

Pedagogical representations may be designed explicitly to provide alternatives to known misconceptions. For example, most beginners learning about electricity tend to conceive of electrical power as flowing from a battery to a bulb (or other user of electricity) and being used up enroute. This "linear misconception" (cf. Closset, 1983) is supported by common experience and by the language used in discussing power sources, e.g., "consumption of power." The correct conception of a circuit through which electricity flows, with equal amounts of current throughout the circuit, is surprisingly hard to teach. Recent instructional research (Johsua & Dupin, 1987) shows that students can induce the proper circuit conception when provided with a model to reason about—for instance, a model of a train on a circular track with so many cars that its front joins its own end. The train must move as a unit; every car must move at the same speed. Resistors placed at various points on the circular track slow the train down, but they slow it down everywhere. At the same time, a power source—men who push each of the cars as they go by a particular point—keeps the train moving. Stronger pushes speed up the train; weaker pushes slow it down. The model provides a meaningful distinction between the strength of the electrical current (speed of the train) and the strength of the battery (strength of the pushes—which are likely to become weaker as the men's muscles fatigue). Johsua's research shows that, using this kind of mental model as an analogy, young students learn the basic logic of electrical circuits with relative ease and either discard or never develop the kind of linear misconception that often interferes with learning. This kind of mental model is a natural for computer displays. Indeed, a version of such a model has been computerized by Haertel (1982). In this computerized model students or teachers can manipulate the parameters of the system, thus giving them a tool for their mental reasoning about the model.

Computerized simulation laboratories can represent more than physical systems. Shute and Glaser (in press) are developing a simulation laboratory, called SMITHTOWN, for investigating principles of microeconomics. In addition to simulating the relationships between economic variables (students can vary price and population, for example, and observe effects on demand), the laboratory incorporates various tools that support students' use of the simulation. For example, a notebook tabling tool that operates like a spreadsheet facilitates data recording and inspection. A graphing tool is available for students to examine relationships among variables. A prediction and hypothesis menu guides the student through the processes of formulating hypotheses, and a review facility allows students to look back over the history of their hypotheses and tests. In SMITHTOWN then, a simulation model of economic theory is linked to various graphic representations and is further supplemented by generic tools that guide and support laboratory investigation.

INTELLIGENT TUTORING:
PROMISES AND LIMITS

We cannot conclude a chapter on what cognitive theory implies for the future of computers in education without explicitly considering the cognitive community's most notable contribution to the field of computers in education. This is what has come to be known as *intelligent computer-assisted instruction* (I-CAI) or *intelligent tutoring*. (See Sleeman & Brown, 1982, for a collection of papers that still virtually defines the field.) All programs described in the preceding sections use machine intelligence in the service of instruction, but for the most part they do not qualify as intelligent tutors in the current meaning of the term.

Intelligent CAI and intelligent tutoring have come to mean computer-assisted instruction in which the machine builds up a model of what the student is thinking and chooses instructional steps (e.g., hints, new problems, new pieces of information, questions) on the basis of this constantly tuned model. In this view, the computer is meant to function as a substitute for a human teacher. In fact, it is claimed that the computer can be *better* than a teacher, because it can tutor or coach each student individually. Actual instantiations of this idea, however, are more limited than some of the rhetoric surrounding the issue would suggest. The tutors developed so far do not build very deep models of what individual students know or why they make specific responses.

Consider John Anderson's LISP (Anderson & Reiser, 1985) and geometry (Anderson, Boyle, & Yost, 1985) tutors, for example. The "intelligent" heart of each is an expert system that works on the same problem the student is solving. When a student's response does not match the expert's, the system interrupts and provides some coaching intended to set the student on the expert's course. To tune this coaching to the student, the tutors also contain systematically *in*expert systems—i.e., systems that perform the tasks with routines that contain "bugs," therefore generating the types of wrong responses that students make. If a student's incorrect response is one that can be generated by a buggy routine, the system infers that the student is applying that routine and then tailors explanations and coaching accordingly (for example, by picking a hint or explanation that is stored with the buggy routine). In a sense, the LISP and geometry tutors diagnose the student's difficulty and tailor instruction to the student. But this process of diagnosis and tailoring is based on very local information. No long-term picture of the student is developed, and it does not appear to be needed. Most users of these and similar tutors seem to feel that the tutor interacts intelligently with them.

For the user, this sense of interacting with an understanding entity can be enhanced when the tutoring system enables students to express their *intentions* and also allows the system to (apparently) respond in terms of those intentions. Even intention-based tutors, however, are still local and limited in their diagnosis and student modeling. An example is Bonar's (1988) BRIDGE tutor for learning PASCAL programming. BRIDGE first helps students refine their informal theories or procedures and then helps them develop these theories into programming plans. All this is done via a "conversation" using a menu of phrases that was developed from students learning PASCAL whose comments and questions had been recorded. Only at the final step must students use the syntax of PASCAL statements.

Are the current limits of intelligent tutoring fundamental or do they only reflect an early stage of development? The answer is not clear. It is certainly true that we have not yet proceeded far enough with the broad venture of understanding human learning processes. This means that our theoretical tools for modeling students are rather primitive. But the problem may be deeper. Searle (1984) and others (e.g., Winograd & Flores, 1986) have raised the question of whether an artificial intelligence system can really "know" anything about a world external to the symbols it manipulates. In other words, there may be fundamental limits on what a system can know about its users (including students). On the other hand, important as such questions may be for theories of artificial intelligence, they may matter less than it seems for educational applications. The purpose of artificial intelligence systems used in education is to interact with *natural* intelligence systems (humans, that is), and humans, we know, will *attribute* human-like intelligence to any system that behaves, on the surface, as humans do. This means that interactive AI systems may be able to help learners construct new knowledge by only "pretending" to know what the learner is thinking. They can, in other words, "fake it" and still be effective learning devices, as long as other aspects of the learning system and broader learning environment provide enough useful material for students' knowledge construction.

INTELLIGENT MACHINES FOR INTELLIGENT PEOPLE: A RECONCEPTUALIZATION

As the preceding discussion suggests, we believe that current discussions of intelligent CAI view the long-term potential for computers in education too narrowly. Intelligent tutors based on on-line construction of student models represent only one of the ways in which artificial intelligence and the expanded computing capacity of the future can be applied to education. We envision a future in which a much broader spectrum of human activities will be performed interactively with computers. Computers will be everyday partners in work and leisure, extending human intellectual power as other machines have extended human physical power beyond the imagination of earlier generations.

The idea of extending human capacity by building tools to do part of the work once done by humans is not unique to the computer age. For example, it is possible to trace the history of navigational instruments, showing how aspects of navigation that initially depended on human calculation and judgment have been transferred to various devices in successive stages of technological development (Resnick, 1987). The results of such development are both enlarged capabilities of the total human/machine system and fundamental changes in the nature of the human intellectual skills required for participating in the system.

In a computer-rich future such as we envisage for the year 2020, it is reasonable to imagine that the line between intelligent instruction and intelligent tools may blur and even disappear. The goal of both will be to extend human intelligence, to make humans more powerful thinkers and, therefore, actors. There are two ways to make human intelligence more powerful through interaction with a computer. One is to use the computer as a temporary device to boost human knowledge or skill, with the goal of bringing students to a point where they can perform complex tasks competently without the computer. This is the classic—and still dominant—view of education. Although the instructor (in this case a computer tutor or other program) is present during a learning phase, eventual independent performance by the students is the goal, and effective teaching requires phasing out interaction with the teacher. This is the only way to imagine using humans as teachers—for neither social expectations nor human resources will support a world in which each individual has a human tutor available whenever a task is performed.

This constraint does not always hold for computers, however, and will hold even less in the future as computers become more widely used in work, home, and leisure. For many tasks it may be much more sensible to think of computers as long-term "intelligence extenders"—i.e., tools to be used habitually to complete certain tasks more efficiently—rather than instructional devices. To consider as *educational* those devices intended to share tasks permanently with humans is to expand the meaning of the term *education*. Yet we think such expansion is called for in projecting a computer-rich future. We must think about the kinds of artificial intelligence that will interact well with human intelligence across a broad spectrum of human activities and then design artificial intelligence systems and training programs for human users accordingly. With this expanded view of the potential role of computers in mind, we can suggest several broad categories of educational applications of computers that should be explored as preparation for the computer-rich future of 2020.

Computers as Conversational Partners. Much learning occurs from conversation with others who either know a great deal about a subject in which one is interested or raise penetrating questions about our formulations. Conversations with computers are awkward at the present time, because the natural language understanding and production capacities of AI systems are not developed adequately and because we have not yet worked out medium-appropriate substitutes for the nonlinguistic and supralinguistic aspects of communication. In addition, we do not know much about the structure of arguments other than those based on formal logic. As a result we cannot yet build systems that mimic the structure of good conversation in much detail. But eventually, we should be able to do so. And meanwhile, because human intelligence tends to fill in the gaps in everyday communication, grasping meaning even in the absence of complete information, there are possibilities for "faking." For example, restricted language and menu-like techniques can simulate conversation in limited domains if the restricted language is carefully chosen and if the computer has not only an extensive knowledge base but also the capability of constructing explanations and justifications for its actions. It is possible, then, to begin investigating the use of computers as conversational partners without waiting for the year 2020 to arrive.

Computers as Devices for Accessing and Organizing Information. People increasingly must access and organize large amounts of information. Computerized library catalogs and search tools are already becoming commonplace. But these still treat the search process and the actual access to the information as separate functions. Electronic storage of information will be nearly universal in the future. As a result, it will be possible to merge information search and information use functions of the computer. What is more, information-access functions can be built into many computer tools. For example, consider the power available to writers from a thesaurus nested inside a dictionary accessible during word processing without exiting from the file in which one is working. Computerized access systems can also be used to help learners and even "browsers" decide what portions of a large library of graphic, audio, and print materials they wish to examine, with networked addressing systems such as *hypertext* providing coherent yet highly flexible pointers among different segments of the information available.

Computers as Conversation Enhancers. Even in a computer-rich world, people will probably continue to do most of their learning from one another. Sociological studies show that most people (academics perhaps excepted) prefer personal sources of information. Instead of fighting this tendency, computers can join it. Properly designed, computers can enhance conversations among people. This is already happening with computer mail systems, for example, but we have only begun to explore the possibilities for using computer networks and computer displays as devices for enhancing human communication. One of the ways computers may alter the nature of thinking in the future is by making it more communal—allowing more cooperative problem solving (cf. Trigg, Suchman, & Halasz, 1986). Computers might serve as intelligent blackboards, allowing people to develop and mutually edit displays that help them to visualize situations or think out consequences of potential actions. Such tools already exist in specialized work environments (e.g., computerized drafting tools) where they are often used in joint problem solving. Such tools can also be viewed as educational tools — by expanding the range of people who have access to them and by designing interfaces that take into account the needs of beginners as well as experts in a field.

Computers as Planning Tools for Problem Solving. Effective problem solving depends on recruiting and organizing one's resources for attacking problems. Research on problem solving has taught us a good deal about the nature of this resource recruitment, ranging from goal analysis to strategy identification, but we do not presently give problem solvers much help in the process. Appropriately designed computer systems could provide much help by supplying a variety of organizing devices for people, along with hints and coaching systems that individuals can call on as needed. Some of the basic computer elements of such planning tools already exist. Hooked to more extensive knowledge bases, systems of this kind could function as planning tools for people at many levels of expertise and in many fields.

Computers as . . . . Although the list could be extended, the thrust of our argument should now be clear. Conceiving of computers not just as tutors but also as collaborators with human intelligence extends the boundaries of traditional definitions of education by modifying the meaning of intelligence and thereby calling into question traditional methods of enhancing intellectual competence. We assume that, as computers become more accessible and necessary, new uses and needs beyond those outlined here will arise. The implications of such developments for cognitive theory as well as for educational practice are enormous. Indeed, if computers really become a part of our daily life outside school — as there is good reason to believe will happen by the year 2020 — our very ideas of what constitutes education can be expected to shift. We have hinted at some of the possibilities here. We anticipate that, as computers become increasingly available as intelligence-extending tools, broad educational uses well beyond those that we have been able to imagine will suggest themselves. History tells us that long experience with certain tools (steam engines, radios, automobiles, for example) functioning as common cultural devices shapes people's sense of the possible in ways that cannot easily be forecast at early stages of development. At early stages, tools are used mainly to do traditional tasks more efficiently. Only as the tools become commonplace do ideas emerge for using them in other ways that few people ever thought to try. Such, we expect, will be the case for computers as developers and extenders of human intelligence.

REFERENCES

Anderson, J.R., Boyle, C.F., & Yost, G. (1985). The geometry tutor. *Proceedings of the 9th International Joint Conference on Artificial Intelligence* (Vol. 1, pp. 1–7). Los Angeles.

Anderson, J.R., & Reiser, B.J. (1985, April). The LISP tutor. *BYTE* (pp. 159–175).

Beck, I., Roth, S., & McKeown, M. (1985). *Syl-la-search III teacher's manual*. Allen, TX: Developmental Learning Materials.

Bonar, J. (1988). Bridge: An intelligent tutor for thinking about programming. In J. Self (Ed.), *Artificial intelligence in human learning*. London: Chapman and Hall.

Brown, A.L., & Reeve, R. (1987). Bandwidths of competence: The role of supportive contexts in learning and development. In L.S. Liben (Ed.), *Development and learning: Conflict or congruence?* Hillsdale, NJ: Lawrence Erlbaum Associates.

Brown, J.S., & Burton, R.R. (1978). Diagnostic models for procedural bugs in basic mathematical skills. *Cognitive Science, 2,* 155–192.

Chrosniak, P.N., & McConkie, G.W. (1985, April). *Computer-aided reading with reading-discouraged children.* Paper presented at the annual meeting of the American Educational Research Association, Chicago.

Closset, J.L. (1983). Sequential reasoning in electricity. In *Research on physics education.* Proceedings of the first international workshop. La Londe les Maures, 313–319.

Cohen, R., Barriere, M., Hafter, C., Naymark, J., Plaisant, C., & Stambak, C. (1987). *Les jeuenes enfants la decouverte de l'ecrit et l'ordinateur*. Paris: Presses Universitaires de France.

diSessa, A.A. (1982). Unlearning Aristotelian physics: A study of knowledge-based learning. *Cognitive Science, 6,* 37–75.

Fleisher, L.S., & Jenkins, J.R. (1978). Effects of contextualized and decontextualized practice conditions on word recognition. *Learning Disabilities Quarterly, 1*(3), 39–74.

Frederiksen, J.R., Warren, B.M., & Rosebery, A.S. (1985a). A componential approach to training reading skills: Part 1. Perceptual units training. *Cognition and Instruction, 2,* 91–130.

Frederiksen, J.R., Warren, B.M., & Rosebery, A.S. (1985b). A componential approach to training reading skills: Part 2. Decoding and use of context. *Cognition and instruction, 3/4,* 271–338.

Gentner, D., & Stevens, A.T. (1983). *Mental models*. Hillsdale, NJ: Lawrence Erlbaum Associates.

Greenfield, P.M. (1984). A theory of the teacher in the learning activities of everyday life. In B. Rogoff & J. Lave (Eds.), *Everyday cognition* (pp. 117–138). Cambridge, MA: Harvard University Press.

Haertel, H. (1982). The electric circuit as a system. *European Journal of Science Education, 4*(1), 45–55.

Hull, G. (1985). *Using cognitive research and computer technology to improve writing skill in low-performing college students*. (Interim report to the Ford Foundation, Contract No. 830-0355). Pittsburgh: University of Pittsburgh, Learning Research and Development Center.

Hull, G. (1986). *Using cognitive research and computer technology to improve writing skill in low-performing college students*. (Final report to the Ford Foundation, Contract No. 830-0355). Pittsburgh: University of Pittsburgh, Learning Research and Development Center.

Hull, G., Ball, C., Fox, J.L., Levin, L., & McCutchen, D. (1985, April). *Computer detection of errors in natural language texts: Some research on pattern-matching*. Paper presented at the annual meeting of the Educational Research Association, Chicago.

Johsua, S., & Dupin, J.J. (1987). Taking into account student conceptions in a didactic strategy: An example in physics. *Cognition and Instruction, 4*(2), 117–135.

Lave, J. (1977). Tailor-made experiments and evaluating the intellectual consequences of apprenticeship training. *Quarterly Newsletter of the Institute for Comparative Human Development, 1,* 1–3.

Lesgold, A.M., Resnick, L.B., & Hammond, K. (1985). Learning to read: A longitudinal study of word skill development in two curricula. In G.E. MacKinnon & T.G. Waller (Eds.), *Reading research: Advances in theory and practice:* Vol. 4 (pp. 107–138). New York: Academic Press.

McConkie, G.W., & Zola, D. (1985). *Eye movement techniques in studying differences among developing readers* (Tech. Rep. No. 377). Champaign: University of Illinois, Center for the Study of Reading.

McConkie, G.W., Zola, D., & Winograd, P. (in press). Computer aided reading for adult illiterates. In M. Pennington (Ed.), Teaching English with computers: First and second language perspectives.

Nesher, P. (in press). Microworlds in mathematical education: A pedagogical realism. In L.B. Resnick (Ed.), Knowing and learning: Issues for a psychology of instruction. Hillsdale, NJ: Lawrence Erlbaum Associates.

Ohlsson, S. (1987). Sense and reference in the design of interactive illustrations for rational numbers. In R. Lawler & M. Yazdani (Eds.), Artificial intelligence and education (pp. 307–344). Norwood, NJ: Ablex.

Perfetti, C.A., & Lesgold, A.M. (1979). Coding and comprehension in skilled reading. In L.B. Resnick & P. Weaver (Eds.), Theory and paractice of early reading. Hillsdale, NJ: Lawrence Erlbaum Associates.

Pettito, A.L. (1985). Division of labor: Procedural learning in teacher-led small groups. Cognition and Instruction, 2, 233–270.

Resnick, L.B. (1986). The development of mathematical intuition. In M. Perlmutter (Ed.), Perspectives on intellectual development. Hillsdale, NJ: Lawrence Erlbaum Associates.

Resnick, L.B. (1987). Constructing knowledge in school. In L.S. Liben (Ed.), Development and learning: Conflict or congruence? Hillsdale, NJ: Lawrence Erlbaum Associates.

Resnick, L.B., Cauzinille-Marmeche, E., & Mathieu, J. (1987). Understanding algebra. In J.A. Sloboda & D. Rogers (Eds.), Cognitive processes in mathematics (pp. 169–203). New York: Oxford University Press.

Resnick, L.B., & Omanson, S.F. (1987). Learning to understand arithmetic. In R. Glaser (Ed.), Advances in instructional psychology (Vol. 3, pp. 41–95). Hillsdale, NJ: Lawrence Erlbaum Associates.

Rogoff, B., & Gardner, W. (1984). In B. Rogoff & J. Lave (Eds.), Everyday cognition: Its development in social context. Cambridge, MA: Harvard University Press.

Rogoff, B., & Lave, J. (Eds.). (1984). Everyday cognition: Its development in social context. Cambridge, MA: Harvard University Press.

Roth, S.F., & Beck, I.L. (1984, April). Research and instructional issues related to the enhancement of children's decoding skills through a microcomputer program. Paper presented at the annual meeting of the American Educational Research Association, Chicago.

Roth, S.F., & Beck, I.L. (1985). Theoretical and instructional implications of the assessment of two microcomputer word recognition programs. Manuscript submitted for publication.

Schwartz, J.L. (1983). The semantic calculator user's manual (Computer program manual). Pleasantville, NY: Sunburst Communications.

Searle, J. (1984). Minds, brains and science. Cambridge, MA: Harvard University Press.

Shaughnessy, M. (1977). Errors and expectations. New York: Oxford University Press.

Shute, V., & Glaser, R. (in press). An intelligent tutoring system for exploring principles of economics. In R. Snow & D. Wiley (Eds.), Straight thinking. San Francisco: Jossey Bass.

Siegler, R. (1978). The origins of scientific reasoning. In R. Siegler (Ed.), Children's thinking: What develops? (pp. 109–150). Hillsdale, NJ: Lawrence Erlbaum Associates.

Sleeman, D., & Brown, J.S. (Eds.). (1982). Intelligent tutoring systems. New York: Academic Press.

Trigg, R.H., Suchman, L.A., & Halasz, F.G. (1986, December). Supporting collaboration in notecards. Paper presented at the Conference on Computer Supported Cooperative Work, Austin, TX.

Vygotsky, L.S. (1962). Thought and language. Cambridge, MA: MIT Press.

Vygotsky, L.S. (1978). Mind in society. Cambridge, MA: Harvard University Press.

White, B.Y. (1984). Designing computer games to help physics students understand Newton's laws of motion. Cognition and Instruction, 1, 1-4.

White, B.Y., & Horwitz, P. (in press). ThinkerTools: Enabling children to understand physical laws. Cognition and Instruction.

Winograd, T., & Flores, F. (1986). *Understanding computers and cognition: A new foundation for design.* Norwood, NJ: Ablex.

Wood, B., Bruner, J.S., & Ross, G. (1976). The role of tutoring in problem solving. *British Journal of Child Psychology and Psychiatry, 17,* 89–100.

9 Putting Knowledge to Use

ROY D. PEA
New York University

> I want to tell you something my brother David, may he rest in peace, once said
> to me. He said it is as important to learn the important questions as it is the
> important answers. It is especially important to learn the questions to which there
> may not be good answers. (Potok, 1986, pp. 295–296.)

Questions about how people learn so that they can use their experiences productively and creatively when facing new situations are at the heart of psychology
and education. These are questions about the *transfer problem*. But these questions have not been met with good answers—if by good answers we count those
that would have enabled us to formulate designs of learning activities and environments that promote appropriate knowledge transfer. Are good answers
available? And will better questions—addressing broader aspects of the transfer
problem than ones about the isolated "cognitive" learner—improve our answers?

Contemplating the needs of education in the year 2020 would give anyone
deep pause in thinking about these questions. Perhaps new kinds of interactivity, or organizations of learning and teaching, or representations of knowledge,
or views of the learner might fundamentally improve the state of knowledge
transfer achieved through educational practices. Although many new worlds
will be technically possible, can we begin to say what features of specific possible worlds might actualize the transfer of learning so long desired?

I believe we are beginning to gain new insights into the problem of knowledge
transfer. These insights have as much to do with recognizing the impacts of
the sociocultural organizations of activities in which learning takes place as
they do with psychological findings from research on learning. To make our

way to these insights, and toward the goal of framing promising directions for educational technologies, I first need to set a historical context for studies of transfer.

To anticipate somewhat, I plan to develop an *interpretive perspective* on the transfer problem. This is markedly unlike the preeminent theory of transfer whose likelihood is defined in terms of "common elements" of the situations of knowledge acquisition (encoding) and application (retrieval). The interpretive view considers the "appropriate transfer" desired as a product of education to be primarily a sociocultural rather than an objective concept. Elements of previous and current situations perceived to be the "same" by a thinker are not intrinsic in the nature of things but "read" in terms of the thinker's category system of problem types. Such a category system is influenced by culture in significant ways.

I first critically synthesize research findings from the cognitive sciences, especially on studies of learning and thinking in situ, and then identify specific features of thinking-skills instruction likely to be effective for promoting transfer. These features include learning about and practicing knowledge application in multiple contexts of use, constructively participating in bridging instruction across school and nonschool problem situations, thinking and self-management ("metacognitive") skills taught within domains, and synergistic integration of learning for different subject domains. Recommendations are then made for developing new learning technologies that build on these conditions for enhancing knowledge transfer.

WHAT ARE THE DIMENSIONS OF THE PROBLEM?

Knowledge transfer is a problem with many faces at the heart of learning and education. It is not only an individual achievement but a cultural problem, encompassing the study of history and its uses. And education as an ideological institution is itself the attempt to transfer knowledge from the culture to the individual. The interpretive or sociocultural perspective on knowledge transfer developed here is designed to accommodate to these complexities.

The knowledge transfer question is most commonly described one-directionally and thus incompletely: How can formal educational knowledge, acquired in the specialized setting of schools, be transferred appropriately to everyday life and work situations? These observations lament common evidence from the workplace, home, community, and from educators' reports, that wisdom acquired formally is not applied as desired outside the schooling context.

From a developmental perspective, we must ask the inverse question. How can formal education ensure use in its settings of the concepts, skills, and strategies that students have acquired or invented and applied effectively already in everyday life and work situations?

Yet another direction of transfer of skills, strategies, concepts, and other knowledge is transfer between the traditional curriculum divisions. Greater curricular synergy is needed so that students may learn and apply knowledge in an integrated manner matching the demands of everyday situations—in which, for example, writing, reading, mathematics, and science may all come to play at once, not during different class periods, much less organized by textbook chapter boundaries.

The crowning direction of transfer is so widespread that it blurs with the very concept of learning: Transfer studies have been used as a means for assessing learning. If students only can solve specifically instructed problems, failing to solve related ones, we do not attribute subject mastery to them.

Any comprehensive theory of knowledge transfer for education will need to encompass these multiplicities.

Knowledge Transfer and Tomorrow's Education

I first examine several influences that have served in highlighting attention to the knowledge transfer problem. Although specific concerns for educators may vary between now and 2020, the transfer problem has been a perennial one. Thousands of years ago the Greek Heraclitus told us that *we never step in the same river twice,* that every event experienced is in some measure unique. The existence of vast computer data bases of text and images, accessible through easily navigated graphical browsers, with search tuned to one's interests (Weyer & Borning, 1985) will not erase these deep theoretical problems or the practical concerns of the transfer problem. Nor is it clear what would be meant by saying that knowledge transfer will become *more* important in future decades—unless one believes that the more knowledge that civilization accrues, the more intransigent the transfer problem becomes. Access to pertinent knowledge for transfer was already vexing and the subject of satirical humor in the writings of Washington Irving, long before the "information explosion" of the mid-20th century.

There is a widespread anxiety, expressed at teacher educator and subject-matter specialization conferences and journals, about the irrelevancy of much of today's curricula, largely derived in their topical divisions and sequencing from 19th-century curriculum theory, and dominated by fact-oriented learning devoid of knowledge application. Such curricula clash with an information age where the basic facts are changing rapidly, where information is stored and conveyed digitally, and in which the "basic knowledge" citizens need is under debate in most curricular fields because computers are capable of carrying out mechanical aspects of problem-solving activities, as in symbolic equation solving in mathematics, or plotting and transforming graphs.

One response to this contemporary fear has been met with grass roots movements initiated by educator organizations to teach "thinking" and "problem-solving" skills. Many curricula with this orientation have largely been developed and taught independently of course content. This approach has led to extreme critical reactions, charging that educators have thereby degraded what students know when they graduate (Hirsch, 1987). From a research perspective, it has become quite clear that transfer of learning with such materials to either valued school outcome measures or to enhancing the quality of everyday life problem solving and action has rarely been evaluated (Chipman, Segal, & Glaser, 1985; Resnick, 1987; Segal, Chipman, & Glaser, 1985). But as we see, in the sections that follow, few cognitive theorists recommend instruction in cognitive skills without substantial content knowledge emphasis.

A third contribution to transfer-problem awareness among cognitive scientists came from comparative cross-cultural studies in the 1960s and 1970s designed to test the cognitive consequences of formal schooling and of literacy. Bruner (1966) had suggested that the decontextualized nature of school thinking, such as mathematical reasoning with symbols and equations, and multiple classificatory schemes for their own sake, fosters abstract thinking and formal operational thought. But contrary to expectations, extensive research generally revealed meagre connections made between what was learned in school and other everyday life problem solving (see review by Laboratory of Comparative Human Cognition, 1983).

A fourth influence came from studies by cognitive scientists and science education researchers revealing that even university physics students tend to regress from Newtonian theory toward mistaken physical explanations based on informal experiences with moving objects. Shaken from the frame of their textbook explanations, they resort to nonformal qualitative explanations frought with inconsistencies (diSessa, 1983). Shweder (1977) presents similar findings for statistical reasoning among presumably statistical literates. Practical cognition is not, it appears, very affected by instruction in formal science or mathematics. Some consider the external validity of much school "learning" questionable if it does not impact on students' practical cognitions.

A fifth, broadly based influence is the belief not only throughout the United States but in foreign educational rationales from Belgium, China, France, Great Britain, Japan, the Netherlands, and Sweden, among others, that learning computer programming will condition the mind to think systematically, precisely, planfully, and more rationally in contexts beyond programming. The current instruction of over several million American students in programming each year is in part a measure of the depth of educators' commitments to this expectation. (As writings by Soloway, this volume, and DiSessa, this volume, make evident, the instructional payoff of "programming" per se will be hard to assess, as trends toward domain-specific programmable tools and activities become realized, and learning to think procedurally—the real breakthrough of programming, Sheil, 1981—becomes integrated within diverse disciplines.)

Although incomplete, this list of contributing factors to the present level of attention in the research and educator communities to problems of knowledge transfer attests to the diversity of influences at work. The historical roots of the dominant theoretical perspective for transfer of learning now require some illumination.

"What's the Same?": Thorndike's "Common Elements" Transfer Theory

Early in the century, Thorndike carried out many learning transfer studies to test William James' (1890) hypothesis on the specificity of learned habits. It was then common for students in school to learn Latin, not so much for its utility as for its anticipated general promotion of "mental discipline" for learning other curriculum topics. The negative findings from these investigations (Thorndike, 1924; Thorndike & Woodworth, 1901) devastated the discipline hypothesis and helped open up a period of vocationalism in American schooling (Cremin, 1961). Similar arguments are pressed today for the study of logic, mathematics, and science, but particularly for computer programming. As in the case of Latin, where spontaneous transfer outcomes have been carefully assessed for programming, findings have not been promising (Kurland, Pea, Clement, & Mawby, 1986; Milojkovic, 1983; Olson & Soloway, 1987; Pea & Kurland, 1984). Whereas more guidance and structure may yield more significant transfer results, these findings come from explicitly training for generalizability of specific reasoning skills beyond programming contexts (e.g., debugging; Carver, 1986).

As an alternative to the belief that learning rigorous topics generally disciplines the workings of a young mind, Thorndike and Woodworth (1901) offered a specific transfer theory based on the idea of identical elements. On this theory, transfer of knowledge or learning will occur between two tasks insofar as the tasks *share* identical elements, particularly perceptual features. Versions of this common element theory have persisted ever since Thorndike's associationist theory came to prominence in education (Brown, Bransford, Ferrara, & Campione, 1983; see Ellis, 1965; Gagne, 1968; Osgood, 1949).

We can now answer, "what's the same?" *Common elements theory* is now common. It is under revival (although often unknowingly, because memories are short for big ideas) in artificial intelligence (AI) theories of transfer of learning, commonsense reasoning, metaphor comprehension, and human–computer interaction. "Elements" today are commonly defined in the knowledge representation programming languages in which such AI reasoning systems are built (Carbonell & Minton, 1983; Winston, 1978, 1979). A common elements approach to transfer also appears in Polson, Muncher, and Engelbeck's (1986) account of learning different word-processing systems.

The units of the transfer metric in such theories differ from the physical or symbolic elements of Thorndike's theory, but the logic of the approach is identical. Instead of common physical elements in situations, theorists now count as indices of "similarity" either nodes in a knowledge network, or overlapping rules in production systems as a measure of the likelihood and direction (positive or negative) of knowledge transfer.

Access and Availability of Knowledge

Cognitive developmental studies have provided other central findings and concepts for an appraisal of knowledge transfer theory. Numerous investigations in a Piagetian tradition had by the early 1970s documented in excruciating detail the conceptual "inadequacies" and "deficits" of preschoolers. They could not reason causally or arithmetically, could not conserve number, had bizarre ideas about animacy, and so on. But under more clever research designs and observer scrutiny, 2- to 4-year-olds demonstrated they had much greater conceptual, logical, and social understanding than previously acknowledged. How did such inconsistencies emerge?

The secret of the revealing studies resided in the construction of the situations for assessing children's skills or knowledge. Working with familiar materials in familiar settings with simpler (if any) experimental instructions, research thoroughly documented the rich and precocious understanding of the world possessed by the preschooler (Donaldson, 1978; Gelman, 1978; Gelman & Brown, 1986). (These works were likely influenced by comparable studies of cross-cultural cognition [see review in Laboratory of Comparative Human Cognition, 1983] that had "experimented with the experiment" [Scribner, 1977] once they "found" the obviously questionable result that non-Western adults could not reason logically with traditional laboratory-derived measures.)

To understand these contrasting findings, the distinction between *availability* and *access* of knowledge, earlier elaborated for adult memory by Tulving and Pearlstone (1966), is central. Its relevance to the transfer problem in education is that the preschooler had available the requisite knowledge to accomplish the experimental task, but it had not been accessed as it should have been — from the experimenter's perspective anyway — in earlier studies.

Two Types of Transfer

Voss (1987) helps clarify the distinctions and data that cognitive science has brought to bear on transfer. We briefly summarize his observations and introduce related findings as appropriate. Voss considers transfer a more fundamental concept than either learning or memory (cf. Ferguson, 1956). He argues that transfer must be viewed in relation to the individual's prior knowledge that is utilized in the transfer situation. As in Ferguson's (1956) definition, we consider any identifiable covariation between any two or more forms of performance as a transfer function.

The study of transfer in psychology and education therefore requires re-evaluation of the traditional transfer paradigm, that is, Learn A, Learn B versus Do-Not-Learn A, Learn B. Voss's observation therefore suggests the following distinction: Transfer may be studied by observing performance as a function of prior knowledge, as in the expert–novice paradigm, or transfer may be studied in the traditional training paradigm, bearing in mind that utilization of prior knowledge is nonetheless taking place. Transfer in these two circumstances is now examined. In either case, we already begin to see complications of Thorndike's picture, because learner characteristics (knowledge, expertise) and not only objective features of situations are presumed to influence transfer.

Transfer Involving Utilization of Prior Knowledge

Knowledge utilization is often assessed by comparing how well learners spontaneously transfer knowledge they possess or have recently acquired to a new problem context. Voss, Greene, Post, and Penner (1983) showed that experts in Soviet political science, when asked to solve a problem of poor agricultural productivity, carry out a two-phased problem-solving process. They both develop a problem representation and state and justify their solutions by means of two fundamental processes: *categorization* and *knowledge retrieval.* In categorization, the problem solver acts to link the problem statement contents to known problems, or some more comprehensive principle in terms of its structural rather than surface features (Larkin, McDermott, Simon, & Simon, 1980). Experts' knowledge is considered hierarchically defined in terms of inclusive problem types and tokens, principles and cases, whereas novices create problem representations based on specific concepts found in the problem statement. Scribner and Cole (1973) argued similarly that formal education prepares the learner to consider new problems as class members rather than as unique.

Voss et al. (1983) also found expert–novice differences in knowledge retrieval. If a problem could not be recognized as a token of a known type, experts but not novices used a goal-directed and constrained search in their knowledge retrieval, guided by specific reasoning strategies such as stating arguments, rebutting counterarguments, qualification, analogies, and problem-solving methods like problem decomposition.

Related difficulties have been documented with knowledge utilization transfer from school learning. Early arithmetic and algebra instruction both provide salient examples of failed knowledge utilization from school learning (Resnick, 1987). For either equation transformation rules necessary for algebra equation solving, or the symbol manipulations required for solving written multidigit subtraction problems (Resnick, 1982), students often have great difficulties. They make errors when syntactic operations they carry out with the formal, written system are not connected to actual problem situations—even when these connections could render the written expressions meaningful. Whereas the point of abstract expressions may ultimately be to allow context-free calculations, the end goal is not a pedagogical recommendation for referentially isolated learning.

Pettito (1985) argues that inappropriate transfer may arise from school arithmetic. Such effects are revealed in Scribner and Fahrmeier's (1982) study comparing the reasoning of dairy workers versus high school students in a series of tasks involving calculations for milkcrate packing. The dairy workers were highly flexible in the arithmetic strategies they used. The high school students were very inflexible: When new practical arithmetic problems demanded revision of calculation strategies for optimization, students continued to apply their school-learned procedural rules.

Resnick and Omanson (1987) have demonstrated through "mapping instruction" that one can provide instructional support for young children's integration of their practical experience in mathematics with school knowledge. Children may display skill in using base-ten manipulables (Dienes blocks) to represent written numbers and carry out matching operations in the two representational media, while nonetheless making errors in manipulating place value in written subtraction and addition problems. The intensive mapping instruction used has the teacher guide the child to link the semantics of the base system with the syntax of the written algorithms. The written form is depicted as marking a record of block manipulations as the children alternate between subtracting the written and the manipulable media. Children with former procedural bugs in written arithmetic did not make errors even 3 to 6 weeks after such instruction. Mapping instruction appeared to have taught children where to look for the links between their practical knowledge of base-ten relationships and the written arithmetic algorithm (Pettito, 1985).

There is a related lack of transfer from invented and everyday mathematics that works to contexts of school mathematics, where performance falters. This was an early finding of Gay and Cole (1967). They showed that Liberian farmers successfully used measurement and calculational systems in areas that affected their well-being in life situations but had little understanding of mathematics as a generally useful abstract knowledge system. And Carraher, Carraher, and Schliemann (1985) recently discovered that young Brazilian children use informally developed counting procedures to solve many arithmetic problems in the marketplace that they cannot solve in school.

Recent ethnographic studies of thinking point to the same results for schooled adults, whose everyday mathematics in practical activities such as shopping, managing money, and dieting (Lave, 1987; Lave, Murtaugh, & de la Rocha, 1984), or loading trucks with dairy orders in the factory (Scribner & Fahrmeier, 1982) works but is not transferred to school tasks such as written mathematics testing. In a related vein, Resnick (1987) notes that many children fail to see that the formal rules taught in school and their own independently invented mathematical intuitions are related.

The sensitive nature of how the thinker *reads* a problem situation as one appropriate or not for transfer of mathematical competencies is revealed in

Lave's (1986) discussion of an experiment by Capon and Kuhn (1979). They attempted to simulate best-buy supermarket shopping outside a store where customers were requested to compare actual pairs of different-sized store containers of a product for a best buy. Lave suggests that subjects' inadequate use of proportional reasoning in the Capon and Kuhn study, which dramatically contrasts with near-perfect performance in her own research group's studies within supermarkets, is due to circumstances in the Capon and Kuhn experiment that reminded subjects of school-learned arithmetic algorithms. Specifically, they asked subjects to write out their work for comparing best buys (process) rather than just selecting the best buy (answer). In reading the situation as one with an activity organization like a school-based task and thus as requiring a particular type of mathematical activity, Capon and Kuhn's subjects did not appropriately transfer the knowledge they (presumably) had available to the problem situation created for the experiment.

This concept of *situation reading* is an important one for the study of knowledge transfer, and it highlights a deep problem in current cognitive theories of transfer discussed shortly.

Transfer Involving Knowledge Use: The Traditional Paradigm

Assessments of knowledge-acquisition transfer provide the paradigm case of educational transfer studies, such as Thorndike's studies on transfer of learning from Latin, or Polson et al.'s (1986) studies of how learning to use a first word processor affects the ease of learning to operate a second one (for reviews of extensive research with this paradigm during the heydays of "transfer of learning" studies, see Gagne, Foster, & Crowley, 1948; Ellis, 1965). Voss (1987) observes that this classic transfer paradigm involves superimposing the transfer instructional treatment (such as Latin, or a programming language; Pea & Kurland, 1984) on the subject's existing knowledge base. Thus, one needs to know how preinstructed knowledge influences subsequent learning. Voss suggests that classical studies of transfer (and, we may add, studies of programming's cognitive effects; Kurland, Pea, Clement, & Mawby, 1986) may yield nonsignificant effects because the new learning is unimportant relative to the influence of prior knowledge in transfer task performance.

This *constructivist* perspective—the conception that learners build new understanding in terms of prior concepts or conceptual systems—has perhaps become most apparent in the case of science learning (Driver, Guesne, & Tiberghien, 1985; Hawkins & Pea, 1987; Linn, 1986; Osborne & Freyberg, 1985; West & Pines, 1985). The widespread finding is that preinstructed knowledge provides a conceptual foundation that instructional processes must meet through diagnostic activities and then build on. The key notion is that the learner's prior knowledge is *generative,* used in an attempt to understand the new information offered by instruction. In the terms of Bransford and Franks (1976), such prior knowledge structures "set the stage" for comprehending what goes on in school, relating that experience in terms of the past but allowing for the articulation of unique aspects of the new situation.

One of the principle ways in which prior knowledge may influence transfer task performance is by means of categorization processes. Insofar as education can promote the formation of appropriate categories of problem types, transfer is supported when a categorization process is used to subsume a new problem under a known type, and an attempt is made to apply prior knowledge about successful strategies for dealing with that type to the present case.

Data bearing on this hypothesis is available from cross-cultural studies of the cognitive consequences of formal schooling. Scribner and Cole (1973; also see Cole, Lave, & Sharp, 1979) found that schooled students were more capable of transferring problem solution methods learned early in a problem sequence to different but related problems than were nonschooled students. But as Pettito (1985) cautions, because the tasks in those studies were all school problems, generalization of learning to practical activities remains an open empirical question.

Relation to Analogical Reasoning

A psychology of *analogical reasoning* is fundamental to an understanding of the knowledge transfer problem (Carbonell, 1983; Gentner, 1983; Holyoak, 1985). The reason is that analogical mapping is a process of recognizing the similarities between a past situation x (source) and current situation y (target), and then using details of one's memory of x to structure and elaborate one's understanding of y. Such analogical mapping consists of transferring information from the source to the target domain. The success of this process requires: (a) that the thinker has rich knowledge of the source domain that is applicable to the target (supporting Voss's claim that an understanding of the prior knowledge base of the thinker is essential to an analysis of transfer), and (b) that there is no radical translation problem between the conceptual schemes of the learner for the source and target domains.

But similarity comparisons of source and target domains may be simplistic: Because novices do not understand the target domain, mapping appropriately onto it may be quite difficult (Carbonell, 1983; Carey, 1986; Ortony, 1979; Schank, 1986).

The Dimensions of Transfer Redefined

The development of intelligence has long been defined as a shift from context-dependent knowledge use, where knowledge and skills resources are "welded" to their initial context of acquisition, to more context-free generalizations of the use of intellectual resources. In this sense, the lack of transfer of learning to new contexts was equated with rigid intellectual functioning, or "mechanization" (Luchins & Luchins, 1959).

But it has rarely been alleged that to transfer knowledge indiscriminately to new situations is a hallmark of high intelligence. More is involved in the transfer problem than transfer in terms of "common elements" regardless of circumstance. *Selective* knowledge transfer, that is "appropriate," which "works," defines the valued outcome of thinking and action. In this section, different dimensions of the knowledge transfer problem are sketched to resituate it as the cultural and interpretive problem it is.

In the cognitive science renderings of the knowledge transfer problem described earlier, the learner is alone and a "cognitive" being. But accounts of transfer restricted to the individual and to only cognitive aspects of transfer must be considered a theoretical legerdemain. Other influential dimensions of the problem involve basic concerns about the sociology of knowledge use and acquisition, anthropological and cross-cultural issues about the interpretation of situations for thinking and learning, and how motivational and attitudinal states may affect the likelihood of transfer.

Important questions arise about the *purposes* of knowledge transfer, and to the related *values* issues lurking beneath the surface of the concept of "appropriate transfer." Because desired transfer is selective, where do the selection principles come from? If we address only the conditions of learners' knowledge states, which causally incline them to knowledge transfer ("cognitive mechanics"), we will fall short of explaining the selectivity of transfer. We are reminded of Dilthey's (1833/1976) insightful remark that "no real blood flows in the veins of the knowing subject constructed by Locke, Hume, and Kant; it is only the diluted juice of reason, a mere process of thought" (p. 162). Insofar as a cognitive mechanics is possible, it will only be likely to suffice for a highly restricted set of knowledge use and acquisition situations. As Skinner (1971) once observed, "the world of the mind steals the show" (p. 12).

Writers often mention "appropriacy" of knowledge transfer but not the social construction of such categorizations. According to Papert (1980, cited in Dreyfus & Dreyfus, 1986) "true computer literacy is not just knowing how to make use of computers and computational ideas. It is knowing when it is appropriate to do so" (p. 122).

"Inappropriate" transfer (often called "negative") refers to cases when one has transferred prior knowledge and "should not" have. But observe that such negation is not epistemic, defined in the nature of things, but deontic, defined in the nature of social meanings. Such prescriptions reveal that "appropriate transfer" is not a natural kind, but defined by cultural and individual value systems. Particular transfers of learning from the learning context to a new situation are never intrinsically "appropriate," but only as judged against a set of conventions reflecting the values of the culture to which the learner belongs (Shweder, 1986).

A continuum of four cases conveys the spectrum of conventions that enter into judgments of the appropriacy of transfer. The child overgeneralizes a lexical term, calling any cloth a "towel" that is wet from a spill. He has confused the incidental and vital features of "towel" because his first acquaintance with the term was with a wet cloth. Judged from community standards, this is inappropriate transfer. But from the child's perspective, these naming tasks share certain "common elements."

In our second case, the grocery shopper who has learned the decision analysis method of multiattribute utility theory in her thinking-skills course applies it to the decision problem of picking a tomato at the greengrocer for making a pasta sauce. She explicitly defines the various criteria that matter to her for judging tomatoes, weights their importance, and evaluates each tomato option by each criterion. Several hours later, after lengthy calculations, she optimizes and selects the best tomato. Whereas we would deem this transfer of a higher order thinking skill inappropriate, because the effort expended is disproportionate to the seriousness of the decision problem, the same approach would be appropriate if the task were diamond selection by a gemstone carver for the queen's tiara, or a site for a new missile silo.

Similarly, the military strategist may think that because people can be counted like objects, they are like objects, subject to cost-benefit analysis, and thus minimizing body counts is a desiderata in battle planning. Depending on one's value theory, this may be considered highly "inappropriate" transfer. Similar cases could be detailed in risk analysis for nuclear or toxic waste disposal, insurance risk assessments, and other science-technology-society problems.

Finally, to take an extreme case, if one taught burglars to define goals, to plan and to do progress monitoring, and to use precision in their thinking, these skills would very likely be transferred to their clandestine thievery work. Such transfer is channeled toward the purposes such individuals consider relevant to their life space. But the burglars' purposes are negatively valued goals for transfer from a prosocial perspective, and deeply inappropriate.

Common Elements as Social Constructions

Hoffding (1892) brilliantly argued against Thorndike's seminal treatment of transfer, urging that the issue is not, as Thorndike supposed, one of measurable physical elements of problem environments, but of the learner's construal of task domain similarity. Although physical similarities can influence likelihood of transfer, *perceived similarity* is fundamental. What matters is how the new situation reminds the thinker of previous situations, which is liable to be quite idiosyncratic.

In this respect, Hoffding's approach is congruent with Dilthey's 19th-century work on "moral sciences" such as history, psychology, sociology, literary criticism, and "hermeneutics," the interpretive methodologies humans apply to understanding the meaning of situations and social phenomena as if they were texts. Similarly, Dewey (1922, p. 131) critiqued psychologies such as Thorndike's that assume that the lists and categories they construct represent fixed collections *in rerum natura,* when lists serve only as classifications for a purpose.

Unfortunately, anthropological study of perceptions of contexts for transfer of learning has been minimal until recently. In contrast, societal influences on the selective principles controlling attention have been a concern linking psychology and anthropology since early in the century (e.g., Evans-Pritchard, 1934; Wilson, 1970). Studies rooted in Marx's observations on this topic were carried out, with special attention to thinking in non-Western cultures, by Durkheim and Levy-Bruhl in France, and by Bartlett, Evans-Pritchard, Malinowski, Rivers, and Radcliffe-Brown in England. For example, as Evans-Pritchard (1932) stated:

> As James, Rignano, and others have shown, any sound or sight may reach the brain without entering into his consciousness. We may say that he "hears" or "sees" it but does not "notice" it. In a stream of sense impressions only a few become conscious impressions and these are selected on account of their greater affectivity. A man's interests are the selective agents and these are to a great extent socially determined for it is generally the value attached to an object by all members of a social group that directs the attention of an individual towards it. It is, therefore, a mistake to say that savages perceive mystically or that their perception is mystical. On the other hand we may say that savages pay attention to phenomena on account of the mystical properties with which their society has endowed them, and that often their interest in phenomena is mainly, even exclusively, due to these mystic properties. (p. 24)

More recently, Cole and colleagues at the Laboratory of Comparative Human Cognition (1979, 1983, 1984) have critically reviewed contributions of developmental and cognitive psychology, anthropology, and sociology to the understanding of how individuals in a culture come to acquire belief systems that specify how experienced events are connected. They argue for a "cultural practices" theory (1983), according to which the kinds of social contexts children participate in contribute to the fundamental categories of experience out of which cognitive development and knowledge transfer arises. These contexts are not defined in terms of physical features of settings, but in terms of the meaning of these settings constructed by the people present. Such an interactional conception of cognition in culture provides an important foundation for investigating the dimensions of the knowledge transfer problem in education.

In the case of current cognitive theories of transfer, this question of interpreted rather than objectively given "elements" serving as the basis for transfer is begged. The productions in production systems modeling human thought or the nodes in knowledge representation networks in cognitive simulations are part of the *theorist's* construction of the problem situation. The question is begged because the problem-solving context is interpreted, not an experimental variable defined invariantly across subjects. If it were so simple, findings of "no transfer" in experimental studies of problem-solving strategies would not be so common. The elements of situations said to determine the suitability of transfer are treated as reified entities rather than as socially constructed, situated realities. It seems likely that using an interpretive approach to the problem of selective knowledge transfer will offer a more productive orientation to educational activities design for promoting transfer than the traditional common elements one.

It is perhaps not surprising that the renowned cognitive studies that fail to find transfer of problem-solving strategies involve puzzle problems such as the Tower of Hanoi and Missionaries and Cannibals, which are "formally identical" (in terms of the problem-solving operations required for their solution) but have different "surface structures" (Reed, Ernst, & Banerji, 1974; Simon & Hayes, 1976). Note here that the "common elements" between such problems are not physical problem features as in Thorndike's initial formulation of transfer theory, but problem-solving production rules. In terms of the important role of problem categorization on transfer likelihood, why should the college student in such studies have seen those puzzle problems as belonging to the same type? They were not taught or discussed as a class of problems of similar type; it is only at an abstract level of analysis that they are formally identical. The same point applies to Gick and Holyoak's (1980, 1983; also see Perfetto, Bransford, & Franks, 1983) work on transfer of problem-solving solutions from a divide-and-conquer battle story, to Duncker's radiation problem and related problem analogs. In each case, subjects had to be prompted that information given to them was relevant to solving the problem posed, for without the prompt they did not use the information.

Need for a Cultural Practices Framework

How do socially organized activities come to have consequences for human thought? No clear theory of the mechanisms by which the social affects cognitive variation is available. But recent theory influenced by Vygotsky's (1978) cultural-historical theory of higher mental functioning suggests one promising direction. Scribner and Cole (1981) have provided an important framework, developed in over a decade of cross-cultural cognitive research, for thinking about how "cultural practices" influence thinking. Rather than focusing on the features of a technology (e.g., formal schooling, written language) alleged to influence cognition, they approach a set of practices, such as literacy, as a "set of socially organized practices which make use of a symbol system and a technology for producing and disseminating it" (p. 236). "Practice" involves technology, knowledge, and skills. It is defined as a particular technology and a particular system of knowledge. "Skills" are the coordinated actions involved in applying this knowledge in particular settings. This framework on cultural practices has dramatic consequences for conceptualizing transfer: "Literacy is not simply knowing how to read and write a particular script but applying this knowledge for specific purposes in specific contexts of use. The nature of these practices, including, of course, their technological aspects, will determine the kinds of skills ('consequences') associated with literacy" (p. 236).

In terms of their framework they can make sense of results of their careful studies on the cognitive consequences of literacy in relation to those of schooling, which documented an asymmetry of schooled and nonschooled literacy effects. School and nonschool contexts for using literacy skills involve different tasks, even for the "same" practice of reading and writing. The most profound effects of schooling were found for experimental tasks requiring verbal explanations for why a problem was solved in a particular way. They suggest that the skills required in teacher–student dialog practices in the classroom contribute to these distinctive school effects of literacy on cognitive tasks.

An important consequence of the cultural-practice approach to transfer is that because cognitive achievements are largely unique in their contextual characteristics, and yet clear influences of prior learning on present activity are evident, one must "look to the organization of the environments in which interactions occur" (Laboratory of Comparative Human Cognition, 1983, p. 341) and recognize that "transfer is arranged by the social and cultural environment. . . . Overlap in environments and the societal resources for pointing out areas of overlap are major ways in which past experience carries over from one experience to another" (ibid). We presently have little research understanding of specifically how "areas of overlap"—categories of situations on which transfer seems to depend—are socially constructed. How are such categories formed? Through what experiences with discourse on events (their "sameness" or "differentness"), and actions in the material and symbolic environments that a culture has composed?

Several conclusions may be drawn from this perspective. First, we may expect that promoting knowledge transfer in education will depend on more effective arrangement of environments for bridging knowledge utilization across contexts of value within a culture. Second, we may conjecture that the new interactive symbolic environments that can be constructed with computers could dramatically extend a student's experiences of the environments in which available knowledge is viewed as appropriate for transfer. How might technologies contribute to our "societal resources for pointing out areas of overlap" across situations for which transfer is appropriate?

On Transfers "Not Taken"

In any given situation, an individual has a vast storehouse of prior knowledge that could be related analogically to the present occasion. Perhaps the biggest unexplained mystery of cognition is the selection process involved in such choices.

In fact, as the dramatist and literary critic Kenneth Burke suggests, it is often "perspective by incongruity"—the conjoining of concepts in unexpected ways—through which novel insights are derived. Any AI theory that works out transfers based only on "common features" in some explicit representational language is bound to miss the provocative and interesting novel insights that unexpected juxtapositions of concepts can yield. The history of creative thought in science, mathematics, and literature is rife with such cases.

Furthermore, many potential transfers are never contemplated, and not all transfers that the thinker contemplates are actually followed through, either in thought or action.

So why are some transfers "not taken"? Two answers to this difficult question are explored for present purposes: (1) Because they are not "appropriate," (2) because they "take too much effort." The cultural groundings of each are briefly discussed.

Appropriacy of Transfer. Culture dictates constraints on appropriate transfer in its conventions and mores. Sometimes transfer applications are censored because of taboos that vary cross culturally (e.g., on dirtiness, rawness, sexuality, incest). Some potential transfers of knowledge are so incongruous and unexpected that they serve not to illuminate the worlds of science, but the human condition, and its ways of reflecting on itself, as in humor or exotic literature, revealed in writings such as those of Eugene Ionesco, James Joyce, or Jorge Luis Borges. Conceptual disputes between different ideological communities may also center on what particular transfers are appropriate, e.g., whether certain metaphors for how society functions, or how the mind works, or how light behaves are legitimate. Members of such a community may not make some transfers then, because of ideological constraints on their appropriateness.

It is common to read that students need to acquire "skills of analogical thinking," of generating analogical connections from knowns to unknowns as a means of understanding. This crucial "fluency" aspect of intellectual functioning was stressed in the writings of divergent thinking theorists such as Duncker and Wertheimer and is the subject of much experimentation in modern cognitive psychology (e.g., Sternberg, 1985). But that is only half the issue. What is less commonly noted is a complementary evaluative skill that is required if analogical thinking is to support the learning and problem-solving activities of the learner. Not only should the learner be able to productively generate analogies, but the learner should be able to evaluate the utility of the generated analogy for the purposes at hand. In other words, not all analogies are good ones. Most importantly, *the goodness of the analogy depends on the purposes of the analogizing.* Whether the analogical transfer of knowledge is judged to be good depends on who is doing the evaluation and why. The goodness or utility of a transfer depends on the satisfaction criteria for the thinking task.

Halacz and Moran (1982) argue, for example, that in learning about software such as word-processing programs, not all analogies are useful, and some may lead to negative transfer and detrimental miscomprehensions. But they tacitly assume learning efficiency as their utility criterion. Many analogies people use are misleading and may, as in electricity, even be deadly if assumed to be true (Gentner and Gentner, 1983). Resnick (1987) notes how overtransfer of taught reading strategies can disrupt reading if overapplied. In the cases of word processing and reading, sociocultural standards provide cognitive control schemata for judging transfer appropriacy. At the other extreme, the impact of objective standards in evaluating whether transfer works is made strikingly evident by the case of electricity.

The cognitive economics of transfer is another complex of factors, too little researched from an educational perspective, that may influence whether contemplated transfers of knowledge are pursued or not. The pervasiveness of the principle of minimal effort in mental as well as physical action is well documented. In relation to contemplated transfers of prior knowledge to the present problem situation, the thinker asks, even if he or she thinks the transfer might work: Is it worth the costs to carry it out? I may project that the mental work of analogical mapping is sufficiently difficult that it does not outweigh the possible benefits I could derive from the transfer.

Evaluations of such simulated mental effort may influence the likelihood of knowledge transfer even when students have availability and access of transfer-relevant knowledge. Such mental-effort conservation is fundamentally cultural because perceived transfer benefits are value dependent. What one considers transfer of learning to be "worth" in one's effort calculations (whether tacit or explicit) is influenced by cultural concerns such as the value of time, and accountability to others. Determination of such costs will in part depend on an individual's idiosyncratic history of costs and benefits for knowledge transfer in what he or she perceives to be similar situations to the current one. To complicate matters, the veracity of one's projections of the likely cognitive effort of knowledge transfer activities is itself probably influenced by the sophistication of one's prior knowledge. One can be more or less accurate in the estimates one makes of how much work will be involved in transfer.

On a related point, diSessa (1983) describes the potency of *phenomenological primitives* (p-prims) in transfer. These are schemata for understanding situations that are purpose relevant for the reasoning one does in one's "niche" of problem-solving situations. Thus, if one has available a set of p-prims for everyday physical reasoning and is then presented with formal physics problems in school, there may be no mapping between the two contexts because of a radical translation problem across the two problem representation systems (see in particular, Clement's 1986 attempts in physics education to fill such gaps with bridging examples).

There are additional issues in cognitive economics concerning broad-scale conceptual change. What is the new value of the formal physics concepts and methods for the physical reasoning I consider important? Is there significant payoff to adapt my current conceptual schemes with these new ideas? Or do I just learn formal physics as a separate conceptual system with school-linked conditions of application?

Transfer Attitude

Additional influences on knowledge transfer may be introduced. Earlier the distinction was made between one's access to and the availability of knowledge and skills during a problem situation. Critical to the access problem are affective and motivational factors that are ill understood. How students feel about their capabilities of performance in learning tasks can drastically affect their interest not only in knowledge transfer but in learning itself. How is the disposition to engage in persistent memory search for transfer-relevant knowledge in a problem situation influenced by self-efficacy, fear of failure, anxiety, intolerance of mistakes, or other emotional blocks (e.g., Meichenbaum, 1977)?

Research on *achievement motivation* indicates that if children conceive of intelligence as a stable "entity" whose adequacy is revealed through performance, rather than an "incremental" set of skills to be increased through effort, then they are likely to view errors as personal failures and approach problem-solving events not to learn from, but as occasions to look smart or to fail (Dweck & Elliot, 1983). Diener and Dweck (1978) have distinguished "mastery-oriented" and "helpless" strategies for processing failure feedback in problem solving. Brunstein and Olbrich (1985) make an analogous distinction between the action-oriented strategy to go on to new events, and the state-oriented strategy of dwelling on events.

We unfortunately know little about how such different achievement goals arise. Yet the entity view, the helpless strategy, and the state-oriented strategy can all have crippling consequences for learner motivation when the false starts that are inevitably ingredient to learning and knowledge transfer are viewed as failures (also see Papert, 1980).

Sternberg (1983) makes the important observation that, unlike in education, the need to provide positive motivational conditions for transfer of skill training has been well recognized and effectively handled by behavioral psychologists dealing with treatment programs aimed at overcoming obesity, heavy smoking, and drug addiction.

Even such limited findings as these suggest promising research strategies. The sociocultural orientation to selective knowledge transfer outlined here implies that such affective and motivational influences on knowledge transfer are best studied in the cultural systems that give rise to them rather than as traits of individuals. This runs counter to the common treatment in the literature of children as "intrinsically motivated" or not, or the tendency to seek out the characteristics of a software game that cause intrinsic motivation (Lepper, 1985; Malone, 1981).

Toward Solving the Redefined Transfer Problem

Various sociocultural dimensions of the knowledge transfer problem have been acknowledged. What might education do to better provide for the kinds of activities and emphases that will support students in learning for appropriate transfer? Some clues are suggested by psychological research on instruction in thinking skills for transfer.

Generalizable thinking skills can be successfully taught, including problem-solving heuristics in mathematics (Schoenfeld, 1985); word list learning and recall strategies (Belmont, Butterfield, Ferretti, 1982); planning, goal monitoring, and revisionary strategies in writing (Bereiter & Scardamalia, 1986); reading comprehension skills (Palincsar & Brown, 1984); and skills of allocating effort while studying (Dansereau, 1985; Weinstein & Mayer, 1985). What are some of the elements of success in these efforts? Many directly address aspects of Dweck and Elliot's (1983) statement of children's learning difficulties for intellectual tasks (in contrast to physical ones): "children may be less likely to know what they are aiming for [goals], why they are aiming for it [purpose], how to get there [method], and when they have gotten there [evaluation]" (p. 677).

In the next part of the chapter, I summarize arguments for recommendations about how one might foster the development of appropriate transfer of learning from education. A variety of measures are suggested. They include acquiring knowledge in functional contexts, providing multiple-domain knowledge application examples and experiences, creating bridging instruction across school and nonschool problem situations, and integrating subject learning with synergistic design. The higher order goal of creating cultures of transfer thinking in which these measures play enabling roles is briefly characterized.

Where is Learning Spectacular and Transfer Common?

In seeking to identify features of an effective education, Bransford, Sherwood, and Hasselbring (1985) begin by asking where learning is *spectacular.* It so happens that where it is, one can find remarkable transfer of what is learned. Such spectacular learning occurs in the first 5 years of life. Then children quickly acquire concepts, language, and motor, spatial, and social skills with minimal explicit intervention. They also appear to willfully learn with little obvious effort. And they do so despite lack of knowledge, few available conscious learning strategies, and probable limitations on working memory (Case, 1985). Bransford et al. (1985, November) describe distinctive features of these spectacular learning contexts:

1. Learning takes place in context. Children learn during the first 5 years while involved in culturally meaningful ongoing activities and receive immediate feedback on the success of their actions.

2. Learning is often effectively mediated. Parents, friends, and peers serve not only as models for imitative learning but help the children learn by providing structure to and connections between the child's experiences, highlighting task-relevant information in a situation, and establishing continuity to functional learning contexts in which children can come to take over part-activities of a whole problem-solving task (Bruner, 1983).

3. Learning is functional. (1) and (2) together help provide children with an understanding of the functions of information for problem solving. Concepts and skills are acquired as tools with a range of purposes.

To Bransford's description of features of spectacular learning settings, I would add that the functions of new knowledge are not only shown but are also often explicitly stated. For example, successful studies for teaching thinking skills for transfer have been explicit in describing for learners the need for and purpose of these new learning activities, e.g., that they will benefit performance (Bereiter & Scardamalia, 1986; Brown et al., 1983, p. 129f; Palincsar & Brown, 1984; Pressley, Ross, Levin, & Ghatala, 1984; Schoenfeld, 1985). These findings suggest that we should explain to students that the transfer of the knowledge they are acquiring is important and why. Otherwise, student improvement tends to be highly task specific. This technique may be effective because orienting children toward what they perceive as high-value learning goals, regardless of their level of perceived self-competence, leads to mastery-oriented striving (Dweck & Elliot, 1983).

The instructional implication is that one should teach concepts, strategies, or skills in problem-solving contexts in ways that make their functions apparent. Such "functional presentations" and the emphasis on learning-by-doing will make it more likely that the knowledge will be accessed and transferred to new problems. Students are provided with real problem-solving situations (or in some cases, models) that engage the concepts and skills under instruction in situations analogous to their desired targets of application.

The Utility of Multiple Examples and "Bridging Instruction"

Multiple contexts of acquisition and application of new knowledge (e.g., in different problem domains) are important because then the encoding of that knowledge in memory has multiple functions associated with it for future retrieval. Consequently, the likelihood decreases that the knowledge is welded in memory to a specific problem context (Brown et al., 1983; Gagne, 1985). Experimental results from learning studies support this prediction (Cheng, Holyoak, Nisbett, & Oliver, 1986; Gick & Holyoak, 1983; Homa & Cultice, 1984).

Gagne (1985) offers the (by-now familiar) suggestion that learning transfer is a circumstance influenced by the number of common cues between the learning and transfer situations. Transfer is said to be enhanced if the cues available in the situation in which transfer is appropriate are increased at the time of learning, by linking rules with other concepts, or to a more meaningful context such as a schema. Gagne's account is similar to Thorndike's "identical elements" theory. Even though more "interpretive" in its consideration of situation elements, Schank's theories of dynamic memory (1982) and explanation patterns in reasoning (1986) also take a multiple-cue approach.

There is an added complexity to the recommendation of providing multiple examples in knowledge acquisition for subsequent knowledge transfer. Not just any combination of multiple examples will suffice, and which *range* of examples is chosen, and the *sequence* in which the examples are offered, will probably influence the breadth of selective transfer one will observe students making. Yet very little research has systematically examined desirable characteristics of example selection for maximally appropriate transfer.

Some research suggests that representatives of the natural *variability* of category instances should be captured in examples used for instruction (Elio & Anderson, 1984; Fried & Holyoak, 1984), since a single rule can but rarely express the complex "family resemblances" (Rosch, 1978) among situation category members for which transfer is appropriate.

From another perspective, one case suggests the importance of the sociocultural relevance of the examples offered. Children's native cultural experiences were used as bridging activities in the successful school-based KEEP program of text comprehension instruction with Polynesian Hawaiians (Jordan, 1985).

In contrast, de Bono's (1985) CoRT program to teach thinking skills offers multiple examples. But they are all real-life situations such as planning for holidays or choosing a career, and one considers unlikely the spontaneous transfer of such thinking skills to school topics such as mathematics or language arts. Glaser's (1984; also see Frederiksen, 1984) recommendations that higher-order thinking skills be taught primarily within subject-matter domains appears overly restrictive in the reverse direction.

Until more instructionally-relevant research is available on the issue, it seems reasonable to suggest that a representatively broad range of contexts for transfer, deemed culturally-appropriate, including in-school and out-of-school problem situations, should provide the examples used for instruction. Contrast cases of transfer considered inappropriate should also aid in student's category formation and knowledge representation. It is presently ill understood whether explicitly stating principles or rules or definitions in addition to such positive or negative examples is helpful, or sufficient without examples. The transfer payoff of such explicitness has been shown to vary with subject matter and subjects' prior knowledge (Gick & Holyoak, in press).

Feuerstein, Rand, Hoffman, and Miller (1980) train for transfer of concepts or skills in their precollege thinking-skills program with "bridging." Bridging involves teaching a general principle and then helping students see how it works in multiple situations, e.g., in semantically rich science or social encounters.

Bransford, Stein, Arbitman-Smith, and Vye (1985) discuss how Feuerstein's program, principally used with children with learning difficulties, has students create their own examples and evaluate the adequacy of the examples others offer. These bridging activities have four rationales: (1) They prompt students to draw on their own experiences; (2) they restrict the potentially infinite range of application of principles of the students' life experiences; (3) students' generating examples serves to diagnose their understanding; and (4) instantiating the principle in a variety of contexts encourages transfer. Brown and Campione (1981) describe this approach as explicit instruction in the *range* of knowledge applicability. The assumption is that this instructional strategy will encourage access of transferable knowledge and skills in the future.

Bridging is only one small part of the transfer problem, however. Perhaps more difficult as an educational barrier to promoting transfer is the problem of radical translation between two different situation-perception systems: the child's — derived from everyday experiences — and those promoted by the specialized situations of the formal education of schooling. Establishing the appropriate mapping between the familiar and unfamiliar domains in metaphor comprehension is a challenging process.

Although such bridging activities appear promising as an instructional technique for promoting knowledge transfer, little is known about what may be the best ways (given particular purposes) to convey these bridging relations, for example, through knowledge network diagrams, or verbally (as in Feuerstein, 1980), or in terms of multimedia materials such as interactive videodisc (Bransford, Sherwood, & Hasselbring, 1985).

But conflicts exist between this approach and influential proposals of why schooling has powerful consequences for cognitive abilities as measured by experimental tasks. Bruner (1966) argued that it is the very removal of everyday life experiences from the formal learning situations of school that makes possible deeper learning for its own sake rather than as a subgoal of practical activity. Lave (1986) suggests that the accepted wisdom is that school must provide preparation for life in context-free terms; as it does, then cross-situational transfer will follow. The specific social organization of knowledge utilization should not, by this classic account, affect its meaning, value, or use. The enhancement of abstract symbolic representations taken to undergird the power of formal reasoning through schooling presumably depends on this detachment from the here and now.

Pettito (1985) suggests resolving this conflict by considering that schooling offers learning of rules and principles for *potential* transfer if appropriate links can be made to practical knowledge. In designing a future education to promote transfer, we will need to synthesize the *abstract* treatment of reasoning considered as the support for transfer of learning, and the *situational embedding* of concept learning in problem-solving activities taken from everyday life. Otherwise, students may not notice occasions for school-type reasoning outside school settings.

Cognitive Self-Management Skills

From cognitive research in the past decade, we have come to understand in a way we never did before the specific characteristics of thinking that define an independent, directed, effective learner and thinker. Cognitive studies of how experts regulate their mental processes when defining and solving problems, as well as instructional interventions designed to teach and coach general cognitive self-management skills, reveal that such skills do exist, can be taught, and are transferred to new materials and domains of study. Many difficulties that learners have are not due to lack of basic knowledge or to unavailability of relevant problem-solving strategies alone, but to "executive" problems with not managing their mental resources effectively. Recent studies show that learners need to acquire not only problem-solving strategies but self-management skills for autonomously guiding thinking and learning episodes.

Consider that when Belmont and Butterfield (1977) reviewed 114 studies on cognitive strategies instruction, none taught executive, self-management strategies and none achieved transfer of skills taught. Since that time, many investigations have directly taught self-management cognitive skills and found dramatic and maintainable transfer of learning effects (reviews by Belmont, Butterfield, & Ferretti, 1982; Brown et al., 1983). For example, Brown, Campione, and Barclay (1979) taught self-monitoring techniques for estimating test readiness and found learners transferred these new skills from word list learning to prose recall.

Our ultimate goal is for learners to become teacher-independent thinkers, learners, and problem solvers. To this end, students need to learn executive thinking skills, such as goal setting, strategic planning, checking for accurate plan execution, goal-progress monitoring, plan evaluation, and plan revision. Yet we know from classroom studies of reading (Beck & Carpenter, 1986), writing (Bereiter & Scardamalia, 1985), mathematics (Schoenfeld, 1985), and science instruction (Herron, 1971), that the fundamental *executive processes* for controlling thinking and learning processes are under the teacher's control, not the students. The contrast case is the effectiveness of the passing on of control processes in the informal education reflected in apprenticeship relations, as in weaving or tailoring (Greenfield & Lave, 1982).

Schools rarely embark on the necessary fading process in which students take over these executive roles for their own self-regulation. Many learners initially require and benefit from explicit support in managing and guiding the complexities of new cognitive activities. Any teaching that aims to foster complex thinking processes should therefore be developmentally responsive in the following sense; that the prompts or other structures it provides for fostering the development of thinking should fade as students manifest capacity to handle these processes autonomously (Collins & Brown, in press-b; Rogoff & Lave, 1984).

Integrate Subject Learning with Synergistic Design

Promising directions for promoting knowledge transfer in education so far considered have not dealt with the topic of interdisciplinary knowledge transfer. Yet many school reformers advocate linking the learning of different subject domains for greater knowledge transfer in contexts of application or acquisition. For example, Ohm's law as taught in introductory physics is rarely introduced as a simple proportional function from mathematics (Brown & Greeno, 1984). Bransford, Sherwood, and Hasselbring (1985) call such curriculum initiatives to overcome such unproductive isolations *synergistic design,* in which the whole is greater than the sum of the parts. The goal is to make interlinked learning offer greater yield of understanding than the study of disaggregated subjects.

As a superintendent of schools during the 1870s in Chicago, Francis W. Parker eliminated the prevalent rote teaching methods in favor of an emphasis on having children observe, describe, and understand curriculum topics by building on their everyday experiences. Because of these emphases, John Dewey considered Parker "the father of progressive education" (Cremin, 1961, p. 129). Parker's program was an astounding success as reading, writing, spelling, and arithmetic performance soared. Parker (1901–1902) also developed innovative approaches to interrelating curriculum subjects to make their significance more obvious to the child. Many of his techniques are familiar today, including children's creation of their own stories for reading and writing, the combination of studies of grammar, penmanship, reading, and spelling in the motivating contexts of conversation and writing, and the interweaving of science studies with art, mathematics, and writing in the service of understanding nature through fieldwork and laboratory studies. Dewey's famed Laboratory School took a similar approach, starting with the familiar and continuing to enlarge its meanings with the bounties of artistic, literate, scientific, and workplace cultural experiences.

These historical notes are significant because these special efforts were by all accounts highly successful at engaging children's interests and their transfer of learning across curriculum boundaries and beyond school walls. From the problems of unrelated learning in the different curriculum subjects discussed in recent commission and research reports, a revisitation of methods for linking the knowledge attained in the study of different subjects within school would be worthwhile. Although it is tragic that the problem of cross-curriculum segregation has not changed much in 110 years, we have much more sophisticated understanding than Parker or Dewey did of the component tasks, knowledge structures, and reasoning strategies that could in principle contribute to more integrated subject-domain instruction. And information technologies can be used, as we note later, as integrated problem-solving tools requiring the use of knowledge and skills across curriculum areas.

Creating Cultures of Transfer Thinking

Bridging instruction, teaching that conveys knowledge and skills in functional contexts, the provision of multiple examples of knowledge transfer, synergistic curriculum design—all these activities could contribute to the creation of an educational culture that encourages transfer-enhancing learning and thinking processes. Unfortunately, the *culture* notion is elusive. It is perhaps more comprehensible when used as a descriptive term by anthropologists or ethnographers than as a prescriptive term by educators, psychologists, and technologists. Yet it seems essential to try to understand how to build such communities or cultures, particularly because we have seen how, descriptively, cultural practices seem to be the guiding forces in a student's "reading" of a problem situation as one for which transfer of previous knowledge is possible, or important, or worth the effort.

It is highly significant that when the American Association for the Advancement of Science (1984; also see Cole, 1987) looked at several hundred precollege programs for teaching mathematics and science in which minorities and women performed as successfully as white males, they found the programs shared a number of features. The statistical picture reveals that successful programs were those in which there was vertical and horizontal integration of the school educational setting with community learning. Vertically, there was continuity across the grade levels up through college in the quality and commitment of offerings and educational practices involving these groups. Horizontally, there was parental, industry and workplace, and community involvement that was invested in having the students' mathematics and science learning work. In essence, these successful programs had been able to define a culture that said to students that transfer of learning has real consequences.

Research is needed on how to create such thinking cultures, which I take to be closely related to the goal of creating cultures for selective knowledge transfer. Resnick (1987) has summarized tacit assumptions for characteristics of such environments for learning to think independently: (a) self-directed classrooms (on what to work on; activity scheduling); (b) discussion rather than lecture–recitation classes; (c) small cooperative group emphasis.

Social interactions in which thinking processes are made explicit, or modeled, seem to provide important fostering conditions for learning to think well and transfer what one knows to new problem contexts within a broad domain such as reading, writing, or mathematics (Collins & Brown, in press-b; Palincsar & Brown, 1984; Scardamalia, Bereiter, & Steinbach, 1984; Schoenfeld, 1985). They appear to enhance the "disposition" to think (Resnick, 1987). The use of such techniques in education is said to create opportunities for *Cognitive Apprenticeships* (Collins & Brown, in press-b). It is still unclear what the locuses of such effects are, but in part they may provide a culture for thinking in which such activities come to be seen as valued contributions (Schoenfeld, 1987).

Observation of modeling alone is insufficient. Students need to try out such thinking themselves and subject their own thinking processes to community reaction and supportive critique. In participating in this social "zone of proximal development" (Vygotsky, 1978), a child may better envision the new capabilities he or she would have if only the knowledge the other person had contributed were acquired. These think-aloud activities may also positively alter children's self-concepts, their beliefs in whether their intelligence can be developed or is a fixed entity, and their feelings about anxiety, failure, and other potentially disabling emotional blocks to either the knowledge acquisition or application sides of transfer of learning. Similar methods have been promoted by Papert (1980).

Teachers will also need to learn to understand how to promote a culture for transfer in their classrooms by teaching knowledge in use, concepts as tools for understanding, and transfer of thinking skills as an activity central to the social contract of active learning.

Such changes to classroom interactions may be threatening to authority structures. For in an education that takes conveying functional knowledge in multiple contexts seriously, and which tries to build on prior experiences the child brings to the classroom from the thought and actions of everyday life, the locus of authority in the classroom will have shifted. The primary discourse of the classroom would need to shift from the familiar "Do you know X?" frame (Mehan, 1979), a continual regurgitative role for knowledge with the teacher in authority role, to one in which he or she plays a functional role, instead stressing "Do you know X to do Y?" or "What can you do with X to arrive at Y?" or even "What can you make of X?" Uncertainties will arise, which, although epistemologically appropriate (e.g., Hawkins & Pea, 1987), fundamentally change the traditional nature of the teacher's role as all-knowing "Oz" to one of collaborative colleague.

Regular working collaborations between the research community and educators and input to the research agenda on knowledge transfer from teachers will be essential aids to this transformative process. In particular, we will need better methods for helping teachers learn how to diagnose knowledge that students already have from everyday experience, for learning how expert teachers already do this well and how they developed such capabilities, and to refocus and build on such prior conceptions for the purposes of thinking toward which education will be directed.

Roles for Technologies in Promoting
Selective Transfer

It is worthwhile asking about possible schemes for using technology to foster appropriate transfer of knowledge in education. Apart from providing new opportunities for process-oriented intervention research on knowledge transfer, as many authors have noted (e.g., Brown & Greeno, 1984), the novelty of computers makes change in the curriculum and in learning/teaching strategies more viable.

There are several directions that appear particularly promising, given what has been said thus far. The general aim is to create tools that enhance the chances that students adopt a self-aware transfer state of mind, and that they be provided with the transfer-relevant access skills and heuristic strategies, and a sufficiently rich taxonomy of problem types for each domain of study to make the application of such search heuristics worthwhile. All the measures I suggest involve the *interpretive* activities of a normative group for a culture (.e.g, teachers, community), whose "situation readings" suggest what transfers are appropriate or not. Such "interpreters" can provide opportunities for students' specific thinking activities to be appropriated into the multiple conceptual frameworks of formal education.

We can also dramatically change the cognitive economics of transfer activities by making the knowledge-application process easier to enact (a common strategy in the design of computer-based cognitive technologies; Bloomberg, 1986). Problem-solving tools could guide the application of prior knowledge, such as equation-solving methods in algebra or composition-planning techniques in writing.

Tools for Building, Linking,
and Revising Belief Representations

One approach is to build tools that make it feasible for students to represent the substantive details and connections between in-school and out-of-school thinking experiences, link their within-school experiences across curriculum domains, and revise these structures as aids to belief revision when experience calls for such revisions. In the future, students will be able to construct labeled graphic representations of their beliefs (e.g., as concept network maps; Novak & Gowen, 1984)—but on an electronic whiteboard that would be used to make transfer possibilties to a current problem situation open for discussion or teleconferencing by teachers and other students. Such representations would be available for the student's use in future problem solving, in a sense as a software placeholder of one's conceptual understanding to be built on, and within which new knowledge would need to be integrated. I predict that the experience of explicitly articulating one's knowledge would render the organization of this knowledge more amenable to retrieval for transfer because it has been given greater structure (e.g., categorical, causal, temporal).

Inquire is a software environment with goals like these under development at the Bank Street College of Education. It will serve as a cognitive technology for structuring and supporting the component activities of whole-task inquiry science by middle school students. Inquiry science includes question and sub-question formulation and cycles of question development, planning of inquiry actions, belief articulation and revision, linking and categorizing notes taken from observational, experimental, and textual research, belief integration in graphical schemes, and the interpretive activities of argument–evidence analysis and scrutiny of quantitative data (Hawkins & Pea, 1987; Hawkins et al., 1987). Annotation facilities of the software will help establish a community of scientific communication and exchange in the classroom, among students and teacher.

Along a more futuristic orientation, and sheerly speculative at the present state of empirical and technical development, would be tools to support "belief revision," building on current research in artificial intelligence on "truth maintenance systems" (e.g., de Kleer, 1986; Doyle, 1984) and "belief maintenance systems" (Falkenhainer, 1987). Some preliminary exposition is required to explain why computer-aided belief revision might be worthwhile to pursue.

Problems of conceptual change are central in cognition, both in the hard sciences and in reasoning toward resolution of so-called "ill-defined" problems of political decision making or design. The major insight of cognitive science research in science learning in the past decade has been that formal science education builds on (or, in the worst case, is acquired in isolation of) a configuration of beliefs about how the world works that is constructed from everyday experience.

Such everyday experience includes not only spontaneous interactions with objects, environments, and persons but socially arranged encounters with informal teaching, memories of explanations offered when questions are asked, and others thinking aloud as they engage in problem solving. These are the resources for the human induction machine of belief formulation.

It is particularly clear that formal science education has paid insufficient attention to students' prior beliefs. Far from being tabula rasas, students come to school with intricate belief systems, often perplexing to the instructor and difficult to ascertain (Osborne & Freyberg, 1985). But the situation is made more difficult because much of science education has bypassed this diagnosis problem altogether, assuming that a well-told story from a curriculum perspective, paying close attention to conceptual prerequisites, and so forth will make for an effective science education. We now know otherwise. Instructional activities should make students' beliefs primary instructional substance. And to serve as primary instructional substance, such beliefs must first be "found." Having been found, learning and teaching activities can then serve — as does discourse in everyday life—to remediate these conceptual schemes through conversational "repair," so that they can function more adequately for the new purposes of formal inquiry for which scientific reasoning is designed.

What to do about this pedagogical situation is a matter of substantial controversy and empirical investigation. First, how to describe the students' belief states? Positive characterizations are possible of why students have the beliefs they do, because these beliefs may serve them well in the "ecological niche" of problems they have been applying these concepts to, and in the imprecise explanatory accounts they have been required to give of events naturally encountered (Hawkins & Pea, 1987). Such emphases are certainly more pedagogically productive than construals of students as beset with "misconceptions," "faulty theories," etc. So in some important sense, students are "rational agents" in the predictions they make and in the explanations they offer for what happens. Such beliefs are often characterizable as "knowledge in pieces" (diSessa, this volume), not integrated, isolated in "packets" by event types, and easily leading to inconsistent prediction patterns if events for which explanations are required are carefully arranged by the experimenter or teacher in soliciting the student's beliefs.

Some researchers believe cognitive conflicts should be induced by "leading" students to see contradictions that their beliefs produce (e.g., Stavy & Berkovitz, 1980). Some researchers believe that promoting such cognitive "disequilibria" through peer problem solving and debate concerning competing accounts of phenomena is a promising method. Yet others consider that students, like scientists historically (as Kuhn, Feyerabend, and Lakatos show), will only let go of their beliefs and move toward conceptual integration or conceptual change, if a new system of beliefs is offered that works for the problems at hand. The comparative values of such a new belief system may need to be shown "competitively" by way of demonstration.

What all these schemes have in common is that conceptual change is characterized by belief revision. The beliefs an individual has are causally used to provide warrants and evidence for arguments an individual offers for *why* things happen as they do, or *will* (by prediction) happen in such and such a way. Such beliefs are brought forward as parts of explanatory accounts, as premises from which conclusions follow by patterns of reasoning (Toulmin, 1958).

But what does it mean to "revise a belief?" One may modify the conditions in which a belief is considered applicable, one may relate that belief in a new way to another belief or to an outcome, one may redefine the objects of the belief (ontology), and so on. But the important fact about belief revision for the educational technology envisioned is that beliefs have dependency relations. For example, one's beliefs about the predictive power of horoscopes depend on other beliefs about the causal influences of patterns of stars and planets and other celestial bodies at the time of one's birth on patterns of activity during a lifetime. Evidence that forces a revision in the basic belief in such causal efficacy should also lead to revisions of beliefs that depend on that belief. That is, belief revisions often propagate through dependency chains (de Kleer, 1986; Falkenhainer, 1987).

Whereas it is clear that belief revision is central to conceptual change, and that belief revision should often have global and not only local reorganizational effects on beliefs when evidence so dictates, research on science learning has yet to take a systematic look at the empirical specificities of belief revision, and the nature of constraints on belief revision propagations. This is not surprising. Such analyses are more common and even then have arisen only recently in the field of reasoning by artificially intelligent systems. For in constructing such systems, one *has* to be specific. It has primarily been through major contributions to our understanding of the nature of qualitative reasoning in physics that the critical nature of belief dependencies and assumptions has been recognized. Related work on nonmonotonic logic and formal theories of commonsense reasoning provides the logical foundations to these studies. These logics are used to judge cases of reasoning that involve assumptions that may have to be abandoned when new information is made available (Doyle, 1983).

Expert systems that reason to come to conclusions (e.g., about diagnoses of faults in electrical circuits, as would engineers) move through inferential steps based on evidence available to them. How does reasoning effectively about the behavior of the physical world (and devices within it) arise? A major problem-solving technique in AI, embedded in such commonsense reasoning systems, is called *dependency-directed backtracking* (de Kleer, 1986). It aims to evade contradictions in beliefs and is invoked as a process when a discovery is made of a currently inconsistent belief state. This method then changes belief states to eliminate the contradiction, by consulting dependencies (inferences performed in the reasoning history) and records of previous dependencies that the method constructed to deal with previous contradictions.

Consider what might happen if versions of such tools were available for students to use in monitoring belief dependencies and to prompt engagement in belief revision activities. One can imagine students running experiments they have designed to test conjectures they have made, and crafting these in such a way to test a specific foundational belief they have made explicit in a belief representation system. Whereas the learning environment designer would be likely to meet with significant difficulties in creating interactive procedures for soliciting students' beliefs, and in graphically representing belief dependency structures for ready comprehension, research could focus on elaborating and testing interface designs so that students could understand and use such techniques.

Modeling of Multiple Bridging Activities in Thinking

Another use of computer technologies of interest involves making transfer processes *visible*. Successful examples of teaching transferable thinking skills by

Bereiter and Scardamalia (1986), Palincsar and Brown (1984);, and Schoenfeld (1985) all utilize methods for making transfer processes explicit (Collins & Brown, in press-b). For a given concept or cognitive skill, live modeling of its application to multiple cases could be recorded via optical disk storage for a selected range of problems or domains, and where one expects the students to make appropriate generalizations from the cases selected. The system would be highly interactive, enabling levels of help if a student had difficulties in carrying on with new knowledge transfer activities after observing modeling of multiple bridging involving that knowledge.

Reflective analysis of the details of one's own transfer performances as well as those of others should be possible, by replaying problem-solving episodes (Collins & Brown, in press-a). The modeling activities selected would ideally be based on task analyses of knowledge application to the problem situations of everyday life (Sternberg, 1986, offers some suggestions) and bridge these with the problem classes of formal education in mathematics, science, and literacy. The phrase "everday life" is a placeholder for the culturally defined norms of activities that constitute cultural practices.

Ethnographic studies are needed to contribute to a theory of situations, what Scribner and Cole (1981) call *cultural practices*, that help shape what people in a culture "read" as the tasks or problems facing them in a situation. How do these interpreted "common elements" of situations come to be understood or perceived? Are there critically different and intrinsic features of school and nonschool environments that will be important to take into account in designing such bridging activities? If we have answers to these questions, our selection of domains for multiple examples of knowledge application and of methods for introducing them could have more theoretical grounding. Because the everyday life settings found will be likely to vary across cultural groups, cross-cultural cognitive studies will be central to the design of instructional activities supported by the technologies.

The few available tutorial software programs explicitly designed to teach problem-solving strategies fall short when judged against these bridging standards. Examples include *Wumpus,* a fantasy game designed to teach skills in logic, probability, decision analysis, geometry, and *Rocky's Boots,* in which students can use compositions of Boolean logic gates of increasing complexity to build machines that come alive on the screen. In neither case are any links made to in-school topics or out-of-school reasoning situations. As one low-cost measure, such "transfer link" materials could be developed through local school system initiatives and enrich the effectiveness of existing problem-solving software, as Pogrow and Buchanan's (1985) work has demonstrated with compensatory programs for elementary school Chapter 1 students.

Some recent software has begun to address these bridging concerns, such as Sunburst's *Survival Math.* It requires mathematical reasoning to solve real-world problems, such as best-buy shopping, trip planning, and building construction. Efforts to meet these criteria were also taken in creating the Bank

Street *Voyage of the Mimi* materials for mathematics, science, and technology education. In this project (supported by the Department of Education, CBS, Sony, and NSF; broadcast on PBS), video, software, and print media weave a narrative tale of a boat odyssey for whale research taken by young scientists and their student aides. Science problems and uses for mathematics and computers emerge and are tackled cooperatively during the adventuresome activities of the group (Char, Hawkins, Wootten, Sheingold, & Roberts, 1983).

One of the programs from Mimi, *Rescue Mission,* simulates navigational instruments (such as radar, and a direction finder) used on the Mimi vessel, and the realistic problem event of navigating the boat. To effectively work together during this software game, students need to learn how to plan and keep records of emerging data, work on speed–time–distance problems, reason geometrically, and estimate distances. Although none of the software cited directly addresses instruction of generalizable thinking skills or models the processes of knowledge transfer across multiple appropriate examples, each case embodies some appropriate bridging conditions for knowledge transfer.

We are exploring the feasibility of a multiple bridging approach in a software research and development project at New York University called *IDEA* (Interactive Decision Envisioning Aid; Pea, Brunner, Cohen, Webster, & Mellen, 1987). Our goal is to help young adolescents learn elementary decision theory for critical application to school and everyday decision-making situations. In this design, familiar specific domains of decision making — family chore planning, consumer purchasing — are used to introduce generalizable aspects of systematic decision-making skills (such as defining the space of alternative choices, establishing evaluative criteria, utilizing analysis of attributes of alternatives). Multiple examples of applications of these and other general decision-making methods are available through the software, so that at any time the learner can explore or be guided to learn generally useful aspects of methods they are learning to apply in these introductory cases and other situations (such as selecting courses, a high school, or voting for U.S. President). We find that with use of *IDEA,* young adolescents spontaneously identify other decision problems (e.g., party planning, allocating study time, producing a movie) for which they expect such systematic decision methods might improve their decision outcomes. We are now studying whether aspects of such techniques that students can carry out without computer support are used appropriately in subsequent decision making.

Computer Tools and Synergistic Curriculum Design

It should be our high priority to provide a generation of interactive thinking tools for students that can be used across the curriculum. Cross-disciplinary integration of methods and knowledge is the hallmark of problem solving and problem definition in today's increasingly complex society and world (Hamburg, 1984). But education, particularly in high school, is a collection of disaggregated topics, without any strategy provided for forming appropriate relationships.

With new technologies, we have the opportunity to fit these topics into a context and to help students understand the nature of disciplinary interrelationships and open systems thinking. Even now, such business tools as idea outliners, word processors, data-base-management systems, electronic conferencing systems and bulletin boards, and multimedia electronic notebooks with integrated mathematics–science report-writing facilities are available.

But these systems are by and large agenetic, presupposing that users possess the various thinking skills and task understanding required for their flexible use. There should therefore be an emphasis in the next several decades on creating developmental cognitive technologies — that will have layers of functions associated with students' competencies that learners will shed like skins as they no longer need them (Pea & Kurland, 1987). They should also incorporate easily programmable options so that learners can mold their tools to serve their unique style of thinking and learning (as we are already beginning to see in the macrocapabilities of writing tools, in the "Calculator Construction Kit," and in games such as "Robot Odyssey"). These developmental technologies will also provide approximations to the kinds of task scaffoldings an expert teacher would offer a novice who is learning the system and its relevant tasks. Such support would fade as the student takes on more control of the system's use and displays proficient task performances (Collins & Brown, in press-b).

Cultural Information Transfer Systems

Today one can get to vast quantities of information in Claude Shannon's mathematical sense of the term, but not so easily to meaningful information given one's goals. It is an intriguing thought that it might be possible in decades to come to create information technologies that offer communal "transfer spaces," organized in networks according to topic and even to purpose.

This challenging concern stems from the recognition that future transfer theory should go beyond the level of the individual mind as the locus of study for the transfer of learning to the organization, community, society, and even world levels. The *social distribution of knowledge* and the potentials of interweaving the knowledge networks of communities and organizations with information utilities recommends hard work toward designing *organizational interfaces* for promoting solution of what might be called the *coordination problem* in large-scale knowledge transfer.

Could information technologies be developed to serve as an "information lens" (a concept developed by Malone, Grant, & Turbak, 1986, for the design of intelligent systems for information sharing in organizations) to focus the yields of others' transfer experiences onto the educational process? How might transfer of learning carried out successfully by others for important cases be used to advantage in an educational system? How should such experiences be stored and accessed? What would it be like to have vast electronic "cultural memories" that have organized for appropriate retrieval and application the prior experiences of individuals within it so that broad gains in transfer to new problems might be made?

Some part of the answer to these difficult questions must lie in classification of problem types, because vertical organization of problem classes is what seems to provide much of the power behind the expert problem-solver's ease in access transfer-appropriate knowledge.

Fortunately, there is research and development work underway on these important questions. Malone and colleagues (Malone, 1985; Malone et al., 1986) have described some of the theoretical and design problems in creating a prototype of an intelligent "organizational interface" for information sharing. Their *Information Lens* utilizes AI concepts such as production rules, inheritance networks, and variable frames but avoids the natural language-understanding problem by offering users a large set of semistructured message templates ("frames"). The initial aim of the *Lens* project is to provide a display-oriented editor system for people to use for filtering, sorting, and prioritizing messages addressed to them, avoiding junk and getting the good stuff. *Lens* has a large number of message-type frames used for composing and sorting messages, and of receivers' interests. Sets of production rules (condition-action pairs) serve as automatic message filters. Defining and using messages and selection-rule types is simplified by their organization in a frame inheritance lattice. In such a lattice network (Fikes & Kehler, 1985), template subtypes inherit field names and property values (such as lists of alternatives, defaults, explanations), and subtypes may have unique fields or different property values. Just as in the case of concepts and words (Miller & Johnson-Laird, 1976), the redundancy of message hierarchies can be exploited economically by inheritance networks to save the effort of entering slightly dissimilar message types anew. (It would seem that a related system of this type might have broad applicability for teacher networking, lesson and activity planning, and other learning-oriented work, such as sharing success and failure stories for techniques that work for particular curricular topics.)

The *Lens* Project and related research and development projects for structured information sharing across electronic communities (e.g., Hiltz & Turoff, 1985; Trigg, 1983) seem to offer promising techniques for the more ambitious kind of information-sharing system proposed here: A Cultural Information Transfer System, the aim of which would be to collect, organize, and disseminate transfer-relevant information and knowledge in forms readily entered and used by individuals. How such a system might be adapted for use in education is too complex a question for analysis here.

Such a Cultural Information Transfer System might even preserve a person's or organization's traces of problem-solving process at an abstract level of analysis, including such details as problem definitions and considered, attempted, and successful mappings of prior knowledge to their current problem situation. These possibilities presume, realistically, that substantial parts of the problem solving will have taken place with computer tools (e.g., financial planning, writing, decision analysis). Wherever an individual has made a mapping between prior knowledge and what they consider to be a new problem, they could register this mapping in the system. Keyword and concept-level "transfer" entry and browsing capabilities would be available for a user's documentation of transfer traces or for directed search through the cultural knowledge traces of knowledge-function relations discovered by others through prior transfer experience and recorded on the system. Individuals could do opportunistic browsing in hopes of being reminded of transfer-relevant knowledge one has, or that one could learn about on the system.

Although considerably speculative in conception, the goal of such a system would be to provide at least an approximate medium of *functional knowledge description and exchange* for aggregating knowledge transfer experience across individuals. Individuals within a culture may have different readings of a problem situation, and the knowledge they each consider as appropriate for transfer application may be different. But at least they share a common language for negotiating the situation's meaning that can then be used to share and critically examine the similarities and differences of their perspectives.

Indeed, it has been suggested that it is *language,* and in particular, descriptions of a task situation across occasions in similar terms, that provides the coding device for capturing a culture's theory of what goes with what—which is then used as a universal resource for organizing an individual's knowledge transfer (Laboratory of Comparative Human Cognition, 1983, p. 341). If this is true, then lexically based information-management systems for aggregating the transfer experiences of a culture, utilizing AI techniques such as those exploited by Malone's *Lens* Project, should ultimately allow for the expansion of the symbolic environments an individual experiences and make more effective knowledge transfer possible.

Conclusions

The analyses of the chapter result in situating knowledge transfer as an *interpretive problem.* We have seen that transfer is not so susceptible to an analysis that reifies "common elements" in problem-solving situations. What observations have led to this conclusion?

The first observation was that transfer is *selective.* "Appropriate transfer" is socioculturally defined for particular purposes, tasks, and thinking situations. When transfer involves more than straightforward knowledge access and application, complex personal issues arise of *cognitive economics* (predicting whether knowlege transfer will be worthwhile or not), *analogical mapping* between prior and present situations, and *transfer monitoring* (evaluations of knowledge transfer effectiveness). These judgments are all rooted in cultural practices and value systems.

The second conclusion is that the "elements" perceived by the thinker as common between a past and present situation—on which knowledge transfer appears to depend because of processes of reminding—are not given in the nature of things. They are "read" as texts, with multiple possible interpretations, according to the thinker's culturally influenced categorization system of problem types. Knowledge transfer thus requires *situation analysis,* a determination of the ways in which prior knowledge bears on the situation because the problem reminds the thinker of previous problem cases or types. There are thus likely to be significant developmental, individual, and cultural differences in the *situation perception* on which knowledge transfer depends. These issues have been insufficiently examined in research, and we should place serious attention on them well before 2020.

The implication is that education could positively influence the likelihood of transfer by addressing these problems directly in its practices, and in the technologies it employs. It might do so by making everyday situations and school situations part of the same classification scheme for problem types, by making explicit the links the student is now expected to draw spontaneously, and by checking to see whether appropriate transfers are made. Such a transfer-promoting categorization method could be implemented for many different curriculum topics.

This is not to say such activities will be easy. Extending the sociocultural approach would involve two major steps: Making explicit (in a symbolic representational system such as a semantic network) a student's situational elements for the targeted task setting, and pedagogical activities to help the student transform their belief-structure so that it corresponds with the conceptual scheme promoted by formal education. More instructional attention should go into defining common perceived elements across the spectrum of problems for which transfer of knowledge such as concepts, procedures, or higher order thinking skills is desired. One could then perhaps teach ways of analyzing situations in school with out-of-school ideas and out-of-school with in-school ideas. This bridging should be considered legitimate, even necessary, classroom activity.

The third set of conclusions involves a series of recommendations with the aim of enhancing conditions for knowledge transfer in education. These directions emerge from a critical synthesis of research findings on teaching thinking skills through content. These conditions include learning about and practicing knowledge application in multiple contexts of use, creating bridging instruction across school and nonschool problem situations, fostering thinking and self-management skills taught within domains, and synergistic integrations of the learning of different subjects. I then pointed to the higher order goal of creating cultures of transfer thinking incorporating these measures and conjectured the likely connection of affective and motivational variables in such an endeavor.

Finally, I sketched what these analyses suggest as promising directions for new techologies that might more directly enhance knowledge transfer than what we see today. Examples included tools for students to use for building, linking, and revising "belief representations" of prior experience in terms of new beliefs acquired through school activities, and interactive systems to help students acquire and practice the application of thinking skills across multiple domains by "live" modeling of multiple bridging activities of new knowledge application. The speculative concept of creating a Cultural Information Transfer System — linking problem descriptions to problem-solving process histories of many individuals and even organizations so that transfer experiences might be broadly shared — deserves closer attention and may be made more feasible by AI techniques.

The prospect of dreaming about education in the year 2020 is a daunting one. We have little reason to believe our visions can begin to touch the possible worlds that may be. Only 30 years ago, behaviorist learning theory reigned, mentalistic terms such as *believe* and *know* were considered taboo in a science of learning, and the filmstrip was the hottest new technology for education. Today we see prototypes of supercomputers with a thousand computers working in parallel, 5-inch optical disks that can store 150,000 pages of text or a full-hour of full-motion video, fiber optics data transmission ready for home installations and for "personal" magazines filtered by interest from newswire and publication services, and personalizable writing and "desktop publishing" systems that can include automatic spelling and syntax checkers, an on-line thesaurus, spreadsheets, graphs, relational data bases, and digitally scanned photographic images. There is a child's doll on the market now that comes with motion, light, and temperature sensors, and which has limited key-word speech recognition ability, all of which are used to cue "appropriate" synthetic speech production; available 64K "insert" cards give her different lexical capabilities.

Given such dramatic changes and the even more rapid trends at work today, particularly in consumer electronics (Pea, 1987), what should we imagine may be available for transfer technologies 30 years from now? In some respects, I suspect it is easy to err in a conservative direction, taking too many present conditions for granted, such as a predominantly school-based education and a predominantly text-based literacy. Cohen (this volume) suggests schools will still be with us. There are some reasons to believe a text-based literacy may not be as dominant as today, as computer screen-based multimedia literacy enters popular consciousness (Pea, 1987).

But what I have sketched seem to me to offer sound orientations for research directions, and for redesigning educational environments — if we desire a more direct approach to enhancing learning for appropriate transfer in classrooms somewhat like those we see today. The actual embodiments of these ideas will surely be influenced, not only by the winds of technological and scientific innovation in the next several decades, but by the willingness of the complex social structures of educational and research institutions to tackle these intricate problems. We can be sure of one thing: Whatever the specifics may be, it will be a truly exciting period for "putting knowledge to use."

ACKNOWLEDGMENTS

I would like to thank the Spencer Foundation for current support of our work on learning generalizable thinking skills with interactive technologies. Portions of this chapter will appear in "Socializing the knowledge transfer problem," *International Journal of Educational Research*, Fall 1987. The U.S. Department of Education, National Institute of Education, IBM Corporation, National Science Foundation, and the Xerox Foundation have also supported earlier research whose results contributed to the perspective outlined here. The views expressed here do not necessarily reflect the policies of any of these institutions.

REFERENCES

American Association for Advancement of Science (1984). *An assessment of programs that facilitate increased access and achievement of females and minorities in K–12 mathematics and science education*. AAAS 84–14. Washington, DC: AAAS.

Beck, I.L., & Carpenter, P.A. (1986). Cognitive approaches to understanding reading. *American Psychologist, 41*, 1098–1105.

Belmont, J.M., & Butterfield, E.C. (1977). The instructional approach to developmental cognitive research. In R. Kail & J. Hagen (Eds.), *Perspectives on the development of memory and cognition* (pp. 437–481). Hillsdale, NJ: Lawrence Erlbaum Associates.

Belmont, J.M., Butterfield, E.C., & Ferretti, R.P. (1982). To secure transfer of training instruct self-management skills. In D.K. Detterman & R.J. Sternberg (Eds.), *How and how much can intelligence be increased* (pp. 147–154). Norwood, NJ: Ablex.

Bereiter, C., & Scardamalia, M. (1985). Cognitive coping strategies and the problem of "inert" knowledge. In S. Chipman, J.W. Segal, & R. Glaser (Eds.), *Thinking and learning skills: Current research and open questions* (Vol. 2, pp. 65–80). Hillsdale, NJ: Lawrence Erlbaum Associates.

Bereiter, C., & Scardamalia, M. (1986). *The psychology of written composition*. Hillsdale, NJ: Lawrence Erlbaum Associates.

Bloomberg, D. (Ed.). (1986, May). *Digests of recent research: Intelligent Systems Laboratory: Mid 1983–Mid 1986*. Palo Alto, CA: Xerox Palo Alto Research Centers.

Bransford, J.D., & Franks, J.J. (1976). Toward a framework for understanding learning. In G. Bower (Ed.), *The psychology of learning and motivation: Advances in research and theory* (Vol. 10, pp. 93–127). New York: Academic Press.

Bransford, J.D., Sherwood, R.D., & Hasselbring, T.S. (1985, November). *Computers, videodiscs, and the teaching of thinking*. Paper presented at the Computers and Complex Thinking Conference, National Academy of Sciences, Washington, DC.

Bransford, J.D., Stein, B.S., Arbitman-Smith, R., & Vye, N.J. (1985). Three approaches to improving thinking and learning skills. In J.W. Segal, S.F. Chipman, & R. Glaser (Eds.), *Think-

ing and learning skills: Relating instruction to basic research (Vol. 1, pp. 133–200). Hillsdale, NJ: Lawrence Erlbaum Associates.

Brown, A.L. (1978). Knowing when, where, and how to remember: A problem in metacognition. In R. Glaser (Ed.), *Advances in instructional psychology* (Vol. 1, pp. 77–165). Hillsdale, NJ: Lawrence Erlbaum Associates.

Brown, A.L., Bransford, J.D., Ferrara, R.A., & Campione, J.C. (1983). Learning, remembering, and understanding. In J.H. Flavell & E.M. Markman (Eds.), *Handbook of child psychology: Vol. 3 Cognitive development* (4th ed., pp. 77–166). New York: Wiley.

Brown, A.L., & Campione, J.C. (1981). Inducing flexible thinking: A problem of access. In M. Friedman, J.P. Das, & N. O'Connor (Eds.), *Intelligence and learning* (pp. 515–530). New York: Plenum Press.

Brown, A.L., Campione, J.C., & Barclay, C.R. (1979). Training self-checking routines for estimating test readiness: Generalization from list learning learning to prose recall. *Child Development, 50,* 501–512.

Brown, J.S., & Greeno, J. (1984). Report of the research briefing panel on information technology in precollege education. In *New pathways in science and technology: Collected research briefings 1982–1984* (pp. 298–317). New York: Vintage.

Bruner, J.S. (1966). On cognitive growth II. In J.S. Bruner, R.R. Olver, & P.M. Greenfield (Eds.), *Studies in cognitive growth* (pp. 30–67). New York: Wiley.

Bruner, J.S. (1983). *Child's talk: Learning to use language.* New York: Norton.

Brunstein, J.C., & Olbrich, E. (1985). Personal helplessness and action control: Analysis of achievement-related cognitions, self-assessments, and performance. *Journal of Personality and Social Psychology, 48,* 1540–1551.

Capon, N., & Kuhn, D. (1979). Logical reasoning in the supermarket: Adult females' use of a proportional reasoning strategy in an everyday context. *Developmental Psychology, 15,* 450–452.

Carbonell, J.G. (1983). Learning by analogy: Formulating and generalizing plans from past experience. In R.S. Michalski, J.G. Carbonell, & T.M. Mitchell (Eds.), *Machine learning* (pp. 137–161). Palo Alto, CA: Tioga Press.

Carbonell, J.G., & Minton, S. (1983). *Metaphor and common-sense reasoning.* Carnegie–Mellon University, Department of Computer Science. Tech. Rep. CMU-CS-83-110.

Carey, S. (1986). Cognitive science and science education. *American Psychologist, 41,* 1123–1130.

Carraher, T.N., Carraher, D.W., & Schliemann, A.D. (1985). Mathematics in the streets and in schools. *British Journal of Developmental Psychology, 3,* 21–29.

Carver, S.M. (1986). *Logo debugging skills: Analysis instruction and assessment.* Unpublished doctoral dissertation, Department of Psychology, Carnegie–Mellon University.

Case, R. (1985). *Intellectual development: Birth to adulthood.* New York: Academic Press.

Char, C., Hawkins, J., Wootten, J., Sheingold, K., & Roberts, T. (1983). *"Voyage of the Mimi": Classroom case studies of software, video, and print materials.* New York: Bank Street College of Education, Center for Children and Technology.

Cheng, P.W., Holyoak, K.J., Nisbett, R.E., & Oliver, L.M. (1986). Pragmatic versus syntactic approaches to training deductive reasoning. *Cognitive Psycology, 18,* 293–328.

Chipman, S.F., Segal, J.W., & Glaser, R. (Eds.). (1985), *Thinking and learning skills: Current research and open questions* (Vol. 2). Hillsdale, NJ: Lawrence Erlbaum Associates.

Clement, J. (1986, July). *Misconceptions in mechanics and an attempt to remediate them.* Bank Street College Working Conference on Physics Learning.

Cole, M. (1987). *Non-cognitive factors in education: Subcommittee report.* National Research Council Commission on Behavioral and Social Sciences and Education. Washington, DC: NRC.

Collins, A., & Brown, J.S. (in press, a). The computer as a tool for learning through reflection. In H. Mandl & A. Lesgold (Eds.), *Learning issues for intelligent tutoring systems.* New York: Springer.

Collins, A., & Brown, J.S. (in press, b). The new apprenticeship: Teaching students the craft of reading, writing, and mathematics. In L.B. Resnick (Ed.), *Cognition and instruction; Issues and agenda.* Hillsdale, NJ: Lawrence Erlbaum Associates.

Cremin, L.A. (1961). *The transformation of the school: Progressivism in American education, 1876–1957.* New York: Vintage.

Dansereau, D.F. (1985). Learning strategy research. In J. Segal, S. Chipman, & R. Glaser (Eds.), *Thinking and learning skills: Relating instruction to basic research* (Vol. 1, pp. 209–239), Hillsdale, NJ: Lawrence Erlbaum Associates.

de Bono, E. (1985). The CoRT thinking program. In J. Segal, S. Chipman, & R. Glaser (Eds.), *Thinking and learning skills: Relating instruction to basic research* (Vol. 1, pp. 363–388). Hillsdale, NJ: Lawrence Erlbaum Associates.

de Kleer, J. (1986). Dependency directed backtracking. *Encyclopedia of artificial intelligence.* New York: Wiley.

Dewey, J. (1902). *The child and the curriculum.* Chicago: University of Chicago Press.

Dewey, J. (1922). *Human nature and conduct.* New York: Henry Holt.

Dewey, J. (1938). *Experience and education.* New York: Macmillan.

Diener, C. & Dweck, C. (1978). An analysis of learned helplessness: Continuous changes in performance, strategy, and achievement cognitions following failure. *Journal of Personality and Social Psychology, 36,* 451–462.

Dilthey, W. (1833/1976). The construction of the historical world in the human studies. In H.P. Rickman (Ed. & Trans.), *W. Dilthey, Selected writings* (pp. 168–245). New York: Cambridge University Press (Originally published, 1833).

diSessa, A.A. (1983). Phenomenology and the evolution of intuition. In D. Gentner & A. Stevens (Eds.), *Mental models* (pp. 15–33). Hillsdale, NJ: Lawrence Erlbaum Associates.

Donaldson, M. (1978). *Children's minds.* New York: Norton.

Doyle, J. (1983). Nonmonotonic logics. In *Handbook of artificial intelligence* (Vol. 3, pp. 114–119). Palo Alto, CA: Kaufmann.

Dreyfus, H.L., & Dreyfus, S.E. (1986). *Mind over machine.* New York: Free Press.

Driver, R., Guesne, E., & Tiberghien, A. (1985). (Eds.). *Children's ideas in science.* Philadelphia: Open University Press.

Dweck, C.S., & Elliot, E.S. (1983). Achievement motivation. In P.H. Mussen (Ed.), *Handbook of child psychology* (Vol. 4, pp. 643–692). New York: Wiley.

Elio, R., & Anderson, J.R. (1984). The effects of information order and learning mode on schema abstraction. *Memory and Cognition, 12,* 20–30.

Ellis, H.C. (1965). *The transfer of learning.* New York: Macmillan.

Evans-Pritchard, E. (1934). Levy-Bruhl's theory of primitive mentality. *Bulletin of the Faculty of the Arts* (Egyptian University), *2,* 1–36.

Falkenhainer, B. (1987, April). *Toward a general-purpose belief maintenance system* (Rep. No. UIUCDCS-R-87-1329). Department of Computer Science, University of Illinois at Urbana-Champaign.

Ferguson, G.A. (1956). On transfer and the abilities of man. *Canadian Journal of Psychology, 10,* 121–131.

Feuerstein, R., Rand, Y., Hoffman, M.B., & Miller, R. (1980). *Instrumental enrichment.* Baltimore: University Park Press.

Fikes, R., & Kehler, T. (1985). The role of frame-based representations in reasoning. *Communications of the ACM, 28,* 904.

Frederiksen, N. (1984). Implications of cognitive theory for instruction in problem solving. *Review of Educational Research, 54,* 363–408.

Fried, L.S., & Holyoak, K.J. (1984). Induction of category distributions: A framework for classification learning. *Journal of Experimental Psychology: Learning, Memory, and Cognition, 10,* 234–257.

Gagne, R.M. (1968). Contributions of learning to human development. *Psychological Review, 75,* 177–191.

Gagne, R.M. (1985). *The conditions of learning and theory of instruction* (4th ed.). New York: Holt, Rinehart, & Winston.

Gagne, R.M., Foster, H., & Crowley, M.E. (1948). The measurement of transfer of training. *Psychological Bulletin, 45,* 97–130.

Gay, J., & Cole, M. (1967). *The new mathematics and an old culture.* New York: Holt, Rinehart, & Winston.

Gelman, R. (1978). Cognitive development. *Annual Review of Psychology, 29,* 297–332.

Gelman, R., & Brown, A.L. (1986). Changing views of cognitive competence in the young. In N.J. Smelser & D.R. Gerstein (Eds.), *Behavioral and social science: Fifty years of discovery* (pp. 175–207). Washington, DC: National Academy Press.

Gentner, D. (1983). Structure-mapping: A theoretical framework for analogy. *Cognitive Science, 7,* 155–170.

Gentner, D., & Gentner, D.R. (1983). Flowing waters or teeming crowds: Mental models of electricity. In D. Gentner & A. Stevens (Eds.), *Mental models* (pp. 99–129). Hillsdale, NJ: Lawrence Erlbaum Associates.

Gick, M.L., & Holyoak, K.J. (1980). Analogical problem solving. *Cognitive Psychology, 12,* 306–365.

Gick, M.L., & Holyoak, K.J. (1983). Schema induction and analogical transfer. *Cognitive Psychology, 15,* 1–38.

Gick, M.L., & Holyoak, K.J. (in press). The cognitive basis of knowledge transfer. In S.M. Cormier & J.D. Hagman (Eds.), *Transfer of learning: Contemporary research and applications.* Orlando, FL: Academic Press.

Glaser, R. (1984). Education and thinking: The role of knowledge. *American Psychologist, 39,* 93–104.

Greenfield, P.M., & Lave, J. (1982). Cognitive aspects of informal education. In D. Wagner & H. Stevenson (Eds.), *Cultural perspectives on child development* (pp. 181–207). San Francisco: W.H. Freeman.

Halacz, F., & Moran, T.P. (1982). Analogy considered harmful. *Proceedings of the Conference on Human Factors in Computer Systems* (pp. 383–386). New York: Association for Computing Machinery.

Hamburg, D.A. (1984, June). Science and technology in a world transformed. *Science,* 943–946.

Hawkins, J., Brunner, C., Chaiklin, S., Ghitman, J.M., Mann, F., Magzamen, S., & Moeller, B. (1987). *Inquire: Software tools for inquiry learning.* Paper presented at the National Science Teachers Association Meetings, Washington, DC.

Hawkins, J., & Pea, R.D. (1987). Tools for bridging the cultures of everyday and scientific thinking. *Journal for Research in Science Teaching, 24,* 291–307.

Herron, M.D. (1971). The nature of scientific inquiry. *School Review, 79,* 171–212.

Hiltz, S.R., & Turoff, M. (1985). Structuring computer-mediated communication systems to avoid information overload. *Communications of the ACM, 28,* 680–689.

Hirsch, E.D., Jr. (1987). *Cultural literacy.* New York: Houghton–Mifflin.

Hoffding, H. (1892). *Outlines of psychology* (trans. M.E. Lowndes). London: Macmillan.

Holyoak, K.J. (1985). The pragmatics of analogical transfer. In G. Bower (Ed.), *The psychology of learning and motivation* (Vol. 19, pp. 59–87). New York: Academic Press.

Homa, D., & Cultice, J. (1984). Role of feedback, category size, and stimulus distortion on the acquisition and utilization of ill-defined categories. *Journal of Experimental Psychology: Learning, Memory, and Cognition, 10,* 83–94.

James, W. (1890). *The principles of psychology.* New York: Henry Holt.

Jordan, C. (1985). Translating culture: From ethnographic information to educational program. *Anthropology and Education Quarterly, 16,* 105–123.

Kurland, D.M., Pea, R.D., Clement, C., & Mawby, R. (1986). A study of the development of programming ability and thinking skills in high school students. *Journal of Educational Computing Research, 2,* 429–458.

Laboratory of Comparative Human Cognition (1979). What's cultural about cross-cultural cognitive psychology? *Annual Review of Psychology, 30,* 145–172.

Laboratory of Comparative Human Cognition (1983). Culture and cognitive development. In W. Kessen (Ed.), *Mussen's handbook of child psychology* (4th ed., Vol 1, pp. 295–356). New York: Wiley.

Laboratory of Comparative Human Cognition (1984). Culture and intelligence. In R. Sternberg (Ed.), *Handbook of human intelligence.* New York: Cambridge University Press.

Larkin, J.H., McDermott, J., Simon, D.P., & Simon, H. (1980). Expert and novice performance in solving physics problems. *Science, 208,* 1335–1342.

Lave, J. (1986). Experiments, tests, jobs, and chores: How we learn what we do. In K.M. Borman & J. Reisman (Eds.), *Becoming a worker* (pp. 140–155). Norwood, NJ: Ablex.

Lave, J. (1987). *Cognition in practice.* New York: Cambridge University Press.

Lave, J., Murtaugh, M., & de la Rocha, O. (1984). The dialectics of arithmetic in grocery shopping. In B. Rogoff & J. Lave (Eds.), *Everyday cognition: Its development in social context.* Cambridge, MA: Harvard University Press.

Lepper, M.R. (1985). Microcomputers in education: Motivational and social issues. *American Psychologist, 40,* 1–18.

Linn, M.C. (1986). *Establishing a research base for science education: Challenges, trends, and recommendations (Report of a national conference held January 16–19, 1986).* Washington, DC: National Science Foundation.

Luchins, A.S., & Luchins, E.H. (1959). *Rigidity of behavior: A variational approach to the effects of einstellung.* Eugene: University of Oregon Press.

Malone, T.W. (1981). Toward a theory of intrinsically motivating instruction. *Cognitive Science, 4,* 333–369.

Malone, T.W. (1985). Designing organizational interfaces. *Proceedings of the CHI'85 Conference on Human Factors in Computing Systems.* San Francisco.

Malone, T.W., Grant, K.R., & Tarbak, F.A. (1986). The Information Lens: An intelligent system for information sharing in organizations. In M. Mantei & P. Orbeton (Eds.), *Proceedings of the CHI'86 Conference on Human Factors in Computer Systems* (pp. 1–8). San Francisco.

Malone, T.W., Grant, K.R., Turbak, F.A., Brobst, S.A., & Cohen, M.D. (1987). Intelligent information sharing systems. *Communications of the ACM.*

Mehan, H. (1979). *Learning lessons.* Cambridge, MA: Harvard University Press.

Meichenbaum, D. (1977). *Cognitive behavior modification: An integrated approach.* New York: Plenum.

Miller, G.A., & Johnson-Laird, P.N. (1976). *Language and perception.* Cambridge, MA: Harvard University Press.

Milojkovic, J. (1983). *Children learning computer programming: Cognitive and motivational consequences.* Unpublished doctoral dissertation, Department of Psychology, Stanford University.

Novak, J.D., & Gowen, D.B. (1984). *Learning how to learn.* Cambridge, MA: Cambridge University Press.

Olson, G.M., & Soloway, E. (1987). Transfer and programming. To appear in *Empirical studies of programming* (Vol. 2). Norwood, NJ: Ablex.

Ortony, A. (1979). The role of similarity in similes and metaphors. In A. Ortony (Ed.), *Metaphor and thought.* Cambridge: Cambridge University Press.

Osborne, R., & Freyberg, P. (1985). *Learning in science.* Auckland, Australia: Heineman.

Osgood, C.E. (1949). The similarity paradox in human learning: A resolution. *Psychological Review, 56,* 132–143.

Palincsar, A., & Brown, A.L. (1984). Reciprocal teaching of comprehension-fostering and comprehension-monitoring activities. *Cognition and Instruction, 1,* 117–176.

Papert, S. (1980). *Mindstorms: Children, computers, and powerful ideas.* New York: Basic Books.

Parker, F.W. (1901–1902). An account of the Cook County and Chicago Normal School from 1883–1899. *The Elementary School Teacher and the Course of Study, 2,* 752–780.

Pea, R.D. (1985). Beyond amplification: Using the computer to reorganize human mental functioning. *Educational Psychologist, 20,* 167–182.

Pea, R.D. (1987, April). *Human–machine symbiosis: Cognitive and cultural implications of hypermedia.* Paper presented at an international conference on Computers, Cognition, and Epistemology, University of Aarhus, Denmark (to appear).

Pea, R.D., Brunner, C., Cohen, J., Webster, K., & Mellen, N. (1987, April). *IDEA: A software system for learning systematic decision-making skills.* Paper presented at the Annual Meetings of the American Educational Research Association, Washington, DC.

Pea, R.D., & Kurland, D.M. (1984). On the cognitive effects of learning computer programming. *New Ideas in Psychology, 2,* 137–168.

Pea, R.D., & Kurland, D.M. (1987). Cognitive technologies for writing. *Review of Research in Education, 14,* in press.

Perfetto, B.A., Bransford, J.D., & Franks, J.J. (1983). Constraints on access in a problem-solving context. *Memory and Cognition, 11,* 24–31.

Pettito, A. (1985, July). *Schooling and cognition.* Unpublished manuscript, University of Rochester, Graduate School of Education and Human Development.

Pogrow, S., & Buchanan, B. (1985). Higher order thinking for compensatory students. *Educational Leadership, 43,* 40–43.

Polson, P.G., Mucher, E., & Engelbeck, G. (1986). A test of a common elements theory of transfer. In M. Mantei & P. Orbeton (Eds.), *Human factors in computing systems: CHI '86* (pp. 78–83). New York: Association for Computing Machinery.

Potok, C. (1986). *In the beginning.* New York: Knopf.

Pressley, M., Ross, K.A., Levin, J.R., & Ghatala, E.S. (1984). The role of strategy utility knowledge in children's strategy decision making. *Journal of Experimental Child Psychology, 38,* 491–504.

Reed, S.K., Ernst, G.W., & Banerji, R. (1974). The role of analogy in transfer between similar problem states. *Cognitive Psychology, 6,* 436–450.

Resnick, L.B. (1982). Syntax and semantics in learning to subtract. In T. Carpenter, J. Moser, & T. Romberg (Eds.), *Addition and subtraction: A cognitive perspective* (pp. 136–155). Hillsdale, NJ: Lawrence Erlbaum Associates.

Resnick, L.B. (1987). *Education and learning to think: Subcommittee report.* National Research Council Commission on Behavioral and Social Sciences and Education. Washington, DC: NRC.

Resnick, L.B., & Omanson, S.F. (1987). Learning to understand arithmetic. In R. Glaser (Ed.), *Advances in instructional psychology* (Vol. 3, pp. 41–95). Hillsdale, NJ: Lawrence Erlbaum Associates.

Rogoff, B., & Lave, J. (Eds.). (1984) *Everyday cognition: Its development in social context.* Cambridge, MA: Harvard University Press.

Rosch, E. (1978). Principles of categorization. In E. Rosch & B.B. Lloyd (Eds.), *Cognition and categorization.* Hillsdale, NJ: Lawrence Erlbaum Associates.

Scardamalia, M., Bereiter, C., & Steinbach, R. (1984). Teachability of reflective processes in written composition. *Cognitive Science, 8,* 173–190.

Schank, R.C. (1982). *Dynamic memory.* Cambridge: Cambridge University Press.

Schank, R.C. (1986). *Explanation patterns: Understanding mechanically and creatively.* Hillsdale, NJ: Lawrence Erlbaum Associates.

Schoenfeld, A. (1985). *Mathematical problem solving.* New York: Academic Press.

Schoenfeld, A. (1987). What's all the fuss about metacognition? In A. Schoenfeld (Ed.), *Cognitive science and mathematics education* (pp. 189–214). Hillsdale, NJ: Lawrence Erlbaum Associates.

Scribner, S. (1977). Modes of thinking and ways of speaking: Culture and logic reconsidered. In P.N. Johnson-Laird & P.C. Wason (Eds.), *Thinking: Readings in cognitive science* (pp. 483–500). London: Cambridge University Press.

Scribner, S. (1985). Knowledge at work. *Anthropology and Education Quarterly, 16,* 199–206.

Scribner, S., & Cole, M. (1973). Cognitive consequences of formal and informal education. *Science, 182,* 553–559.

Scribner, S., & Cole, M. (1981). *The psychology of literacy.* Cambridge, MA: Harvard University Press.

Scribner, S., & Fahrmeier, E. (1982). *Practical and theoretical arithmetic: Some preliminary findings.* Industrial Literacy Project, Working Paper No. 3, City University of New York, Graduate Center.

Segal, J., Chipman, S., & Glaser, R. (1985). (Eds.). *Thinking and learning skills: Relating instruction to basic research* (Vol. 1). Hillsdale, NJ: Lawrence Erlbaum Associates.

Sharp, D.W., Cole, M., & Lave, C. (1979). Education and cognitive development: The evidence from experimental research. *Monographs of the Society for Research in Child Development, 44* (1-2, Serial No. 178).

Sheil, B.A. (1981). *Coping with complexity* (CIS-15). Palo Alto, CA: Xerox PARC.

Shweder, R.A. (1977). Likeness and likelihood in everyday thought: Magical thinking in judgments about personality. *Current Anthropology, 18,* 637–658.

Shweder, R.A. (1986). Divergent rationalities. In D.W. Fiske & R.A. Shweder (Eds.), *Metatheory in social science: Pluralisms and subjectivities* (pp. 163–196). Chicago: University of Chicago Press.

Simon, H.A., & Hayes, J.R. (1976). The understanding process: Problem isomorphs. *Cognitive Psychology, 8,* 165–190.

Skinner, B.F. (1971). *Beyond freedom and dignity.* New York: Knopf.

Stavy, R., & Berkovitz, B. (1980). Cognitive conflict as a basis for teaching quantitative aspects of the concept of temperature. *Science Education, 64,* 679–692.

Sternberg, R.S. (1983). Criteria for intellectual skills training. *Educational Researcher, 12,* 6–12, 26.

Sternberg, R.S. (1985). *Beyond IQ: A triarchic theory of human intelligence.* New York: Cambridge University Press.

Sternberg, R.S. (1986). *Intelligence applied.* San Diego: Harcourt Brace Jovanovich.

Thorndike, E.L., & Woodworth, R.S. (1901). The influence of improvement in one mental function upon the efficiency of other functions. *Psychological Review, 8,* 247–261, 384–395, 553–564.

Thorndike, E.L. (1924). Mental discipline in high school studies. *Journal of Educational Psychology, 15,* 1–22, 83–98.

Toulmin, S.E. (1958). *The uses of argument.* Cambridge: Cambridge University Press.

Trigg, R. (1983, November). *Network approach to text handling for the online scientific community.* Doctoral dissertation, Department of Computer Science, University of Maryland, CSTR-1346.

Tulving, E., & Pearlstone, Z. (1966). Availability versus accessibility of information in memory for words. *Journal of Verbal Learning and Verbal Behavior, 5,* 381–391.

Voss, J.F. (1987). *International Journal of Educational Research.*

Voss, J.F., Greene, T.R., Post, T.A., & Penner, B.C. (1983). Problem-solving skill in the social sciences. In G.H. Bower (Ed.), *The psychology of learning and motivation: Advances in research and theory* (Vol. 17, pp. 165–213). New York: Academic Press.

Vygotsky, L.S. (1978). *Mind in society: The development of the higher psychological processes.* Cambridge, MA: Harvard University Press.

Weinstein, C.E., & Mayer, R. (1985). The teaching of learning strategies. In M. Wittrock (Ed.), *The handbook of research on teaching* (3rd ed.). New York: Macmillan.

West, L., & Pines, A.L. (1985). (Eds.). *Cognitive structure and conceptual change.* Orlando, FL: Academic Press.

Wilson, B.R. (1970). (Ed.). *Rationality: Key concepts in the social sciences.* New York: Harper & Row.

Winston, P.H. (1978). Learning by creating and justifying transfer frames. *Artificial Intelligence, 10,* 147–172.

Winston, P.H. (1979). Learning and reasoning by analogy. *Communications of the ACM, 23,* 689–703.

10 Technology in 2020: Educating a Diverse Population

SHIRLEY M. MALCOM
American Association for the Advancement of Science

"There are many possible futures . . . Not all possible futures are equally probable. Not all possible futures are equally desirable. What is most desirable among the possibilities is not necessarily the most probable in the absence of some concerned effort to make it so."

With that statement, Nickerson prefaces the charge to the panel convened to consider the role of technology in education over the next several decades. I focus on the diverse student population to be served in the Year 2020, their educational needs, and how technology might help to meet those needs.

A TALE OF TWO FUTURES

Raul Gomez walked in the door of his inner-city middle school classroom rather down in the dumps. "Here we go again," he thinks. If it were not for the compulsory education laws and the possibility that his mother could be arrested if he were truant, he wouldn't bother to come at all. He spends a lot of his day sitting in front of the computer doing endless drill and practice.

To increase educational efficiency and to help Raul's teacher cope with 35 students the district put computers in the classroom. Some of the children work on the computers while the teacher works directly with the others. For 14 students, English is not their native language. Among them, there are seven different languages spoken. If he had to go through another set of practice problems and subject/verb agreements, he'd go crazy. Occasionally, just for a

213

change of pace he'd deliberately answer a question incorrectly so he could see the funny little graphics built in to "motivate the user." If he didn't get it right after a couple of times, "the solution" was explained to him. He had figured out other ways to solve the problems, but for some reason the computer never explained it his way. They both got the same answer, but he knew there must be something wrong with his way because the computer never did it like that.

Raul had thought computers were going to be a lot more fun. He first saw one at the Saltmans' house, the family for whom his mother worked. He had gone with her during the summer to help with the yard work and had seen the games and the simulated science experiments. There was an electronic mail feature that had been set up to help team members keep in contact as they prepared for the international mathematics competition. But somehow, at his school it just wasn't the same. He asked Ms. Russell about those neat things he had seen at the Saltmans, but she had said that the students weren't ready for that yet. Besides, doing those things required more time on the computer and there were not quite enough machines to go around.

If only his family had the money to buy its own computer! But there was barely enough money to buy food and clothes and pay the rent for the four of them — Raul, his younger sisters, and his Mom. There was so much he wanted to know about how the world worked, but in his class they never seemed to get to any of the exciting stuff — they always seemed to be getting ready for the next competency test, always having to cover more pages in the textbook. As soon as he could, he was going to quit school and go to work and help his mother with the girls. Maybe he'd get back to school one day. If there were more here for him he wouldn't leave, but it's just a waste of time. What good does it do his family if he knows the names of all the dead presidents?

He had seen a TV program once about Mayan mathematics and about the sun dagger in the Southwest that native people developed to tell the arrival of the different seasons of the year. He asked his teacher about these things, but she said they had to stay on schedule or they wouldn't cover the material in time for the science test.

Sonia entered her inner-city middle school classroom elated. She had just "published" her first book, complete with illustrations. As soon as it had been bound, it would be put in the media center. Imagine that, Sonia Ramirez, AUTHOR. And to think, just 3 years before when she and her older brother and sister had come from Puerto Rico, she couldn't speak, read, or write English, and now she had a book in English and Spanish. The speech synthesis and translation features on the computer had really helped her develop proficiency in both languages. There were enough computers to go around and enough textbooks for everyone to use. Her book was about rain shadows. It was fun when you could do science, geography, English, Spanish, and art at the same time. She had to do a lot of work on her book at home, but that was all right. Sonia had been taking home a loaned computer since she had first entered school here. Computers are a big part of Sonia's life and the lives of her classmates. Her friend Hilda has a computer that speaks for her (and in a girl's voice!): Hilda is nonvocal because of cerebral palsy. Hilda has to use her computer for writing too.

Sonia is learning to play the synthesizer in the school orchestra. The wide variety of software that she can borrow from the library (or that comes with the books) lets her look at all kinds of things that interest her. She and her classmates have developed software, too, which is included in the middle school computer network in their school system.

Sonia and Hilda are interested in birds. Their *Peterson's Field Guide* has a videodisc that goes with it so they can study the birds in flight, listen to the songs, and learn more about their life histories. It really helps to be able to go back and forth between similar species and to have the differences between them highlighted.

Raul and Sonia live in two very different futures. Raul's future was created by extrapolating from the present: the present trends in education, the present educational goals for poor, disadvantaged, and minority students, the present way the technology is used in educating these students. For Raul, overall trends in the technology matter very little when he has so few appropriate tools for his education, and when no concerted effort has been made to address his educational needs. Differences in the educational use of technology further separate the worlds of the Gomez and the Saltman families. On the other hand, Sonia Ramirez has been empowered by education, and the technology has made that education more meaningful and more accessible. At present, Raul's future is more probable though not very desirable. Achieving Sonia's future will not be easy.

The Population to be Served

America is characterized by diversity. Within its borders, one can move from tropics to tundra, from desert to rainforest. In terms of population, one can find peoples from all over the world who speak many different languages. We find such diversity in our schools as well, the children of recent immigrants and the children of native peoples, children of plenty and children of want. They come, each to be educated, to be given the tools that will let them achieve their own version of the American dream.

For millions of Americans the dream continues to be deferred. It is likely that in the year 2020 schools will be populated by a student group that has an even larger percentage of poor and disadvantaged children than today, more children who are members of minority groups, more children from single-parent families, and more children with special needs (Hodgkinson, 1985; U.S. Department of Education, 1986a). The budget deficits at the federal level, a conservative turn in attitudes regarding federal investment in education, and a rearrangement in spending priorities make it less and less likely that the federal government will mount any major national initiative to address the problems of this segment of the society, even as its proportion increases (National Urban League, 1987).

Whereas in absolute numbers most poor children are white, Black and Hispanic children are more likely to live in poverty. In 1983, 17% of white children were poor, whereas 39% of Hispanic children and 47% of Black children were living in poverty.

A 1985 study by the Congressional Research Service reviewed research that showed that "poor children start school less ready to learn than their peers and fall further behind as they progress through school."

Limited English-proficiency (LEP) students have been described as the "fastest growing segment of school age population in the United States." Although the overall population of students aged 5 to 14 declined by 6.2% from 1978 to 1982, the LEP population grew by 10.3% (U.S. Congress, 1987). Projections developed in 1981 show the total number of LEP children ages 5 to 14 increasing 16.7% between 1980 and 1990 and increasing 41.7% between 1980 and 2000 (U.S. Department of Education, 1986a).

If we use today as the baseline to look into the future, we see a school age population that is almost one quarter minority. By the year 2000, minority groups will comprise over a third of the U.S. population. In the state of California the elementary grades of the public school system are, for the most part, predominantly minority as are student populations in 23 of the 25 largest U.S. city school districts. By the end of this century, the entire population of the public schools of California will have a majority of minority group children (Hodgkinson, 1985).

The minority children in our schools are disproportionately poor as are the schools they attend. These students are more likely to drop out of the school system before completing high school. They have lower levels of achievement as measured by standardized tests (National Science Foundation, 1986). If they attend high school, they are more likely to be found in general and vocational tracks than are more affluent white students and Asian American students of any socioeconomic level (National Science Foundation, 1986; Berryman, 1983; U.S. Congress, 1985). They take fewer years of academic level courses, even for those who plan to attend college (Ramist & Arbeiter, 1985), and are more likely to be enrolled in classes that lead nowhere. For example, while Black and American Indian students are as likely as white students to report taking 3 or 4 years of mathematics, they are less likely than white students to report taking those mathematics courses associated with an academic track program (National Science Foundation, 1986). They mark time and then leave the school system essentially unemployable even for low-skilled, menial jobs, due to lack of skills combined with discrimination against them in the job market. (Minorities were estimated to account for 32% of discouraged workers by the end of 1980.) It is not uncommon to find classrooms in our major cities where, for most of the students, English is a second language.

Disadvantaged, poor, minority, limited English-proficient students, and students from single-parent households are often described collectively as being "at risk." "Risk" is certainly not limited to these groups; it is easily shown that the educational system disadvantages other groups of students, for example, by failing to provide appropriate programmatic access to students who have physical or learning disabilities or to female students in certain nontraditional areas of study such as science and technology. At risk students who come to our schools in 2020 to be educated will have the differences separating them from advantaged members of society magnified or diminished by what happens in their classrooms. And what happens in tomorrow's classrooms will depend on the actions of today's researchers, educators, and policymakers. Nowhere is that likely to be more pronounced than with the use of technology in education.

The Educational Challenge of Diversity

What educational needs do poor, disadvantaged, and minority kids have? Although these students bring different and often less rich experiences with them to the schools, they need the opportunity to expand and enrich—the earlier the better. They need to become independent, empowered learners.

These students need positive reinforcement and feedback; excellent teachers and adequate school resources; encouragement and high expectations; cultural relevance; competent instruction; meaning, context, and interrelation, instruction that draws on the experiences those students are likely to have had and the things that are important in their lives; and outlet for creativity and vehicles for independent learning; diagnosis and treatment of specific learning difficulties; and, opportunities for enrichment as well as for filling in the gaps in their present knowledge (see Malcom et al., 1984; The College Board, 1985).

Looking at the list of needs outlined, it is quite obvious that these are, in fact, the things every student needs. These issues must be emphasized for disadvantaged learners because the educational system has all too often had different and lower expectations for these students. Disadvantaged persons are unlikely to have sources *other than the school system for having their learning needs addressed*—there is no other option, no "redundancy in the system." They tend not to have advocates in dealing with the schools or ways of knowing when they are being shortchanged in their education. These students have low tolerance for inferior or even mediocre education, but that's what they get. Where technology can help to meet the educational needs of disadvantaged students, it should be developed along lines to make this happen. But I will go further and say that where technology is developed to address any educational needs, it must be developed to ensure that the needs of disadvantaged persons are met. To do otherwise is to widen the educational differences between "haves" and "have nots" in our society. Experiences from intervention programs in the area of science, engineering, and mathematics indicate that effective practice for minority, disabled, and female students ends up being effective when used with all students (Malcom et al., 1984). Cetron (1985) suggests that concern for equity has enriched educational research for all, such as in looking at effective schools and individualized education plans.

Access to Educational Excellence

Those who are least well served by the educational system, who are "at risk" in our schools, may be further disadvantaged if the promises of educational technology are fulfilled without full, appropriate, and equitable access. Although it has been a traditional federal role to be concerned about equity, there is little within current federal policy or programs to give poor and minority persons hope that the government will promote equity in this instance. The current mood of the country runs against the idea of "special treatment" for targeted populations.

Poor school districts have less access to computers and other technologies than wealthier districts (Center for Social Organization of Schools, 1983). So poor kids do not have physical access in the schools to the technologies they might need to make a real difference in their education. Disadvantaged youth also do not have home access to computers. These factors further disadvantage the poor in competing (or computing) immediately or ultimately with the more advantaged members of the society.

Access is more than just physical, however. The situation for girls and young women with regard to computing underscores this point. Becker talks about the different ways that computers are used in instruction for advantaged and disadvantaged students independent of access to hardware (1983). Students who are disadvantaged are generally given very rigid opportunities for interaction with the machine—such as in-drill and practice. Students who are more advantaged are provided more flexible opportunities for interaction with the computer (U.S. Congress, 1987). Such patterns of use promote powerlessness with the former group and empowerment of the latter—dependence versus independence in learning. Performance measures are highly correlated with socioeconomic levels. Lower teacher expectations for disadvantaged and non-Asian minority students may seal the fate of even the brightest poor and minority youth for whom lack of exposure is interpreted as lack of ability. The "presumption of inability" often extends as well to persons with severe physical disabilities, even where appropriate determination of mental ability has not been made (Redden & Stern, 1983; "Focusing," 1987).

The Promises of Technology—
The Half-Full Glass

In the preceding section, I enumerated some goals for the education of disadvantaged students. Research provides examples of where technology has been used successfully to address many of these goals. A recent staff paper from the Office of Technology Assessment (1987) on the status of computer use in Chapter 1 and bilingual education indicates that:

- Although drill and practice is the predominant instructional application for low-SES and Chapter 1 students, a number of studies document achievement gains when compared with other forms of drill.
- Computer technology seems to enhance motivation for learning. Many researchers and practitioners suggest that this is related to the computer's ability to be nonjudgmental, to provide immediate feedback, to allow self-pacing, and to help raise students' "status" in their schools.
- The computer is an effective learning tool, but it does not replace the teacher.

In addition to providing reinforcement through immediate feedback and a nonjudgmental and neutral learning environment, instructional use of computers can enhance problem-solving and critical-thinking skills. Computers also show special promise in use with disabled students.

The Promises of Technology—
The Half-Empty Glass

Although some exemplary uses of computers in educating disadvantaged students can be found, national statistics suggest that the picture for the most part is less than rosy. The story is one of limited access to computers in school settings; different patterns of use with disadvantaged students; teachers who feel they are poorly prepared to incorporate the promise of computers into instruction; and more limited out-of-school and informal opportunities for computer use.

Research has shown that computer-assisted instruction (CAI) with Chapter 1 students results in educational gains when compared with other forms of instruction, but this research does *not* compare CAI with *other kinds of computer-based instruction* such as simulation, problem solving, or other non-traditional approaches.

Much of the difference in access and usage is correlated with the socioeconomic status of a school, which translates into lower levels of student performance, compensatory education that focuses on basic skills, and different expectations for the students. But differential access is not just a factor of poverty. The gender differences in computer utilization have been clearly documented, especially during free time after school when informal use is dominated by boys. This research stands as testimony to the importance of seeing computer use not only in terms of physical access but also as a programmatic and psychological issue; that is, one needs to ask:

- Are the computers available?
- Are computers available to accomplish the full range of educational purposes, particularly those that the computer can accomplish uniquely?
- Are computers available in a setting that is appropriate and friendly to the user?

Pointing the Way:
Possible Points for Technological Intervention

Research suggests some leverage points in the education of disadvantaged and minority children. It might be useful to think about how technology can play a role in these areas.

Early childhood—Disadvantaged children need good beginnings—a source to augment the home for learning and reinforcing developmental skills such as identifying colors, shapes, letters, numbers, and relationships, all with appropriate interaction. Much of this kind of activity is provided in good early childhood programs and some in quality television such as the Children's Television Workshop program, "Sesame Street." In the absence of good early childhood programs, or when parents do not know how to assist their children's learning at the appropriate developmental level, technology can provide children with important options. The growing proportion of teen parents among American Indians, Blacks, and Hispanics means that there is an increasing number of parents who are underprepared educationally to guide their children's early learning experience. If technology can help adults figure out the best way to teach a child or can provide examples and approaches that can be used by teachers, parents or other significant adults, so much the better. The success of programs such as "Writing to Read" with disadvantaged students has made a number of educators extremely hopeful. Educational technology would be an adjunct to the teacher rather than a substitute or replacement for important interaction with caring adults. Conversely, researchers point out that use of technology may avoid or neutralize some aspects of negative classroom interaction that may discourage "at-risk" students—technology plus teacher can come close to achieving this "best case."

Early Exposure and Experience with Ideas and Phenomena. Growing up poor in America means not having available to you those experiences that are often taken for granted by mainstream society. In addition, it often means not having people directly available to you who have been successful in that society. How do you get your questions answered? Who tells you things? Who sees to it that you have certain important experiences? This does not mean that poor and disadvantaged children are lacking a cultural base. It means that they may lack the specific culture necessary to navigate the economic and social mainstream. Technology provides alternative sources for this information. Television has done much to broaden the world view of disadvantaged persons but in a limited number of directions, mostly noneducational, and not all necessarily positive. The motivating aspects of the various media can be combined in an educational setting to provide meaningful learning alternatives and adjuncts for disadvantaged students.

Learning Style. Different people learn in different ways. Obviously, the most effective mode of instruction would be to find the style of the individual learner and begin teaching using that style. Whether there are group-based styles of learning has been the subject of much discussion and debate. Politically, many fear such research questions as whether males use one learning style and females another, or whether Blacks learn by one mode and American Indians by another. "Different" has come to mean, "deficient" in our society and in an educational system that is normed by and for the majority. So the fears of those not in power, who would likely be the objects of study rather than the subjects may be well founded. On the other hand, if educational technology can address different ways of learning by individuals or groups without adding the judgment "deficient," we will have a powerful tool for addressing educational needs of a diverse student population.

Technology in Education: Choosing a Future

The issue originally proposed for exploration in this chapter was the question of differential home access to technology. The topic was expanded to include differential school access to technology, largely on the premise that these two issues are inseparable. Full access to computers in our schools is as yet not a reality. Present policy directions do not lead us to believe that the computer-access problem for students in poor inner-city and rural systems will be resolved in the near term. For disadvantaged students, initial contact with technology, especially for educational uses, is likely to come in the school. Home demand for computers would likely result from in-school exposure. The way that a student interacts with the technology in school is likely to influence the way the student interacts with the technology (or expects to) out of school. For disadvantaged persons home is unlikely to be an alternative place for access to the technology. Even if costs of technology decrease significantly, access is not assured. Furthermore, even among advantaged persons, home (and school) has been a less likely place for access to computers for girls than for boys. Resources, experiences and societal expectations all affect who will or will not get to use computers in their education.

The preferred future is one in which educational technology can help address the specific educational needs of poor, disadvantaged, minority, disabled, and other "at-risk" kids, where the technologies can expand the experiences, increase learning opportunities, and otherwise help "level the playing field" for the disadvantaged, where access is real and appropriate. Access means having technology-based options for learning that are meaningful, culturally relevant, that build on prior experience, that respect differences, and provide powerful tools that encourage independence in learning.

For the "have nots" in our society, developments in educational technology can cut both ways, yielding help or harm depending on how the technology is used. If we are really successful in increasing the effectiveness of technology in education, if we can greatly enhance student access to and use of information, understanding of concepts, integration of knowledge across fields, exploration of relationships, and so on, I would fear for those on the short end of the technology stick—those who have also been shortchanged in their education and who lack real and meaningful access to the technology today.

On the other hand, if concern for equity were infused throughout the discussions about the role of technology in education, if equity concerns determined research priorities, target populations, test populations, and if research, development, and policies are being carefully considered for their impact on equity, I would be encouraged and excited to see the development of powerful educational tools. Such tools have the potential to narrow the educational gap and to help *all* students achieve at the maximum of their potential. This will require creative research, and strategic planning that begins now—planning that begins with an examination of the issues of equity and impact.

Many of the short-term trends in technology are relevant to education and are important in determining the potential of technology to positively affect disadvantaged populations. Obviously, as computers go down in cost and size, more and more people will be able to afford them and to use them. One need only remember the changes in the market and in access as a result of cost reductions in televisions and telecommunications. The possibility of computer equipment being loaned by community science centers, libraries, museums, and the schools themselves also becomes real. But it is at best naive to assume that lowered cost and greater physical access to computers will be sufficient to affect the computer's impact on education. Whereas most homes have televisions (including disadvantaged homes), the viewing patterns of high-SES and low-SES homes are not the same. What one watches on television is a function of socialization, not just equipment availability. Cetron (1985) points out that in samples taken in the eastern United States, 90% of parents whose income is in the upper 10% had bought a computer, disk drive, a printer, and educational as well as business software for their homes, whereas only 20%

of parents whose income is in the lowest 10% had bought a computer—usually with a joy stick and some games.

The availability of an extensive variety of software increases the likelihood of obtaining that which fits the preferred style of learning or preferred cultural perspective of diverse student populations. Mixing media would likely enhance the motivational aspects of the technology and allow students to use multiple sensory inputs in their learning. These are all aspects of learning situations that have been shown to have positive impact on minority, disadvantaged, and disabled learners (Malcom et al., 1984). On the other hand, widespread use of computer-based information services such as job posting, want ads, and the like will probably have disastrous effects without concern for equitable access.

It is important that students be provided with the skills that make the power to interact with large data bases meaningful; students must first be taught what questions to ask and what to do with all the information that is obtained. The current educational system too often fails for "at risk" students because it attempts to impart discrete bits of information with no prior cognitive scaffolding on which to hand them—a stress on knowledge, skills, and short-term improvements of test scores, rather than on understanding and application of knowledge. Texts are written like this; students are taught like this; and students are tested for these fragments of information.

If the emphasis of the coming decades increasingly will be on learning how to learn, how can we use technology to develop these skills and how can we ensure that the goals of education are high and consistent for all children? When we consider disadvantaged learners, we become aware of the importance of "affect"—"wanting to learn" and "liking to learn." If the educational setting makes one feel successful, if it does not denigrate one's prior experiences no matter how limited or different, if it does not require the dissolution of ties to one's culture or community, if it allows students to find out what they want to know and gives them knowledge that is important to have, if it is nonjudgmental, if it permits multiple modes of expression, then it is likely to make the student want to face the challenge of acquiring new knowledge. These are issues closely tied to motivation, and they affect whether a student will take educational risks. (For example, why should I take physics when it is not required, unless I find something about it that I like or it allows me to do something that I want to do, especially if I think it is going to be hard.)

Looking Ahead

In the charge to the panel, Nickerson outlined a number of questions about how education could or should be influenced by technology over the next few decades. Many of these questions have a direct bearing on the educational choices for disadvantaged persons and the changing meaning of access.

The Purpose of Education. Some persons contend that minorities and disadvantaged persons often want to get an education so they can get a job. Acquiring knowledge for its own sake or for future management of one's life may not be stressed for these groups either by those within (e.g., peers, parents) or those outside the group (teachers, counselors). As the knowledge explosion continues, the balance between what to learn and how to learn may shift toward the latter, given the impossibility of knowing everything about anything. As the educational requirements for a job and higher education converge (College Board, 1984) precollege education should become more similar for all learners and options for further education thus preserved for a longer period of time. The economic and social needs of our country will force us to provide for many the kind of education previously reserved to the elite few (Carnegie Task Force, 1986).

New Knowledge and Curriculum Changes It Will Require. In addition to the sheer increase in the amount that we know, a major feature of change in domain content will be the loss of boundaries between fields. There will likely be more interdisciplinary and cross-disciplinary work. Where interconnections are made in instruction, where problems and issues are encountered that look like "the real world," minority and disadvantaged students seem to perform quite well, usually because this kind of teaching necessarily builds on and requires its own tightly constructed models and framework.

A New Form of Literacy. If literacy means the ability to function in the world using the commonly agreed on tools and symbols for commerce, citizen participation, personal interaction, and further acquisition of learning, then the computer becomes an end as well as a means to other ends. The computer and other media would not replace other ways to learn but would provide new and exciting options to the learner. The electronic storage and transmission of information will likely be the sole province of business and the professions unless and until a highly literate nation of learners is produced by our schools. *This expanded use of computers will have to be socialized into the culture much more widely for education and other purposes.* As machines become more portable, learning and enriching the senses through leisure-time or free-time use of purse-size computers becomes more likely. We may see workers using "computotes" while commuting to their homes or offices, or as wireless terminals to transmit to the office if a "call comes in." Such technology can serve personal or private purposes when machines are used like diaries or journals, or it can provide us with an ever present link to the rest of the world. Such personally liberating uses of technology, to provide options, are not now available to the disadvantaged. They generally confront technology as something that controls, paces, monitors, or replaces them on their job (Gilliam, 1984; Hartmann, Tilly, & Kraut, 1986; U.S. Department of Labor, 1985).

Clearly, the technology must create its own market by helping to create highly literate people among all sectors of society—among those who have been socialized to love learning and to want to learn throughout their lives, and who see the computer as an accessible and useful machine to facilitate that process.

There are many individuals who need continuing education to help move them into new jobs, hold their present one, or acquire new skills. But they are often the very people who do not seek out opportunities for training until they are forced to because of a threatened or real loss of their jobs. If they were not successful in school, or are embarrassed by what they do not know, or do not have access to courses at the time or place that is convenient for them, or have family responsibilities that preclude being away from home (such as child or elderly care), home access technology may greatly expand their educational options.

New Ways of Representing Information. I have been intrigued by the developments in hardware and software that have been created to meet the needs of persons with physical disabilities. The variety of inputs and outputs that have been devised to assist persons with particular sensory or motor impairments only begin to suggest possibilities to us. The important thing, I believe, is that the successful technologies were driven by human need, involved the users in their conceptualization, design and testing, and were flexible enough to be particularized. These features speeded acceptance and utilization of the technology. We must be aware of the learning needs first; after that, specific aids can be developed in concert with potential users to make information available in a form to meet those needs. There are many opportunities, as there are many unmet needs, for example, among persons with learning disabilities and limited English-proficiency students. Adults who cannot read or write also provide a ready audience for such developments, not only to improve reading and writing, but also to give them other ways to learn content, process, and skills.

Environments Conducive to Learning. Clearly, an expectation of success is one of the most important aspects of an environment that supports learning, as is the competence of the teacher as guide and facilitator. Other features that seem to be important are the opportunity for interaction with peers, where cooperative as well as competitive formats are available, where responsibility for one's own learning as well as responsibility to each other can be fostered. Where technology can provide one with different kinds of options for learning, including those that require teamwork, a variety of cultural styles can be accommodated and the value of group responsibility can be instilled.

Technology and Individualized Instruction. I believe there are several ingredients necessary for technology to be used to individualize instruction: (1) machines that are flexible in the way that a student can interact with them in terms of input and output; (2) a wide variety of software that retains some level of flexibility; and, (3) a skilled teacher who knows how and when technology can be effective for what student. There needs to be the option for generating situation-specific software as well as for using a programming language or special purpose packages. There also need to be a much more culturally, racially, an ethnically diverse group of people involved in the development of software for educational purposes, and a tolerance on the part of the market-place for software that has a more "limited" commercial audience (orphan soft-ware). The teacher as internist, perhaps with the assistance of sophisticated assessment instruments and the educational equivalent of a PDR (*Physician's Desk Reference*), is key to effective individualization of instruction. Even the process of matching existing computer-based technology and software to accom-modate a specific physical disability or disabilities could be facilitated by devel-oping an expert system that provides individualized configurations. The legis-latively mandated IEP (Individual Education Plans) for special-needs students in the schools would then take on new meaning.

Technology in the Classroom. The various questions about the use of technology to motivate, to develop independent learners, to ensure understanding of con-cepts, and to integrate knowledge across traditional disciplines depend for an-swers on teachers and the skills they possess for managing the educational pro-cess. Of course, we must presuppose that we have the research base for knowing how to do these things and the software developed that draws on the research. But without the teacher to put these together with the student in a supportive environment, the existence of the technologies will be irrelevant. This is espe-cially true for poor and minority students who usually do not have an indepen-dent, alternative source for instruction. In an 1985 national survey of mathe-matics and science teachers, Weiss points out that most teachers, independent of grade level taught, reported feeling totally unprepared or somewhat unpre-pared to use computers as an instructional tool (Weiss, unpublished). Teachers in urban schools, and those in schools serving 50% or more minority-student population, were more likely to report feeling totally unprepared to use com-puters as instructional tools than those in suburban or predominately majority schools. Mathematics teachers in suburban schools (grades 7–9) were more likely to report having college coursework in computer sciences than teachers in rural or inner-city schools.

If technology is one tool of instruction, and if human choice exists as to how much, under what circumstances, and in what ways it is used, the possible dehumanizing effects can be reduced. technology can be a means of socialization rather than a deterrent to it, as in the case of a deaf student in a summer science program who used the computer to make social arrangements for after class. As long as real choice exists and flexibility is maintained, technology can play a positive, exciting, and enriching role for students.

There are many different opportunities to teach even while getting domain-specific knowledge into students' heads. For example, history, biology, and the behavioral and social sciences all contain important messages about conflict, its causes and consequences, and about cooperation and competition. Many exercises, especially when couched in biology (a "safer" way of exploring them), are easily adaptable to simulation (e.g., changing the proportions of predators and prey, or altering carrying capacity, or increasing gene frequencies). It is important to balance the increase in students' knowledge with their sense of responsibility to each other and the world in which they live. A number of area high schools for the academically talented have added a requirement for community service as a mechanism to ensure that such balances will be maintained. It is the choices humans make about the purposes and methods of education and the tools they use to accomplish it that are the most important issues. Technology is a tool, like paper and pencils and books. Technology is a tool, unlike paper and pencils and books. Its power to expand the capacity of the human mind is undeniable. But, its success at providing *better* education will depend on the choices that are made about its use, including who will use it and to what end, and who has first claim on the research and development. Equity and universal access must be among the highest priorities. If technology serves to widen the gap between the "haves" and "have-nots," we will fuel social instability. A democratic society cannot long endure with a large number of young, poor, embittered, illiterate, and disenfranchised people, and neither can a knowledge-based economy.

Achieving the Preferred Future

There are a number of recommendations for policy, research, and development that I would propose for achieving real access to educational technology.

1. Funders must support research in teaching and learning that can determine the weaknesses, strengths, and needs of diverse student populations. There must be more in depth knowledge about the relationship between prior experience and knowledge acquisition by specific subpopulations. At the same time researchers must be sensitive to the needs of different groups of learners and determine what works in their education. Research methods should be carefully constructed and target populations carefully drawn to provide comparative data by different group characteristics (e.g., students of different racial/ethnic groups, gender, socioeconomic levels), including research on effective practices. Efforts should be made to involve a diversity of persons in this research, including undergraduate work-study and minority-student assistants; this may be an effective mechanism for attracting them to the issues and to the research.

2. In view of the pivotal role of the teacher in selecting and using technology in the classroom of the future, present efforts to reform teacher preparation must include incorporation of technology and its role in teaching and learning. If the Carnegie plan or efforts of the Holmes group are

successful, then large proportions of experienced teachers of the year 2020 will likely have attained board certification. The use of technology in education must become a part of the preservice and inservice professional education and certification requirements of teachers.

3. The teaching workforce of the year 2020 must be broadly representative of the population of students to be educated. Three teachers must be involved in developing and disseminating knowledge on effective practice for diverse student groups as well as in serving as role models who are actively engaged in learning (as well as teaching). Included in the education of *all* teachers must be specific methods that will allow them to be effective in the education of *all* students. These methods should include appropriate use of technology.

4. A variety of software should be developed based on different and multiple learning styles, different interests and experiences, and cultural differences for culturally diverse student populations, as well as being available (for LEP students and foreign language immersion) in foreign languages.

5. Efforts should be made to bridge the intergenerational gap in attitudes toward and uses of computers. If we are successful in making disadvantaged children in-school computer users and independent learners through the use of technology, we must avoid permanent chasms between their experience and those of their parents. Opportunities should be created where parents and children can explore learning together, using computers in nonthreatening settings such as out-of-school programs (e.g., Scouts, Girls Clubs), community computing centers, church-based learning centers, malls, libraries, and museums. Trends toward lowered costs and more portability can facilitate development of such programs.

6. As technology assumes a greater role in teaching and learning, questions about the financing of education and equity among local districts in a state or among states in the nation to support this kind of education system become critical. The federal role in assuring that students with special needs have special claim to resources must be reestablished. Computers will have to become like books or band instruments, loaned free or available for minimum rental fees based on the ability of parents to pay. Only in this way can student access to equipment for in-school uses (and homework) be guaranteed. The availability of computers for education of adult learners might similarly be accomplished through job training or employment centers, library use, or rental. Technology in education may not live up to its potential in the near term because of hardware costs, software limitations, and development costs, and lack of preparation of teachers to take advantage of the present capabilities. I am presuming that by 2020 we will have overcome these impediments and started to realize real productivity increases in education as a result of the technology. We are currently engaged in various R&D efforts to move us toward this end.

It is not clear, however, that impact and equity are being considered sufficiently in this planning and development. Given what we know about current student needs as well as use and access patterns of the technology, priority should be given to demonstration projects, pilots, and research on "at risk" learners — to explore how higher level cognitive skills and real understanding can be developed among minority and disadvantaged learners and to see how performance gaps might be narrowed.

What will come first, the development of the R&D base for technology in education or concern about equity? If we proceed to explore the potential of the technology without immediate and concurrent concern for equity, we do serious harm by further widening the gap. The disadvantaged have always been forced to play catch up. If we have a tool that can help students overcome previous disadvantage and reach their educational potential, we have a moral obligation to give priority to this purpose.

REFERENCES

Becker, H.J. (1986). *Instructional uses of school computers* (Reports from the 1985 National Survey, Nos. 1–3). Baltimore: Johns Hopkins University, Center for the Social Organization of Schools

Berryman, S. (1983). *Who will do science?* New York: The Rockefeller Foundation.

Carnegie Task Force on Teaching as a Profession. (1986). *A nation prepared: Teachers for the 21st century*. Washington, DC: Carnegie Forum on Education and the Economy.

Center for the Social Organization of Schools. *1983 National Survey of Instructional Uses of School Computers*. Baltimore: Johns Hopkins University.

The College Board. (1984). *Academic preparation for the world of work*. New York: Author.

The College Board. (1985). *Equality and excellence: The educational status of black Americans*. New York: Author.

Cetron, M.J. (1985). *Schools of the future: How American business and education can cooperate to save our schools*. New York: McGraw-Hill.

Focusing on communication aids and techniques. (Summer, 1987). *Communications Outlook, 9*(1).

Gilliam, D. (1984, February 9). Technogap. *The Washington Post.*

Hartmann, H., Tilly, L., & Kraut, R. (Eds.). (1986). *Computer chips and paper clips* (Vol. 2). Washington, DC: National Academy of Sciences Press.

Hodgkinson, H.L. (1985). *All one system*. Washington, DC: The Institute for Educational Leadership.

Malcom, S.M., Aldrich, M., Hall, P.Q., Boulware, P., & Stern, V. (1984). *Equity and excellence: Compatible goals* (AAAS Publication 84-14). Washington, DC: American Association for the Advancement of Science.

National Science Foundation. (1986, January). *Women and minorities in science and engineering*. Washington, DC: Author.

National Urban League. (1987). *The condition of black America*. New York: Author.

Ramist, L., & Arbeiter, S. (1985). *Profiles of college bound seniors*. New York: The College Board.

Redden, M.R. & Stern, V. (Eds.). (1983). *Technology for independent living: Volume II. Issues in technology for daily living, education, and employment*. Washington, DC: American Association for the Advancement of Science.

U.S. Congress, Office of Technology Assessment. (1985). *Demographic trends and the scientific and engineering work force: A technical memorandum* (Publication No. OTA-TM-SET-35). Washington, DC: U.S. Government Printing Office.

U.S. Congress, Office of Technology Assessment. (1987). *Trends and status of computers in schools: Use in Chapter 1 programs and use with limited English-proficient students* (Staff paper). Washington, DC: Author.

U.S. Department of Education, National Center for Education Statistics. (1986a). *The condition of education.* Washington, DC: U.S. Government Printing Office.

U.S. Department of Education, National Center for Education Statistics. (1986b). *High school and beyond.* Washington, DC: U.S. Government Printing Office.

U.S. Department of Labor, Women's Bureau. (1985). *Women and office automation issues for the decade ahead.* Washington, DC: U.S. Government Printing Office.

Weiss, I. (1987). *Report on the 1985–86 national survey of science and mathematics education.* Research Triangle Park, NC: Research Triangle Institute.

11 Educational Technology and School Organization

DAVID K. COHEN
Michigan State University

INTRODUCTION

It is plain from the newspapers and trade journals that the new technology is the educational phenomenon of the moment. American schools always seem to have at least one such animal in residence, and microcomputers may retain this favored position for some time. But it also seems likely that this new technology will not work precisely as its sponsors hope: Perhaps it will not be adopted as widely as they wish — or more quickly, or widely, than anticipated. In addition, many teachers will not use it in the prescribed doses. Evaluations, of course, will show that the new technology is "working" for some schools and students, but "not working" for many others. Educators and policymakers will want to know why. Researchers will be invited to investigate and explain.

Readers with an acute attack of deja vu may stop here, feeling that they have been on this roller coaster before. But that is one point of this chapter: Barring any unexpected and amazing developments, this new educational technology will become embroiled in problems of adoption and use. We may be able to learn something about these problems from a consideration of similar problems in the past — the problems that Americans are now in the process of forgetting. New technology, after all, is an old educational enchantment. One part of the story begins late in the 19th century, when the rise of a new industrial technology excited imaginations everywhere. Educators thought that new methods of production already had increased what managers, citizens, and even ordinary workers needed to know, and they envisioned much greater increases in the near future. If schools did not enroll more students and teach them more — how to work with the new technology, how to manage it, and how to understand it — grave political and economic trouble would ensue. This theme has lost none of its appeal. Education for the new industrial technology is still a favorite American incantation, one that critics and fans of education both recite, as they bash and boost the schools.

The uses of new technology in education is quite a different part of the story. This one dates back at least to the 1820s, when educators enthused about the production of more books, and their wider distribution. They were excited about the pedagogical possibilities of more diverse materials, more directly available to students and teachers. But educators' romance with new technologies of instruction warmed up as time passed. Since the end of World War II, educators, reformers, and school critics have seized on one technical innovation after another, seeing fabulous opportunities for better education in each. Changes in publishing that made cheap books widely available was an early case: The paperback revolution was announced as a way to free students and teachers from the texts, lectures, and recitations to which they had been chained since McGuffey. Educational television was another early hope, but prophecies of new freedom for teachers and students were quickly followed by stories about TV sets languishing in school closets. New curricula and texts in the sciences and mathematics may seem quite conventional in comparison to television, but they were nonetheless an important innovation in the technology of education. Computer-assisted instruction was much more exotic, though one remembers CAI more for its impact on large corporations (it encouraged several to create expensive but unsuccessful subsidiaries to develop and promote educational technology) than for its effect on school instruction. The successes of Sesame Street and its progeny soon distracted commentators from the dismal performance of both the new educational technology firms and CAI. But Americans had just gotten used to the new programming when microcomputers burst on the scene, the newest new technology. Promises of computerized educational revolution quickly put most of the older new technologies in the shade.

This second story is my subject here. Like any good love story, it has had many ups and downs. Some of the new technologies have been widely used, whereas others have been generally ignored by educators. But even the technologies that were used were not always employed as their sponsors had planned, or hoped. The sponsors often have been heartbroken by the abuses their offspring have sustained, in liaisons with schools. But these uses, misuses, and nonuses are all useful, because they can help in telling my story. I focus on two issues: What kinds of matches have been made — or frustrated — between technology and schools? What explains why some marriages have lasted, while others limped along, and still others never made it to the altar?

PATTERNS IN TECHNOLOGY USE

It seems only fair to begin with books. They are the oldest new technology in education. They are widely used, and they have persistently been advertised as having many of the same virtues now ascribed to computers. Books can be used very flexibly, after all. The great variety of books available means that students in a single class often can study the same subjects, or even the same topics within a subject, by reading very different books. Modern publishing also makes it possible to produce such variety quickly, where it does not already exist. The technology thus permits students to adapt their studies to differences in taste, talent, and time. Even when an entire class uses the same book, the technology is quite flexible. Each student can read at his own pace, with few queuing problems. Readers can flip back and forth for particular points, or review, with great ease. Books can be carried around and used at the student's discretion, read for hours at a time, studied in bits on subways and buses, or put aside for consultation with a teacher. They can be used individually or in groups. Books also can be published relatively inexpensively, and cost can be further reduced by reuse.

Given this remarkable technology, it seems reasonable to ask: do schools use books in ways that capitalize on their flexibility?

Yes and no. Teachers have capitalized on the flexibility of books, but they did so in ways that preserved rigid instruction for many students while reducing it for some others. First, the books most commonly used in public schools are texts. Despite the many different kinds of books that are available, texts dominate book use in public elementary and secondary schools[1]. And despite the many more flexible ways in which the material printed in texts could be published—in smaller and deeper paperbacks, for instance—most of the material that students read is in texts.

A second point is that these texts are commonly prepared and employed as complete instructional packages. Although teachers select topics within texts, and sometimes use supplementary materials not connected with the text, it appears that in most cases the text, along with associated workbooks and worksheets, comprise the entire *materiel* of instruction. The great flexibility afforded by more mixed materials is typically foregone. One most commonly sees such mixed materials in high school advanced placement classes. There are amazing opportunities for students to diversify their readings within subjects or topics, and possibilities for further expanding these opportunities. But few of these opportunities are seized.

A third point is that texts and other reading materials are mostly used within a rigid lecture–recitation–seatwork organization of classroom work[2]. This is the

---

[1]Cuban, L. (1984). *How teachers taught* pp. 1–11. New York: Longmans.
[2]Cuban, *op. cit.*

the very organization that many advocates thought would be swept away in a flood of paperbacks. But the deluge did not have this effect, something that might have been inferred from inspection of earlier episodes in the same drama. At the beginning of the 19th century, educational reformers argued that American schooling would be greatly improved by the then-novel practice of printing texts and other books for students' and teachers' use. New points of view about subjects and how to teach them could be introduced, and reliance on whole-class work—dominated by teacher talk and slates—could be reduced. Classrooms could move away from lecture and recitation to more individualized work. But by the middle of the century educational writing was full of complaints about the rigidity of whole-class teaching, the prevalence of teacher talk, and the lack of much attention to individual students.

Publishing was more sophisticated by the later 19th century, and many reformers, amazed at the flood of new students in elementary schools, saw salvation partly in the greater variety of texts and other books that were becoming available. The more varied student population could be accommodated by using these materials to permit students to work at their own pace. Plans for flexible grading, grouping, and promotion proliferated: The Dalton Plan, the Winnetka Plan, and others offered ways to individualize learning within a mass-education system, through a combination of flexibly scheduled assignments, individualized evaluation of students' work, personalized learning contracts, and diverse instructional materials. But when educational researchers began investigating classroom work shortly thereafter, early in our own century, they found virtually no trace of these plans. Classrooms were rigidly organized for lecture and recitation. Texts and teacher talk ruled supreme. Researchers complained that they saw none of the flexibility promised by new plans for organizing instruction, and few flexible uses of printed materials[3].

Textbooks and other print materials improved, diversified, and grew in volume between the World Wars. Great stress was placed on devising materials that would meet and excite the interests of an increasingly diverse body of students. According to researchers and educators, considerable progress was made in this area. But studies of classroom work sang the same sad tune, as teachers and students did not take much advantage of the greater flexibility that was available. Most classrooms seemed as rigid as they had been decades before[4]. Classroom researchers sing the same tune today, after a revolution in publishing that produced an unprecedented avalanche of diverse material.

Ironically, one reason things turned out this way is that books are a very flexible technology. They can be easily adapted to a variety of instructional

---

[3]One of the earliest studies was a doctoral thesis at Columbia, concerning the persistence of traditional recitation: Stevens, R. (1912). *The question as a measure of efficiency in instruction.* New York: Teachers College.

[4]Powell, A., Farrar, E., & Cohen, D.K. (1985). *The Shopping Mall High School* pp. 266–67. Boston: Houghton Mifflin.

organizations. The very attribute that innovators thought would revolutionize education made it easy for schools to adapt this innovation to existing organization and purposes[5].

My point in this little recital is not that public education is an organizational mastodon, frozen in its own cozy little glacier. It has changed swiftly and fundamentally in some ways. For instance, an entire system of public secondary education was built between 1890 and 1940, and a new mass system of public higher education was built between World War I and 1970. But, as Larry Cuban has shown, the more intimate organization of instruction has changed much less dramatically than the large organization of school provision. During this same period, reforms that sought more flexible, child-centered instruction in schools seem to have produced only small changes: the style of work in most classrooms today appears to be strikingly similar to that of 8 or 9 decades ago[6]. And this conservatism has persisted in spite of a print technology that progressively opened up more and more opportunities for flexibility in the organization of instruction, and in spite of steadily increasing demands for such flexibility.

We can probe this point a bit further by considering the ways in which innovative content in this technology (one might think of it as new software for textbooks) has been used. My example is the new curricula that were devised in response to school criticism in the 1950s—in part because it seems timely, and in part because there are some data.

The chief worry then, as now, was that quality education was getting short shrift in schools, as the result of a flabby egalitarianism. One leading response was an unprecedented national investment in new curricula. Some of the best minds in the country went to work on what students would read, and within a relatively short time much new material was in print[7].

In some important respects the results were a real success. The textbooks greatly improved subject matter content and presentation over what had gone before. These improvements encouraged more and better instruction at the top of the high school curriculum. More students with the will and the wit were able to study advanced science and math, for instance. Such courses multiplied rapidly between the middle 1950s and the early 1970s. But these changes did not occur at the instructional core of public education. The top track was marginal to that core. It also was the one place where there was both support for change and no powerful opposition to it.

There also were some broad adoptions of the new texts: Biology books seem to have found homes in high school classes for students at all levels. And some other books seem to have stimulated change more by inspiring imitation in

---

[5]For a nice discussion of this point, see Cuban, L. (1986). *Teachers and Machines* Chap. 3. New York, Teachers College.

[6]Cuban, *How teachers taught, op. cit.*

[7]Powell *et. al., op. cit.*, (pp. 282–92).

commercially written texts than by supplanting them in the market. The new curricula were thus successful in several different ways: They were a substantive improvement; they were used widely in some cases and deeply in others; and they were imitated.

But successful invention, diffusion, and adoption are only the first steps for any innovation. They make a novelty available for use, but they guarantee nothing about how it will be used. How were the new materials employed in teaching and learning? Whereas research on this point is embarrassingly thin, the available evidence is much less impressive than the data on diffusion and adoption. For the instructional uses of the new materials seem to have diverged from authors' and sponsors' expectations in several different ways.

First, little seems to have changed in the actual organization of instruction. Whole-class, lecture–recitation continued to be the order of the day. Teachers seemed to talk just as much after using these materials as before. The livelier and more inquiry-oriented content did not seem to much change classroom discourse.

Second, most teachers seem to have used these materials as packages. There were explicit and implicit invitations to diversify reading and other work. There was some diversification at the margins, in AP and honors classes. But there seems to have been little diversification in most classes.

Third, when we turn to the content of teaching and learning, the results seem to have been quite mixed. Some teachers understood the new content and used it to good advantage. But many more appear instead to have taught these inquiry-oriented materials as literal truth. For instance, a math text might present three different ways of representing the answer to this problem in the multiplication of two-digit numbers:

$$12 \; times \; 12 \; = \; ?$$

$$4 \; times \; 12 \; = \; 48 \qquad 12 + 12 + 12 + 12 + 12 + 12 + 12 + 12 + 12 + 12$$
$$3 \; times \; 48 \; = \; 144 \qquad 12 + 12 = 144$$

$$10 \; times \; 12 \; = \; 120$$
$$\underline{2 \; times \; 12 \; = \quad 24}$$
$$144$$

Such different representations seek to encourage understanding of the nature of multiplication, rather than just memorization of the conventional algorithm. But most teachers seem to have taught such thoughtful stuff by having students memorize it, just as they would have directed memorization of the conventional algorithm, or the 13 causes of World War I. The means of instruction would thus defeat the novel content of the materials, perhaps introducing more confusion about multiplication than the old method of instruction alone would have done. The texts intended to open up subjects for inquiry and argument, and to introduce students to critical thinking about them. But most teachers seem to have used the texts instead as a vehicle for their established, much more traditional approach to instruction, submerging the new conceptions of subjects in the old ones.

So, while the new curricula were used, they were used within the extant organization of instruction. In a minority of cases this meant they were used intelligently and sympathetically, but even in these cases the new content did not bring radical change in the ways that classes were conducted, that teachers taught, or that students learned. But in most cases, the new curricula were assimilated to an inherited and rather rigid organization of subject matter, teaching, and learning. In either case, it seems fair to say that the new materials seem to have changed the organization of instruction in any dramatic way. More often than not, the extant organization changed the materials. In a sense it is fair to say that the new materials failed, despite the opportunities they created to free students and teachers from whole-class, lock-step, batch-processed instruction. But it is also fair to say that the curricula failed precisely because they created such opportunities. Classroom work changed little because the new materials were flexible and could be adapted. Had such adaptation been impossible, use would have been much less. In any event, by the early 1980s most traces of the new content appear to have vanished, carried away on later waves of innovation[8].

I return to these points a bit further on but wish first to consider one other educational technology — television. What do we know about the uses of television that was devised for schools?

Larry Cuban has shown in his recent book on teachers and technology that despite extravagant claims for the revolutionary effects of educational programming in this medium, it has been used only a little in the schools[9]. He explains this result in part as the result of a poor fit, between the kinds of materials that were available for viewing and the demands of regular classroom instruction. For instance, programs were not keyed to the curricula that teachers had to use and did not fit into the school schedule well. His account suggests that innovators attended more to the new technology and its possibilities than to the organization of instruction in which the technology would be used.

This point can be amplified a bit in the uses of television in higher education. For this technology is used as a medium of undergraduate instruction in many American universities. When so used, TV seems to be an ancillary means of extending a conventional pedagogy: Professors' lectures are videotaped, and cassettes are made available to students for viewing at their convenience. I have found courses in which more than 4,000 students are taught in this fashion. In other cases, lectures are broadcast live to students watching monitors in other rooms; or both. There are few reports of such technology

---

[8]Stake, R., & Easley, J. (1978). *Case studies in science education* (2 vols.) Vol. II, pp. II:4–5. Washington: U.S. Government Printing Office.

[9]Cuban, *Teachers and machines, op. cit.*

use in small colleges, or in selective private universities. TV seems to be used more often in large public institutions, where huge classes are more common. This seems utterly unsurprising: everyone can think of reasons why Brown and Wesleyan would be allergic to practices that Indiana or Michigan State would embrace.

Why do high schools not follow the Big Ten example? After all, most secondary schools closely resemble land grant universities in ideology, and organization: Both are inclusive; both offer extraordinarily comprehensive curricula; and both aspire to provide a peoples' education. Pedagogy in both also seems well adapted to a flat-footed use of TV: Most teachers talk while students listen or at least don't disrupt the lecture.

At least part of the answer is that university teachers are no longer assigned custodial responsibility for their students, whereas high school teachers still have heavy duties in this department. Leaving a room full of high school adolescents alone with each other and a television set would still seem problematic today. But we have gotten used to the idea that doing the same thing with their slightly older brethren in college is not likely to cause trouble—or that if it does, the trouble is not their teachers' business. This view is a relatively recent development in the history of higher education. For a long time, colleges and universities assumed extensive responsibility for student manners and moral discipline. Had there been educational television in 1890, it might have seemed as troublesome in universities as it now seems in high schools.

My account, admittedly speculative, suggests that the social organization of education is an important influence on technology use. In institutions that have given up most social and moral oversight of students, and in which student discipline is not seen as an educational matter, an instructional technology that permits students more autonomy from their teachers—even if it is a curiously routinized and even remote autonomy—is not problematic. But technology that permits such autonomy presents difficulties for educational institutions that make student discipline a central educational mission.

Adult and continuing education programs have capitalized somewhat more on television's possibilities for decentralized instruction. The Open University, for instance, uses television to deliver higher education to adults. Students can watch at home, do assignments and exams by mail, and work to a large extent on their own schedules. The technical capacity for this mode of delivering higher education exists in many American public higher education systems, and some universities use TV to deliver some of their lifelong education programs. But these are kept quite separate from undergraduate and graduate education—the academic and budgetary core of U.S. universities. There is no technical reason for such separation: Undergraduate or graduate students could take their classes in their rooms, their parents' homes, on in downtown hotels. It would be cheaper and easier to wire up a university for educational TV than for computers. Indeed, universities could reduce many of their costs if they seriously used this technology. Why has no one seized the opportunity?

At least part of the reason is that each advantage of such an innovation is also a serious organizational drawback. For one thing, radical decentralization of instruction could eliminate many classes. While this might not be a great pedagogical loss, given the quality of instruction in most universities, it would be a great change in the organization—and the theatre—of higher education. And the change would raise questions about the value of university campuses, dedicated as they are to classrooms. It also would raise nasty questions about the faculty. For if classes can be preserved, packaged, and rebroadcast, why keep the likes of us around, soaking up salaries by annually offering courses that might better be taped once every 5 or 10 years? And finally, this technology would eliminate the need for universities to provide daycare for superannuated adolescents: The costly and burdensome administration of dormitories, health services, counselling, and related services could be reduced or eliminated. But such measures might produce hostile reactions among parents and students, eager for relief from each other.

These considerations suggest some reasons why TV has not captured the heart of university education, and they help to explain why it has spread instead at the periphery. Continuing education is a sector of higher education in which the organizational barriers to this technology are weak. For these programs rarely have permanent faculty. They have few students in need of a home away from home. They have no great costs sunk in physical plant. And they have few alums wishing to renew fond memories of dozing through Western Civ in Blow Hall 100.

Past Uses of Technology

What does this discussion suggest about patterns of technology use in education?

First, there is plenty of evidence that technology is used. If educational television did not deliver on its promises for elementary and secondary schools, it is used in higher education. If the new curricula were often not used as intended, some were taken in sizable does, nonetheless. In thinking about the newest technology, we should be as prepared to explore unintended uses and nonuse as faithful adoption.

How can these things be described? Explained? In the recent past, adoption and use have most often been explored in terms of what might be termed organizational management: Variations in use have been ascribed to the extent to which the change process accommodated the interests, concerns, and situations of the various parties involved[10]. This concern seems appropriate,

---

[10]There has been an outpouring of research along these lines in the past 15 or 20 years. One of the chief studies was Berman, P., & McLaughlin, M. (1977). *Federal Programs Supporting Educational Change* (Vol. 7). Santa Monica: RAND. Another was Weick, K. (1976). Educational organizations as loosely coupled systems. *Administrative Sciences Quarterly, 21,* 1–19.

but it might usefully be broadened. In the cases just sketched, for instance, it often looks as though very broad organizational considerations that reach beyond the change process—such as the structure of adult and continuing education, or the social organization of higher education—may help to explain the uses and nonuses of technology. And in other instances it seems as though very specific features of the organization of instruction—such as the demands of whole-class instruction—also affect technology use.

In what follows, I explore the relation between the social organization of instruction, writ large and small, and instructional technology. This is a tall order. Researchers have probed each of these departments in some detail, but they rarely have explored them together, or explored their connections. With a few exceptions, researchers have not tried to understand the relations between what we call practice (the instructional form or content of a technology, or the organization of instruction itself), and what we call policy and organization (programs to reform instruction, the structure of school systems, and the like). This is a messy subject, but a fascinating one.

One issue concerns the relative importance of technology and social organization: Much of the programmatic literature on new technologies portrays them as powerful interventions into troubled or moribund organizations. But many studies of innovation tell stories about new instructional technologies being swamped by the organizations into which they were introduced[11]. Can one make sense of these contrary claims?

The dominant view, at least in America, is to regard technology as a powerful independent force for organizational change. The impact of new manufacturing technology on the creation of assembly line production is the classic example of this view. But it is not the only example. Nearly all the new technologies pressed on schools since WW II, from paperbacks to microcomputers, have been advertised as agents that would change education by making students less dependent on teachers, and by reducing whole-class, lockstep, batch-processed teaching and learning. Americans persistently dream about the liberating effects of technical innovations. There is a St-Simonian, almost utopian quality about these hopes, a sense that technology itself can break the chains that bind us to a dreary, work-a-day routine. Much of the promotion for microcomputers, among other educational innovations, attends little to their potential for school instruction, focusing instead quite selectively on their most extraordinary possibilities.

This view of technology seems more plausible if one focuses just on the possibilities for learning and teaching that new technologies might open up. But new possibilities alone will not drive social organizations to realize them. Incentives are required to encourage the changes that new technology requires; work often must be reorganized to accommodate new modes of production;

---

[11]Cuban, *Teachers and machines, op cit.*, presents such a story for most technical innovations in education.

decisions must be taken. A little analysis of the old assembly-line example reveals that technology did not drive change in the organization of production. It only opened up opportunities for such change. Workers and managers still had to decide whether changes would be made, what they would be, and how they would be made. Work still had to be reorganized to accommodate these changes. Technology alone reorganizes nothing. If we view technology as an enabler rather than a driver of organizational change, we can ask a question that enthusiasts and commentators alike have often ignored: What might it take, in addition to the possibilities opened by the new technology, to change an organization so that it could take advantage of the new technical possibilities?

Such a query would be salient in the study of technology and social change in any sector of society. It would be particularly salient in sectors whose production technology was relatively weak (whether because it was weakly understood and thus poorly used, or simply weak). For in such sectors we would expect that the lesser influence of technology on production might be complemented by a greater influence of nontechnical, social factors. Education is such a sector. In addition, posing that question would encourage us to consider differences, among sectors, in the capacity of organizations to take advantage of new technical possibilities. Public education seems relatively poorly situated in this respect. Unlike most private firms, it is not organized as a market activity. Therefore decisions about technology use, among others, are not much affected by economic incentives. And, unlike most private firms and some public organizations, education does not have results that can be relatively easily summarized in things produced, services performed, net sales, or profit and loss. Nor have educators been able to find means to reliably produce the results they do seek.

Under these circumstances, one would expect that the innovations most widely adopted would be those that presented the fewest problems. For lacking other powerful incentives to adopt and use a new technology, and suffer through the attendant disruptions, one powerful influence on the uses of any novelty would be its general compatibility with ongoing practice.

One way to illustrate this point is to compare CAI with the more recent microcomputers. CAI was little used. Yet it was only a slightly earlier incarnation of a technology that, even after only a few years, is now fairly widely used. Why?

CAI was problematic in part because computers were expensive and scarce. But worse, they were relatively inflexible. Most ordinary schools or classrooms would have had only one terminal. Because most instruction is whole-class work, most teachers could not have used the new machines without creating queuing problems. Even if teachers already knew everything they required to use CAI, they would have had to cope with turntaking at the terminal, and its impact on what everyone else would be doing. That would have added another classroom management problem to the many teachers already had. That would have chilled the enthusiasm even of teachers who desperately wanted CAI.

By contrast, the new technology can easily adapt to the social configuration of school instruction. Because the new machines are relatively cheap, and getting cheaper while getting better, some schools already can afford to have all students in a class work simultaneously on their own machines. More may be able to afford it in the near future. And because the technology is much more powerful than it was 15 years ago, and getting more so, it is already possible to program computers so they can be used quite flexibly—in some cases, nearly as flexibly as books. The machines are much more capacious and much smaller. Partly as a result of their greater capacity, the programming is more flexible, and sometimes quite ingenious. As a result, there are quite a few programs that allow students to work at their own pace, without disturbing others. There are some programs that even allow students to work, by themselves, on topics that might interest them. My point is not that all schools will adopt computers. It is only that they could, without creating the kinds of organizational problems that CAI would have produced.

But if technologies vary, so do organizations. Although public education generally exhibits weak incentives for the adoption of innovations that would cause internal stress, it is not utterly homogeneous in this respect. There is internal variation in possibilities for educational innovation.

What type of variation? I find it useful to distinguish between the core and the margins of educational organizations, when considering the adoption and use of new instructional technology. The barriers to serious innovation in the core instructional program are imposing. But many innovations have found a home on the margins of the schools. They do so by defining a distinctive clientele and a distinctive instructional approach, and enclosing them in an organizational subunit that is not seen as central to the organization's work.

Support for this view can be drawn from studies of high school organization, and from evidence on educational innovation more broadly defined. The research on American high schools that Arthur Powell, Eleanor Farrar, and I reported recently, in *The Shopping Mall High School*, noted rather sharp differences between kinds of instruction that could be found in various boutiques—i.e., programs for students whom the schools saw as "special"— and the instruction found in the much larger programs for ordinary students. Some boutiques offered crack academic work, some offered vocational studies, and others were for special education students. But teaching in the boutiques often was more personalized and of good quality. By contrast, instruction in the core was much less personalized and only infrequently did it rise above the routine. Instruction at the margins also was much more likely to incorporate various recent instructional and curricular innovations.

We noted some organizational differences between boutiques and supermarkets. The boutiques were small and specialized, but the supermarkets were large and unspecialized. The boutiques seemed to be on the fringes of the schools' organization and purpose, whereas the supermarkets were at the core[12]. Even though they were less good and less distinctive, these large programs for ordinary students were the educational mainstream.

What does that mean? Part of my assignment in *Shopping Mall* was to investigate why high schools had turned out as they had. I noticed two telling developments. Between 1890 and 1950, enormous energy was devoted to creating an organization and instructional forms that were specifically designed to accommodate students who were thought to be uninterested in learning very much, or untalented at learning very much, or both. The result was an educational program that was almost entirely vocationalized—that is, although there were different subspecialties, nearly all were aimed at different occupations, and most course work was turned in a practical, vocational direction. Only the small, top, academic track included courses aimed at mental cultivation, and even these were thought to point toward professions. Most high schools had four or five curricula, but most sought to provide practical studies, easily completed, for students who were thought to care little for learning. All this was thought to be a great victory for democracy over aristocracy and classicism in education[13]. It still composes the core of instruction and organization in secondary education.

But between 1950 and the 1980s, the schools were struck by wave after wave of criticism and reform. They responded by permitting or encouraging change around the edges of the already-established core. In a few cases this required only the adaptation of an extant subunit, as in the case of better course work for the college bound in the 1950s. More solid courses were added to this small segment of the organization, and existing courses were redefined. In most cases it required the creation of the new educational specialties and/or organizational subunits. One such departure was the Advanced Placement Program. This was a new organization of instruction for the most talented students, inspired by 1950s concerns about poor instruction in high schools. It was a bold departure in several respects. Though offered locally, it was in some respects a national program. Teaching and curriculum in special classes were referenced to uniform national examinations. In addition, the program linked high school performance to college work in a hitherto unheard-of way: Students' scores on these exams could gain them credit for work in the first year or two of college. The first of these changes marked the advent of a selective, European-style approach to education in a distinctly un-European system of mass-access higher education. And the second marked an effort—unique in this open and forgiving system of mass higher education—to offer strong incentives for quality work in high schools, and to tie them to specific measures of performance in specific curricula.

---

[12]Powell *et. al.*, (pp. 9–65).
[13]*Op. cit.*, (pp. 245–79).

These remarkable changes owed a good deal to the marginality of the concerned students, teachers, and curricula. For by the early 1950s secondary education was already mostly oriented to weak academic performance. The high schools had abandoned their selective character five or six decades before and oriented most offerings to a clientele that was believed to have neither the will nor the wit for serious academic work. The system of secondary education that was built by the late 1920s was a large-scale, batch-processing enterprise, oriented to getting the largest number of students in and out with the least difficulty. By the 1950s that had been the core of secondary instruction for more than a generation. The genius — and the chief limitation — of the AP program was that it opened up new possibilities for high-quality work within such a system, without challenging the core of the system. It did so by creating a new educational specialty at the margin. The program has proved to be quite effective, and durable.

A similar account could be given for a wide range of innovations. Consider special education, for instance. Prior to 1968, handicapped students typically got more warehousing than instruction in public schools. Many students were kept in separate rooms — margins of a kind. The changes made since then have been called mainstreaming — i.e., bringing disabled students out of various educational closets into regular classrooms. This picture is not incorrect, for PL 94–142 increased contact between disabled and regular students. But it is somewhat misleading. For instance, many high schools now offer something close to an entire curriculum for special education students. Special classes in elementary schools have increased, not diminished. A new subspecialty of teachers, who teach only disabled students, has developed. They see themselves as a cadre: Specially qualified, with a distinctive mission, teachers who are different and better than their regular colleagues. Many students spend all or most of their time with these teachers.

Although mainstreaming is a good slogan, a better description is that a new subsector of education has developed. There has been some mainstreaming of students, but special education was not absorbed in the mainstream. It is mainstream in the sense that it is out of the closet, near the center of debate and discourse, relatively well funded and prestigious. But it is not at all mainstream in the sense that special education has been diffused in the central core of education, or of individual schools[14].

---

[14]The subsector reaches beyond schools to special education research, development, teacher training, and evaluation, All have multiplied, improved, and made connections that cross the boundaries of governments and educational organizations. And all are part of a remarkably effective political network, dedicated to secure better services for disabled students that has grown up to protect, revise, and extend the legislative and legal victories won two decades ago.

Other examples of the same phenomenon come easily to mind: bilingual education, Headstart, and Upward Bound. These are marginal in the several senses used here. The students are special and are highly identifiable populations. They are believed to require unusual treatment in schools because of some special condition or problem. They have well-organized constituencies that have

The point can be extended to the two-year-old struggle to improve education for disadvantaged children. The available analyses seem to show that there has been little or no sustained improvement in students' academic performance as a result of exposure to ESEA Title I (now Chapter I) programs. The reasons adduced for this rather modest showing cover everything from fragmented programs to inadequate resources. But my arguments about innovation suggests that Title I remains a problem partly because it failed to create a distinct subsector, in which distinctive educational services could be provided for a special population. Instead, program advocates launched a frontal attack on the way disadvantaged students were managed within the educational mainstream. Innovators were thus in the odd position of demanding special attention for students who were agreed to be different in some sense, but also rejecting the strategies that would have made such attention organizationally feasible and appealing. "Pull-out" programs a few hours a day were permitted, but no distinctive subunits, teaching cadre, or instructional approach were developed. In this respect, the program may have been a victim of the egalitarian ideals with which it always has been associated.

Innovations do succeed at the core of public education. But they tend to be superficial. Many have swept across the nation's schools, quickly finding thousands of adoptions but disappearing equally quickly, leaving few traces of their existence. The best current case is effective schools programs. They have been packaged by many entrepreneurs so that a district can "adopt" the innovation by hiring a consultant and making an announcement and disseminate it by holding a few workshops. Another favorite of bygone years was the filmstrip, along with other "audio visual technology." These could be adopted by purchase and disseminated by renaming school libraries: They became "media centers," with the new technology filed inside.

My point is not that instructional change is impossible. It is that there are different kinds of change in instruction, and different organizational locales for it. There is a continual busy flutter at the heart of public education, as one infatuation after another holds sway. While everyone deplores these little romances many must find them enticing, for they persist. But when substantial pressure has been mobilized for change at the margins of education, the results often have been fairly impressive. My account suggests that the margins are a flexible and changing locale: As the 20th century has progressed, they have become more densely populated. One implication of my argument is that if we looked for significant instructional innovation in these subregions, rather than looking for it on average, everywhere, we would find more of it.

---

recently compiled a decent track record in getting what they want from governments. They have cadres of teachers who think of themselves as specially qualified and committed and able to deal with extraordinary demands. Finally, these programs married some important changes in educational technique or technology to important changes in the organization of instruction. A glance over these attributes reveals that they also apply to Advanced Placement programs, honors courses, and the like.

What does my argument imply, concerning the use of the newest new technology?

Chiefly that its great flexibility may make it easy for schools to adapt this technology to the inherited organization of instruction. Many fans of the new technology see its flexibility as the key to its revolutionary impact, but they may well be disappointed. Consider the technology's prospects, in light of the main features of the instructional core that I have been discussing:

1. Most instruction occurs in groups of 25 to 35 students. It tends to be scheduled in small segments of 45 to 50 minutes. These segments seem to be irreversible in high school, and somewhat more flexible in some elementary schools.

2. Classroom instruction is either whole-class work or completely individual; there are few cases in which subgroups' work varies greatly, or that they have had a large role in shaping. There is grouping within classes in elementary grades, but work in these groups generally seems to consist of faster or slower versions of the whole-class agenda.

3. Instruction is teacher dominated, whether whole-class or individual. Whole-class work consists chiefly of lecture and recitation, rather than discussion or other formats in which students take extensive responsibility by setting the terms of instruction, probing issues, and the like. Teacher talk dominates such instruction. When students do talk, it usually consists of brief answers to teacher questions. There are few opportunities for teachers to probe students' thinking, to explore the nature of misconceptions, mistakes, innovative ideas, and the like.

4. Most individual work is seat work, in which students labor alone on hand-outs that are either devised or selected by teachers. The content and format of these worksheets is generally such that teachers dominate as much here as in recitation; students have little responsibility for setting the terms of work, or opportunities to probe issues. As in whole-class recitation, they respond briefly to teacher queries. There are few opportunities for teachers to explore students' thinking.

5. There is a mental organization of instruction that typically accompanies this social organization. In it, academic competence is construed in what some would regard as minimal terms. Knowledge is represented as the mastery of bits of information, and isolated, mechanically mastered skills. Intellectual performance is represented as the correct recapitulation of those bits, and display of the skills.

The new technology can easily fit into the instructional organization. It can be used within the whole-class format discussed previously in points 1 and 2, without disruption due to queuing. Although not yet as flexible as books, the machines and software already available seem to work well within the lecture–

recitation format (point 3). Much of the software currently available is, in effect, an individualized recitation.

But the new technology would not be used widely unless it also was compatible with the intellectual organization of instruction described here (point 5). All reports are that the most common instructional programs are drill and practice. If this industry responds to demand in roughly the same way that other publishers have, such software will continue to be the most popular, simply because it can be easily integrated into mainstream classrooms (point 4). This suggests that the chief barriers to the widespread adoption and use of the new technology may turn out to be financial or administrative, rather than organizational or intellectual.

There are, of course, exceptions to these patterns. Teachers in AP classes, or Special Education classes, some vocational classes, and teachers who specialize in various subject areas all are potential markets for more specialized and possibly more sophisticated software. When instructional software that aims at more than drill and practice is used, it probably will be in such marginal areas of the instructional organization, not in the mainstream. Of course, there are some teachers at work in standard instructional settings whose practice is demanding and sophisticated, and they may use innovative software.

Explanations

Explaining the failure of reform has been an important theme in educational research since the turn of this century, when reformers and commentators first noticed that important instructional innovations were not having the intended effects. Such work developed into a sizeable social science industry in the late 1960s, when a large national program of national educational reform seemed to flop. Three kinds of explanations have been advanced. The oldest refers reform failures to the materials of reform itself: inadequate curriculum, insufficient teacher preparation, too little time, or not enough money. This has long been a popular explanation, perhaps because it permitted reformers and partisan investigators to chalk the persistence of old patterns up to teachers' perversity or stupidity, or to the absence of good alternatives in curriculum or instruction[15]. But these explanations are no longer easy to accept, for as Larry Cuban and others have pointed out, the old patterns of teaching have persisted through the provision of many of the alternative curricula and instructional improvements that reformers demanded. They have persisted as well through dramatic improvements in the education of American teachers. This suggests that the barriers to instructional reform are either located elsewhere or are more deeply rooted.

---

[15]John Dewey himself was one of the early figures to use this argument, in explaining the slower-than-earlier-imagined progress of his "new education." See *Experience and education* p. 90. New York: Kappa Delta Pi, 1938.

A second line of work focuses on frailties in the reforms. One common explanation is inadequate management of change in schools and innovative programs, and another is inadequate adjustment between reforms and schools. This line of work is popular, perhaps because the research seems to suggest that reform can work if these problems are repaired[16]. A last line of investigation locates obstacles to change in the schools' organization. The favorite explanation is weak interdependence among subunits of local schools—loose coupling, in one inelegant formulation. This approach seems to imply that reform will not succeed unless schools are reorganized[17].

All these approaches seem sensible in some respect. Each points to problems that have been found in some instructional reforms and might be found in many more. But other explanations have been offered that have had less attention. I explore three of these next.

Incentives

One explanation for the persistence of traditional instruction is that societies get the schools they deserve, or want. If incentives for serious academic effort are generally weak, it would be foolish to expect anything but superficial innovations, and the continuation of inherited forms. Incentives for instruction can be grouped in three rough categories: those that are broadly social and operate ubiquitously on education, those that are specific to the system of public education and operate within that system, and those that are specific to the terrain of instruction and operate in classrooms, or wherever instruction occurs.

Ubiquitous Incentives. Education is an object of both public needs and private wants. State, local, and federal governments make policies for schools, but parents and students shape education simply by the weight of their private preferences. Both affect the incentives for instruction, but their effect has been paradoxical in America: We are enthusiastic supporters of public schools, but indifferent or hostile to intellectually demanding education. This situation can be seen in public policy, where Americans have pressed public schools to solve social and moral problems more than they have pressed for academic quality[18].

---

[16]This has been especially true of the line of research associated with Berman and McLaughlin's work, (*Federal Programs Supporting . . .*).

[17]Weick, K., *op. cit.*

[18]In debates about whether education should be a public responsibility, in the 1830s and 1840s, juvenile crime and immigrants' alleged lack of proper morals and respect for authority were higher on many reformers' agendas than students' academic performance. Indeed, some early crusaders for public education, like Henry Barnard, argued that public schools were needed to repair a moral crisis, not to improve intellectual performance. Early in the 20th century, the expansion of public education was justified partly as a solution to problems of child labor and family instability. More recently, drugs, teen-age pregnancy, and race relations have become important items on the schools' agenda. These problems may be appropriate for schools to attack, but none require stiff academic standards for their solution.

It also can be seen in the content of private attitudes, in which students and adults consistently give vocational preparation and social adjustment much greater importance than academic work. This preference also pops up in passionate popular crusades against sophisticated literature and cosmopolitan curricula, and for the promulgation of simple pieties in public schools.

Higher education is another important source of incentives for elementary and secondary instruction. One way colleges and universities exert their influence is in the education of teachers for the lower schools, an activity to which they consistently give a very low priority. They devote few resources to the cultivation or study of expert pedagogical knowledge, either in their own faculties or among teachers in the lower schools. And the higher schools impose the weakest standards in admission to teacher education programs, and permit a disproportionately large share of weak candidates to complete their programs and enter the teaching profession. Such teachers have a limited capacity to encourage strong academic performance from students, either by their own example or by more deliberate means.

Colleges and universities also affect incentives for performance in the lower schools with their entrance criteria. These can shape high school performance standards for those students who want to go to college, and perhaps for others in their vicinity. The influence of admissions standards has changed dramatically in our own time: Between 1940 and 1970, a small and rather selective college and university system became a huge and mostly unselective system. American secondary education thus went from a situation in which, on average, only a few students in each high school were directly affected by college admission standards to one in which, on average, perhaps a third or a half the students were so affected.

That seems a vast increase in the leverage that higher schools had on their lower counterparts. But the strongest post-WW II expansion occurred in the weakest academic sectors of higher education: community colleges, state university branch campuses, and state universities. By the late 1960s or early 1970s, students in high school virtually anywhere could get into something called a college, as long as they had graduated from high school. Other academic qualifications were irrelevant. This forgiving system has several advantages when compared with more selective approaches found in most other nations: It offers many students a chance at higher education and thus offers many who have done poorly in high school another chance, or two. But considered as a system, U.S. high education does not reinforce solid standards of academic performance, either within its boundaries or in the schools below.

Labor markets are a third source of generalized incentives for instruction. The old romance of technology and education tells us that technical and industrial progress push the need for education ever higher. But while skill and knowledge requirements have increased in some technical and professional jobs, they have not increased, and probably declined, in many other jobs. This development sends a mixed message: Studying hard will pay off for a minority who will win skilled jobs, but not for many others who will work in various service industries, or as laborers in old or new industrial firms. We know little about the extent of economic rationality among high school students, but recent studies reveal that many students know that youth unemployment is high, and that skill requirements for many jobs are low. Many know they can get jobs without doing much in school; others doubt that they can find any decent work and wonder why they should do schoolwork[19].

There are incentives for demanding teaching and learning, then, but they are not general through the society. They are found only in selected social pockets. The more ubiquitous incentives are those that encourage or tolerate weak academic performance.

School System Incentives. The organization of education systems also affects incentives for academic performance. The U.S. system is inclusive: Everyone old enough to attend is expected to do so, and no admission standards save age are imposed. Universality tends to weaken incentives for academic performance. For in the competitive society, goods or services that are universally available tend to be assigned a lower value than those that are more scarce, other things being equal. Goods or services that are available to all but can only be secured by some, as the result of special effort or achievement, are more highly valued than those that anyone can have without special effort or merit.

Universality alone is not controlling: Internal standards of quality can strengthen performance incentives, even within universal systems. Japanese elementary and secondary schools are roughly as inclusive as our own and so might seem to offer few incentives for strong academic performance. But Japanese schools are organized around highly selective school entrance and leaving exams. These create incentives for academic work because students' educational status, and their progress toward careers depend on their exam performance. Japanese schools balance an emphasis on inclusiveness and diverse educational opportunities with a stress on academic performance[20].

By contrast, American schools have only minimal standards for internal progress and school leaving. Historically, schools' standards of quality have been eroded, or their formation has been precluded, as education became more popular. As elementary school attendance moved toward universality in the late 19th century, for instance, standards for promotion and graduation steadily weakened. By the end of the century, promotion was based more on social than academic grounds, and graduation could be achieved simply by completing the grades, rather than by producing evidence of adequate academic

---

[19]Sedlak, M., *et. al.* (1986). *Selling students short.* New York: Teachers College. Some evidence on these points is summarized in pp. 59–63.

[20]Rohlen, T.P. (1983). *Japan's high schools.* Berkeley: University of California, especially part I.

performance. Roughly the same story was repeated for secondary education in the first four decades of our own century. By World War II, internal standards for promotion and school leaving were so weak that students could complete the required 12 years of education with only minimal academic accomplishments[21]. Incentives for weak performance due to the system's inclusiveness are not balanced by pressures for strong performance due to internal selectivity.

Weak incentives for academic work also can be traced to compulsion in education. Students cannot learn much, and teachers cannot teach well unless they make serious commitments to do so. Although such commitment can be encouraged and supported, it is difficult to compel in a relatively free society. For in such a society commitment is associated with choice, and compulsion with punishment, incapacity, or both. Most ordinary law enforcement uses compulsory punishment as its sanction, and mental illness or incompetence also are often dealt with by compulsory assignment to custodial or treatment institutions. But activities that require great personal commitment for success are rarely compelled. Military service is a seemingly contrary case, but the units that require the greatest commitment typically require choice. Membership in elite units, such as the Air Force, paratroopers, commandoes, and the like, are the result of mutual choice: The recruits must apply, and they must also be chosen. In such cases mutual choice helps to build mutual commitment to the goals of the units, to hard work, and to high performance, This is also the case with selective schools, and with some selective programs within schools. But most of public education is compulsory. Indeed, compulsory school attendance originally was motivated in part by fear of delinquent and potentially criminal youth, and by the hope that schools could resocialize them and save society from destruction. Compulsory schooling later grew with renewed worries about delinquency, child labor, and youthful competition with adult workers. Organizations built on such compulsion tend to defeat rather than build commitment to hard work and high performance, save perhaps in times of crisis.

The incentives that are specific to the organization of the public education system are thus one-sided. The corrosive effects of unselective access and the absence of strong internal standards are reinforced by compulsion.

Classroom Incentives. The organization of teachers' classroom work also generates incentives for weak academic performance. One reason for this is that public school teachers have enormous problems of coverage. Most elementary teachers work with a relatively modest number of children, 25 to 35, on average; but they have enormous problems of subject-matter coverage, for most teachers are responsible for all subjects. One can cover mathematics, reading and writing, geography, social studies, and physical and biological science if

---

[21]Powell *et. al., op. cit.*

one more or less blindly follows a text. But it would require extraordinary talents to know all those subject well enough to teach them in an intelligent and demanding fashion. The extraordinary demands of subject-matter coverage in elementary schools presses teachers toward superficial, rote teaching.

High school teachers need not cover so many subjects: Most teach no more than two. But they must cover many more students, not uncommonly 150 or more every day. These students come in four or five daily batches of 20 or 30 each, for 50 minutes per batch. This organization permits deeper knowledge of subject, but it does not encourage thoughtful or demanding teaching of those subjects. Because the constraints of time, schedule, and student numbers make it prohibitive to give much attention to students' written work, teachers are pressed to use simple multiple choice or fill-in-the-blanks student assignments and discouraged from making many writing assignments. The constraints also discourage much attention to students' ideas about subjects, save whether their answers are right or wrong.

These pressures are multiplied by the common tendency of school managers and parents to hold teachers responsible for classroom discipline above all else. Teachers are expected to keep their classes friendly and quiet, and to manage discipline problems by themselves. Many principals and parents associate noisy classrooms, or students sent out because they will not work, with teachers' inability to manage competently. These expectations put teachers in a bind, for many of their students have little interest in academic work. Such uninterested students are a potential discipline problem in any event, and their potential in this department increases as teachers increase academic demands. Teachers thus must often trade off academic demands for classroom peace, and protection from complaining parents and principals

I am not advancing an organizational determinism. Teachers work within and around the constraints that I have described in many different ways. But much of this variation in teaching lies on other dimensions than academic quality. Some teachers do overcome the constraints and produce impressive classes. They are relatively rare exceptions, though. The incentives that affect public elementary and secondary schools encourage superficiality in teachers' and students' contacts with each other, and with academic subjects.

Under these circumstances, one would expect that demanding reforms of instruction would take hold only under special conditions, and that inherited instructional forms would persist. One also would expect that to find widespread adoption and use, innovations would have to make only modest demands of students and teachers and require only modest change in inherited approaches to teaching and learning. The implications for the new technology seem straightforward: Cost and promotion aside, if widely used in ordinary school settings it seems likely to be used for standard and relatively undemanding activities, usually lumped together under the rubric of drill and practice. if used in the service of academically demanding instruction, it seems likely to be used chiefly in special circumstances, such as those that I earlier termed the margins of public education.

BARRIERS TO INQUIRY-ORIENTED INSTRUCTION

One of the most powerfully appealing features of the new computer technology is the sense that it opens up many possibilities to make teaching and learning more exciting. Many fans see the new technology as a way to nourish students' intellectual curiosity and feed the hunger for learning that is believed to be blocked by backward practice, or inadequate materials. These ideas connect the new technology with two old themes in American efforts to reform instruction and learning. One is that students are naturally curious and inventive, and that school is dull because these attributes are suppressed rather than encouraged. If they were just offered interesting curriculum, students would approach instruction with the same appetites they bring to ice cream. The other theme is that it is not difficult to make teaching lively and interesting while still packing it with deep intellectual content. If teachers could be clever about pedagogy and knowledgeable about their subjects, everyone would learn and love it. John Dewey was the first really famous preacher of this gospel, but he had many predecessors as well as battalions of followers[22].

Enthusiasm for the latest new technology incorporates many of these old ideas about educational practice. Like many earlier reformers, designers of computer software and advocates of inventive design want to devise materials that would encourage students and teachers to become active inquirers. They want instruction to be inquiry oriented. This is a slogan that covers a multitude of tendencies in educational practice and theory, but most of them share a view of students as active constructors of knowledge, of knowledge as open and evolving, of academic learning as exciting and vital, and of teaching as a stimulus to curiosity and a model of inquiry[23].

There are, however, important barriers to the success of such instruction that have been little examined, either by reformers or students of instructional improvement. Some arise from the extraordinary intellectual and emotional

---

[22]This section draws on research for a book in progress that I have tentatively titled, *Teaching: Policy and practice*. Some parts of the argument are sketched in an essay delivered at The Benton Center at The University of Chicago that is to be published by The National Society For The Study of Education: "Teaching Practice: Plus Que Ca Change . . .", June, 1987.

[23]These ideas have animated many academic efforts to reform instruction. They include the early 20th century Progressivisms of Dewey, George Counts, W.H. Kilpatrick, and others, to the later curriculum reform efforts of Jerome Bruner and his many co-workers and sympathizers, and recent "constructivist" and "cognitivist" psychologists and curriculum reformers. These advocates have found much to argue about with each other, but they seem more similar than different when considered against the background of teaching practice in most public schools.

demands that such teaching makes on teachers and students. The other arises from the weak roots that these reforms have in the social organization of instruction in the U.S. I take up both problems in the following sections.

Instructional Barriers. Some clues that inquiry-oriented teaching and learning may be problematic regularly surface in studies of instruction. Many teachers who seek more thoughtful and exciting classes find that they cannot produce them — the work is too tiring, or otherwise demanding. In addition, students often demur. They complain that the teaching is too demanding, too difficult to understand, or not to their taste[24]. One could dismiss these reports as the result of either teachers' inadequate skill or determination, or students' laziness. No doubt both explanations are sometimes appropriate. But there are other explanations as well. Learning to understand multiplication strikes academics as more gratifying than merely learning to do it. But learning to understand multiplication requires that students take on a formidable intellectual agenda. They must learn several different ways to represent this arithmetical operation. In regular classes it requires that students consider each others' representations, and it quite likely also requires that they probe each others' reasons for representing the procedure in one way and not another. Understanding multiplication also requires that they make plausible arguments, to their teacher and perhaps their classmates, about the representations they have devised.

These requirements strike many professors as exciting — cracking puzzles is our stock-in-trade, after all. But school and university classrooms abound with evidence that students often find such work problematic. Many will tell observers and teachers that they prefer rote learning, in part because it is simpler, easier, and less uncertain. Most reformers and many researchers interpret such statements as evidence that the teaching simply was not good enough, and they redouble their efforts to develop the techniques, or to discern them. There is a sense in which one wants to reject the students' comments: Multiplication learned by rote is deeply mysterious. No explanations for following the procedures are offered, save that the teacher or text says so, or that they produce the right answers. This offends the inquiring mind — or at least the mind that inquires about mathematics. But note that those same minds often reject their garage mechanic's efforts to explain why their Saab stalls in damp weather, or the dishwasher repairman's effort to show them how to load wine glasses properly, or the cleaning person's effort to explain why wax remover, not soap and water, is needed for the kitchen floor. The desired objects of understanding are not equally weighted for all minds. So when many students say they find procedural learning less mysterious, and that they want to only learn the right algorithm, they may only be doing to teachers what many teachers and researchers to do mechanics or cleaning people. When students resist efforts

---

[24]Cohen, *op. cit.,* (pp. 33–63).

to elicit their understanding of ideas and seek the easier surface of academic knowledge, they may be expressing a deep preference, not just reflecting laziness or the lack of adequate instruction.

In addition, inquiry-oriented learning can be as risky as it is difficult. It requires that students tolerate considerable uncertainty: about the nature of arithmetical problems, about the procedures for solving them, about what the answers are, and about how implausible answers can be detected and plausible answers defended. It also requires that students expose themselves more, simply because they must adopt trying out—i.e., hypothesis framing and testing—as a way of life in learning. But many students find it difficult to accept that knowledge entails the acceptance of uncertainty. They find it risky but also contrary to their conception of knowing. Many also resist the exposure of self that a trying-out approach to learning entails, even in tutorial situations. Many more resist in whole classrooms, when a large audience watches and listens. The prefer the certainties of mechanical learning to the risks of more adventurous work.

Turn now from students to teachers. One reason that teachers often find inquiry-oriented approaches to instruction very difficult is that so many students seem allergic to it. For in order to make inquiry-oriented instruction succeed with such students, teachers must take on a large agenda. They must wean students away from the safety of rote learning. They must instruct students in framing and testing hypotheses. And they must build a climate of tolerance and curiosity about unusual answers, among other things. Teachers who take this path must work harder, concentrate more, and embrace larger pedagogical responsibilities than if they only assigned text chapters and seatwork. They also must have considerable additional knowledge and skills to pull it off effectively. They must, for instance, deeply understand the material and grasp how students think about it. They must be able to comprehend students' interpretations of problems, their mistakes, and their puzzles. And, when they cannot comprehend, they must have the capacity to probe thoughtfully and tactfully. These and other capacities are required to present the material in ways likely to engage students' minds, to help students to frame fruitful hypotheses and discard unfruitful ones. None of this would be needed if teachers relied on texts and worksheets.

In addition, even if none of their students resist, teachers who seek to open up subjects as fields of inquiry must still take unusual risks. If they proceed in the standard instructional format, they can rely on the authority of text or official position in disputes with students, or when uncertain about how to proceed. But if they offer academic subjects as fields of inquiry, they must support their actions and decisions as intellectuals, not merely as functionaries or voices for a text; that is, they must appeal to rules of inquiry, methods of proof, and canons of evidence for resolving disputes and settling uncertainty. To do so, teachers also must be prepared to share authority. For how could students become active inquirers if their solutions and approaches were not taken seriously, accepted if plausible and well defended, and rejected only if demonstrated to be implausible? If academic subjects are to be taught as fields of inquiry, students must become inquirers, learning how to frame problems and decide disputes rather than learning how to get the right answer. They must therefore be encouraged to assume the authority that comes with intellectual competence, rather than to fly blind on the authority of texts and teachers.

Sharing authority is difficult for many teachers and students. They find it unsettling, even threatening. But when teachers embark on an inquiry-oriented pedagogy, they open up an entire new regime, one in which students have more autonomy in several dimensions, and in which teachers depend on their students more visibly and acutely. For if students are to become inquirers, they must take a large responsibility for producing instruction—it is, after all, their ideas, explanations, and other encounters with the material that become the subject matter of the class. If students do not pick up these broader intellectual and social responsibilities, this approach to instruction simply will not work. But if students do pick them up, teachers depend on these students more, for the students must produce more of the instruction, and teachers must rely less on texts and worksheets, or even their own lectures, among other things. This is risky stuff: At the same time that teachers' responsibilities expand and their authority seems to become more precarious, their dependence on students increases.

These arguments suggest that inquiry-oriented reforms of instruction make more extraordinary demands on students and teachers than most innovators and researchers have thought. These demands would incline many students and teachers to rather traditional approaches to instruction, whatever the organization and incentive structure of instruction. In the case of U.S. public education, organization and incentives actually amplify these conservative tendencies in practice[25], rather than reducing them.

Historical and Social Barriers. Educational reforms that seek to orient instruction to inquiry struggle against an old and deeply rooted scholastic inheritance. In this inheritance, teaching is telling, learning is accumulation, and knowledge is facts, strung together by rules of procedure. Contrary to most reformers' beliefs, these views elicit profound attachment from many children and adults. And the attachments do not arise merely from the difficulties of inquiry-oriented teaching and learning sketched earlier. The conceptions and practices that reformers wish to replace are not simply obsolete, boring, and stupid impositions, as Dewey and most reformers since have argued. Traditional approaches to instruction contain coherent and defensible views of knowledge, teaching, and learning. They represent views and practices to which many teachers, students, and parents have deep attachments.

One part of this scholastic inheritance is the widely shared conviction that valid academic knowledge consists of facts. Facts are found in books and

---

[25] *Op. cit.*

teachers' lectures. Efforts to suggest that there is more to academic knowledge than facts—that it consists of ideas about facts, or that facts have no meaningful status unless embedded in ideas about them, or that students are authors of ideas and therefore creators of academic knowledge—violates this view. For if knowledge does not consist of facts, well established and stored in authoritative locations, how can it be trusted? Anyone can make up ideas. If knowledge is composed or constructed—which is to say, made up—by little children, or even by schoolteachers, how seriously can it be taken? In addition, such a view of academic knowledge raises questions of authority: if knowledge is made up by ordinary people—even by people who are not grownup or much experienced—then how trustworthy can it be?

Another part of the inheritance is the notion that teaching is telling. The teacher is a voice for authoritative knowledge, which originates elsewhere. She is a pipeline for Truth. Teachers' assignment is to pass that knowledge on. Reforms of teaching and learning that reconstruct the teachers' role as interpreters of others' knowledge, and as facilitators of students' knowledge creation, cut across the grain of this view. If teachers are not a voice for what is authoritatively known, then what is the source of their authority to instruct? If teachers are only handmaidens to students' inventions, then how valuable is their contribution to education?

A third element in this scholastic inheritance is the idea that learning consists of accumulation. Students are supposed to assimilate knowledge that has valid sources elsewhere. Learners are seen as immature and marginal members of society, not innocents whose fresh perceptions offer a clearer view than inherited ideas and prejudices. Children are regarded as incomplete, undisciplined, and potentially dangerous—impressionable and easily misled. To assert that children construct knowledge is, from this perspective, either to say that their knowledge is not valid or authoritative (precisely because it was constructed by those who are marginal and immature), or that the learners are more mature and/or less marginal than had been assumed. Neither alternative is acceptable to those who hold this view.

These ideas have deep roots in medieval and early modern instructional practices and religious beliefs. They also have sources in passive epistomologies of early modern Europe, and the psychologies later built on them[26]. They are ancient and well established in academic habit. They contrast strongly with the intellectual sources of inquiry-oriented instruction. These reforms draw their inspiration chiefly from relatively recent academic theory and research in the sciences and psychology, and from elite literary and aesthetic culture. They have some sources in the new physics and philosophies of science of the late 19th and early 20th centuries; others in conceptions of the individual, and the power of individual imagination common to Romantic literature and philosophy; and still others in the more recent "cognitive revolution" in

---

[26]*Op. cit.*, (pp. 15–22).

psychology and information processing. The new ideas are powerful and compelling for many academics and cosmopolitan intellectuals. They have relatively quickly become an important part of academic work in the great centers of university research. But while professors there carry on Romantic traditions of critical individualism in the humanities, and more recent traditions of steady revolution in the physical and biological sciences, theirs is an academic, not a popular tradition. It lacks deep roots in popular thought and culture. By contrast, there is a popular culture of teaching and learning that has broad and deep roots in social practice, in inherited popular ideas and values, and in pedagogy in both the lower schools and the higher academy. This popular tradition lacks the elaborate expositions and justifications with which academics have endowed the new ideas about learning and teaching, but these seem not to be required for its continued vitality.

With respect to the new academic traditions, it appears that most of the inspiration and core ideas for inquiry-oriented instructional reform have emanated from academic intellectuals in elite institutions of higher education. These institutions are the sources of most academic research, whether in the sciences, the social sciences, or the humanities. They also are the most prestigious educational agencies in the United States. Harvard, MIT, The University of Chicago, The University of Illinois, and similar institutions were the source of much criticism of public education as mindless and boring in the late 1940s and early 1950s. They were where the curriculum reforms of the late 1950s were born, and where much of the curriculum development was carried out. They are the institutions in which much subsequent criticism of educational quality in the lower schools has originated, and from which many proposals for reform have been launched. And they are the institutions in which the new psychology, now widely regarded by academics as the chief rationale for instructional reform, now flourishes. These institutions are the center of the academic universe. The knowledge that is produced in them and the academics who produce it would therefore seem to have great standing and influence.

They do. But this standing and influence are sharply limited, at least for the purposes of reforming instruction. For one thing, these central institutions are quite remote from the thousands of higher and lower schools in which nearly all teaching and learning occurs. These other schools are peripheral in terms of prestige and knowledge production, but they are central agencies of instruction and learning. Few faculty members at the top research universities have been graduates of state university branch campuses or community colleges. Few able advanced-degree recipients from the great research institutions spend most of their careers at such low-prestige agencies of mass higher education. By contrast, few public schoolteachers are graduates of these great institutions at the academic center; most get their schooling in colleges and universities in which little research and much teaching are the rule. To the extent that the education and recruitment of new faculty are a source of influence for the great research institutions, then, that influence seems to be contained within a relatively modest circle of similar institutions of higher education. The great mass of schools, universities, and colleges find their faculty, and thus many of their ideas about knowledge, teaching, and learning in other institutions that are further from the center.

The elite centers also are remote from instructional practice in most educational institutions because they have devised a unique mission: research. Their distinction is tied in part to the discoveries and academic production of their faculties, and to their education of new generations of producers and discoverers. But the great mass of colleges and universities, like nearly all elementary and secondary schools, exist to teach, to provide day care, to prepare students for further specialized education and work, and to grant degrees. Knowledge production is not part of their mission, nor their faculties' assignment. As a result, the consumption of new knowledge that has been produced in the great centers is not a high priority either. It is, in fact, superfluous for most purposes of life and work in the academic hinterlands. It can be a way of "keeping up," and staying in touch. But for those who do not write—which is the huge majority of American teachers, whatever their institution—it is a matter of personal preference, not occupational necessity. Most teachers at the periphery have no good reason, save curiosity, to consume the products of the central academic institutions. And their teaching assignments offer many incentives to read little and write less. This difference in organizational mission and individual work impedes the influence of ideas, produced at the center, on thought and practice at the periphery.

Although new knowledge is produced at the academic center, then, it has more prestige than influence in the institutions of mass higher and lower education in which most instruction occurs. In addition, the universities at the center give little special attention to instruction. The study of education always has been academically marginal in these places, and the improvement of instruction, even in their own classrooms, never has been a high priority. Whereas they speak with great authority in many matters, few academics in these agencies have any special knowledge about or competence in instruction. Few have carefully or even casually studied teaching. These reforming academics have little to offer their colleagues whose careers have been devoted to teaching, aside from critiques. Although criticism can be an essential stimulus to change, it is rarely sufficient.

The relative weakness of inquiry-oriented reforms is not due simply to the social isolation of its chief advocates. It also stems from the existence of a powerful and deeply rooted popular culture of instruction that exists outside academic institutions. In this culture children are supposed to listen and not speak out; adults have answers; children learn by absorbing the answers. These ideas bear a marked resemblance to the scholastic inheritance sketched previously, and they seem to be quite popular in America. Studies of child-rearing and educational attitudes find them at all levels of society. They find them most commonly in those sectors that are least cosmopolitan—i.e., in less urbanized regions, among more religious elements, and by members of the working and lower middle class[27]. The recent revival of Protestant evangelism—among other contemporary religious renaissances—has helped to revitalize and refurbish these views of teaching and learning, and to install them in new fundamentalist schools. Recent demands for a return to "basics" also echoed elements of this old inheritance. These ideas are a lively feature of both the politics of education and the daily business of schooling. Pressure groups and public officials push them on school boards, administrators, and teachers. Parents press them on children before they go to school and later when they knock heads over homework.

These attitudes can plausibly be viewed as elements of an old scholasticism. It had accumulated over many centuries, and, contrary to the views of many academic researchers and reformers, it does not rest on outmoded scholarship, nor does it consist only of obsolete teaching techniques. The old scholasticism is transmitted as much by general education as by schools. It rests on a popular culture of knowledge, teaching, and learning that has been passed down unwittingly, and even unwillingly. This inheritance cannot be changed simply by changing research or teaching methods, for its roots are deeper and more extensive than either.

Unlike other professions, then, teaching is taught and learned as part of a popular culture over which professional agencies and official policies have little influence. It is picked up partly in the ordinary transactions of family life, which are little affected by educational policy or professional practice, and partly in the ordinary business of the lower schools, which lie mostly beyond the reach of professional education. There is an informal curriculum of teaching that has a historical life and influence all its own, apart from the curriculum of professional education.

A similar argument can be made about learning. Reformers of instruction have concentrated much effort on the texts and other materials in which academic knowledge is formally presented, trying to make the contents more attractive and up-to-date. Although this makes sense, nearly a century of research has shown that students arrive in school with reasonably well-developed views about what knowledge is, which they have acquired from parents and others, along with ideas about how things are taught and learned. While reformers have concentrated on changing practices in the schools, researchers have been revealing the extensive nonschool influences on learning—which are at least as important as teachers and textbooks. Traditional conceptions of knowledge, like conceptions of teaching, are passed along inside the stream of schooling by teachers and students who are committed to those conceptions. But they also are passed along across generations, outside the stream of school-

---

[27]*Op. cit.*, (pp. 22–27).

ing, by families. Although such conceptions can be affected by formal educa-tion, they cannot be easily or quickly affected.

My point is not that these reforms should be dismissed. If my account is correct, we may have seen only the opening chapters in a story of continuing crusades to reform teaching and learning. The leaders of these endeavors might usefully be viewed as missionaries for reform, crusaders for new ideas. The curriculum reforms of the late 1950s and early 1960s might be viewed as the academic missionaries' first large-scale foray to the rest of education. Current efforts to press the new electronic technologies into schools may be a second such crusade, though its magnitude remains to be determined.

The missionary metaphor makes sense in part because academic reformers of instruction and learning have been a committed but isolated vanguard. It also makes sense because this cadre relies on the word for authority and results. The reformers are thoughtful persuaders, not arm-twisters, vote-counters, or even demonstrators. They seek conversion by the word and often are startled when it does not work. The missionary metaphor also makes sense because these reformers have been strangers in the lands they sought to convert. They are an elite that is separated from most avenues of intellectual influence within education by great barriers of social organization, occupational specialization, and intellectual culture. They have made considerable progress in one depart-ment: Their new ideas have begun to carry the day, in research and writing, in the academic disciplines in the leading institutions of higher education. The new message about learning has begun to percolate through a few of the disci-plinary channels that comprise the chief intellectual organization of higher educa-tion: Academic psychology, for instance, is revising doctrines about learning, and some approaches to research. But the new doctrine has made little progress anywhere else. Ideas about the nature of knowledge and learning have only just begun to change in the much larger intellectual hinterland of higher education.

In addition, the new ideas have barely established a beachhead in teaching practice, or even in the study of teaching practice, in the elite institutions from which they are broadcast. They have even less of a purchase in the thousands of institutions in which teaching masses of students, rather than producing new knowledge, is the order of the day. For most teachers in these schools picked up much of their subject-matter knowledge and conceptions of practice a generation or more ago, in institutions on the academic periphery. Most teachers are still educated in these peripheral institutions, far from the sources of new ideas about knowledge and learning.

It seems likely, therefore, that these missionaries—including fans of the new technology who relish inquiry—will continue to cry in an academic wilderness for some time, despite their influence and position. And it seems likely that their doctrines will have only slow and modest effects on the instructional prac-tices they wish to change. Mass education institutions are likely to select those technology applications that fit established practices of teaching and learning.

CONCLUSION

Entanglements between the story of the new instructional technology and several older tales has been one theme in this chapter. One is a tale of hope recurrent: Like many earlier innovations, microcomputers have crystallized an exciting vision of schools in which teaching will be challenging, learning will be playful, and creative thinking will be abundant. Another is a story of hopes dashed: Earlier innovations were not used, or, when they were used, instruction did not improve as expected. Still other stories seek to explain these persistently unhappy endings. I have tried to sketch some outlines of a few of these older stories, in hope of relating current efforts to those already forgotten.

A second theme has been the importance of the social organization of instruction to instructional innovation. I sketched an analysis of this organization that distinguished between an instructional core that accommodates most students in a relatively homogeneous, batch-processing instructional format, and an increasingly differentiated set of marginal entitities oriented to various special curricula, teachers, and students. I noted that the differences between core and margins include organizational, historical, and curricular features. And I argued that this organization mediates between innovative policies and programs on the one hand, and the instruction that is worked out between teachers and students on the other.

This organization might therefore be viewed as a net, through which innovations are filtered, or as a medium in which they must subsist. But in either case, my account points to some features of practice that will be salient to the adoption and use of innovations (such as the mental structure of content, formats of instruction, and working definitions of purpose). It also suggests some features of innovations that may affect their adoption and use (such as whether they define a specialized clientele and curriculum, and how flexible they are). And it has some implications for understanding patterns in the adoption and use of innovations. Contrary to many reformers' dreams about the revolutionary effects of very adaptable instructional media and machines, the most flexible innovations have piled up very impressive records of large, lasting, and relatively inflexible use. One reason for this perverse result is that the more flexible the instructional technology, the more easily it can be adapted to the instructional organization of the core. Another reason is that public education lacks strong incentives for innovations that enhance productivity; this gives organizational considerations even more influence than they have in market-oriented firms.

A third theme has concerned the instructional value that many advocates of the new technology press, and the place of those values in the social organization of teaching and learning. I associated these values with what I termed inquiry-oriented instruction. Even before Dewey began writing, academic reformers had sought to replace traditional conceptions of knowledge and instruction with more student-centered, constructivist approaches. Partisans of these reforms more or less naturally turn their attention to schools to implement them: schools, after all, are the chief organizations of formal instruction, and they are maintained by the state. They seem an obvious lever for change. But academic reformers chronically overestimate the power of these scholastic agencies. Schools do affect knowledge and its transmission, but this work is affected, and often impeded, by broader social organizations of knowledge.

One reason is that knowledge is everywhere: its transmission is part of the ordinary work of ordinary life. Children learn a good deal about knowledge, teaching, and learning before they ever get to school. They continue this ordinary learning all through school. Much research has shown that these ordinary sources of knowledge are at least as powerful an influence on children's learning as their school instruction. And in large parts of America, this ordinary knowledge is quite traditional and is closely tied to the instructional practices that inquiry-oriented approaches to reform have sought to replace. In these cases, reforms must fight against informal instructional practices that children learn before going to school, and regularly relearn outside of school. And in the lower schools, the reforms are at a further disadvantage because the curriculum is quite vulnerable. It is vulnerable to ordinary knowledge because most of the elementary and much of the high school curriculum is relatively unspecialized: The traditional intellectual culture has ready alternatives to constructivist conceptions of arithmetic, or Progressive versions of social studies (though it does not have such alternatives for more advanced and specialized materials, like underwater archeology or advanced algebra). The curriculum also is vulnerable because Americans are deeply, even passionately, attached to the traditional culture of knowledge and instruction and have not been hesitant to press their views on neighborhood schools and locally elected school boards. The lower schools' intellectual vulnerability to the pressure of popular ideas is compounded by their organizational vulnerability to popular political pressures.

Instructional practice in schools thus subsists in popular cultures of instruction that are old, deeply ingrained, and powerful. Even if reformers successfully captured a great deal of the formal instructional program in schools, many children would do poorly, or resist, in part because of the influence of this other culture. But few reformers have even gotten that far, for the reforms also have been undernourished by their own shallow roots in the social organization of academic instruction. Most teachers in the lower school are situated at the distant periphery of an extensive system of formal educational agencies, while most leading advocates of revisionist instruction are situated at the system's center. These two groups are divided by great gulfs: Those at the center practice criticism and research, while those at the periphery practice instruction. Those at the center place the highest priority on producing and consuming new knowledge, or new critiques of old knowledge, while those at the periphery place the highest priority on producing students, degrees, and grades. These differences alone make it exceedingly difficult for the leaders of instructional reform to speak a language that makes sense to practitioners of instruction. The difficulty is compounded by the great gulf of prestige and position that separates leading investigators at the great research institutions from lowly instructors in the undistinguished mass of teaching institutions, higher or lower. Even if there were a common language to speak, it would not be easy to arrange regular and fruitful communications across this imposing—and treasured— gulf.

Instructional practice in American education is therefore removed from major influence by the leaders of revisionist thought about learning and instruction. It also swims in a sea of popular traditional practices of teaching and learning. Considered from the perspective of practice, this has meant that teachers who tried to implement inquiry-oriented reforms typically did so without much helpful leadership, and frequently with much unhelpful resistance inside and outside school. Considered from the perspective of the latest technology, my analysis suggests a paradoxical conclusion: The features that promise the greatest intellectual gains may make the smallest instructional headway.

BIBLIOGRAPHY

Berman, P. & McLaughlin, M. (1977). *Federal programs supporting educational change* (Vol. 7). Santa Monica: RAND.

Cohen, D. (1987, June). Teaching practice: Plus que ca change . . . Chicago: The National Society For The Study of Education.

Cuban, L. (1984). *How Teachers taught.* New York: Longmans.

Cuban, L. (1986). *Teachers and machines.* New York: Teachers College.

Dewey, J. (1938). *Experience and education.* New York: Kappa Delta Pi.

Powell, A., Farrar, E. & Cohen, D.K. (1985). *The shopping mall high school.* Boston: Houghton Mifflin.

Rohlen, T.P., (1983). *Japan's high schools.* Berkeley: University of California.

Sedlak, M. (1986). *Selling students short.* New York: Teachers College.

Stake, R., & Easley, J. (1978). *Case studies in science education,* (Vol. 2). Washington: U.S. Government Printing Office.

Stevens, R. (1912). *The question as a measure of efficiency in instruction.* New York: Teachers College.

Weick, K. (1976). Educational organizations as loosely coupled systems. *Administrative Sciences Quarterly, 21,* 1–19.

12 Teachers' Assistants: What Could Technology Make Feasible?

JIM MINSTRELL
Department of Science and Mathematics
Mercer Island High School

AN ALL TOO TYPICAL SCENE

Too many students view school as boring and irrelevant to their lives. To them the content of courses does not seem to relate to their present or to their future. The pace of the teaching, which may be aimed at the middle, is too fast for many and too slow for others. The methods by which they learn are too often teacher controlled and the learner is put into a passive role of recipient of information rather than as an active participant who is responsible for her or his own education. Individuals who have ideas are not often given sufficient opportunity to share them with another caring, but analytically critical, student or teacher. Frequently, students report the greatest benefit of school is that it is a place to be with one's friends.

Caring teachers feel overworked and misunderstood. It often seems their purposes are to count students to justify state financial support, to control students so that the school appears orderly for the administration, to march through the curriculum to meet the coverage prerequisite for the next level, and to keep the students occupied and out of mischief while parents are away during the day.

What I Want for My Students

I come to the writing of this chapter with a wealth of classroom experience but with very limited experience in the use of technology to enhance educa-

265

tion. If technology is to assist in making a positive change in education, it will need to deal with the dominant views presented in the preceding paragraphs. It will need to assist in the creation of a very different environment, not just be another object in the old environment. The new environment that I want for my students would value engaged, active participation, not the mere presence of a body. Bureaucratic activity for students and teachers would be relegated to a low priority, only taking valuable time when it contributes to the development of the participants. By contrast, physical, emotional, cognitive, social, and even moral development of the participants would be the highest priorities. The several facets of a student's multiple intelligences would each be analyzed and fostered on an individual basis (see Howard Gardner's chapter). The environment would respond to individual needs and create an advocacy for responding to each of those needs. Instead of evaluation being represented by a test score or a letter grade at the end of the year, evaluation within this environment would be ongoing and would represent a much more complete assessment of each individual's several understandings and capabilities. This assessment would be the joint responsibility of the individual and his or her peers, with the teacher playing a less central role than is the current practice. The environment would strive for transfer of understanding between school learning and the world outside of school and would be integrated across content domain (see Roy Pea's chapter). The main cognitive aim would be the development of learning and thinking skills with much less emphasis on the memorization of material. Participants would develop abilities to access and process information, to generate new ideas and apply learned ones, and to inquire in novel contexts.

These are some of the purposes of the environment I would like to see available to teachers and students in the year 2020. Whereas technology is neither necessary nor sufficient for the creation of such an environment, technology would increase the ability to respond to individual needs and desires. Machines would offer the opportunity to make the learning experience more humane.

To capture the vision for the learning environment I have begun to describe, I offer the following brief story. It reflects the need and potential for having different ways of reaching and challenging both students and teachers. It models an environment in which the participants are responsible for their own learning and are active in assessing that learning. The roles of the student and teacher are different from those typically seen today. Students and teachers work together so that each develops a deeper understanding of the subject matter and of learning. The students take a more active role and the teacher is freed from bureaucratic duties to create environments that challenge students.

The machines that are described in the story are not necessarily those that are needed. The critical feature of the technology is that it extends the environment of the students. The machines serve as sources of information, enhancers, and processors. They should enable learning to occur. The machines are only part of the environment. They do not necessarily decrease the amount of time students or teachers are engaged in the learning experience, but the work that is done is more clearly related to personal development.

The ideas are presented in story form because it allowed me to dream about the future. I hope this style will assist readers in bridging the gap between the reality of today's schools and the potential of tomorrow's learning environments. Readers are cautioned not to limit their own dreams to the tasks described or to the capabilities of the machines depicted in the story.

A STORY ABOUT A FUTURE LEARNING ENVIRONMENT

It is in the fall of the year 2020. Matt Jones, the physics teacher for Middleburg School District, enters his school, passes the administrative office, and walks the extra 100 meters to the door of his work station. After placing his hand on the ID touch pad, he enters. Inside, the lights come on automatically as he sits down in front of the organization and management computer terminal, OMAC, and logs on. To allow him the flexibility of moving about the room, he selects audio input/output mode. Then, while he hangs up his jacket and reorganizes equipment from the previous day, the soft voice of the terminal speaks the messages for the day. Bored with the bulletin, Matt interrupts the machine with "Halt" and then says "Faster, 2 times," to move more rapidly through the announcements.

When the more personal messages begin, he slows the rate to normal, occasionally interjecting a comment like "Halt, remind 5 minutes before the meeting with the school management executive," or "Halt, remind on November 17th to confirm final draft of instructional goals for the next year," to get the system to page him when it is time to respond to specific activity. Then, the machine stops, awaiting the next command.

Matt calls for "Mail." The machine reads a list of mail sources, then waits. "Scan *The Physics Teacher* for current electricity or rotational dynamics," sends the machine into a search for articles related to topics of interest to the teacher. When the machine reports that it has found one article on teaching rotational dynamics, Matt issues the command "Abstract, print" and the machine scans the article and prints the highlights of the article. Matt pockets the page for reading later in the day.

After calling for "participation," he reviews potentially troublesome patterns of student inactivity. Student participation levels have been assessed by monitoring the times students have logged on or touched the ID touch pad. Matt knows that students don't always remember to "touch" in or out, and sometimes they touch in but are not really engaged.

It's time to finish preparations for today's teaching and learning. Matt leaves OMAC and goes into the next room to engage TACFU, his teaching assistant computer for understanding. One can tell that Matt has a special affection for this machine, or at least for its capabilities. With the help of the team at the National Institute for Cognitive Studies, TACFU has been specifically programed to assist Matt in teaching the physics program his way. The TACFU system has been left sufficiently open that Matt can change the system by adding problems/activities or by altering the logical criteria for classifying students' solutions or for identifying their abilities. He can also change the prescriptions for subsequent activities for investigation or evaluation of understanding when classroom experience suggests a better route.

The physics content of the program that is built into TACFU is based on an international curriculum development effort with participants from 56 countries. The effort, which took the first decade of the new century, was based on research and development designed to determine the physics content most helpful to general intellectual development and most useful for fostering subsequent learning in *all* areas of knowledge. Research identified which ideas and thinking processes were investigated at various points in the effort. An ongoing identification and inclusion of the content most applicable to other disciplines is a feature of the program, as well as updates every 5 years. These applications and appropriate developmental levels are important to Matt because the learners with whom he interacts come from a broad range of ages, ethnic backgrounds, and interests, including bright 10-year-olds interested in science, general education middle and high school students, and adults preparing for a career change. The context applications help students identify possible career areas in which they may want to work.

The TACFU system has Matt's particular style and emphases built into the program and that is something he takes pride in. Although well prepared for his teaching assignment, Matt is stronger and more interested in some content areas than others. The system allows him the flexibility to incorporate his unique capabilities. To a fair extent TACFU can also compensate for Matt's weaker areas. Students who want or need even greater opportunities in some content may enroll in similar programs or portions of programs centered at other institutions.

TACFU, connected to the phone line, has been monitoring student progress wherever students log on with their electronic notebooks (a personal hand-carried computer that can communicate with large-frame computers) to accomplish their assigned work. Some students study at home or at work where they are exploring careers relating to their interests, abilities, and giftedness in one or more facets of their intelligence. Some parents are still demanding their children be in the schoolhouse between the hours of 8AM and 3PM, and some students, who cannot appropriately manage their own time, are required to be there during those hours. The majority of students do much of their work at home, recreation centers, community libraries, or other neighborhood meeting places. On other projects, students may be working at larger facilities like the local science center, zoo, museum, or a nearby research lab in a business, industrial, or academic institution.

Students are given the opportunity of engaging with the large-frame computer most any time of the day or night. This allows TACFU and Matt to collect large amounts of data on students and to construct student profiles they can use to guide individual and group learning. But, out of respect for individual freedom, students may choose not to log on, and they may choose to erase any portion of their recorded interaction at any time. Such a choice would limit the profile of understandings and capabilities in each student's record, but this is a price one has to be willing to pay for remaining a free society.

Matt requests individual responses for nearly every student activity. That takes an incredible amount of reading, analysis, synthesis, and response. Once again TACFU proves useful. Since class started for these beginning physics students, TACFU has been monitoring all their communication. In the case of papers TACFU has identified errors in writing mechanics, leaving the content primarily to Matt. For problem situations, TACFU has kept a record of each solution given by every student when he or she was logged onto a large-frame machine. The collections of answers have been synthesized into a Framework of Knowledge Profile for each student for each concept area. These frameworks were constructed out of past research on the conceptual understanding of novices and the development of those conceptions toward expert thinking. In addition to describing, in depth, typical knowledge structures, past research suggested diagnostic questions and procedures for tentative identification of conceptions held by students. Having TACFU do this is important to Matt, because it allows him to more accurately select the appropriate activity that can challenge the student's present understanding. Of course, the research did not suggest that every student was thinking exactly the same, but there were common "glitches" in understanding, common facets of experience that could yield more successful conceptions that had not yet been integrated into or differentiated out from the conceptual beliefs of many students.

Back in 1985 researchers were listing students' misconceptions. They were looking at student thinking from the standpoint of formal physics. Early in this century they became quite skilled at understanding student thinking from the more naive point of view. They gave up classifying students as Aristotelean, Impetus theorists, Newtonian, Einsteinean, Unified Field Theoretical, etc. and began characterizing their thinking *de novo*. They began to describe the intellectual structure from within the students' culture, similar to earlier studies done by anthropologists.

Because students' thinking is a product of their experience as processed by their cognitive system, the resulting understandings are many and varied. Their initial conceptions function well enough in the domain of their experience. Thus, to promote intellectual growth, teacher developers like Matt wanted to extend the experiential domain of each student. TACFU contributes greatly to this extension of the students' environment, because it provides a rich assortment of problems and because it frees Matt to spend more time interacting with and challenging individual student's conceptions. It is hoped that the result is a more powerful ecology of conceptions that could be applied more generally and successfully to solving the planetary problems or probing the cosmos.

Matt sees his role as one of fostering general intellectual growth rather than merely passing on traditional content. The research on the integration of general thinking skills with content understanding helped form a base for the programs that keep TACFU probing for development.

TACFU describes students' thinking, diagnoses possible difficulties, and suggests experiences that would foster development for each student. Matt compares his own assessments of the status of thinking with assessments done by TACFU.

There is a list of students who are just beginning to distinguish between action on a body and property of a body. Matt smiles as he considers how much easier it will be for those students to understand the formal notions of net force and resulting acceleration. Even more satisfying will be their ability to describe the various actions necessary to cause an object to travel with a constant velocity, the similarities and differences in the actions required while the object is cruising through the relative molecular void of space compared with plowing through ambience of various densities. Perhaps, knowing this, the students will appreciate the government regulations restricting speeds on land and water for within atmosphere vehicles.

That's another of Matt's goals, to develop in the students a functional understanding of the universe in which they live. Fortunately, the multimedia, interactive curriculum of 2020 includes kinesthetic, auditory, and visual modes for learning, and TACFU has developed a sense of which of these will best help each of the different students. TACFU also enables lessons that will foster students' abilities to learn by other modes, so they are not limited to one style of learning but can benefit from all. The lessons also will foster development in their areas of lesser intelligence. Brain research helped in this endeavor. TACFU will help suggest a sequence and pace appropriate for the development of each individual, beginning with some concrete experiences. Matt and his students consider these as they develop sets of experiences of greatest interest or benefit.

At each of Matt's requests to know which differentiations or integrations of knowledge have or have not yet been made, TACFU responds with data, both anecdotal and statistical, to support each psychological inference. Matt and the Cognitive Studies Institute Staff developed the operational procedures by which the inferences are made. Frequently, on the basis of classroom experience, Matt alters those operational procedures. TACFU also recommends activities from which Matt will choose. His choice is based on the materials and equipment available, including the interactive simulations available through TACFU. Because Matt has grown to trust the research-based decisions of TACFU, in most instances he goes with the machine's suggestions. In some cases, however, Matt chooses to override the machine because he feels he has more recent or pertinent information. He has, after all, been spending his time working with individuals in the laboratory and in rich human discussions. Like the teachers of old, Matt spends much of his time interacting with groups or with individual students. These days, however, the teacher has much more information to help him or her direct the learning of the groups or individuals. Also, some students still do not relate to a machine and TACFU still has trouble understanding their language and their thinking. The program is not yet as receptive to free response as it might be.

Between TACFU's input and his own, Matt decides what activities to recommend to the student. From these several suggestions, the student will choose her or his assignment. In that way Matt can be more certain that Melinda, who is interested in athletics and in working in a social group, and Michelle, who enjoys projects, and James, who prefers working with equipment (physical and simulational), will attack the assignment in a way that will be appealing to each of them. Back in the old days, the teacher could only offer one or a few choices because grading had to be done by comparing students with each other. To grade students fairly, teachers gave the same assignments or tests. Now, because TACFU can help Matt keep track of what the students do or do not know, more flexibility is possible. Grouping reflects the cognitive knowledge structure, not whether students have memorized what they've been told. It's not the answer that is the focus, but the structure and process of thought.

Consistent with this focus on structure and process is the form of evaluation. It consists of a description of knowledge and skills exhibited by the individual learner. The students, with the help of their peers, take responsibility for their own evaluation. They choose problems from TACFU's bank and attempt to elaborate their understanding of the situation by listing assumptions and identifying what is given and what can be inferred. TACFU keeps track of all this, the order of events, and any analogies or problem heuristics imposed by the student. TACFU socratically probes the student's understanding of the problem until he or she feels as though the whole situation makes sense. Periodically, the student, with TACFU's help, creates a concept map showing relationships between ideas. In TACFU, the student keeps a log of all new questions that come up and need answering in subsequent study sessions. Because TACFU is a machine, students don't hesitate to ask their own questions, no matter how "dumb" they might appear. From these interactions with his or her peers and with TACFU, the student gains knowledge of what he or she does and doesn't understand.

Matt periodically monitors the individual progress of each student. At various levels of detail, TACFU can give Matt a review of the students' progress, individually or collectively. He scans the computer record for inconsistencies with his daily observations in the laboratory and in discussions. The teacher does not have to "give" the student a grade but will assist him or her in a personal assessment. At the end of a term or course, a record of the student's structure and processes of thought in this subject area can be duplicated for the student to carry with him or her to the next level of education.

There are still approximately 2 hours of large-group activity each week. These times are used for presentations or discussions. About once every 2 weeks, Matt's classes are able to use the total experience Hemidome theater, wherein various scenarios can be chosen and played out to see "what would happen if." In this theater the audio/video presentations are interactive. Film and simulations are based on scenarios of greatest curiosity to the group. The teacher/facilitator and/or the group of students have access to audios, visuals, and olfactories from the past and present. Also, they can choose to experience animated scenarios based on data previously entered, or based on trends, and future speculation done by students or by professionals. These allow the students not only to experience the past but also to experience various futures, so they can actively participate in advocating conditions that will bring about their choices. Matt is concerned that his students develop a social conscience as they expand their responsibilities as citizens.

While seated within the Hemidome, students may have their electronic notebooks plugged into the Hemidome computer. In this way students voice their choices, and the general choices of the class are available to the group. With this device, Matt engages the thinking of his students as they make predictions of specific outcomes or general trends.

In addition to the 2 hours per week of large-group activity, students meet in small groups for another 2 or 3 hours. This is time spent in discussions, group problem solving, and physical laboratory work. Groups can arrange for laboratory/classroom space as best it fits their schedules and those of other students.

The community still believes that school is one of the primary modes of socialization for human cultures. People need to learn to speak and listen to others, to argue constructively, to nurture, love, and care for others and their needs. The problems and solutions of the planet and solar system are so complex they require the cooperation of international, intellectual communities. Learning how to cooperate can come from the family and from the school socialization time.

The physical laboratory situations are based on research that determined what experiences are best learned in the natural world and that can be simulated. Also determined were which simulations are best preceded by natural world experiences. At some levels of development, simulations are more effective than at others, so depending on the physical, emotional, and intellectual needs and capabilities of students, there are different degrees of physical experience required for individual students.

With these kinds of machine support, Matt can concentrate on using his human qualities. He does not have to be a truant officer, an accountant, a clerical secretary, a grader, or a librarian unless he chooses to be. He can focus on being warm, understanding, cooperative, emotional, caring, respectful, witty, dramatic, creative, thoughtful, and inquiring, as well as helping students learn. In this environment Matt can be a model for what it means to be a learner, because he too is actively involved in learning. Side by side, Matt and his students can probe their environment. He can be an advocate for students. He can spend his time being human.

At the end of the school day, Matt touches out, the lights go off, and he begins his walk to the commuter tube. He feels pleasantly tired from the total engagement of the stimulating environment.

13 The Use of Technology to Improve Two Key Classroom Relationships

WILLIAM H. BOSSERT
Harvard University

INTRODUCTION

Those whose attention we seek in our attempts to further the applications of technology in improving education have every right to be suspicious of us. Throughout the history of computer-aided instruction, or educational technology as we now call it to wash ourselves of past sins, they have been sold ideas without products, products without curricula to which they may be applied, and curricula developed without regard for the institutional constraints of an overall educational policy. We have regularly put the cart before the horse by developing technology first and then searching for educational problems that might be relevant to the advance. In this chapter I identify some problems with current educational techniques and point out how they might be solved in a high-technology educational environment achievable by 2020. Of course, in assuming a technologic environment I am also guilty of "putting the cart before the horse," but I hope in the course of the presentation those who buy the cart might gain some confidence that something will be there to pull it.

Current educational techniques do not manage the relationships between the classroom and the external intellectual environment and between students on an intellectual basis within the classroom very well. Promoting these relationships is important; the resources of a classroom have always been and will always be limited, relative to those of the larger environment that include museums, libraries, news media, and the summed family experiences of a student group. There is also the simple motivational message that what goes on in the classroom is based on and prepares one for the outside world. Improving these external relationships has been a goal of educators for some time, as witnessed by such institutions as "show and tell," field trips, and current event reports. Unfortunately, these institutions are notoriously flawed in opening the classroom to the larger intellectual environment. Show and tell, which I attack again shortly, is more of a minor theatrical experience than an attempt to put students in touch with a diversity of personal and family backgrounds and behaviors. Current events exercises based on popular journalistic media do not structure information on a topic over time, so that only acute situations and causal relationships are regularly discussed. The long time-horizon studies that could make current events a tool for investigating general sociologic and economic mechanisms are not well supported by newspapers, television, and news weeklies. Field trips, at nearly every educational level, are more a lesson in mob control for students and teachers alike than contacts with art, science, or industry. The logistics of moving groups about becomes more involving than the external environment being sampled. The time available for the experience allows only the most superficial and often misleading impressions to be gained. Might high-quality data and audiovisual access to resources outside the classroom remove some of the logistical problems of external study? Might computer programs aid students in the structuring of information gained from these external experiences so they could be easily communicated to others and be accumulated to achieve new general as well as specific understanding?

The relationship between students within the classroom is even more poorly managed. The best interstudent relationships are formed and exercised outside the classroom and are largely social in nature. The values of scholastic athletics and other extraclassroom activities are argued to be the development of team skills, including the understanding of group goals, the recognition of the needs of others, the ability to assess one's ability to move the group toward its goals, and to meet responsibilities to others. Why can't these be done in the classroom as well, with intellectual rather than physical goals? Very little time is allotted for interstudent communication in a typical public school classroom. Moments of recitation, such as show and tell, are more for the edification or embarrassment of the speaker than for the enlightenment of the listener. One to one communication, either verbal or through notes, is usually frowned on and is therefore rarely related to the curriculum (except in the case of cheating). Interstudent relationships are also hindered by the significant differences in ability within the classroom. Just as it is difficult to find a position for the less physically gifted student to play in a team sport, it is difficult to find a role that will be of educational value for a less intelligent student in a group curricular activity. Might a computer program aid in structuring the interactive solution of a modular problem by members of a group? Might computational or algorithmic cognitive aids help level the abilities within a group so that less able students might take on tasks that would be viewed by others as meaningfully furthering the group activity? Might a simple computer mail system allow notes to be passed between students without disrupting the class?

My response to these questions is, of course, an optimistic "yes." Before describing scenarios related to these problems for the future, I set a technologic context for the rosy extrapolations. Following them I dampen the optimism by recognizing the substantial barriers that stand in the way of the several applications of technology.

The Technologic Context

On the basis of a review of the past 30 years, most technologists will refuse to predict the technologic environment 30 years in the future. An exception might be made in the case of the elementary or secondary school classroom. Educational systems have proven so technologically conservative that we can safely conjecture that the 2020 environment in the classroom is state of the art now. We learn this lesson from the delay in the use of film or closed-circuit television in the classroom. The latter is still not widely used despite the availability of relatively inexpensive equipment and recorded curricular materials. The new technologies we might hope would be included in a typical 2020 classroom are the personal computer and the broad-band communications networks, similar to the best now available. The only advances postulated are cost reductions that would allow the devices to be treated in the same manner as textbooks are treated today; that is, they would be considered precious but expendable with reasonable life.

The hardware environment will include a small processor, a keyboard, a simple graphical input device, a self-contained, nonvolatile storage device of a few tens of megabytes, and a high-resolution color LCD display for each student. The system will be portable and make up, along with lunch box, the student's take-home kit. It should have one high-speed external interface for access to external graphical communications facilities and perhaps a low-speed one to serve interstudent and student–teacher mail needs.

The classroom should have ample ports for access to data and audiovisual services sponsored by national museums, libraries, news services, curriculum distribution services, and the like. More important than the details of the communications hardware technologies are the software support systems for these external information sources. As discussed in the next section, they will guide investigatory probes into the data and will accumulate and structure output according to the needs of the student.

The personal software complement in the student's kit will include a mail service system, a data-audiovisual network-access controller, a super calculator appropriate to the attainment and needs of the student, a notepad-based word processor, interactive audiovisual language-instruction programs, and, for younger as well as for secondary students, a flow chart-based simulation system. Managing this cornucopia will be an individually tailored shell that will control and facilitate use of the body of software, for example, by selecting an audiovisual network service, simplifying the inquiry commands to the minimum required for the investigations appropriate to the current curriculum of the student, and filtering the network response, also to match the ability and needs of the student at a particular point in time.

This is not an infeasible dream. All components of the projection are currently available or producible with current engineering methods. Only the cost is now inconsistent with its nonexperimental implementation. Reasonable extrapolations of real cost of such a dream make it comparable in 30 years with today's curricular support materials of textbooks, existing libraries, and audiovisual enrichments. It can be in place then if there are good reasons for it to be.

The *In Touch* Classroom

The possibility of putting students and the classroom in touch with the external intellectual environment is one of the most exciting promises of communication and computer technology. A field trip to anywhere can be as easy as pressing a key on a student's personal processor. If major museums and libraries had digitally encoded copies of their possessions and simple means of network access, there need be no rich or poor schools. With the logistic problems of the field trip removed, there could be more of them and they could be open ended for individual students.

My feelings about field trips are deeply influenced by an experience I had in the Museum of Comparative Zoology at Harvard University, a popular field trip objective for schools throughout central New England. While passing through the collections one day I saw a lone young man, perhaps a third or fourth grader, intently studying a display of a closely related group of insectivorous bird species. He seemed to be measuring the beaks of the birds, and maybe his mind was moving on to question why the species differed so markedly in this characteristic. His study was interrupted by an angry adult, perhaps his teacher, who rushed up to him, grabbed him, complained that he had fallen behind the main group and was going to throw the whole schedule off. He was rushed off to the pack with no chance to complete the formulation of one of the more important questions of ecology today. I wanted to run after them and pull him back, but I realized that the supervisor had grounds for upset. An experience had been planned, and probably carefully planned, to make use of limited time to sample the resources of the museum and, whatever problem he might have caused the group, he was going to miss something himself if he tarried too long in one place. If only he could have returned to his focus of interest by merely browsing with a keyboard at some later free time there would be no problem.

Just as an example, suppose the Museum of Comparative Zoology could be accessed remotely by network, with catalogs, high-resolution graphics, and perhaps even specimen data available. The access would be selected by catalog for older students or by pictorial maps for younger students. The student could browse by picking through the catalog or moving a cursor over a map, selecting higher or lower resolution display, or textual backup information. A field trip might begin with one of a set of well-planned survey tours from which individuals could specialize. The investigation could proceed to an intensively detailed study of a particular specimen or display, or more general comparative views of several similar or contrasting displays. Every student need not focus attention in the same way. At present very little specialization is possible anyway. The "trip" would not have to begin at a special time, end at a special time, or even be done at one sitting. An audit trail of the student's activities could be kept, as a souvenir for the student to share with others, and as a medium for review, evaluation, and guidance by a teacher. Field trips of this type would cease to be a financial burden for the system and a logistic headache for the teacher. Given an adequate array of networked resources and related curriculum materials, such as the guided tours, much more of the curriculum could be directed outside the classroom than is conceivable now, with the classroom time spent more on individual and group reflection and analysis of the external experiences. The increased flexibility of external investigations would be of special importance to the more gifted students who might find more useful employment of their free time due to quick completion of standard drills, and who would feel less trapped by the classroom structure and the activities of others than they do at present.

I would like to give another example of the use of technology to keep in touch with the external world in analogy to current events studies in today's classroom. The curriculum device would be the access to a large, in time and topic, news service data base. Passage through the data would be chronologically or by topic, with references to topics threaded together over time and from one topic through related topics. The exercise would be the construction of a short history about a topic, leading to a document that could be shared among students. For younger students it might be largely practice in reading with vocabulary development assisted by accumulating individual dictionaries. The dictionary, or current vocabulary, could function as a filter on the access to data to avoid a confusing dive into data that was beyond the limits of understanding. For the older student it would involve the analysis of causal and collateral relationships that could be generalized over several topics at a given period. For either age, the product would be a written report constructed in hierarchical fashion from notes selected by cutting and pasting from the examined sources guided by an interactive grammar and style tutorial program. The access to such information in this way is simply too laborious without a structured data base at this time.

The examples cited here have no particular importance in themselves and are probably not as imaginative or as effective in meeting skills and understanding developmental needs as others concocted by teachers on the firing line. They do illustrate the major potential benefits of pointing the educational experience more to the outside than is possible with current methods and curricula.

The *Interactive* Classroom

Technology should permit more communication of an intellectual nature and of different styles between students — one to one, small group, or one to a group recitation — than is feasible today. The problems are to structure student activity so that the participants have something meaningful to talk about, and to provide media for the communication ranging from speech, which could be disruptive if there is too much of it in a small space, to short informal memos, to longer formal written presentations. I propose that a useful teaching device is the group solution of a large, modular problem that is multifaceted in the kinds of techniques required for solution, in the intellectual ability required for any particular module completion, and in the types of interactions required between students in the detailed definition and solution. The problem should require frequent interaction with the problem statement and frequent interaction between students who tackle modules of the problem individually or in small groups. As before, it is easiest to illustrate the idea through several simple examples, and, as before, the examples themselves are of no special importance.

First, consider the problem of planning and ordering the food for a week's menu at a summer camp. Components of the problem are nutrition, consumer acceptability, scaling up quantities from individual recipes, scheduling staff and campers for preparation, service and cleanup, cost budgeting and accounting, among others. Each module leads to some more traditional academic questions: nutrition to biology and health, consumer acceptance to sociology of diversity of values and perhaps survey methodology (the class could pretend to be the object of the effort), scheduling to algorithmic thinking, recipe scaling to mathematics, and so on. No part of the solution can be completed in isolation; for example, the accountants must know what the nutritionists are doing. Nearly every component of the solution could be done in simplistic fashion, or with greater sophistication through the support of preprogrammed procedures. For example, one could schedule by arbitrarily assigning people without concern for optimizing anything, by discovering a scheduling algorithm that might match talent to assignment or equalize work load, or by using a well-documented scheduling program that fits the problem. For each component, the level of solution would be adopted by the person or team to match their abilities. This decision has some important implications, particularly in the possibility of using preprepared algorithms to gain a quality of result not otherwise attainable.

We classify students frequently according to their ability to create algorithms.

Then too often we place gifted and less gifted students in situations where they are required to perform in the same way. The alternative of using instead of creating an algorithm provides a crutch that allows the less gifted students to take on just as hard a module to produce just as good a result as the gifted students. The term *crutch* has such a negative connotation in the educational environment that I hesitate to use it; it almost suggests cheating. The fact is that this alternative is a realistic introduction to how problems are solved outside the classroom and requires enough attention to instructions and guidelines for application that the use of the "crutch" has possibility for intellectual development. It is certainly better for the less able student to take a normal role in the receipt and generation of information in the team than to sit on the sidelines.

The procedure for the interactive solution of a problem would involve group definition of the problem, setting the scope and identifying the modules or subproblems, then assigning responsibility for the modules. The relationship of the modules to each other would be defined and used to imply intergroup communication requirements. At regular intervals module team representatives would come together to chart progress, realign their solution designs, and begin to integrate the component solutions. The test of the solution, as well as a detailed statement of the solution, might be the computer simulation of the system.

A problem of the complexity of the food service example would be suitable only for secondary school students. Younger students might find the writing of a short instruction manual for some device in the classroom more appropriate. Again, the procedure would involve some problem definition and modularization by the establishment of a table of contents. Continued interaction with the problem and with each other might center around experimenting to find out just how the device works in the first place, the design of illustrations to be used by several content headings, and so on. A third example, suitable for classes of any age that can do arithmetic yet allowing elaborate statistics at the high end, is the establishment of actuarial tables from newspaper obituaries. Life expectancies could be presented numerically, statistically, or graphically. Modules for the solution could be distributed over data gathering in different times and places, computation or the development of computational tools and data presentation. In both of these last examples, there are adequate opportunities, actually requirements, for communication between students, and the possibility of supporting components of the solution with previously prepared aids. These would be the criteria for the identification and preparation of good problem topics.

The Barriers to Cross

As mentioned earlier, technologic or economic barriers to the implementation of these scenarios do not seem to be inhibiting. The hardware and system software can be produced on a mass scale and reasonable projections place its cost in line with current curricular support expenditures for public education. Even the large network data bases seem both technologically and economically feasible and are likely to come into being independently of educational needs in response to a general business and public entertainment demand. It is difficulty with the design, distribution, adoption, and teacher acceptance and execution of the curricular materials themselves that is likely to delay or deny the establishment of the scenarios presented here, and others like them.

The integration of individual curricular products, designed and tested by a large number of independent authors, into comprehensive hardware and software control systems is a completely new requirement. Inserting a camp food services project into a personalizable shell, with what tradition tells us will be nonstandard hooks, is akin to requiring that today's authors take into consideration the cover designs on books that might be used for other purposes in the same classroom with theirs. Only pervasive industry or government-directed standards will allow such systems as proposed here to come to fruition.

Even given a feasible environment for the design of materials, there is some question just who will actually do it and how they will be compensated. So many different skills will be required with programming, communication scheduling, graphics design, and so on, added to the creation of an idea that serves a need and the experience to insert that idea into a broader curriculum. The easiest concept to accept for this design task is that it will be carried out by a team of educators and technologists based in a school of education or established as an industrial unit. I worry that such a future team, even in a school of education, would become, and be viewed as, professional producers of educational software rather than professional teachers, and that their products would be as out of touch with practical classroom possibilities and needs of 2020 as we are today. I have always hoped that curricular development would become the responsibility of teachers, albeit the most gifted, rather than the responsibility of professional textbook authors, professional society committees, or educators at a grossly different academic level as happens most often today. If my hope is to be realized, it would require some sweeping changes in the roles of at least some public school teachers. They would have to be given time, i.e., very light teaching loads and frequent, extended sabbatical leaves, recognition, and compensation appropriate to their productivity. Some public school positions would have to be competitively attractive with the best university professorships to ensure that teachers would be available to provide a regular supply of the most imaginative, yet practically effective, materials. I do not know enough about public school institutions to know if this is possible or impossibly farfetched. I am hopeful, but I expect significant time lags, perhaps a generation of teachers before it might happen.

Given sound curricular software, who will distribute it? Traditional publishers have regularly failed to deal satisfactorily with the distribution of computer software materials. This stems, as others have discussed, partly from their conservatism, their past commitment to a particular medium, and their tangential relation to content, but also to problems with computer software such as copyright insecurity and much higher design costs that are inconsistent with their traditional marketing and pricing practices. They missed a fine opportunity to sponsor and further the market for another potentially valuable educational tool, the programmable, frame-addressable video disk. There is really no indication that publishers will ever adapt to new modes of delivery.

Hardware providers and the major software houses with whom they cooperate do not seem to be a probable medium for distribution either. They have shied away from accepting responsibility for highly diverse applications software, usually claiming that they did not want to compete with smaller firms who use the core operating systems that they do market. The real reason for their reluctance to enter the production or serve as the focus for distribution of a wider range of materials is more likely the concern that one or two poor products in a large line can reduce consumer confidence in the primary functioning units that they feel are their bread and butter. Smaller software houses on the other hand, although successful in distributing games and office products, just do not have the market strength to establish and enforce the necessary standardization. If future educational software production is to follow the cottage industry model set by games and diverse office products, it will have to be guided and constrained by larger institutions, the federal government or major professional societies. There have been few actions on the part of either to date to suggest that something might happen in the near future.

Given that we had good products and reliable chains of delivery, who would buy them? The major state and city Boards of Education that can cause a boom or bust for a particular publisher's line are even more conservative than their traditional suppliers of curricular materials. It is easy to find cause for their risk aversion in the tight financial and political situation in which most of them are placed. We must also recall the history of unfulfilled technological promises mentioned in the introduction. The unwillingness of these institutions to take the role of enlightened consumers in creating an instant market for promising developments of their choice is a barrier we may never cross. Although it is controversial, the addressable video disk mentioned earlier is a perfect example of a promising technology that is valuable in its own right and is certainly a step on the path to many of the *in touch* classroom concepts that excite me. It has floundered more because of the neglect of the major curriculum consumers than for any other reason. Only a large-scale post-Sputnik-like outcry of popular demand for improvements in elementary and secondary education could carry sufficient political weight to force more innovative behavior among the administrative leaders of public education. I do not sense such a state of urgency in the general public or in the media.

Given that we did have the technologic context and specific curricular materials put in place by demanding and discriminating local school administrations, we might still lack teachers with the skills and motivation to execute the system effectively. Training teachers to structure extra- and intraclassroom relationships as discussed here would require considerable changes in the programs of schools of education. The retraining of teachers may not be easy, as witnessed by the slow implementation of past changes in mathematics and social science curricula for younger students. We may face, as with diffuse creative design of materials, a whole generation's delay before this continually critical barrier can be overcome. A generation means 25 to 45 years. The year 2020, which seems so distant when we extrapolate our technology, is perhaps too soon to expect that the kinds of applications presented here could become normal practice. If only one or two of the potential benefits postulated could actually be achieved — bridging the gap between what people do in the classroom and what they do beyond it; providing resources to all students, particularly the more gifted; developing team spirit and communication skills around intellectual pursuits; or providing algorithmic support to less gifted students so they can participate more fully in the classroom — then the barriers, however imposing, would be worth picking apart now.

14 Technology in Education: Possible Influences on Context, Purposes, Content and Methods

RAYMOND S. NICKERSON
BNN Laboratories Inc.

INTRODUCTION

Much discussion about technology and education has focused on the question of how technology can be used to facilitate teaching and learning. But technology relates to education in many ways, the connection with educational *methods* being only one of them. Education takes place within a sociocultural *context*, the nature of which is determined by technology as much as by anything else. To the extent that the *purposes* of education are determined by the context in which it occurs, technology, by virtue of its role as an agent of social change, is a force in shaping them. Technology also affects the *content* of education, because among the objectives of education is that of making understandable the world in which one lives, and we live in a technological world.

At the end of the introductory chapter of this book are some questions that were posed in the interest of stimulating discussion on specific ways in which technology could influence education over the next few decades. The contributors to this volume address these questions, as well as others that could have been included in the list, though not in a question-by-question fashion. Each author has focused on one or a few issues from his or her particular vantage point. In this summary chapter, I will view the relationship between technology and education from a broad perspective and discuss the several connections mentioned above in light of the preceding chapters and with the questions raised at the outset in mind.

THE CONTEXT OF EDUCATION

Education occurs in a sociocultural context, and that context influences not only what people learn, but why and how. The context in 2020 will surely be different in many respects from what it is today. In attempting to anticipate what the world will be like 35 years hence, it is instructive to reflect on how it has changed during the past 35 years and on how few of those changes would have been predicted 35 years ago. Much has happened since the middle of this century. In 1950:

- Commercial television had barely made its debut.
- Commercial aircraft were all propeller driven.
- Open-heart surgery, organ transplantation, and test-tube babies were still in the future.
- Sputnik had yet to be launched; the idea of men walking on the moon was still in the realm of science fiction.
- IBM had yet to bring its first computer to market; timesharing, personal computers, and computer networks were hardly figments of anyone's imagination.

In looking to the coming 35 years, probably the only truly safe prediction is that there will be some surprises—that any attempts to anticipate developments will overlook some of the most consequential ones. But we must do the best we can to understand the possibilities if we are to hope to shape things at all to our liking. The introductory chapter notes some of the more obvious technological trends; the following are a few of the possible consequences of those trends that, in the world of 2020, could have significant implications for education.

- Many of the tasks now performed by humans will then be done by machines. Perhaps automation will be pervasive: Certainly it will encompass, as Landauer[1] notes, many cognitive as well as noncognitive tasks.
- If the recommendations of the National Commission on Space (1986) are implemented on schedule, by 2020 the Space Station will have been in operation for 25 years, spaceports will be orbiting the earth and the moon, manufacturing operations will be ongoing on the moon, a human outpost will have been established on Mars, and a full base on that planet will be less than ten years away.
- It could be possible to travel anywhere on earth in less than two hours.
- People will be faced with moral and ethical problems that we can only vaguely anticipate. Medicine will be much more accomplished at organ replacement than it is now and it undoubtedly will be able to keep people alive, by some definition, much longer than is now possible. Genetic

---

[1]Citations without dates refer to chapters in this book.

engineering will no longer be a nascent discipline, but will have been around for several decades. Much will have been learned about the implantation and control of specific genes. (Branscomb's [1986] view of the future includes the mapping of the entire human genome before the end of this century and its availability to biologists for about $10 on a CD ROM disc shortly thereafter.) Experimentation with organic or semi-organic computing devices probably will have been going on for several years.

- The world population will be roughly double what it is now, or about 8 billion. Almost 17% of the population in the U.S. will be over 65 years of age, compared with about 12% in 1986. The median age is expected to be 39.3 years, compared to 31.7 at the midpoint of this decade. These projections do not assume revolutionary breakthroughs in cellular and subcellular biology. If Drexler (1986) is right, people who are younger than age 65 in 2020 will have a good chance, thanks to nanotechnology and cell repair machines that can slow or reverse the aging process, of living in good health for a very long time.

- Raw computing resources will exist in superabundance. The number of transistors that can be placed on a single silicon chip has increased by roughly three orders of magnitude per decade over the past two decades, and the cost per transistor has been dropping commensurately. Extrapolating this growth pattern would make the number of transistors on a chip in about 250 years greater than the estimated number of atoms in the universe, so we know this cannot continue indefinitely. The end is not yet in sight, however, and it seems reasonable to expect that by 2020 an inadequate supply of computing cycles will seldom be a problem for anyone.

- The software that will be available in 2020 should be far more versatile and powerful than what exists now. It seems likely still to be the case however, that the primary challenge then will be, as it is now, to find ways to realize the potential of the technology more fully.

- Children who enter public school in 2020, assuming there are public schools then as we know them now, will have had experiences already with machines that talk, that play intellectually-demanding games, and that do other things that were once thought to be uniquely human capabilities. When we who are adults today see machines do such things, we do not take them for granted because we remember a time when machines did not have such abilities. We do not know quite what to make of these developments, but we at least perceive them as developments. Children of the future will take machines with such capabilities for granted. What effects this will have on children's perceptions of themselves as human beings, we do not really know, although there has been some speculation about the matter (Turkle, 1984). It is a question well worth thinking about.

What will the implications of such developments be for education? What will it mean to be educated in such a world? What should the prospects of these developments mean for forward-looking educators and educational researchers now? Questions of these types have been addressed in many of the chapters of this book, and some of them will be noted in subsequent sections of this summary. One generalization on which there seems to be nearly universal agreement among not only the contributors to this book, but others who have written on the subject as well, is that the future is very likely to present challenges and opportunities to education that cannot be met effectively with the approaches and methods of the past.

PURPOSES OF EDUCATION

Education — institutionalized education in particular — serves many purposes. Among the more prominent of these purposes are preparation for work, preparation for citizenship, and enablement of intellectual growth and independence. Serving these purposes has meant developing basic competencies including literacy and certain procedural skills; exploring the content of various knowledge domains; instilling certain values, perspectives, attitudes, and beliefs; and, sometimes, fostering the ability to learn and think effectively on one's own. This is not to suggest that all these things have been done wonderfully well or even that they have invariably received the attention they deserve. What gets emphasized is likely to depend on the particular purpose that is considered paramount. When preparation for work in highly structured situations is the overriding concern, for example, we should not be surprised to see an emphasis on procedural skills, domain-specific knowledge, and "work-ethic" values, with less concern for the development of independent thinking ability.

Preparation for work has long been recognized as a major purpose for education, although there have been significant differences of opinion regarding how explicit and direct the focus on knowledge and skills that will be useful in the workplace should be. At one end of this continuum is the vocational or trade-school philosophy, which has taken preparation for specific jobs as the primary purpose of education — at least for some students — and put relatively little emphasis on instruction or learning that does not directly serve that goal. At the other end is the liberal-arts tradition, which has taken a much broader view of educational purpose and seen preparation for work as a secondary or derivative objective; acording to this view, education should provide one with a foundation of knowledge and skills that is sufficiently basic and broad to equip one to learn the specifics of whatever vocation or profession one selects.

The idea that a literate and informed populace is essential to a democracy was also a force behind the development of the public education system in this country. If citizens are to participate meaningfully in the governance process, if only through the ballot, they must have the ability to inform themselves on the issues, which, at least before the days of radio and television, meant being able to read, comprehendingly and critically. Being a good citizen has meant also having certain values and beliefs considered to be fundamental to a democratic way of life, such as those articulated in the U.S. Constitution and Bill of Rights.

"The enablement of intellectual growth and independence" sounds somewhat platitudinous, but it represents a serious educational purpose nonetheless. Education for its own sake is an old and durable theme. One need not deny the pragmatic value of learning to believe — as some have long believed — that knowledge has intrinsic value. Learning not only prepares one to be a useful and productive member of society, it enriches one's life. This is not to say that all learning is equally desirable, but it is to deny unequivocally that utility — at least in the ordinary sense of that word — is the sole measure of educational worth.

It seems highly likely that all of these purposes of education will still be valid in 2020, although some shifting of emphasis could occur. One such shift could be from utilitarian considerations to a greater willingness to think of education as an end in itself, or as a means of enriching the intellectual life of the individual. Landauer argues that preparing people for a vocation will diminish as a purpose for mass education, because much of the work that has traditionally been done by humans will be done by machines. In his view there will be a need for a few highly skilled technologists and a few managers, but not for a large work force for production operations; the major employment opportunities for most of us will be in human-to-human service-provision activities that are valued precisely because of the human involvement. Cohen also predicts that although some of the jobs in the high technology society of the future will demand a high degree of skill and knowledge, most will not. Feurzeig, in contrast, emphasizes the substantial demand for workers with scientific, mathematical, and linguistic competence that he believes new computer technology will make and does not explicitly anticipate a countervailing increase in mundane jobs. Both Landauer and Resnick see preparation for leisure as an increasingly important purpose of education.

We do not really know what the future holds by way of job opportunities and the needs of the workplace. Several scenarios are plausible, and in the sizeable literature on automation one can find reasoned defenses of quite disparate predictions. Perhaps the moral is that we must be prepared for a range of possibilities, and that an educational system that is to prepare young people adequately for the future should not overlook any of them.

The citizenship argument should carry as much weight in the future, I believe, as it has in the past, if not more. As the world shrinks and the problems it faces grow increasingly complex, the need for educated citizens (people who not only know a good bit about the world, but have the ability to think critically) becomes more acute. Landauer makes the interesting argument that, somewhat paradoxically, the need in an increasingly technological society may not be so much for more technical education as for education with a more humane, social, and cultural orientation. I find this a thought-provoking observation, inasmuch as a major problem (perhaps *the* major problem facing us all in the coming decades) will be that of figuring out how to get along — individuals with individuals, nations with nations — in a world in which knowledge of how to amass destructive power of various sorts has far outpaced our knowledge of how to control our destructive instincts.

The intrinsic value argument is perhaps the most durable of all the arguments that are advanced in support of education. If learning has intrinsic value, that value is, by definition, not a function of time or circumstance.

THE CONTENT OF EDUCATION

A general educational problem is that of how to ensure that students spend time learning the "right things." The logically prior problem, of course, is that of determining what the right things are; what exactly *should* students learn? To what extent should all students be expected to learn the same things? These are old questions within education, but that does not mean that we now know the answers. Looking ahead, the old questions take on a new sense of urgency for several reasons. New knowledge is being acquired at an explosive rate, and that fact, some argue, makes selectivity in learning imperative even for relatively young children. The information explosion also accelerates the rate at which some knowledge and skills become obsolete, which increases the importance of foundational skills — skills that will equip one to learn throughout life on one's own. Technology is bringing into existence not only new knowledge but new tools, some with rather remarkable cognitive abilities; what should we teach students in school, in view of the kinds of tools that are likely to be available in their lifetimes?

Need for Selectivity

Gardner speaks of the necessity of acknowledging a "cruel truth," namely that "it is simply impossible for anyone, no matter how gifted, to gain competence across the range of domains of knowledge." We must give up, he argues, the ideal of the Renaissance individual who was prized for his versatility. Knowledge has accumulated too rapidly in the recent past for this to continue to be a reasonable ideal. We are forced to choose between knowledge-in-breadth and knowledge-in-depth, between knowing a little about a lot and a lot about a little.

DiSessa takes the position that the best possible general education is the appropriate goal for precollege years, but he argues also for a greater emphasis on depth rather than breadth: teach less, but teach it well. He is careful to point out that he does not mean by this a simple reduction in coverage; in fact he would like to see most standard subjects remain in the curriculum, but to have the teaching of each emphasize deep understanding of some aspect of the subject rather than superficial coverage of it all. He speculates that focus on depth in this sense might actually lead to broader coverage in the long run.

DiSessa proposes that academic subject matter be selected on the basis of "aesthetic criteria—the perceived beauty and enjoyment that students will feel having learned the subject" rather than on the basis of "imagined prerequisites to prerequisites to competent professional work, work (like professional mathematics) that the vast majority of students never approach." The proposal not only makes one think about what the criteria should be; it also evokes the old, though not always popular idea, that learning should be considered an end in itself. Faced with the very practical need to survive in a highly competitive world, most people have probably been more attuned to the more pragmatic consequences of learning such as enhancing ones chances of finding a desirable job, but if, as some futurists anticipate, the need for human labor—both skilled and unskilled—decreases dramatically in time, perhaps aesthetic reasons for learning will become much more significant for people in general; and if they do, then aesthetic criteria will naturally be important factors in deciding what should be learned.

I agree with much of Gardner's and diSessa's analyses. Knowledge, particularly in the sciences, has indeed been accumulating at a great rate over the last few hundred years and especially during this century. Unquestionably, providing most individuals with more than superficial understanding of many of the areas of human knowledge is more than we have been able to do, given our current methods of informing ourselves. I agree also with the idea that young people should be encouraged to begin to go deeply into some area of human knowledge relatively early in their education, "to make a serious commitment to become good at something—to become active participants in some discipline area," as Feurzeig puts it. I would argue, however, with the assumption that the goal of deep knowledge across the board is no longer a reasonable one, and would resist what I would consider an overemphasis on specialization that rests on the belief that we have discovered the limits of human learning and have found them to be very severe.

What should we assume about how much an individual human being of normal intelligence can learn? And what determines the limit? In my view, there is little evidence to support the assumption that we learn as little as we do, relative to what there is to know, because of fundamental limitations of our brains to assimilate, retain, and use information. The cruel truth to which Gardner refers is true enough, but the cruelty may reside more in the limitations of educational know-how and technique then in the limitations of our minds. As Landauer points out, our current primary means of knowledge acquisition—reading coupled with library access—is excruciatingly slow. We really do not know what we are capable of learning and cannot rule out the possibility that, with much more powerful techniques for storing, accessing, and representing information, for assessing what people know, and for combining instruction and exploration in mutually reinforcing ways, that capability might be very much greater than our experience to date would lead us to believe. Given proper teaching and learning methods, might not individuals be able to acquire deep knowledge (at least by today's standards) in several areas? In the absence of compelling evidence to the contrary, I would argue that this assumption should motivate our efforts to exploit technology for educational benefit. It will be more important in the future than in the past, in my view, for a significant fraction of the population to be well informed in a variety of domains both technical and nontechnical. The challenge to educational researchers is to develop the methods that will make this possible, and it is not clear that this is a futile quest.

Skill and Knowledge Obsolescence

Technology has created new jobs that require high levels of knowledge and skill. It also has decreased the requirements of many occupations and, as Cohen and Landauer point out, may do so even more in the future and decrease the economic and occupational incentives for academic learning in certain areas as a consequence. Is the ability to do arithmetic already being devalued with the ubiquity of pocket calculators? Will typing become a useless skill when speech becomes a practical input medium for computer-based systems? What about the highly specialized knowledge that some professionals now acquire at considerable effort, time, and expense?

Many of the instructional systems that are being developed, and other systems that are being used for instructional purposes, are designed to relieve students of the necessity of performing "low-level" tasks, thereby freeing intellectual resources that can be devoted to the more cognitively-demanding aspects of the tasks of interest. Some of the programs that are used to teach writing skills, for example, relieve students of the necessity of focusing on penmanship, spelling, and other mechanical or manipulative aspects of the process and permit them to focus on higher-level aspects of composition, such as expressing ideas clearly, organizing and sequencing thoughts, editing and modifying text. Similarly, in the areas of mathematics, the Algebra Workbench described by Feurzeig relieves students of the need to carry out either numerical or symbolic calculations and permits them to focus on the identification of the algebraic operations that are to be performed. Resnick and Johnson also mention the possibility of having a machine perform lower-level aspects of mathematical tasks while having the student do the higher-level planning and the task specification.

The fact that such unburdening capabilities are available for use in the classroom raises a question about the value of teaching students how to do those low-level tasks that can be done for them by machine. If the machines are available for use in the classroom, presumably they could be available wherever else they might be needed. Is it still important for students to learn how to add, subtract, multiply, divide, find square roots, and so forth? Landauer asks this question. Should the calculator be thought of as qualitatively different from pencil and paper or chalk and slate? In teaching basic math we are willing today to assume the availability of pencil and paper, so the procedures that are taught make use of these tools; should we not have the same attitude toward calculators? And what about when everyone can have a symbol-manipulating computer?

One gets uneasy about going down this path too quickly because it seems to lead to the conclusion that there will soon be nothing—at least in mathematics, to stay with a particular discipline—left to teach. But that is not necessarily so. The nonmathematicians among us probably tend not to think of mathematics as a rapidly evolving knowledge domain; after all, what could be more stable and unchanging than arithmetic? Schoenfeld reminds us, however, that mathematics is anything but static and notes the impossibility of predicting what the subject will encompass very far in the future. (Stanislaw Ulam has estimated that about 200,000 mathematical theorems are published per year. Most of these remain in the obscurity of esoteric journals, but a few influence the future direction of subfields of mathematics. What determines what will fall in the latter category is not clear [Davis & Hersch, 1981]). But while the products of mathematics change over time, Schoenfeld suggests, the processes and predilections involved in doing mathematics remain fundamentally the same. Teaching mathematics with an eye to the future, therefore, means more than teaching the facts and procedures of contemporary mathematics; it means also teaching general problem-solving strategies in the Polya (1957) tradition, techniques for managing cognitive resources (one's own and those to which one has access, say, in a computer) and monitoring one's performance, certain beliefs or predilections that collectively motivate the use of mathematics whenever appropriate in or out of the classroom, and strategies for learning on one's own.

But suppose that computer scientists succeed beyond all expectations in their attempts to codify knowledge and expertise and to develop computer systems that can play the societal roles that human experts currently play, even better than most human experts play them. Will this make learning by humans in these areas pointless? Suppose for example, that medical diagnosis could be performed routinely by computer, and imagine that the diagnoses performed in this way were more accurate than those currently done by physicians. Does it follow that there would no longer be a reason for physicians to acquire the knowledge they now must have to function as diagnosticians? More generally, if the time comes when expertise in many areas is well represented in and readily accessible from computer-based systems, will there be good reasons to make sure that it is stored also in human heads?

I believe the answer to this question is yes. My first reason for believing this follows from the belief that learning and knowledge have intrinsic value to human beings. We desire to understand for the sake of understanding, and the fact that a body of knowledge resides in one person's head (or in a machine) does not satisfy the curiosity of another. But there are more pragmatic reasons for believing that human knowledge will be important even if expert systems become very expert indeed. One of several arguments that can be made that I find particularly compelling is that expert systems, no matter how deep or broad their expertise, are tools. To use them wisely will require an understanding of their capabilities and limitations, which implies a substantive knowledge of the domain.

In passing, it is interesting to reflect on whether people have become less physical as the need for physical labor has decreased. I do not know the answer to this question, but I find plausible the possibility that they have not; possibly, with the great interest in participatory athletics, exercise classes, jogging, and other activities, we are more physically active today, on the whole, than were our predecessors. People certainly live longer today, on the average, than in the past. Whatever else one may conclude from this, it is clear that a decrease in the percentage of the population involved in manual labor has not resulted in widespread atrophy of human muscle; on the whole people are probably healthier and more physically able today than at any previous time. Might we expect a comparable course in the area of the intellect if people find it less and less necessary to engage their brains for the purpose of making a living? Might they spontaneously seek ways to exercise their minds? To stay in shape mentally, as it were?

Thinking and Learning Skills

In the past it may have been reasonable to argue that if the primary purpose of a particular educational program was to prepare one for a specific type of occupation, the content should be primarily the knowledge and skills that would ensure one's success at that occupation, whereas if the goal was general intellectual development, the content should probably be broader and more emphasis should be put on the cultivation of the ability to think creatively and critically. According to some views of the future, this contrast becomes blurred: High level cognitive skills will be important objectives for everyone.

Reich (1983), for example, has argued that America is facing a new challenge on the world economic scene, and that meeting it will require much less emphasis on huge-volume production and standardization and more on the production of specialized high-value products—"goods that are precision engineered, that are custom tailored to serve individual markets, or that embody rapidly evolving technologies." Such a redirection of industrial focus, according to this view, will require a highly skilled, adaptable, innovative labor force and an organization of work that is more flexible and less hierarchical than in the past.

Stability for mass production, which has been a primary goal of industry heretofore, will have to give way to flexibility, and the ability to adapt effectively to rapidly evolving technology. America's current system of public education, Reich contends, is inadequate to the task of preparing people for the kind of flexible labor force that the future will require.

If this view is appropriate for our time frame, then preparation for work will continue to be one of the major purposes of education, but the implications for content will be quite different. The emphasis will have to be on the kinds of knowledge, skills, and attitudes that will increase individuals' flexibility and enhance their ability to adapt to change. This means greater emphasis on the acquisition of effective learning skills—a shift of emphasis from *what* to learn to *how* to learn, to use Malcolm's terms—acceptance by students of greater responsibility for their own education, and a view of education that sees it as a life-long process. It also increases the importance of general thinking ability and of problem solving skills that are applicable across a variety of domains.

Interest in the teaching of "higher-order cognitive skills" (reasoning, problem solving, decision making, planning, composing, evaluating, learning, and other aspects of what it means to think effectively and well) is quite high currently within the American educational community. Evidences of this fact are seen in numerous symposia, conferences, workshops, teaching programs and books (Baron and Sternberg, 1986; Chance, 1986; Chipman, Segal, & Glaser, 1985; Costa, 1985; Dillon & Sternberg, 1986; Nickerson, Perkins & Smith, 1985; Schwebel & Maher, 1986). The interest is motivated in part by disappointing findings from several national studies with respect to the thinking ability of students at all educational levels and in part also from a sensitivity to the rapidity with which specific knowledge and skills that are required in the workplace become obsolete in today's world. The assumption that people can learn enough during 12 or so years of schooling to equip them fully for a lifetime vocation has been considered untenable by many observers for some time. It is becoming increasingly apparent that formal schooling during one's youth should be viewed as one stage of a lifelong learning process, and that among its primary objectives must be that of providing students with the tools and attitudes that will facilitate the continuation of that process. Reflecting on the production and significance of the "Nation at Risk" report, Holton (1984) noted that "the concept of formal education as the preparation for a lifetime of continued self-education in a rapidly changing world is a key to understanding the report's recommendations," the first of which was "that schools seriously aim to prepare every student, *whether college-bound or not,* to enter and participate in the Learning Society through tested competence in the 'new academic basics', so that he or she would have the confidence and motivation to use these tools for further learning" (p. 10, 11). The new basics to which he refers were specified in the report as four years of English, three years each of math, science and social studies and half a year of computer science.

But suppose, as Landauer argues, the demand for human labor decreases to the point of representing only a tiny fraction of the potential work force, so preparation for work—at least in the traditional sense of the word—would no longer be a major purpose of education for most students. What would be the implications for the teaching of thinking? My answer to the question is that even if preparation for work does diminish as a purpose for education, there seems to be little reason to expect the other traditional purposes—preparing for citizenship and realizing the intrinsic value of intellectual development—to do likewise.

The citizenship argument may become even more important as the world continues to shrink and the notion of the responsibilities of world citizenship gains currency. What will it mean to be a good citizen—of a municipality, of a nation, and of the world—in the 21st century? How might education help prepare people for that role? One thing it will surely require is the ability to reason critically. Many issues will be debated at local, national, and international levels during the next few decades that will affect our future and that of our children and theirs. Disarmament, population containment, resource and energy conservation, pollution control, world health, international disaster control, are just a few of the issues that are too important to leave in the hands of a few politicians. A citizenry capable of understanding the issues and forming reasoned opinions about the efficacy of proposed approaches to their resolution will become increasingly essential if the various imaginable undesirable futures are to be avoided. Information technology may make it possible for average citizens to participate more directly and more effectively in decision-making processes through electronically-mediated referenda and international communication, and in numerous other ways. Many of the issues confronting us today are extremely complex and there is little reason to expect their complexity to decrease in the future. Rational involvement in decision making with respect to such issues can be based only on opinions that are well informed and carefully reasoned by intellectually able participants.

How does the idea that education has intrinsic value relate to the teaching of thinking and learning skills in the future? Thinking and learning skills are enablement skills. They equip individuals to use effectively what they have learned and to continue to learn throughout life. If education has intrinsic worth, thinking and learning skills obviously do also; and their importance increases with the amount to be learned. And if, as several contributers to this book have suggested, information is increasing at too great a rate to permit people to assimilate it explicitly, what people need to learn is how to represent multitudinous facts in theories that incorporate them by implication, and what the educational process should produce—as diSessa puts it—is more theory builders, not fact managers.

Cognitive Tools

The idea of technology-based cognitive tools is a key one in many of the chapters in this book. The term has an interesting and useful ambiguity, connoting either tools that have some cognitive properties or tools that are usefully employed in the performance of cognitive tasks. I think both connotations are intended. Although a tool need not be cognitive in nature to be used to advantage in the performance of cognitive tasks, some of the tools that are anticipated will have some cognitive abilities of their own.

Among the tools of interest are those, as already noted, that will perform some of the more mechanical or manipulative aspects of certain academic tasks (e.g. mathematical symbol manipulators, spelling correctors, grammar checkers) leaving the student free to work on more strategic aspects of their tasks. Other tools, mentioned by Feurzeig, include tools to aid knowledge acquisition (articulate expert systems that can play the role of master to an apprentice), tools to aid thinking and learning (practice guides, performance monitors), and tools to aid exploration and independent learning (microworlds). Still others that could be added to the list include style critics, music-composing tools, programming aids, diagnostic and debugging aids, process simulators, information-finding aids, memory aids, decision aids, reading and comprehension aids, data organizers and manipulators, and on-line dictionaries, thesauri, fact books and encyclopedias. Taking advantage of some of the new cognitive tools that will be developed undoubtedly will require new skills and new ways of thinking, as Landauer suggests; if so, teaching them will be a new challenge for education.

Programming and Computer Science

Today computer programming is a highly marketable skill. Programmers are much in demand in the workplace; few corporations of any size can get along without them. Programming is used for vocational or recreational purposes by large numbers of people, especially young people. Most universities and colleges have offered elective courses in programming for several years, and more and more secondary schools are now doing so as well. Here and there some instruction in programming has been made a requirement for graduation.

How might we expect the situation to change by 2020? Will the demand for professional programmers be as great then as it is now? Or greater? Or will it decrease as the result of the development of much more efficient ways of producing programs, including automated and semiautomated techniques? How much interest will there be in programming for avocational or recreational purposes? How important will it be for people who have no interest in programming either professionally or for fun to have some understanding of programming? How will instruction in programming fit within school curricula?

One of the difficulties one encounters in trying to address such questions is the fact that the term *programming* subsumes a broad range of activities. At the most general level, programming means instructing a computer, specifying precisely what it is to do. But instructions can be expressed in many forms, ranging from machine code to statements that resemble somewhat stilted natural language. Numerous "higher-level" languages have been developed that permit the programmer to express instructions in a symbology that is easier to use than is machine-code, and translator programs are available to transform the higher-level representations into sequences of machine code instructions. Some of these higher-level languages are intended to facilitate programming for any purpose; others are designed to support quite specific applications.

Soloway argues that, inasmuch as the computer is a general purpose tool that will be applied pervasively in the future, much as mathematics is applied across disciplines, it will be important to understand it and to know how to use it effectively. He makes the point, as do Resnick and Johnson and Landauer, that by 2020, many of the things that people do in their day-to-day lives will be done *through* computers, and wonders how much people will have to know about them in order to use them effectively. He dismisses the argument from analogy that effective use of computers will not depend on extensive knowledge of how they work, just as effective use of other complex machines, such as cars, airplanes, and microwave ovens, does not require such knowledge. The analogy is not sound, Soloway argues, because computers are qualitatively different from other machines with which we are familiar; in particular, they are multipurpose and readily modifiable. Knowing how to use computers, Soloway suggests, involves knowing how to build things—synthesis skills—which is what programming is about. Programming in this context does not necessarily mean writing instructions in machine code or even in a higher-level language like BASIC, Pascal, or Lisp: It does mean customizing the computer's operation, perhaps by means of an applications-oriented language, for the task at hand. "Thus, skills in specifying actions, putting pieces of action sequences together, debugging them, and so forth will all be necessary." Soloway argues further that in order to be able to write programs, even in a high-level problem-specific language, an understanding of some basic computer-science notions will be necessary. He emphasizes the importance of viewing the computer as a tool that will be used by many professions and consequently as one that students must be taught to use. DiSessa proposes that computation (computers) be developed as a new, dynamic, and interactive medium for representing and disseminating knowledge, and he sees widespread ability to program as an integral aspect of this development. In Landauer's view, all intellectuals of the future will need some competence with computers and that competence should be viewed as a basic intellectual skill.

Pea suggests that the current interest in teaching programming in schools in the United States and elsewhere is, in part, due to the belief that learning to program will enhance thinking ability generally, that it "will condition the mind to think systematically, precisely, planfully, and more rationally in contexts beyond programming." Several contributors note the possibility of using the teaching or learning of programming as a way to mediate the development of other types of competencies or skills. Feurzeig, for example, talks of programming as a conceptual framework for mathematics, his rationale being the correspondence he sees between the concepts underlying mathematics and those underlying programming, especially when the latter is done in a language, such as Logo, that was designed to highlight this correspondence. Like Schoenfeld, he argues that programming also is well suited to foster the development of heuristic skills in the Polya tradition and to help make students more self conscious of and articulate about their own problem-solving performance. Soloway also notes the possibility of using programming to teach generally useful metacognitive skills such as problem decomposition, problem simplification, simulation, and boundary case identification. He, like Pea, notes that there is little empirical evidence that problem-solving skills learned in the context of programming transfer to other domains, but claims that the issue has not been adequately explored.

There can be no doubt that in order to do well at writing programs of any degree of complexity, one must engage in some of the types of behavior that are typically emphasized in discussions of generally useful thinking skills and specific problem-solving heuristics. These include planning, problem decomposition, hypothesis generation and testing, working backwards, testing extreme cases, finding analogous problems, using diagrams, and so on. It is less clear, however, whether what is learned in the programming context transfers, or is transferable, to other contexts. It is important here to distinguish between two questions: (a) Do skills learned as a consequence of learning to program transfer spontaneously to other domains, and (b) can the teaching of programming be used intentionally to foster such transfer? These are quite different questions and failure to distinguish between them can make for confusion. The answer to the second question might well be yes, even if the answer to the first one turns out to be an unequivocal no.

METHODS OF TEACHING/LEARNING

Instruction Versus Discovery

Instruction and discovery are sometimes treated as mutually exclusive alternative approaches to learning, and often when they are, discovery is put forward as the preferred one. The evidence is quite convincing that people are more likely to remember what they actively discover than what they are told. As Resnick and Johnson point out, however, the assumption that people must construct their own knowledge, rather than simply receive it from others, does not require the rejection of instruction. If we could not learn from instruction we would be in serious trouble, because some information is better acquired by simply being told: One should not have to learn by discovery, for example, the consequences of eating the wrong types of mushrooms. There is need in education for both instructional and discovery techniques and, as some of the contributors to this book suggest, especially for approaches that combine instruction and exploration in reasonable ways.

Feurzeig argues that the idea that "exposing students to a semantically rich microworld will spontaneously generate discovery and invention . . . is a wildly romantic and unreal view. Without the aid of a teacher, most students do not learn from working in a microworld environment." Elsewhere, Feurzeig (1986) contrasted the philosophy that lies behind the development of microworlds with that behind conventional, or even "intelligent," computer assisted instruction: "the microworld focus is on exploration and investigation rather than knowledge acquisition, on constructing rather than receiving knowledge, on learning rather than teaching" (p. 252). He cautions against the simplistic adoption of either approach to the total exclusion of the other. Learning, he reminds us, can benefit from varied instructional approaches: "Achieving an appropriate balance between giving students the direction they need and permitting them the freedom to explore and to make their own instructional decisions is the fundamental problem of the teaching art." Both expert tutors and explorable microworlds have something of value to offer, and either by itself is inadequate to the full spectrum of educational goals. Feurzeig anticipates a convergence of the two approaches, perhaps via the route of intelligent microworlds (Thompson, 1985) that contain knowledge both of a domain and of the student, but he sees the approaches retaining "significant vestiges of their different origins — one from a teaching, and the other from a learning paradigm. The intelligent microworld will still be focused on exploration, though the emphasis will be on guided exploration so as to help ensure that learning really occurs" (p. 253). Striking the right balance between directed instruction and exploratory learning is, in Feurzeig's view, the fundamental problem of teaching.

Schoenfeld touches also on the issue of instruction versus discovery in his discussion of future plans relative to Dugdale's "Green Globs," a program that produces graphs of algebraic functions on command. This capability is embedded within the context of a game, the objective of which is to define curves algebraically that will pass through points displayed on a coordinate grid. It is hoped that by playing this game, and becoming adept at moving curves around on the grid by changing the parameters of corresponding equations, one will increase one's understanding of how the graphic representations of equations relate to their algebraic form. Schoenfeld represents the pure game environment in which the student is completely on his own and a purely didactic environment in which a tutor provides strong direction as opposite ends of a continuum and proposes to find a middle ground, "where the game remains motivational but the student gets the 'right' kind of help when necessary or appropriate." I think that Schoenfeld's analysis is right and that a middle ground is exactly what is needed. It seems likely that a student could use Green Globs, or other manipulatable microworlds, for a long time without ever thinking to ask some important questions that the software is capable of answering through its reaction to appropriate explorations. It might be advantageous for the tutor, not only to offer help when it senses that the student is having difficulty with a particular idea, but, on occasion, to point a student in quite a different direction than the one he has been exploring, to introduce new ideas, to suggest questions the student might consider, to describe approaches the student has not yet discovered that should be tried, and so on.

Computer-Based Tools for Instruction and Discovery

A major reason for the assumption that information technology can be used to advantage in the teaching and learning of subject matter is the belief that this technology opens new possibilties for the representation and presentation of information in ways that are better suited to human assimilation then methods available before now. Here, I believe, is one of the most significant challenges and greatest opportunities for technology to facilitate learning and understanding. With the computer comes the possibility of representational media that are dynamic, adaptive, and interactive to degrees not really feasible in the past. One can easily imagine a facility that would permit the user to move readily among various representations of a given entity (structure, process, event) examining it from different perspectives at different levels of detail, accessing, when it is helpful to do so, clarifying or amplifying information that itself is available in a variety of forms (text, pictures, simulations).

From a digital representation of a three-dimensional structure, the computer can generate views from specified perspectives. It can produce partial representations (e.g. cross sections), and it can show an object rotating at a controlled speed around a designated axis. Graphics combined with the computer's ability to simulate dynamic processes provides the basis both for tutorial demonstrations (as opposed to descriptions supplemented by static pictures or diagrams) of processes of considerable complexity and for learning via student-directed exploration and manipulation. Processes can be shown dynamically on a specified time scale or in step-wise fashion. A student can explore the consequences of changes in the parameters or characteristics of a system of interest. If one is learning about turbulence in liquids, for example, one might explore the effects of changes in temperature or viscosity by simply varying these parameters over a considerable range and observing the effects.

The feasibility of watcing a graph being developed in real time while simultaneously watching a simulation of the process the effects of which are being graphed (Schoenfeld) is rich with possibilities for exploitation in education. Use of this capability should make the connection between graphs and the variables they represent more direct and easily grasped. Schoenfeld cites applications of real-time graphing in physics in which graphs of distance, velocity and acceleration are connected to concrete referents. Having simultaneous multiple representations of the same phenomenon (Schoenfled) or yoked representations (Resnick and Johnson) are also very promising ideas. These approaches should be useful in making clear the relationships between a variety of variables that people encounter in their daily lives and perhaps in precluding some of the common misconceptions that people have about the ways things work.

There now exist the technological means to develop simulated laboratories in various domains that would support investigative study of those domains much as do real laboratories at the present time. Without denying that simulated laboratories may be limited in some ways that real laboratories are not, we can recognize that they may also have some distinct advantages. Time can be compressed, for example, so one does not have to wait for months or years to obtain the results from an experiment on, say, (simulated) agriculture or genetics. Conversely, time can be expanded so a process that is too fast to be observed in the real world can be studied in detail. The spatial scale can also be adjusted so as to bring the very large and very small into comfortable viewing range. Experiments that are not feasible in real laboratories, perhaps because of considerations of cost or safety, can be simulated. And there is the possibility that simulated laboratories could be made available to students (and others) everywhere, to be used at the individual's convenience, whereas well-equipped laboratories are not readily accessible to most people and are totally off limits to many.

In short, information technology makes feasible the development of artificial worlds that resemble or differ from the real world in specific desired ways. This flexibility in modelling natural processes permits calling the student's attention selectively to specific aspects of those processes without being distracted by other aspects of the same processes that are not of interest at the moment. It allows also for those aspects of a process that are of interest to be highlighted (exaggerated, embellished, marked in various ways) in the hope of increasing the probability of understanding and retention. Structures can be seen from perspectives not possible in the real world.

Resnick and Johnson refer to one such microworld, developed by diSessa (1982), in which objects displayed on a graphics terminal behave as they would in a frictionless environment. The only forces at work in the environment are those specified by the user. In the absence of such forces, objects at rest (relative to the frame of reference of the display) remain at rest, and objects in motion move at constant speed in a straight line. Application of a force to an object, either moving or stationary, will cause it to respond in accordance with Newton's Law, $f = ma$, which is to say the object's acceleration will be proportional to the magnitude of the applied force and inversely proportional to the object's mass.

The use of microworlds for instructional purposes permits one to begin with highly simplified abstractions and to complicate them progressively as increases in the student's knowledge base warrant their complication. Microworlds can also be embellished and given extra features in the interest in enhancing their instructional value. An example from White (1984), who explored the use of diSessa's microworld to teach certain aspects of Newtonian mechanics, illustrates the point. The objects whose motion was the focus of interest in the microworld she used were spaceships. This scenario was selected because it was assumed that students would find it easy to think of the environment in which spaceships operate as being frictionless. The embellishment that White used was to have the spaceships leave visible trails, thus the effect of application of an impulse force on the direction of motion of a spaceship would be apparent not only from the ship's movement, but from the visible record of its entire path. Another feature incorporated by White was the option to suspend the activity of the microworld and to freeze the display. The student thus had the option of stopping the system, examining and reflecting upon the state of the microworld, then having it resume activity whenever and however often it was useful to do so.

Discussions of the use of microworlds and simulated laboratories for educational purposes appear, for the most part, to assume that students will discover with these tools things that are already known (though not to the students). That is to say, what students are expected to learn is what might also be learned from textbooks, albeit less efficiently or effectively. There has been little talk of the possibility that such tools could be used to facilitate new discoveries, discoveries that are new not only to the individual but to the field. But microworlds are proving to be useful investigative tools for serious research scientists. Learning to use microworlds for educational purposes could, in the future, be a step toward using them to do bona fide research on such topics as population genetics, high energy physics, the evolution of galaxies, prey-predator relationships, conflict resolution, and a host of others.

Motivation

Few educators will quarrel with the sweeping generalization that people who are strongly motivated to learn are more likely to learn than people who are not. The question is how to motivate students to learn. Several contributors to this book see computer technology being helpful here. DiSessa believes that computers are intrinsically engaging. Feurzeig says that students find the activity of building their own programs compelling and believes that computers can be used to create motivating learning environments.

Many developers of educational software have embedded the tasks that are intended to teach specific skills in game-like contexts. Several of the computer programs described by Resnick and Johnson illustrate the point. These investigators raise the question of why some recent programs to train automaticity of word recognition, such as those developed by Frederiksen and by Beck and their colleagues, have yielded some promising evidence of effectiveness when many previous efforts to train automaticity had not been successful. They speculate that the answer lies, in part, in the motivational consequences of the game-like nature of these programs, and, in part, in the fact that the programs adapt to the pace and competence level of their users.

Game playing has been a favored pastime of people of all ages in all cultures from very ancient times. And the possibility of turning this interest to educational advantage is also not an entirely new idea. The "educational game" market is a thriving one, as a visit to any toy store will confirm. Whether the games that are advertised as having educational value accomplish what their promotion claims may be questioned in many cases. But the fact that educational games and toys sell so well testifies to the widespread hope, if not belief, that children can learn something of value while having fun. There can be no doubt that they learn; the question is whether they learn anything other than how to play the game, and even when they learn skills (of planning, strategizing, etc.) that are clearly relevant to other contexts, whether those skills transfer to those other contexts.

The hope of teaching through game playing has been energized considerably with the appearance of computers on the scene. Clearly it is possible to produce computer-based games, especially with the help of computer graphics and some of the tools produced by workers in artificial intelligence, that are intrinsically interesting and highly motivating to players. We know that time on task is a key variable in the learning of any skill, and we know also that a major problem in many conventional learning situations is that of lack of motivation on the part of the students. If the engaging properties of computer-based games can be turned to educational advantage, the leverage that is realized could be great. Unfortunately, there is an abundance of demonstrations of the fact that simply bringing up a game on a computer and declaring it educational is not enough to assure the realization of this possibility.

The question of transfer is a fundamental one for any approach to education, as Pea so effectively reminds us, and it applies, of course, to educational games as much as to any other approach. The problem may be lessened somewhat, however, when the game situation is such as to foster explicitly the direct acquisition of the desired knowledge or direct learning of the target skill. Consider, for example, a word game designed to promote the learning of new vocabulary words. If the enlargement of one's vocabulary is considered a legitimate educational objective in its own right, then transfer in this case is not an issue. (Although "having a word in one's vocabulary" need not mean always being able to access and use it skillfully.)

Resnick and Johnson describe several computer-based games that have been developed to help automate certain aspects of reading (Beck, Roth & McKeown, 1985; Frederikson, Warren, & Roseberry, 1985a,b; Roth & Beck, 1984, 1985). Having tried some of these games and watched others play them, I am convinced of their holding power. I suspect that word games, as a class, represent limitless possibilities for development of software that could be highly effective in improving one's vocabulary and more generally increasing one's command of a language while providing the player a great deal of enjoyment. We have some evidence that word games are quite popular. According to one report, about 30 million Americans attempt to do crossword puzzles on a more or less daily basis (Miller, 1975). It is easy to imagine computer-based crossword puzzles, Scrabble, and other word games—not only from among the many that exist but from among the countless ones waiting to be invented—calibrated to the skill-level of the player and designed in such a way as to ensure that the player not only has the fun of playing the game but learns something—becomes a more proficient word user—in doing so. A problem with many educational games is that they put players in the position of demonstrating what they already know, instead of teaching them something new. But it should not be difficult to design enjoyable puzzles and games that will extend one's language skills rather than simply exercising those that already exist.

In assessing computer-based educational games, one challenge is to distinguish between those aspects of the game situation that contribute to its educational value and those that do not. It is conceivable that some of the more engaging visual aspects of many of them have little, or even negative, educational value. The fact that a game is simple does not make it bad, nor does the fact that it is complex necessarily make it good. Those features of a game that are included strictly for motivational effect also should be considered critically in an effort to determine whether they do in fact contribute to the game's effectiveness, even indirectly by increasing its holding power. The possibility should not be overlooked that game-like features of programs that are included for strictly motivational purposes can sometimes become an encumbrance. When a student is highly motivated to learn what a particular program has to teach and wishes to use the program for that purpose, aspects of the situation that do not directly contribute to the learning experience may be perceived not only as superfluous, but as annoyingly distractive.

Transfer

The problem of transfer is often viewed as *the* methodological problem for education. Pea reminds us that the problem is a multifaceted and general one, involving transfer from the culture to the individual, from the classroom to non-school situations, from nonschool situations to the classroom, and from one curriculum domain to another. He notes that with respect to the classroom and nonschool situations attention has been focused primarily on the question of how to effect transfer from inside the classroom to the outside and that the equally important question of how to ensure transfer in the opposition direction has been largely ignored. He notes too the neglected issue of appropriateness of transfer and the importance of being able to judge same, especially in analogical reasoning. All in all, the problem of transfer—appropriate transfer—is much more complicated than has typically been acknowledged, and consequently it is not likely to be solved in any simple way.

Pea suggests several ways in which technology might be used to foster appropriate transfer. His emphasis in this context, like that of several other participants, is on the development of tools and in particular "tools that enhance the chances that students adopt a self-aware transfer state of mind." These include tools for representing knowledge (and for linking and communicating representations), tools for bridging between various contexts (in school vs out of school, across content domains) over which one wants transfer to occur, and interactive problem solving tools that can be used across the curriculum. With respect to the last category, Pea notes the desirability of tools that can support a scaffolding approach to the development of competence, as do Resnick and Johnson and Feurzeig. And he notes the possibility that computer technology might be used to facilitate transfer by providing interactive environments that give the student more experience in recognizing situations to which the transfer of specific knowledge is appropriate.

If, as several of the contributors predict, the use of computer-based tools will become increasingly commonplace in all walks of life, this could have implications for the issue of transfer. Resnick and Johnson make essentially this point in noting that although human tutors traditionally have tried to make their students independent of them, inasmuch as they (the tutors) are not expected to be available for long, the situation may be different in the case of computer-based tutors. Computers will be around indefinitely and people will work with them not only during the years of their formal education or training, but throughout their adult lives. This being so, becoming independent of the teaching device may no longer make sense as an educational goal; the goal now may become learning to use effectively the tools that they will have at their disposal not only during their formal education, but afterwards as well.

Teachers and Other Facilitators

What does the prospect of major technological innovations in education mean for teachers and other professionals who will have important educational roles in the future? Presumably a variety of things. It can mean the obsolescence of some existing knowledge and skills, and the need for a different type of training, especially training in how to use technological innovations (Malcolm, Soloway). It can mean a threat to the teacher's unique role as knowledge dispenser or learning facilitator. It can mean new tools, and opportunities for innovation. It can mean relief from the burdensomeness of certain mundane chores and the possibility of more time to do those things that really require a human touch (Bossert, Minstrell).

Numerous observers have predicted a growing shortage of good teachers over the next decade or so. Among the causes of this trend that are cited are relatively low teacher salaries (as compared with salaries of some other professionals with comparable education), the stress associated with many classroom situations especially in inner city settings, and the generally low esteem in which the teaching profession seems to be held in the U.S. Evidences (e.g. SAT scores) that teacher training programs are not attracting the nation's top students are also disturbing. There is the possibility too that the most serious shortages could be in the areas of mathematics and the hard sciences, in part because opportunities for professionals in these areas are so numerous. In some disciplines the severity of the shortage could be great. According to Borke (1987), for example, the United States is currently graduating only about one fifth as many math teachers as it did 10 years ago.

Several chapters in this book note the possible emergence of new roles that relate to education and the possible need for new types of professionals. Among these are various mediational roles that involve connecting learners to resources from which they can draw. Gardner discusses the role of a student-curriculum broker, who would help students make decisions about courses to take and out-of-class activities in which to engage, and that of a school-community broker, who would be a source of information about learning opportunities outside and beyond school: "apprenticeships, mentorships, software and hardware for purchase, journals, self-administered courses, clubs, friendship networks, computer networks and the like." Cohen describes potential new roles for libraries and librarians. The library, which typically is thought of as a place where books are kept, might be made into a dynamic collection of learning resources, including technologically-based ones, accessible to the student who wants to use them. The librarian could be, not primarily a custodian of books and documents, but a keeper of educational tools who can provide the motivated student with easy access to them. All of these roles might be encompassed in the generic notion of a learner-resource broker whose function would be to connect individuals to resources that can serve their educational objectives. The job of such a broker could be aided by computer data bases that would store large amounts of information about educational resources and would provide assistance in matching them to individuals' interests and needs. These, in my view, are very exciting ideas.

SOME ISSUES

Equity

Malcolm addresses the extremely important issue of equity in educational opportunity and notes the disturbing possibility that the next few decades could witness a widening of the gap between mainstream and disadvantaged children in this regard. There is not equal access to computers at the present, she notes, and the kind of access disadvantaged students have when they have it, is often qualitatively different from (more rigid and constrained than) that provided to their advantaged counterparts. To compound the problem, the percentage of students classified as poor or disadvantaged could well be greater in 2020 than it is today. What can be done to insure that such a future, although among the possibilities, is not the one that is realized?

If technology succeeds in producing educational tools that are truly effective, and if such tools are more accessible to some segments of society than to others, it follows that the educational opportunities will be greater for those segments that have access to the tools than for those that do not. And if the latter group is composed primarily of students who are already disadvantaged for one or another reason, then the effect will be to amplify such inequities as currently exist. This would be an unfortunate future indeed, not only for the students who happen to be on the short end of this imbalance, but for society as a whole. It is a future that must be avoided.

Part of the answer must be political in nature, but are there some useful steps that can be taken by the technical community as well? Presumably one major obstacle to equitable access to any resource is cost. As long as educational technology is expensive it is likely to be more readily accessed by the more affluent segments of society than by the less affluent, and this in spite of any government or societal efforts to the contrary. So one goal should be to make these resources as inexpensive as possible. Costs are not entirely under the control of technologists, although they may be influenced somewhat by the attitudes and practices of developers of educational resources regarding the sharing of ideas and even more tangible assets. What will probably do most to drive costs down, however, is to have many capable people working hard to produce software and other resources that can be competitive in a mass market. Of course, one would feel more sanguine about this if it could be assumed that the mass market will be highly selective on the basis of quality. Nevertheless, the cost of educational resources, good and bad, is very likely to vary inversely with the amount produced.

Another way that technologists can address the equity issue is to focus effort on the development of tools and programs designed explicitly for the benefit of disadvantaged groups. Malcolm makes this point and notes the potential of technology to improve the education of people with learning disabilities and help address the problem of adult illiteracy. A recent report from a workshop convened by the Adult Literacy Initiative of the U.S. Department of Education focuses on the latter topic and discusses a number of ways in which information technology might be used to help teach adults with poor literacy skills to read and write (Nickerson, 1985). I believe that technology, and computer technology in particular, has enormous potential for mitigating many of the disadvantages, both educational and other, that stem from physical and mental disabilities and especially from communication disorders of various sorts. Although some promising starts have been made on applying technology in this way (Bowe, 1984; Gergen & Hagen, 1985; Goldenberg, 1979; McWilliams, 1984; Redden & Stern, 1983; Schwartz, 1984; Stern & Redden, 1982), the potential remains largely unrealized, and the goal of realizing it deserves more attention from policy makers at all levels than it has received.

The issue of equitable access to educational technology is not to be confused with another equity question that bears a superficial resemblance to it. The second issue involves the question of how our expectations regarding the effects of the application of educational technology should relate to individual student abilities. This question is independent of the question of equitable access. As far as we know, students differ significantly in their intellectual potential, and the full range of potentialities is found in all segments of society, whether the division is made along socio-economic, racial, geographical or any other grounds. There is some possibility—a rather good one I think—that the natural consequence of making powerful educational resources uniformly available to everyone will be to amplify the differences in intellectual development between individuals with greater and lesser potential. This is a different type of split between the haves and have nots than the ones that usually concern us, but it is a split nevertheless, and one that should not be overlooked.

My own reaction to this possibility is that all students, regardless of whatever pigeonholes they may find themselves placed in by the various ways in which we classify ourselves, should have the opportunity to develop their potential to the maximum degree possible, whatever that potential is. While this could have the effect of amplifying individual differences, at least as measured by ability to perform intellectually demanding tasks of various types, the more important consequence is that it could benefit everyone to an unprecedented degree. That assertion is based on the assumption that given the ways in which we currently educate ourselves, very few people, if any, manage to realize more than a small fraction of their potential. Universal access to much more powerful educational techniques than we now have might well differentially benefit individuals with outstanding potential, but it should benefit everyone significantly. I believe we have little idea of what the learning potential of garden-variety human beings, which includes the vast majority of us, really is. I do not believe we have the evidence to rule out the possibility that it is very much greater than we realize.

Quality

A much higher percentage of young people graduate from college or university today than did so 50 years ago. A college education today is, in many respects, a less unusual achievement than was completion of high school a half century ago. There are many reasons for this, not least of which are the greatly increased affluence of the society as a whole and the much greater accessibility of higher education to the average young person. Accompanying the manyfold increase in the number of young people attending institutions of higher learning has been a significant decrease in the admissions requirements and, many would argue, in the quality of the education obtained. Perhaps there still exist the high-quality programs that were in place in the first half of this century, and what has happened is a disproportionate growth in less demanding programs. On the one hand, the effect has made higher education possible to a much larger segment of society, thus democratizing the educational process, in a way; on the other, it has diluted the significance of a college degree.

Although quality of education has been deemed a newsworthy topic by the media from time to time in recent years, the American public and its political leadership have been remarkably complacent about conditions that one commissioned report described as "a rising tide of mediocrity that threatens our future as a Nation and a people" (National Commission on Excellence in Education, 1983, p. 5). Why are we as a society not more insistent on educational excellence? DiSessa suggests that our complacency results from the fact that the deficits of education are decoupled in people's minds from the problems they cause; more proximal causes, which can always be identified, tend to get the attention. Although the educational establishment is often criticized, seldom are specific societal problems identified as direct consequences of the quality of education received in the nation's schools.

Will technology help improve the quality of education in the future? I believe this to be an open question. That technology offers opportunities for qualitative improvements of very considerable degree seems clear; whether these opportunities will be seized remains to be seen.

Impediments to Change

New technology by itself is not a sufficient cause of change in institutionalized education: This view is most explicitly and strongly expressed by Cohen, who argues that the style of organization and work in classrooms has changed very little since the 19th century, with its emphasis on lecturing (teacher talk) to sizeable classes, student recitation, rote memorization and objective testing, and its neglect of inquiry-oriented approaches. Although new materials and approaches have been developed over this time, they seem not to have had much impact on the way most classes are organized and conducted.

There is a truly striking contrast when one compares how some aspects of our lives have changed over the past 35 years with the degree of change that can be seen in institutionalized education. Transportation has been revolutionized with the advent of commercial jet aircraft; home entertainment is totally different from what it was prior to television, audio, and video cassette players; commerce has been transformed by the application of computer technology—a technology that was in its nascency in 1950 and is now entering its "fifth generation"; medicine had been transformed, small pox erradicated, open-heart surgery made routine; we have learned how to get quite good cross-sectional photographs of the body by jiggling its hydrogen atoms in clever and noninvasive ways. Meanwhile in the classroom, things continue pretty much as they were: teachers talk to students, students take notes, go to study hall, take multiple-choice tests, get grades, and so on.

"New technology," Cohen notes, "is an old educational enchantment." All the recent hoopla about information technology is reminiscent of past high expectations for applications of new technologies to education that came to nought. The potential that technology has for use in education has never been realized very fully, in Cohen's view. Even the possibilities (e.g., for flexibility and individualization) inherent in technologies that have been used for some time — books, print technology more generally, diverse curriculum materials — are not exploited effectively, for the most part. Standardized textbooks, lecturing, rigid classroom organization, and lock-step instruction persist in spite of developments that could have supported much greater flexibility. The fact is, Cohen concludes, "new possibilities alone will not drive social organizations to realize them." Technology *enables* but does not *drive* organizational change.

But computer technology is different from other technologies, some would argue, and there is reason to expect that it will be more instrumental in effecting change than have other technologies in the past. Computers are knowledge machines, machines of the mind (Feurzeig), and within them is the potential for far more radical change than would have been enabled by any previous technology. But, Cohen suggests, the very flexibility of the computer may facilitate its nonintrusive assimilation within established patterns of educational practice and thereby diminish its impact as an agent of change.

Cohen's observation that technology does not cause educational change but only enables it, is disheartening news to the technologist, who believes or wishes to believe, that the primary challenge is to develop the tools for a practitioner community that is ready and eager to use them. His message that the mere existence of tools, no matter how promising their potential, is not sufficient to guarantee their adoption and use is one that no one interested in educational innovation can afford to ignore. But if enablement is not a sufficient cause of change it is a necessary one. Tools cannot be used if they do not exist, and the primary challenge to the technologist, as technologist, is indeed the development of those tools.

VISIONS FOR THE FUTURE

Throughout this book are visions of new and powerful tools that could be put to use for educational purposes by 2020, of new knowledge and know-how that could help produce more effective approaches to teaching and learning, of developments that could at least enable, if not cause, significant change. It is interesting that one of the most optimistic of these visions comes from a high-school teacher. Minstrell paints a picture that includes schools using research-based curricula, knowledgeable computer-based teacher assistants, teachers intent on fostering intellectual growth instead of just passing on traditional content, students taking responsibility for their own learning and for managing their own time, and sophisticated evaluation techniques. The technology that is assumed to be available to support this vision includes computers that will be able to recognize speech at least enough to process multi-word continuous-speech commands; to search journals for articles on specific topics; to extract highlights from journal articles; to describe students' thinking, diagnose difficulties in it, and prescribe development-enhancing experiences; to support interactive multi-media large-group presentations and learning experiences. It includes each student having a personal computer ("electronic notebook"), and doing much work at places other than school. Although the computer is ubiquitous in this vision, it should not escape our notice that the human remains in control.

Bossert's vision of what is possible for the future also includes ample computing resources for every student (a powerful computer possibly with several processors and certainly many megabytes of memory, a very high resolution display, and speech production and understanding capability), as well as the tapping (electronically) of many resources outside the classroom. It includes the idea of a personal factotum for every student that could serve as a knowledgeable intermediary between the individual and the universe of computer-based resources. Bossert notes the possibility that high-quality data and audio-visual access to resources outside the classroom will remove some of the logistical problems that limit the effectiveness of techniques that are currently used to bridge the gap between the classroom and the external world, such as "show and tell," field trips and current-events reports. Virtual field trips, made possible by electronic linking of the classroom libraries, and museums, which will have their holdings available in electronic (or photonic) form, is part of this picture. Putting students in better touch with the external intellectual environment is one of the most exciting promises of information technology, in Bossert's view; another is the use of computer-based message technology to facilitate inter-student communication and collaborative problem solving.

In addition to the visions such as these that have been described explicitly, there are numerous other possibilities and prospects implicit in what has been said by the various contributors to this book. Here I shall try simply to list what appear to me and/or other contributers to be some ways in which technology — which I interpret sufficiently broadly to include new scientifically derived knowledge — could enable significant educational changes over the next few decades. Which of the possible changes will be realized, and to what degree, are likely to depend on a variety of factors that are largely beyond the technologist's control.

- A very large amount of software will exist that was developed for educational purposes. This will include microworlds and electronic exploratoria, as well as tutorial programs and programs with both exploratory and tutorial capabilities, for a variety of domains including, but not limited to, the sciences and math. Some of this software is likely to be very effective.

- Expert systems will be in use extensively by business, industry and various segments of the service sector, although they may be referred to by other terms reflecting a greater awareness of the ways in which these systems differ from human experts. As a consequence of the work that will have gone into the development of these systems, much of the knowledge that constitutes expertise in specific domains will have been codified and represented in machine-accessible form.

- Wideband two-way communication channels (fiber optics and satellites) linking homes to information resources of various types (libraries, museums, national and international data banks) will be a reality. Perhaps there will be software that will act as an effective intermediary between the user and such resources, making it much easier than it now is to find specific information when one wishes to do so.

- Electronic pocket fact finders may exist that contain the kind of information now found in almanacs, fact books, year books, and other repositories and are able to provide answers to questions of fact immediately on request.

- There undoubtedly will be electronic books that can present conventional prose and also, on request, explanatory and elaborative information regarding specific parts of the text—definitions, explanations, maps, simulations, answers to specific questions regarding what has already been read, answers to questions about the time, place, circumstances of referenced events, and so on.

- Super courses probably will have been developed by pooling the capabilities and techniques of the best teachers, adding computer-based dynamic process simulation capabilities and real-time access to various information resources.

- There should be classrooms without walls, in which students from different geographical areas—including different countries—interact in real time through wideband communication networks.

- There may be much more effective techniques than now exist for assessing the knowledge and abilities—potential and real—of individuals. There may also be more effective ways of probing depth of understanding and of identifying specific misconceptions.

- Perhaps the diagnostic techniques that are available will be capable of distinguishing more clearly than we now can between difficulties that stem from inadequate knowledge and those that result from limitations of reasoning processes.

- There should exist better models of conceptual difficulties commonly encountered by students at specific levels of mastery of a subject and of specific misconceptions that are likely to arise.

- We should understand better the determinants of intellectual competence, how they relate, and the extent to which they can be traded off against each other.

- We can hope that principles of learning will be somewhat better understood, although it will be surprising if new knowledge does not also bring a greater appreciation of the depth of our ignorance of how the mind works.

- The roles that metaphors play in learning—both useful and detrimental—may be understood better, permitting more productive use of them.

- We can hope that there will be more effective ways to improve interperson communication and to enhance our ability and increase our desire to cooperate with others toward common goals.

We do not know as much as we would like about what constitutes an environment that is conducive to learning, which is not to say that we know nothing about it. One hopes that by 2020 we will know a good bit more than we do now. On the basis of what we do know it seems clear that technology has something to offer in this regard. It can help make learning situations more responsive, providing students with immediate feedback regarding the accuracy of their understanding of a concept or process. It can deal with misconceptions and errors in a nonjudgmental way. It can help one explore ideas and test hypotheses in simulated worlds. It can put one in touch with extensive information resources.

Contributors to this book, and others who have written about information technology and education, have cast the computer in a variety of roles including those of tutor, assistant, critic, advisor, motivator, competitor (in game situations), communication facilitator, information accessor, and specific system simulator. It can serve all these functions, and more. How well it serves any one of them in any particular instance will depend of course on many factors; the computer's involvement is, by itself, no guarantee of quality or effectiveness. Nevertheless, the versatility of the machine does set it apart from others and invites expansive speculation about the possibilities. It is easy to imagine, for example, the in-touch interactive classrooms described by Bossert, the multi-faceted teacher's assistants portrayed by Minstrell, the ever present intelligence extenders foreseen by Resnick and Johnson, the intelligent microworlds and scholars' workstations mentioned by Feurzeig. Some of these possibilities already exist in rudimentary form.

Among the most exciting prospects of the continuing development of information technology, in my view, is the possibility of making information far more accessible—efficiently and effectively accessible—to the average individual than it now is. Some of the critical ingredients of greatly increased accessibility are coming into place. They include (a) large repositories of information in electronic or other computer readable form, (b) communication channels of sufficient bandwidth to permit rapid transmission of high-resolution pictures, including movies, (c) versatile cordless user terminals, and (d) sophisticated and extremely fast information search, abstracting, organization and presentation techniques. The first three of these ingredients are likely to be highly developed long before 2020; how quickly the fourth will come along is more questionable. Its development will probably depend on major advances both in artificial intelligence and in the design and use of massively parallel machines.

Throughout this book there are truly exciting glimpses of the many ways in which technology could impact education for the better in the foreseeable future. There are also warnings, caveats and cautions, and a generous dose of skepticism regarding the probability of radical change in institutionalized education over a period of a few decades, irrespective of what happens in the world of technology. If there is a single conclusion to be derived from the various points of view expressed, it is that the future is rife with possibilities for major technology-enabled improvements in institutionalized education, but that many of these possibilities probably will not be realized unless adequate attention is paid to the nontechnical factors that tend to control change in the educational world. Both the contributors to this book and many other observers of the current educational scene convey a sense of urgency regarding the need for radical change. Making sure that it occurs represents a major challenge of the future to technologists and non technologists alike.

A question for the immediate future and beyond that will require the collaborative attention of technologists and educators is that of how to couple computer-based tools with other teaching/learning resources so as to support an integrated approach to specific subject matter in the classroom. It is a temptation to the technologist to take a piece-meal approach, because some aspects of almost any subject lend themselves more readily to a computer-based treatment than do other aspects and, not surprisingly, people who develop educational software are likely to focus first on those aspects of a subject for which a computer-based approach seems most natural. There already exist many pieces of software that appear to do a good job of teaching some aspects of specific academic subjects, but because they teach them in isolation from other equally important aspects of those subjects, teachers often find it to be more trouble than it is worth to figure out how to fit the use of that software into a structured approach to teaching the subject as a whole. What is needed are some serious attempts to develop curricula and instructional approaches for entire courses taking into account the technology that exists. The question should not be: What aspects of physics, say, can we best teach using a computer; the question should be: How can we best approach the problem of teaching physics, given the computer technology and other resources that exist. More generally, the suggestion is that if technology is to be used to maximum advantage in the classroom in the future, it will be necessary for technology and pedagogy to advance together.

REFERENCES

Baron, J., & Sternberg, R.S. (1986). *Teaching thinking skills: Theory and Practice.* New York: Freeman.

Beck, I., Roth, S., & McKeown, M. (1985). *Syl-la-search III teacher's manual.* Allen, TX: Developmental Learning Materials.

Borke, A. (1987, February). The potential for interactive technology. *Byte,* 201–206.

Bowe, F.G. (1984). *Personal computers and special needs.* Berkeley, CA: Sybex Computer Books.

Branscomb, L.M. (1986). Science in 2006. *American Scientist, 74,* p. 650–658.

Chance, P. (1986). *Thinking in the classroom.* New York: Teachers College Press.

Chipman, S.F., Segal, J.W., & Glaser, R. (Eds.). (1985). *Thinking and learning skills, Vol 2: Research and open questions.* Hillsdale, NJ: Lawrence Erlbaum Associates.

Costa, A.L. (1985). Toward a model of human intellectual functioning. In A.L. Costa (Ed.), *Developing minds: A resource for teaching thinking.* Alexandria, VA: Association for Supervision and Curriculum Development.

Davis, P.J., & Hersch, R. (1981). *The mathematical experience.* Boston, MA: Houghton Mifflin.

Dillon, R., & Sternberg, R.J. (1986). *Psychology and curriculum design.* New York: Academic Press.

diSessa, A.A. (1982). Unlearning Aristotellian physics: A study of knowledge-based learning. *Cognitive Science, 6,* 37–75.

Drexler, K.E. (1986). *Engines of creation.* New York: Anchor Press/Doubleday.

Feurzeig, W. (1986). Algebra slaves and agents in a logo-based mathematical array. *Instructional Science, 14,* 229–254;

Frederiksen, J.R., Warren, B.M., & Rosebery, A.S. (1985a). A componential approach to training reading skills: Part 1. Perceptual units training. *Cognition and Instruction, 2,* 91–130.

Frederiksen, J.R., Warren, B.M., & Roseberry, A.S. (1985b). A componential approach to training reading skills: Part 2. Decoding and use of context. *Cognition and Instruction, 3/4,* 271–338.

Gergen, M., & Hagen, D. (Eds.) (1985). Computer technology for the handicapped. *Proceedings of the 1984 Closing the Gap Conference.* Henderson, Minnesota: Closing the Gap.

Goldenberg, E.P. (1979). *Special technology for special children.* Baltimore: University Park Press.

Holton, G. (1984, Fall). 'A nation at risk' revisited. *Daedelus, 113*(4), 1–27.

McWilliams, P.A. (1984). *Personal computers and the disabled.* New York: Doubleday.

Miller, M. (1975). Puzzling people. *Boston Globe,* July 13, B1.

National Commission on Excellence in Education (1983). *A nation at risk: The imperative for educational reform.* Washington, DC: U.S. Government Printing Office.

National Commission on Space (1986). *Pioneering the space frontier.* New York: Bantam Books.

Nickerson, R.S. (1985). Adult literacy and technology. *Visible Language, 19,* 311–355.

Nickerson, R.S., Perkins, D., & Smith, E.E. (1985). *The teaching of thinking,* Hillsdale, NJ: Lawrence Erlbaum Associates.

Polya, G. (1957). *How to solve it* (2nd ed.). New York: Doubleday.

Redden, M.R., & Stern, V.M. (1983). *Technology for independent living II.* Washington, DC: American Association for the Advancement of Science.

Reich, R.D. (1983). *The next American frontier.* New York: Times Books.

Roth, S.F., & Beck, I.L. (1984, April). *Research and instructional issues related to the enhancement of children's decoding skills through a microcomputer program.* Paper presented at the annual meeting of the American Educational Research Association, Chicago.

Roth, S.F., & Beck, I.L. (1985). *Theoretical and instructional implications of the assessment of two microcomputer work recognition programs.* Unpublished manuscript.

Schwartz, A. (Ed.) (1984). *Handbook of microcomputer applications in communication disorders.* San Diego: College-Hill Press.

Schwebel M., & Maher, C.A. (1986). *Facilitating cognitive development: International perspectives, programs, and practices.* New York: Haworth Press.

Stern, M.R., & Redden, V.W. (1982). *Technology for independent living I.* Washington, DC: American Association for the Advancement of Science.

Thompson, P.W. (1985). Mathematical microworlds. In *ICAI Proceedings of Conference on Moving Intelligent CAI into the Real World*, Burroughs, Canada, PPD MH-85-83.

Turkle, S. (1984). *The second self: computers and the human spirit*. New York: Simon and Schuster, Inc.

White, B.Y. (1984). Designing computer games to help physics students understand Newton's laws of motion. *Cognition and Instruction, 1*, 1–4.

Author Index

Frederiksen, J., 111, 140, *120, 166*
Frederiksen, N., 189, *208*
Freyberg, P., 177, 196, *210*
Fried, L. S., 189, *208*
Furnas, G. W., 17, *24*

G

Gagne, R. M., 173, 177, 188, *208, 209*
Gardner, H., 28, 29, 32, 34, 35, *41*
Gardner, W., 146, *167*
Gay, J., 176, *209*
Gelman, R., 174, *209*
Gentner, D., 156, *166,* 178, 185, *209*
Gentner, D. R., 185, *209*
Gergen, M., 308, *316*
Ghatala, E. S., 188, *211*
Ghitman, J. M., 196, *209*
Gick, M. L., 182, 188, 189, *209*
Gilliam, D., 224, *229*
Glaser, R., 160, *167,* 172, 189, *207, 209, 212,* 295, *316*
Goldenberg, E. P., 104, 115, 116, *119,* 308, *316*
Goldsmith, L., *41*
Gomez, L. M., 17, *24*
Gowen, D. B., 195, *210*
Grant, K. R., 201, 202, *210*
Grant, R., 103, *119*
Greene, T. R., 175, *212*
Greenfield, P. M., 146, *166,* 191, *209*
Greeno, J., 192, 195, *207*
Groen, G. J., 111, *119*
Guesne, E., 177, *208*
Guilford, J. P., 29, *41*
Gullo, D. F., 104, *119*

H

Haan, B. J., 106, *120*
Haertel, H., 160, *166*
Hafter, C., 153, *166*
Hagen, D., 308, *316*
Halacz, F., 184, *209*
Halasz, F. G., 164, *167*
Hall, P. Q., 217, 218, 223, *229*
Hamburg, D. A., 201, *209*
Hammond, K., 140, *166*
Hartmann, H., 224, *229*
Hasselbring, T. S., 187, 190, 192, *206*
Hawkins, J., 177, 194, 196, 197, 200, *207, 209*

Hayes, J. R., 182, *212*
Herron, M. D., 191, *209*
Hersch, R., 293, *316*
Hiltz, S. R., 202, *209*
Hirsch Jr., E. D., 172, *209*
Hodgkinson, H. L., 215, 216, *229*
Hoffding, H., 180, *209*
Hoffman, M. B., 189, *208*
Hollan, J., 85, *96*
Holton, G., 295, *316*
Holyoak, K. J., 178, 182, 188, 189, *207, 208, 209*
Homa, D., 188, *209*
Horwitz, P., 112, *119, 120,* 154, *168*
Houde, R., 81, *96*
Hull, G., 150, 151, *166*
Hutchins, E., 85, 96

I

ITMA, 80, *96*

J

James, W., 173, *209*
Jenkins, J. R., 140, *166*
Johnson-Laird, P. N., 202, *210*
Johsua, S., 160, *166*
Jordan, C., 189, *209*

K

Kaagan, S., 36, *41*
Kaput, J., 80, *96*
Kehler, T., 202, *208*
Kraut, R., 224, *229*
Kuhn, 177
Kurland, D. M., 104, *120,* 173, 177, *209, 211*

L

Laboratory of Comparative Human Cognition, 172, 181, 183, 203, *210*
Landauer, T. K., 16, 17, *24*
Larkin, J. H., 175, *210*
Lave, J., 146, *166, 167,* 176, 177, 178, 190, 191, 192, *209, 210, 211, 212*
Lawler, B., 111, *119*
Lee, S., 99, *120*
Lepper, M. R., 186, *210*
Lesgold, A. M., 140, *166, 167, 207*

Subject Index